Dolores

They Say You Can't Get Here from There!

Dolores Curry

Edited by Bruce Roy
Cover design by Author
and Larry Fox

Library of Congress 2013908150

Curry, Dolores
A biography
Second Edition

ISBN: 9781496166500
ISBN: 1496166507

Acknowledgements

The first person I must acknowledge is Ed Krick, a long time friend from Trinity Episcopal Church in Easton...but wait...that Church is probably the first entity that prompted me to write the book. It was there I met Ed and shared musings and stories of my life. He persuaded me that I *must* write a book. He said, "You have a story to tell, Dolores!"

After that the encouragement and assistance is vast. There were the short-lived writing groups at Innisfree, the first being Katie Arrants and Kathleen O'Shea and me, which went into oblivion because of changes in our lives. Later, again at Innisfree, Tom Clay, Katie Ford, Lisa Gerlits and I had a few sessions, wherein I was encouraged because they accepted me and gave me gentle instructions on how to make my writing better. At the same time I was admonished because their writings were astounding.

No-Shame Theater in Charlottesville gave me the courage to put myself out there, in the public, unabashed. And certainly thanks for that goes to my long time writer-friend, companion and lover, Sherwood Ross. His ongoing support is invaluable.

When I came to a wall against feeling, remembering and writing, in December 2005, I was rescued by my sister, Rosie, and became a member of her household. The dam against the writing wall broke when I attended a Creative Writing Group at Trinity Episcopal Cathedral in Sacramento, where I became a born-again writer which I credit to encouragement of The Reverend Lynelle Walker and the other writers in that group. After the dam broke, Rosie

Dolores Curry

was the impetus and driving force that kept me going. Her selfless hours given to reading, re-reading, editing and remembering for me, were indispensable to the completion of the book. Long hours of proofreading by Teresa Grubl-Graves, Ann Scott and Ann Rothschild were greatly needed and appreciated.

Last, not because of importance, but because he was the most recent driving force, and without whom this book would not be, is Bruce Roy, my precise and prescient editor and friend, thank you.

A Letter To My Readers

Dear Reader,

The book that follows is a love letter to my life. It is also a love letter to my family, my friends and to those who were part of the story. It is a love letter to places and events that were necessary to carry out the entire adventure.

If my life were a quilt, it would be a crazy quilt. It would have odd shapes, many different fabrics; the entire spectrum of colors would be in it. Textures would vary from rough wool flannel, to fine silks and satins, and occasional velvet. It would have surprises tucked in odd places and it would all be held together with an unbroken golden thread.

Not in the way of an apology, but in the way of explanation I tell you that it is a story; not a chronology, not a history.

The first two chapters are memories of what my mother or grandmother told me, repeatedly. My own memory begins in the sand box when I was four years old. After that the story is my story. It tells how I saw things, how I remembered events, and the impact they had upon what followed. I have attempted to tell of events that were nodal points of my development; in religious language, a *metanoia*.

No one has been more surprised by my life than I. Ah! My beautiful life, the life I have loved. As the printed version of it goes to press I will be in the ninth decade of my life. I still am suspended in wonder, awe and abundant thanks for having had the privilege of living on this earth for this amount of time and experiencing what I have experienced. Yours truly, Dolores

Table of Contents

CHAPTER 1

The Beginning–
Curry Canyon

Violet walked deliberately up the rocky foot-worn path from the icy mountain spring toward the little tarpaper shack a quarter of a mile away on a hillside in Curry Canyon. It had been warm for the entire month of January and into February that winter of 1933. The weather this February was unusual enough to cause her to ponder. It was not a typical winter for South Dakota. She walked slowly and carefully because she was carrying new life in her womb, and a bucket of water in each hand. The baby was about a week overdue by her calculations. She hoped it would arrive before the menacing cold and snow bore down on them.

Thoughts darker and colder than the unusual winter lurked further back in her mind. She tried to keep those thoughts from breaking through, but like clouds on a clear day they appeared from nowhere and obliterated the blue sky. What was the meaning of the look that passed between Margaret, the hired girl, and Bob, Violet's adored husband? At a deep level she knew what it meant; that look exchanged between male and female since the first sign of self-consciousness appeared in the species; that signal of the body's deepest longing. Violet told herself that she was just imagining things. Pregnant women often do that. It meant nothing! She told herself that she had more important things to think of and pushed the malevolent thought back.

One of those important things to think about was her mother, Hattie, who would be coming soon according to the post card she received in the mail last week. Violet hoped with all her heart that Hattie would get there before the baby was born. Also she had to think about where Hattie would sleep. There wasn't much choice. Their little shack had been divided into two rooms by a bed sheet. She and Bob slept in one of the two rooms. The three children slept on a pallet on the floor in the other room which also included the table, chairs and the stove. Hattie would sleep with the children. Violet could think of no other way.

Her thinking was not so much as to where her mother would sleep but she wished she had a better place, with more privacy for her mother. Bob and Hattie did not get along very well; a typical mother-in-law, son-in-law relationship, but Violet told herself, that they would get through this. Hattie knew that she would have to sleep with the children and accepted that as part of her duty to be with Violet and part of the privilege of welcoming the gift of a new grandchild. Bob and Violet would keep their bedroom where the birth would take place. Violet knew that she needed the privacy more than her mother did, yet it was difficult to assume status above her mother. It felt like a major shift in the universe.

That thought led her to the next, which was wondering how the birth would go. She had given birth to three daughters before; Bobbie, six years ago; Mary Lou, five years ago and Kitty just twenty months ago. Bobbie and Kitty had been easy births. Mary Lou was different. Both Violet and the baby barely made it through, but they did survive. Violet felt she could get through anything after that. She said a little prayer and focused on the baby to be born as she lumbered up the hill. Perhaps this baby would be the boy child that Bob so earnestly wanted. She would love to please him that way.

In a little while she arrived at the root cellar Bob had excavated in which to store their food. She checked the venison from the deer he had snared during a cold spell in January and was glad to find that the warm weather had not thawed it out. It was a large part of their food supply for the next three or four months. It would be supplemented by the canned goods she had processed in the summer, by the milk from their goats, and pork and lard from the pig they had slaughtered in October. Occasionally her sister, Mary, would bring some eggs and a chicken from her farm out on the prairie. Bob brought staples such as flour, cornmeal, oats, sugar, molasses, salt and baking powder from the court house in Hill City where the Government supplied food during the depression. Violet mollified her anxiety about starving over the winter. They would be all right.

Bob earned sixty dollars a month from Pennington County driving the road grader. His job was to keep the roads clear in the winter. They were all dirt roads and were often difficult, occasionally impossible to travel. His was an important job because all the children of Curry Canyon and the nearby area went to school in Hill City about five miles down the road. It was also where the only doctor for miles kept his practice. There was no hospital closer than Rapid City thirty-five miles away, nor were there any paved roads closer than that.

They had been married for eight years, Bob Curry and Violet Michelson. Of course, she was now Violet Curry and quite proud to be. Her husband was one of the few men in the county who had a full time job that winter. The Great Depression hit South Dakota later than it had in the East, and was coupled with a severe drought. Together those events brought the people of the Black Hills to their knees, struggling along with the rest of the nation.

Violet loved Bob for many reasons; one might say it was "passion of the flesh" and that would be true, but also she loved him because he was fun to be with; just to see his laughing eyes and wide smile lit up her life. He was the best guitarist, mandolin, and banjo player that she or most of the people she knew had ever heard. He had a good heart, too. Hadn't he hired Margaret Schmidt, the fifteen year old girl who lived up the canyon to help Violet this winter because the Schmidt family could not feed all of their eight children? Also Violet needed help with their three children and another on the way.

Margaret was now in 8th grade and planned on going to high school next year. This made Violet jealous as school was no longer an option for her.

There was a reason she had dropped out of school after eighth grade. It went back to first grade when she came home from school every day and taught her younger sister Mary all she had learned. The next year when Mary entered first grade she knew the curriculum and at the end of the year was promoted, not to second grade, but to third, the same grade as Violet. For the next five years, Mary surpassed Violet academically in every subject. Their father, Jay, introduced them to people saying, "This is Violet, my pretty daughter, and this is Mary, the smart one." The final blow to Violet's self-esteem came at the end of eighth grade when she failed because of math. Mary passed and was making plans for high school. Violet was devastated and went to work in the hay fields for her father.

Early in the summer Bob Curry came to work in the hay fields. He fell for the pretty girl, Violet. She saw a way out of her humiliation and despair. And it was easy to fall in love.

Now, seven years later, love was not enough. She yearned for the assurance, self-confidence and independence that education had given her sister Mary. She told herself over and over again that he was worth it. Hadn't Bob, just last month, when he got his check, bought each of them a new dress? Margaret had worn hers the night before when the Civilian Conservation Corps (CCC) men came over to play music. Violet would wear hers after the baby was born, perhaps by Valentine's Day. Bob was good to her most of the time. Every now and then he would surprise her with a bag of books from the library in Hill City. She would devour them hungrily, and was grateful for his thoughtfulness. If only he would not insinuate that she was not smart enough to understand what she read. If only he would stop threatening that he would not to bring any more books if the house was too messy. If only...

The one thing about Bob that worried her most was that he operated a still far up in the canyon. Booze, moonshine, hooch... whatever it was called, it was illegal. Those who made it worked by moonlight as the smoldering fire at night was not so apparent to the G-men who loosely scouted the hills for this activity. They seldom patrolled at night or on a Sunday, but one particular Sabbath afternoon they showed up at the shack and asked about Bob's whereabouts. Violet lied and said she thought he was giving someone a ride home from church. She hated to lie. She was Catholic and would have to confess to Father McNamara. Of course, that Sunday Bob was at the still tending his corn mash. Sunday was his only day off from the road job. She did have to admit that the money he got for his moonshine afforded them luxuries that the neighbors could only dream of, such as a new dress once or twice a year for her and the girls. Their children had shoes and overshoes which were beyond what most of the local families could afford for their children. She and Bob could go to a movie in town once a month and they owned a Model T Ford. At Christmas each of the children got their own doll and a little red wagon to share.

Bob's rationale about his still was that it was none of the government's business what he did with his corn or his time off. He felt that Prohibition was a very bad law and that the government was sticking its nose in where it didn't belong. He intimidated Violet when she brought it up.

Violet knew that if he were caught Bob would lose his government supported job. They would also lose their lease on the government land where he had erected the little shack, and which they would eventually own if they continued living there and improved the property every year. The government did not consider the still an improvement.

She loved their location in the deeply forested hills, the majestic evergreens, pines and spruce and the sweet mountain spring that ran all year around. In the summer all manner of wild berries offered them lush desserts. She and the children would spend hours, sometimes whole days, gathering them. Those were precious days with as much laughing and playing as there was work. There was such an abundance of berries that they had all they wanted to eat on the gathering day and enough to preserve so she could make pies and sauces for the winter. The vegetation around their shack was enough that they could keep a few goats which supplied their milk and cheese. This was a good place to raise her children and she wanted to stay.

Violet remembered how hot and dry it had been working in the hay fields on the Hart Ranch, where the prairie meanders off to the east and the hills rise up to the southwest. When they moved up here into the Black Hills, she was overcome with the joy she found in their little mountain home. She was glad to have brought her children out of the dusty, parched hay fields. Mary Lou especially had not been healthy there. She was fragile at birth and the severe conditions, the heat, and the hay dust at the ranch had not helped her. Since they moved here, Violet could see her blossoming. Mary Lou and Bobbie went to school in Hill City. They loved the stimulation of other children, and they loved learning to read. Almost two years old, Kitty was still at home and was the one Bob adored. He would take her out on the road grader with him. Once Kitty donned his hat and boots and said, "Dod dammit, now I'm Daddy."

The best times for the trio of little girls were when they were all together, playing with their dolls on the soft yard, carpeted with the pine needles, the fragrance of spruce, fir and cedar enveloping them. Bob would be strumming his guitar, the wind whispering soft words to the music. Violet, always involved, might be shelling peas or folding clothes. Those were the good days of summer, spring and fall.

So many things to ponder, as Violet trudged up the hill. The air had changed during her trek. Now it bore a cool crispness and she knew the weather would be different by morning. Not a surprise! This was winter in South Dakota, after all!

Indeed in the morning it was quite different. Fine snowflakes were drifting down, gently at first, through the evergreen branches, sparkling in the morning sun. She was admiring the beauty of it when it occurred to her that it was her birthday, her 24th birthday! She thought of the many birthdays that had dawned like this one, with snow falling gently and then, later in the day, in awe-inspiring abundance. When it started with these fine glistening tiny flakes, it meant that they would keep coming all day and soon all the earth under their feet would be covered in deep snow. Oh! How she hoped her mother would get here today! That was the birthday present she really wanted.

Bob left early that day to get a jump start on clearing the roads. Violet and Margaret got the children off to school after getting the wrinkles out of Mary Lou's lisle stockings, about which she was so particular, and finding Bobbie's hat and mittens which were stored under the mattress on the floor. Kitty was bored; she whined and called after Bob until Margaret ran down the road and persuaded him to take the toddler on the grader with him. He took Margaret to school as well.

Violet did the dishes, made the beds, straightened up the house, and settled down to her books. This might get her worries off her mind. Worry about the snow, the impending labor and birth, and the arrival of her mother; they whirled about in her head. She could not concentrate on what she was reading so she busied herself by starting a batch of bread, mixing the yeast, water and sugar and watching it work until it was covered with bubbles. She then added the flour and salt and set the dough on the warming oven to rise. She went to the root cellar and brought up a jar of green beans, some potatoes, turnips and onions. This was all she could carry because of her large belly which was very quiet inside today. She went back to get a package of frozen venison. The air outside was cold, grey and menacing.

Back inside she put the stew ingredients in a large cast iron pot and placed it on the stove. A little while later she kneaded the risen dough and put it back on the warming oven for a second rising. By then the shack was cozy and filled with wonderful aromas. She lay down on the bed and read a book, pausing once to shape the dough into loaves and allow them to rise. One more chapter, she told herself; then she would put them in the oven.

Soon she heard Bob come into the yard on the grader. It was a little early for him to be home, and she quickly hid the book. Although he brought her the books, he often seemed irritated to see her reading them. He would, on those occasions, harangue her about her housekeeping. It started with, "My mother would never...," or "My mother always...," and lately it was, "Margaret does..."

Today he came in carrying Kitty, put her down, gave Violet a sidelong glance, and washed up in the wash basin. He quickly ate a piece of the old bread as the new loaves were still in the oven; then he went out. He hooked the wagon to the grader. She went out to watch him hoping he would talk to her. He said, "I'm going to get the kids. This is going to be a big one," glancing at the sky. She watched wistfully as he drove away, without so much as a tender word or gesture.

Inside, Violet and Kitty had some cheese and bread after which Kitty went down for a nap. This gave Violet a chance to read again. She tried to keep her mind on her book but kept looking up at the little window. It didn't look good out there. She paced the floor. She kept feeding the fire and it kept eating up the wood supply. The wood pile was going down fast. She went out and got a load in her arms but it was so hard to bend over that she could carry only a small load, and she wondered if it was worth opening the door of the shack and letting the cold air in. She darned a pair of socks and mended a pair of overalls. Then she cleaned the cupboards. It was a long afternoon.

She heard the grader before she could see it, and a ripple of relief went through her, as she knew the little girls would be home and out of danger. When it came into sight she could see that there was another adult in the wagon besides Bob and Margaret. A wave of joy swept over her, as she realized it was her mother! Too burdened by her belly to jump for joy, she was doing so, emotionally. As the grader arrived in the yard, she shouted, "You got here! You got here in time!" Tears ran down her cheeks. "Oh, Mama, I haven't seen you in so long!"

Her mother looked at her and said, "And it looks like I'm just in time. You are about to have that baby. You had better go get the doctor, Bob,"

Bob ignored that advice, but Violet answered, "I haven't had any pains or signs, but it is due any day. A little boy would be a great birthday present but I think he is too late for today."

"So you are sure it is a boy," her mother said.

Bob answered, "It better be. We have enough girls already!"

Hattie replied, "But we don't get to call the shots on that, do we?" Then she looked up at the sky, "How about the doctor, Bob?"

"Not going to do that until there are some signs," Bob said. "You know he charges by the hour."

Anyone could see that Hattie was a bit peeved by that remark, but decided to bite her tongue. Too early in the visit to start anything. She turned to Violet. "Happy Birthday!" and handed her a parcel. Violet exclaimed, "You didn't have to bring me a present. You are my present!"

When the coats were hung up on the wall pegs and hands warmed at the stove, the women set about getting supper ready.

Bob took Margaret up the canyon to her family since it was Friday night and she usually spent Saturday and Sunday at her home. Also the shack was crowded, now that Hattie was there.

Bob was gone a long time, so Hattie and Violet fed the children first and then ate by themselves at the table. The children played happily at their feet. They were relishing the company of each other. Violet opened the presents and was thrilled by the hand-made apron and blouse Hattie had made for her. Hattie was happy to get off work for a month, even though it was without pay. She worked as a maid at the Custer State Game Lodge, where Gutzon Borglum and his crew were staying during the sculpting of Mt. Rushmore. They had stopped the operation for February as weather prevented them from climbing up the mountain and blasting. Hattie was telling Violet about her work when Bob came in, ate his meal, went to the corner and strummed his guitar. Bedtime came peacefully.

The little girls settled down on a mattress near the stove. Bob and Violet went to their makeshift bedroom. Hattie sat by herself gathering her thoughts, and then lay down by the children on her own pallet on the floor. By the time they were all settled down, the wind had picked up and they went to sleep listening to the wind howling through the canyon like a hungry coyote.

About two in the morning, everybody was awakened by Violet shouting, "It's starting! My water's broken! Get me a towel! Bob, get the doctor!"

Mayhem ensued with Hattie looking for a towel, the children crying in fear, Bob stumbling awake, swearing while lighting the kerosene lamp, pulling on his overalls, shirt and sheepskin coat, and trying to open the door with his mittens on. The door wouldn't budge. A bank of snow about four feet high was piled up against it. Outside was an eerie darkness washed with forbidding whiteness. "God dammit! Why tonight, in the middle of a blizzard?" he muttered. Grudgingly, he began to pick away the snow which was blocking his exit.

Hattie had managed to find the towel and calm the children. But she was not calm on the inside. She had never been on this end of a birthing by herself. As was the experience of most country women, she had helped deliver calves, colts and lambs, but never a human baby. She knew of several women who delivered their own and she remembered the birth of Violet, her first born. She had very little time for reminiscing but that memory flooded in, all in one piece.

Thus she remembered how she, Hattie, at sixteen years old had practically delivered the baby by herself, while her husband, Jay Michelson, and the midwife played pinochle. Jay had extensive experience delivering farm animals, and the midwife was thoroughly trained in midwifery, but neither of them expected the short time this one would take. The baby was so small that labor was nearly imperceptible. Young Hattie called out from the bedroom, "Something is happening!" Jay and the midwife jumped up from their game and swung into action. The midwife took care of Violet and Jay took charge of the very tiny baby. Hattie remembered her wee baby daughter whose first weeks were spent in a grape basket on the warming oven of the stove, except for the times when she was brought to her for nursing. Violet weighed only three pounds when the doctor stopped by a few days later. He proclaimed her to be healthy, but did not have much hope that she would survive the rest of a South Dakota winter.

Violet did survive and was here twenty-four years later, doing the very essence of a woman's work. Hattie now felt some comfort and confidence. It seemed possible, even probable that it would be all right. She put a kettle of water on the stove, picked her way over the children and asked Bob to find her some string before he left. Grumbling, he found the string she asked for. She put it in the boiling water as the disgruntled father stomped out the partially blocked door to get a doctor.

With Bob gone, Hattie collected herself and calmly and efficiently went to attend Violet who looked as healthy as any woman in labor can and did not appear to be in any unusual distress.. She asked Hattie what time it was and realizing the new day had come she said, "Missed my birthday," in between labored breaths.

Hattie replied, "There will be plenty more birthdays," as she wiped her daughters face, hoping with all her heart that what she said was true. She wished she could pray.

Bob came storming into the shack, "Damn thing won't start. Not the Ford, not the grader, not a damn thing. Must be forty below out there!" He stomped his feet, warmed his hands by the stove, and swallowed a shot of whisky from a jug up on a high shelf. He headed back into the night, God-knows-where to do God-knows-what. He didn't want to be inside. The moaning woman, the accusing mother-in-law, the three sets of wide blue eyes in those scared little faces, brought to silence and awe by the enormity of what was happening. All of that was just too much for him to endure.

He dug out a sheltered place in the snow on the windward side of the grader. Then he built a fire in that shelter with hope that the crank shaft of the grader would thaw out. The walls of the shack were so thin that he could hear most of what was going on inside. Not the actual words, but the tones of the voices and the shuffling of feet and the heavy breathing and the groans. No place for a man to be.

He tried again to start the grader. He fiddled around the fire. He tried not to think, not to feel. At that moment he believed that there is nothing more humbling to a man than witnessing a woman giving birth to a life he has fathered. A man feels powerful and exultant when he plants the seed, but utterly helpless at the harvest.

Finally the frozen grader choked and sputtered. Bob jumped onto the seat and drove down the canyon about three miles where there was a telephone. He called the doctor who sleepily answered his phone. "Bob, are you crazy? There's no way I can make it. I can't even get out of my house, much less the driveway!" Bob, filled with anger, drove back to the shack, engulfed in fear and dread. What would he do if...if... The thought trailed away, too horrible to imagine.

He had been gone about two hours when he got back to the yard. Then he heard it. The unmistakable sound of the great heaving breath that ushered new life into the world. A fleeting thought, "I wonder if it's a boy," passed through his alert mind. He waited. He heard no sound. He raced inside, instinctively avoiding the children on the mattress on the floor, flung the partitioning sheet aside, and found Hattie holding the squirming blue-grey body of his newest daughter.

Hattie said, with great authority, "Get over here and cut the cord! Right now, *now!*" Bob obeyed mechanically. Hattie turned the baby upside down and scooped her finger in the tiny mouth. Violet, Bob and Hattie smiled broadly as the first wail of life erupted from this precious gift and the flush of new blood turned the little body as pink as the dawn of a new day.

Hattie said, "Another one, another girl, and a healthy one too!"

"Just what I wanted," Violet said weakly. Bob looked awkward and felt silly. Again he felt as an intruder on what he felt was essentially women's work.

He went out of the curtained-off space to stoke the fire, and met the faces of the three little girls on the mattress. Their eyes were wide with wonder, fear and eagerness, mixed together.

He said, "You have a new little sister"

In chorus, "Can we see her, can we see her?"

"In a little while," he said, "Just a little longer."

Hattie stayed with the baby and Violet for about fifteen minutes, then appeared holding the small bundle and beckoned to the children to come over and look.

Bobbie said, incredulously, "Another one?"

"What shall we do with her?" Bob asked.

Kitty said, "Send her back!"

Mary Lou said, "Oh keep her, keep her!"

Hattie was very pleased with herself. She had done what had to be done, and it had turned out all right, better than all right; it was perfect. To see her and hear her, one would think she had done the entire thing all by herself, from start to finish. She asked Bob what they would name the baby. He told her that they would wait until his folks could get up to see her so they could help pick out a name. Hattie held her tongue.

After everybody had settled down somewhere on the floor of the little shack and Violet was alone with her baby, she put her hand gently on the little head nestled in her arm and said, "I baptize thee, Baby, in the Name of the Father, and of the Son and of the Holy Ghost." This was a conditional baptism that had been taught to Violet by her Aunt Chrystal.

Violet and her sisters had not been indoctrinated in any faith at all. Hattie was not a believer in church since her father, Henry Holmes, had abandoned her and her mother, Millie, and four siblings when Hattie was about six years old. He had run away in the company of a woman involved in a tent revival meeting; not an uncommon occurrence out on the prairie in the late 1800's. The tent revival meetings were an innovation to fill a religious vacuum in the early days of settling the West. Many pioneers, perhaps Hattie's father, attended because of a spiritual hunger, others out of curiosity. These events were not like attending a church today. To attend a Tent Revival you drove many miles and stayed for days. They were fiery, loud, exciting events. Probably many were converted to a religious belief, some to deeper spirituality. However, for the many who were abandoned, such as Millie and her children, left at home to attend to the harsh realities of life on the western frontier, the result was disgust, bitterness and revulsion of organized religion. Violet's conversion came from the other side of the family; it was Chrystal Michelson Minnick who was Violet's spiritual guide. Chrystal was Jay Michelson's older sister.

It was days and days before the snow melted and the roads cleared up. The tension of seven human bodies cooped up in that little shack should have been enough to expand the walls, but they seemed to close in. Hattie and Bob had a visceral dislike for each other. Their only cooperation was to keep a wide berth between them, but the house was small. It was more of an emotional distance and that didn't make it any easier. When the snow melted down to knee high, they all found outside work to do. They were chopping wood, breaking up ice, fetching water, clearing the way to the main road, whatever they could do to get out of the house. The little girls built numerous snow people, snow rabbits, snow dogs, snow angels, wherever they could find a clearing. Some of the snow banks were eight feet high.

About ten days later the doctor drove his Model T into the clearing. Hattie flew out the door and shouted in the voice she used to shoo the goats away, "Shoo! Go away! We don't need you and we are not going to pay you five dollars for an exam. I did it by myself."

Hattie was as proud of me as she was of herself. She always told people that I got up on my hands and knees the first day, and had wiggled off the table a few days later, and didn't even whimper when I landed on the floor. She claimed that I was the best-natured of all her seven granddaughters. She had no grandsons at this time and through the years acquired only two before her death.

When I was two weeks old the family came on a Sunday afternoon. On Bob Curry's side were his adoptive parents Lou and Mary Curry, who we always called Grandpa and Grandma Curry. They drove forty-five miles south, from Tilford SD, where he was station master at the railroad station. On my mother's side of the family were Aunt Mary and Uncle Oliver and their daughter, Dorothy who drove seventy miles southwest from Hereford, out on the prairie to Curry Canyon. They all gathered there to welcome me into the world and to name me.

I like to think of Aunt Mary and Uncle Oliver being there because according to our family story, she was the Pillar of Intelligence and Wisdom and he the Paragon of Virtue and Kindness. After the storm and the consequent tension in the little shack they were needed to bring a semblance of civility and festivity to the event. I didn't know Uncle Oliver because he died of pneumonia when I was two years old. However he grew in stature after his demise. In the telling of his life and death, he became more real and had more influence on me than many of the living men in my life.

That uncharacteristically warm Sunday allowed the children to play in the clearing and the adults to sit on logs arranged in a circle. They began their task of the day, naming the baby. Several names were suggested but my mother and Aunt Mary held out for the first name to be Dolores after a famous movie star, Dolores del Rio who was popular for a few years around 1933. There were not many movie stars then and few movies came into the Black Hills. However, one movie, *Flying Down to Rio*, starring Dolores Del Rio, played in Hill City and a few other places in western South Dakota that year. Dolores became a favorite name for little girls, most of who were of Scandinavian extraction. I never went to a public school where I was the only Dolores. Usually there were three or four, and once, six of us in the same class. None of them looked anything like the glamorous raven-haired beauty, Dolores Del Rio! Most were tow-heads; that is, blond, blue eyed, fair skinned, while bearing that exotic Spanish name.

There was some friction, perhaps competition between the two grandmothers, Hattie and Grandma Curry, right from the beginning of the day: where to put the food, when to serve it, each of them trying to achieve a measure of status slightly above the other. The choosing of the name added to the chafing. It was quite a struggle for Violet, Hattie and Aunt Mary to prevail and assert that the middle name would be Hattie. Their rationale was that Hattie had been my deliverer, and that was reason enough. Grandma Curry was a bit peeved, and when it became apparent that Hattie was the chosen name, she said, "Well, she's scrawny as a turkey. Probably won't last the winter. Doesn't matter much what you name her." She never really warmed up to me.

The whole truth is that she didn't warm up to anyone. The tragedy that contributed to her disposition was that for a long time it seemed that she was barren. Then, surprisingly, she became pregnant and gave birth to a baby girl who lived only a few days. She and Lou wrote to the orphanage in Sioux City, asking if they could adopt a baby girl. The reply was sent by mail saying that the orphanage would send the baby with a warden by train and gave the date they could expect to receive it. One cold day in February the train stopped at the station and Lou received the baby bundled in blankets. The person from the orphanage went on without coming into the house. When they took the wrappings off, they discovered a baby boy. At first they intended to send him back, but he was ill. They nursed him back to health and decided to keep him. Grandma Curry was always disappointed that Bob was not the little girl she wanted.

Even Grandma Curry could not maintain her dour attitude when the wonderful food was brought to the table. Aunt Mary brought a big bucket of fried chicken and a frosted cake. Bob's parents had brought real cream and coffee, rare treats in those hard times. My mother got some special relish and pickles she had canned the summer before. After dinner Bob played his mandolin and guitar. Some of the CCC men came over with their instruments to play music. The music from the men and their instruments were counterpoint to the squeals of laughter from the children playing nearby under the pines.

By the end of that beautiful sunny February day in the Black Hills I was named Dolores Hattie Curry. I was passed around the circle and each one who held me looked deeply into my eyes as if to gain wisdom or a spiritually coded message that was carried over to this realm from a distant purer place.

What a party! What a beginning!

Hard times were to follow; very hard times, but no one could foresee such things on that perfect sunny Sunday afternoon in 1933.

CHAPTER 2

The Dark Ages—
Rapid City

Of course, that Sunday didn't go on forever. It was February in South Dakota. Midweek after that lovely Sunday, winter showed its true character. It was below zero most of the time. Days were short and nights long and cold with high winds and snow, snow, snow.

Hattie was supposed to leave right after the naming party but on the day she was to catch a ride to Rapid City with the mail truck, Bobbie and Mary Lou came home from school with terrible hacking coughs, so she said she would stay to help out a little longer. In a few days Kitty came down with the same ailment. My mother and Hattie thought that because I was being nursed I would not get it. However, the house was small and the ventilation poor. The only ventilation was when someone had to go outside and a blast of icy air entered the little cabin. Inevitably, I too, began to have the long hard coughing spells and fever.

Bob's reaction to this, the sick children, the typical mother-in-law, the messy crowded shack, was to work more and longer hours on the grader. Pennington County probably never had winter roads as clear as they were in the winter of 1933. When he did come into the cabin, he was as tense as a guitar string tuned a half octave too high. He did have a temper and a foul mouth.

After the coughing and fevers persisted for several days, Violet begged him to go for the doctor. He refused saying, "All kids get sick, and then they get better by themselves. Why should we give the doctor money for that?" Finally he relented and made the call. The doctor came to the little shack and examined the older children and diagnosed it as whooping cough. He administered medicine and left a bottle for future dosages. He looked at me saying, "She's just too little, there is nothing I can do for her."

So on and on it went. Violet and Hattie held me all the time, taking turns so the other one could do necessary chores and take care of the older girls. Bob railed at them, "You're just spoiling her rotten." At one point he wanted to spank me, but Violet ran out of the house with me wrapped in a blanket, and Hattie restrained him. No one was getting enough sleep to be rational.

I feel sympathy for all of them. Violet was recovering from the birth and constantly worried about the life and health of her children, her need for her mother at this time, and the knowledge that it was getting on Bob's nerves. Hattie was out of her own abode, sleeping on a pallet in a crowded shack and contending with a nearly intolerable son-in-law. Bob, yes, I have sympathy for Bob, too. For him, being in the shack with all the noise and smells and the quarreling must have felt as if he had entered some level of Hell. The Blessing of Children? He had heard that phrase but it rang hollow in his ears.

It was an intolerable situation. One night while Violet was rocking me, I had a coughing spell and coughed up more phlegm than anyone could imagine a baby's lungs could hold. Immediately I could breathe better and began to improve, and so did my sisters. The whooping cough had run its course. Hattie went home a couple of days later, and Margaret came back as our hired girl.

Eventually spring returned to the Hills. Bob had made enough money with his overtime on the grader during the winter that he could set up a sawmill near the shack. It was the improvement that he needed to make on the property to maintain the contract with the government. He was around the property a lot more now. He hired a few men to help out at the sawmill.

For Violet there was always the nagging discomfort about Margaret being there. She tried to squelch her jealousy, as Bob told her it was stupid of her to feel that way. Margaret, he said, was just a sweet kid who needed someone to pay attention to her. But when he taught Margaret to drive his Model T, Violet was hurt. When Violet had begged him to teach her to drive, he said, "You are not smart enough to drive, and anyway, women don't need to drive."

Margaret and Bob spent long periods of time out at the sawmill and seemed to always be playful and lighthearted. Violet could hear them from the house where she was busy cooking, tending the children, doing the laundry by hand, diapers and all, in two washtubs for which she had to carry the water and heat it on the stove. When she mentioned to Bob that she could use Margaret more in the house, he said, "Lay off! Give the kid a break. She's been working hard at school all day!"

In retrospect, the winter looked easy compared to what Violet was enduring now. Back in the winter she felt like a real woman. Now she felt awkward, redundant and afraid of what was coming next. It may have been spring out there, but it was bitter winter in her soul.

There were a few bright times in all this turmoil. My earliest memories are of the music. Sometimes in the evening the men from the CCC would come over at night and exchange songs. These young men were recruited by the government from the legions of the unemployed throughout depression era. They lived in work camps in places such as the Black Hills and did projects having to do with forest preservation, water management, and other useful and enduring projects in exchange for their room and board, medical care and a very small amount of money. Most of them were malnourished and had few prospects before joining the Corps. While there, in the Corps, they grew strong and healthy and learned skills that would serve them the rest of their lives. Many stayed on in the Black Hills after the Depression when the CCC was disbanded. They became entrepreneurs, supervisors, workers, farmers and cowboys throughout the area.

The young men of the Corps came from all parts of the nation and brought songs and music that would not have reached the Black Hills for years, if ever, without their migration. Sessions in our little shack on cold nights and in the yard when the weather permitted, were song exchanges whereby folk music spread throughout the country, years before radios and recordings were available. I remember being in my crib and hearing *Down In The Valley, Little Mohee,* and one in particular, called *Oh My Pretty Quadroon.* I can still call up in memory and hear the mournful words:

Oh, my pretty quadroon,
The flower that faded too soon.
All broke like the strings on my banjo,
Is my heart for my pretty quadroon

We, in South Dakota, would probably never have heard the word *Quadroon* if not for those young men from the South singing songs with my father. A Quadroon was a person who was one quarter Negro. It was a term used during slavery and reconstruction times in the South, mainly in Louisiana, before 1900. We learned a great deal about the cultures from which these young men came and they learned from ours.

I know there were other good times because a few old snapshots show our family looking happy and interacting with each other. Pictures were taken only when someone came to visit us and took pictures. There is one of my family, intact, in 1935 in front of Mt. Rushmore when it had only one face on it. My father has Kitty under one arm and me under the other. His face is barely visible under the brim of his hat; my mother looks anxious and sad with a slight forced smile on her lips. I have wondered who took the picture. Margaret? Whose camera? We did not own a camera for years.

One old memory is of a dog we had. My mother told me that I couldn't have been more than about eighteen months old. We had a little mongrel that looked as though he carried Scottish Terrier ancestry. Of course, we named him Scotty. In this episode Scotty had tangled with a porcupine and was left with painful quills in his nose. I remember his pitiful howling; I remember the whole family standing around in a circle on a floor of pine needles; I remember the smell of the pines and the sound of wind whispering above through the towering tree tops; I remember someone calling for hot water and towels and my father holding those steaming towels against Scotty's nose and finally getting the quills out, thereby freeing the poor creature from his pain. Bob did have a soft side, especially when it came to animals.

By the spring of 1935 the love affair between Bob and Margaret was in full bloom and out in the open. Bob told Violet he loved Margaret and wanted a divorce. Violet stubbornly resisted; she wouldn't even talk about it. When he was gone from the shack she cried bitterly most of the time. She was Catholic! Catholics didn't get divorced, and if they did they were excommunicated from the church. She had talked with the priest in Hill City. He told her there was nothing he could do to change that. He said, "That is just the way it is." She was in spiritual turmoil about the Catholic Church. She loved the church because it stood for something; it did not bend with the wind of human change or desire. It really stood for something! She wanted with all her being to be a part of something so solid. Yet she was so angry with her dilemma that she also hated the church. Could they not make one concession for her? She believed that if she were excommunicated, she would be without solace of any kind. She prayed and prayed for a way out of this quandary, but God didn't answer her; not then. Something had to give!

That something which opened the way to a vast change came in a roundabout way. Seventy miles from the Black Hills where all this turmoil was taking place, another drama was being played out on the prairie

On their farm Aunt Mary and Uncle Oliver lived the idyllic life. This life has since been much enhanced in the tales of the settling of the West. They do not usually tell of the deprivations or of the toil to keep going. What Mary and Oliver had that kept them going was that they were very much in love, had many friends and a darling little girl, my cousin, Dorothy. Their farm was coming along and promised a good life in a few years. That was the story of most of the farms in the '30's on the prairie...coming along and promising a better next year.

One day in late spring Uncle Oliver went swimming in the pasture dam. He loved swimming and was one of the few farmers who could. There was not enough water in South Dakota to encourage swimming as a sport, and seldom enough leisure time to encourage it as a skill. Nevertheless he could swim and he did on that day in June. He came home with a chill and said the water was a lot colder than he expected. He thought he would warm up after a while, but he just got colder. He was trembling and became incoherent.

By morning he had a fever and that evening was delirious. Aunt Mary, holding Dorothy in front of her, rode her horse over to the closest farm, three miles away, which was owned by Dolph and Evvie Behrend. Dolph was Oliver's uncle. They asked Dolph to go to the nearest phone, another two miles away, and summon the doctor, but Dolph said he would take them into town in his Model T. The three of them, Dorothy, Mary and Dolph, hurried back to Mary and Oliver's farm, put Oliver on a makeshift bed across the back seat of the Model T and drove as fast as possible, forty miles to town in a car with maximum speed of thirty miles an hour. When they reached the doctor's office, they got Oliver inside. Mary held him in her arms as he breathed his last labored breath. He died of pneumonia, the doctor said.

The death devastated Mary and Dorothy and their many friends and family. Violet and Bob went to the funeral, but Violet had no recollection of any particulars about it, except that it was the largest funeral anyone on the prairie had ever seen.

Violet and Bob went back to the Hills. Aunt Mary operated the farm mechanically for a few weeks. She seemed to be emotionless; "stoic," people said. Violet, at home in the Hills, went further into deep depression and slept most of the time. The older children got themselves off to school with Margaret's help. Kitty, age four and I, age two, were, essentially, caring for ourselves and one another. Mother stayed in bed and slept most of the time.

A month later Mary and Oliver's farm and equipment were auctioned off. Mary could not keep the farm alone. She took a job teaching in a one-room country school out on the prairie.

One of the men who worked the sawmill with Bob took Violet to the auction of Mary's farm, in Bob's Model T. After the sale was over, while she and Violet were sweeping out the attic, Aunt Mary finally broke down and sobbed for hours while her sister Violet held her in her arms. It seemed that two hearts were breaking beyond repair. The day after the sale and the therapeutic cry, Mary resumed her characteristic competence; she seldom displayed emotion. She was a stoic.

When Violet returned to the sawmill she fell back into depression. About a month later, Bob approached her again about the divorce. This time he had papers for her to sign. This time she said, flatly, with no affect, "Whatever you want. I don't care." She signed the papers without even reading them.

I was two years old at the time of the divorce and do not remember all that happened in the next few years. My first memories of that time are of Mother and I living in a little tarpaper shack on St. Patrick Street on the south side of Rapid City. What I remember most acutely is missing my sisters. Oh! How I missed them. It certainly felt as though major parts had been amputated from my body. Hattie, my grandmother and deliverer, lived a couple of houses away keeping house for an old man named Van Loan. Mother and Grandma sewed flags at the county courthouse for the Works Project Administration (WPA), part of the New Deal Program that President Franklin Roosevelt initiated to alleviate the poverty of the Great Depression. They alternated their workdays so that one of them was at home to take care of me. For their work we received commodities, which consisted of flour, canned milk, cabbage, bacon, beans, dried prunes, applesauce and some fabric remnants and sewing supplies. Mary Lou was with us for a short time on St. Patrick Street, and then she too was gone...gone to Montana with Bob, Margaret, Kitty and Bobbie.

My memories of that time are cloaked in darkness. When I was at home with Mother, the house was dark; most of the time she was asleep in the back part of the house, curtained off by a sheet. She was still in deep depression. Often I was looking for something to eat. I remember going to a cupboard and finding a can of milk. When I pulled it off the shelf, along with it came a beautiful pink carnival glass bowl and shattered on the floor. It was the only beautiful thing in the house. I feared her reaction, but nevertheless, went to her bedside to tell her. Her flat response, "I don't care," was more devastating than any scolding or punishment would have been.

After Bob had been gone about six weeks he came back to see her. He was contrite about what he had done. He wept and tried to hold her. She turned away with scorn as he said, "If you ever loved me you would let me hold you." She replied, "I never loved you." One of the few times in her life Mother ever told a blatant lie.

Dolores

During that dark time, I had a severe case of bronchitis, and was very ill. I was in bed with a mustard plaster on my chest. Mother sent word, through Grandma who was working at the Court House, that we needed a doctor. The County sent Dr. Redeusch, a woman doctor, a rarity in those times. She told Mother that my chances of survival were slim. After the doctor's visit I remember waking up to see Mother sewing. I asked her what she was making. Most of our clothes were red, white or blue or some combination thereof, as they were made from remnants of the flags at the court house. This, in contrast, was of light blue silk material, so in spite of my illness, I was curious. She said she was making a dress for me. Later I learned that she had cut up her wedding dress and was making from it a dress for me to wear in my coffin. As it turned out, I didn't need it; I survived. Soon I was well and played alone in a sand pile outside the little tarpaper shack. I was lonely and missed my sisters.

One day, while playing in the sand pile, I became fully conscious; conscious of life itself. I understood what my personhood meant, apart from Mother and Grandma, and apart from my sisters. The memory of this is clear: I was wearing a little blue sweater and was playing with my favorite toy, a Barber Green, a miniature earth-mover, which had been given to me by Aunt Mary for Christmas. Grandma walked out of the house on the path to the outhouse. I watched her move, and looked at her objectively. Then I looked at myself, there in my blue sweater, observing my own legs, arms and body and I understood what it mean to be a person in my own right. It was as though I had become fully hatched that day. I now knew about my person-hood, my boundaries, my autonomy, my separate self.

Little by little, the light began to come into our lives, one glimmer at a time, and I began to fit the pieces of life together.

CHAPTER 3

Light—St Patrick Street

Oh yes, light did come into our lives, and as light usually comes, it was shot through with a commensurate measure of darkness. That was how it came to me and my family.

Bob left us in a little tarpaper shack south of Rapid City on St. Patrick Street, with no support. The street had only two other houses on it. I heard the story of how we got there, either through Mother telling me, or listening in as she and Grandma and Aunt Mary talked. Initially he and Margaret were fleeing South Dakota with all four of us, Bobbie, Mary Lou, Kitty and me in the back seat of his car.

He wanted to get across the state line into Montana where custody laws and things such as child support were more lenient to fathers. Aunt Mary and Mother chased them for a while but his car was much faster so she turned back. Bob made it across the state line with his daughters. However, after I had been screaming for twenty-four hours he left Bobbie and Kitty with Margaret somewhere in Montana. He took Mary Lou and me back to Mother.

After a few months he came back for Mary Lou. She was willing to go with him because she missed her sisters and felt that Montana would be a great adventure. After Mary Lou went back to Montana I was altogether without sisters or a playmates.

To fill the bleak void in my life, I created an imaginary playmate, Rose Marie, with whom I talked and played for the next few years. There were other children about a half mile away but I was not allowed to play with them. I was never told the reason and it was a time when I did not oppose my elders, so I did not even plead to go there. It would have been unbearably lonely if not for my imaginary Rose Marie; she who was more real to me than life itself.

I didn't know why my father was allowed to take the children. I did learn the legal term, "custody." What it meant to me was that my father had my sisters and we couldn't get them back. We couldn't get them back because of a phrase I heard exchanged among my mother, Aunt Mary and Grandma: "Possession is nine tenths of the Law."

We were poor then, poor in spirit and poor in material goods. Even families that had a father in the home were impoverished during these times, but if their families were intact, it seemed to me they had everything.

I was about four years old and Christmas was coming, I was aware of the holiday and had some faint memory of it being a time of special presents and food. There were no preparations for such an occasion in our humble circumstances.

However, the day before Christmas, Bob unexpectedly dropped my sisters off and said they could stay a couple of days. We all were ecstatic, Mother, Grandma and I and my sisters! We had a marvelous evening; telling jokes, singing songs and simply enjoying each other. I couldn't stay up as late as the older children could, so they put me to bed, as if I were one of their dolls. The next morning my sisters presented me with an adorable set of five dolls. They had drawn faces on the round end of five clothespin, and glued some black yarn on their heads, wrapped each in pink flannel, and told me they were the Dionne quintuplets. I was thrilled. The famous Dionne quintuplets, born in Canada were just one year older than I. I was fascinated and always eager to hear anything about them. Their pictures were often in the papers and magazines that Aunt Mary brought us. I named my little clothespin dolls Emily, Annette, Yvonne, Marie and Cecilia, after the actual quintuplets.

On that happy Christmas Day, after a breakfast of oatmeal and canned milk, Mother bundled us warmly and sent us off across the big field of snow north of our house to attend services at St Joseph's Catholic Church. She could not go with us because she had been excommunicated from the Catholic Church. She was a divorcee. At the time, neither I nor my sisters saw anything wrong with this. It was just the way it was. We accepted it without question.

We had a wonderful time walking to church, laughing, playing and making snow angels on the way. My lasting impression of a church was formed on this day. I thought it was heavenly... the colors, sky blue and ruby red, the gold leaf decorations, the paintings, stained glass windows and incense. It was the most beautiful place I had ever seen. Mary Lou loved it too and insisted that the statue of the Virgin Mary spoke to her. I was sure that it was true. Kitty and Bobbie were not as enchanted with the church as were Mary Lou and I. We were enraptured. None of us could take communion as we had not gone to confession. Communion and Confession were perplexing words for me to ponder for the next few years.

After the Mass we went home across the snowfield and re-entered our tarpaper shack. We had left it just two hours before, and found it completely transformed! There was a huge decorated tree with wrapped presents underneath. The house was full of wonderful smells of turkey roasting and there was an abundance of other sumptuous foods; apples, nuts, ribbon candy, fruitcake and bottles of fresh milk! There were presents for everybody! For me there was big rag doll, almost my size, that I named Jimmy and incorporated in my play with the quintuplets and Rose Marie. It was a glorious day. We ate and played bingo, and made little dramas with our dolls. We laughed uproariously over anything at all. Throughout the day we thanked the Salvation Army.

After Christmas when my sisters were gone again, I was not quite as lonely as I had been during their absence before. I had my imaginary companion, my quintuplets and my new doll, Jimmy. Also I had hope and expectation that my sisters would return. Now I had hope and good memories to sustain me.

Aunt Mary and Dorothy visited every other weekend. Aunt Mary was teaching school in a little town named Keystone, close enough that she could come to see us on Sundays. Dorothy and I were close friends as well as first cousins. She was smart and competent. She got straight A's at school and her handwriting was like a work of art to me. And she could draw wonderful pictures. I loved those Sunday visits. Aunt Mary paid particular attention to me. She usually brought some groceries and we always had good Sunday dinners when they were there. On those days Mother would be alive and animated. Sometimes Aunt Mary brought me a toy or clothes that Dorothy had outgrown. Aunt Mary earned twenty dollars a week, which was considered to be a good teacher's salary in 1937. She owned a little Ford coupe. By now she had come out of the disaster of losing Oliver with a positive, albeit stoic demeanor.

Grandma was often at our house. She gave me an abundance of genuine, warm, loving care. She took me to parades and once, even the circus. She did household tasks that Mother could not do...simple things like sweeping the floor, doing the dishes and washing clothes. Grandma was keeping house for a man named Van Loan in one of the other houses on St. Patrick Street. That house was separated from our house by a big, empty white house, which he also owned. When summer came I had more freedom and could go out to play by myself.. I could play in that big empty house. It was exciting to run through the halls and feel the expansiveness of it compared to our little one-room shack.

At first I simply delighted in running through the empty house--all that wonderful space and the echoes through the empty rooms and hallways. It was the first house I remember having a second story. It was positively intoxicating. Then Van Loan would chase me and we would play hide and seek. After the long dreary winter, it felt so free and friendly. Eventually, Van Loan put me on his shoulders and carried me around the house. We would laugh and laugh. Abruptly the tone of the laughter changed. Little by little his fingers slid up my legs and went to places where they shouldn't have. I wish I could say that I screamed and ran to my mother for safety. I didn't. Not only did I not run from it, but the next day I went back, and the next day and so on.

I don't remember how long it went on...perhaps a week, maybe two. I was not hurt physically but I knew it was wrong. It ended after Dorothy had been there on a weekend. She played the chase game in the big white empty house and then Van Loan put her on his shoulders. She told me what occurred and asked me if the same had happened to me. When I confessed, she told me that what he had done was very, very bad. Then she gave me a lecture that I probably should not have received for another seven years, but circumstances made her sure that I needed it right then. She told me the difference between men and women and how babies were made...all of it. Dorothy was discerning and very wise for her years. Afterward I felt dirty, sullied and inferior to other little girls. I became afraid of men. I knew that I knew too much. When I met other little girls I envied them for their innocence. I never felt free from that degradation.

My life went on but not as innocently. I became very interested in going to school. Aunt Mary taught me to read. I remember the day as clearly as I remember yesterday. It was summer and I was sitting on her lap while she was reading a Dick and Jane primer to me. She was running her finger under the words and I came to recognize the words. Soon I was reading the book to her. She was excited, elated. "Violet!" she said, "This child can read," she exclaimed proudly. "She's only four years old!" I basked in her excitement and admiration with a feeling of accomplishment.

Dolores

I remember how the words looked on the page. Something exceedingly important became real to me, as though a curtain had just been lifted and I could see a new world stretching out before me. I was invincible! I could find out about things! I would learn things! From that day on I read anything that came into my line of sight. I read signs; I read labels; I read catalogs; I read the True Romance magazines that were left around the house. I read anything and everything I could lay my eyes upon.

When fall came that year, I insisted that I was ready to go to school. There was a little white clapboard schoolhouse across the field to the south of our house. That was where I was determined to go. Mother complied with my desire and even made for me a little navy blue coat with a red lining and collar to wear on my first day.

When the day finally came I started off alone across the field, in my new coat, with a note in my pocket and lunch in a paper sack. It was a hot September day and there was a bull with horns in the field through which I must pass to get to the school. I thought the bull would chase me because of the red collar, so I took my coat off and hung it on a fence post, carefully taking the note from the pocket, and continued cautiously across the field.

I was relieved and excited to reach the school, and loved that first day. Never had I been in the company of so many children. There must have been ten of them. The entire school was in one room, serving first through eighth grade. I enjoyed the fact that I could read and keep up with the first grade class just fine. On my way home I had to cross the field again, and discovered that my little navy blue coat was gone. I was bewildered. Would someone really take my coat? I could scarcely believe that. I decided the bull must have eaten it. Mother didn't even scold me. She seemed amused by the coat issue and very happy that I had a successful first day at school.

The next day I returned to school, minus my coat. This time I skirted around the field. I got through the morning fairly well, although it wasn't quite as good as the day before. After lunch we had reading class and I didn't recognize the word "eggs." The *g's* were not printed the way I had always seen *g*. I was indignant and decided I did not want to attend a school where they didn't even know how to make their *g's* properly. I politely told the teacher that I would be going home. That was all there was to it. No parent-teacher conference, no papers exchanging hands, no counseling. What an elegantly simple system! It was not deemed a failure on anyone's part. For me it was an adventure than ended with my dignity intact. South Dakota had not yet accepted the idea of Kindergarten so I didn't go to school until another year and a half.

There had been one little girl at school I liked who lived nearby. We played together a few times after I dropped out. She invited me to go to Sunday school with her one day and Mother gave me permission to. However, when I brought home a picture we had been given to color, labeled as a picture of God, Mother objected. She indignantly said, "No one knows what God looks like. No one should even try to know! It is a mystery!" She would not allow me to go back to Sunday School nor play with the little girl. It left me with a hunger to know more about God and to belong to a church.

Before I officially started school, a new worry came into my life. Tom Hudspeth began showing up at our house. The first thing he did was to bring a bag of groceries. He was quite a bit older than my mother, and was a quiet dignified man...a southern gentleman. He was born in Alabama and had very good manners. He treated my mother with great respect. They had met when he came to the sawmill my father had up in the Hills. Tom ran moonshine which meant that he took the "shine" made at the still and transported it over the state line to Wyoming. Everyone respected Tom, even Bob Curry.

Tom found a soft spot in his heart for my mother years before when he had seen her at the sawmill, but never made a move to engage her while she was still married. However she awakened in him the desire to take care of her, to make her life better than it was. After Bob was out of the state and started his new life, Tom approached my mother and began courting her.

Tom and I had a cautious relationship. From the start each of us wanted all of my mother. Each of us knew she loved both of us and by demanding more we each feared we might lose her altogether. We never said mean words to each other. As a matter of fact, we seldom said any words at all. Neither of us could express our feelings without hurting mother, and neither of us wanted to do that. Our high regard for Mother stymied any relationship Tom and I might have had.

He was at the house often. He always came late at night. Tom owned a card shop in Rapid City. Common in the West in those times, they were known as cigar shops and later on as pool halls. They were dark places that smelled of tobacco, beer and newspapers. Men played cards, shot pool and talked with each other. They did horse and car trading and made all manner of business deals there. He went to work in the early evening and showed up at our house after midnight.

Looking back I know that Tom was a bright ray of light coming into our lives. Mother emerged from her depression. Now she laughed, cooked and kept house. She also started making herself look attractive and well kept. She had his love and respect, things she had never known from a man before. A new sense of pride and self-worth entered her life. Their relationship fostered independence in me, probably because Mother's attention was elsewhere.

One day Mother was called to the phone by our next door neighbor who was the only one in the neighborhood to have a telephone. This was always exciting. Phone calls usually meant that someone had a baby, got married or from the darker side, was critically ill and dying. Grandma and I waited eagerly for her to come back. I looked out the window to see her face and how she walked. From that I could tell if it was a good call or not. She was practically dancing on air as she crossed the yard. "Tom called and asked me to bring him his car. He wants *me* to drive his new Packard downtown to meet him!"

He had been driven into town by a friend earlier in the day, and left his car in our yard. She put on her best voile dress and some lipstick and jauntily ran to his car. As she was backing out of the yard, with many interested eyes following her, I could see she was going right into the ditch between the road and the houses.

She was flustered, and went back to the neighbors to call him and confess her mistake. She came back from that phone call in wonderment. "He said someone will come with a winch and get it out and I should just try again. He wasn't even mad at me. He said 'It's only a car.'"

After the extrication she drove off with a smile on her face. Tom was amused by the incident and told the story in a loving and caring way. My mother was no longer the beaten-down woman she had been for so much of her life. She was on her way to becoming the confident, wise and attractive woman she was to be for the rest of her life.

The next Christmas Tom brought me a baby doll. He and Mother woke me in the middle of the night for the presentation. I was elated. It was the new Betsy Wetsy doll that I had read about in the Montgomery Ward catalog. It was beyond my dreams. It drank from a bottle and wet itself and I had to change its diaper. I loved that doll and named her Suzy. She replaced the Dionne quintuplets and the rag doll, Jimmy, who were worn out. She did not, however, replace Rose Marie, who continued to be my best friend and confidant for years to come.

One day Mother asked Grandma to stay with me all day. This was somewhat unusual. The day felt different. Grandma was no longer working for Van Loan. She now worked as a cook for the Garlik Hotel in the middle of Rapid City. She took the afternoon off. A couple of hours after Mother and Tom left, my father came to visit. I hadn't seen him in three years and was shy and tongue-tied. He took me out for a ride and gave me a little wooden rabbit on wheels. I didn't know what to say to him. I wanted to ask, "Where are my sisters," but was too choked up to even get that out. He asked me if I liked Tom. I couldn't answer.

It was an awkward situation for a child of five. He brought me back to Grandma and I was relieved to be home. Later I learned that my mother and Tom went off to get married that day. It was only by coincidence that my father came the same day.

In the middle of a cold February night, Mother got me up out of bed and asked me if I wanted to go stay with Grandma for a while. Eagerly and without question, I said, "Oh yes, yes!"

Knowing that Grandma was a cook in the hotel, I believed it would be fun to stay there. I did not question the strange hour or why they seemed to be excited and in a hurry. I simply accepted it as one more adventure. Tom, Mother and I got in the car and they dropped me off at the hotel where they woke up the desk clerk and asked him to get Hattie Michelson. Grandma came down the stairs and laughingly greeted me. I must have been very sleepy because I remember nothing else about that night.

I did indeed have a good time staying in the hotel with Grandma. The first morning she said I could have anything I wanted for breakfast. I ordered French toast, waffles, pancakes and Rice Krispies. She tried to explain that you couldn't have those four things for one breakfast. It didn't make sense to me but I accepted her offer to have waffles and syrup, something I had never had before. It was clear to me that this was going to be a special time.

The one thing that was difficult for me was that I was supposed to stay in bed until seven, even though Grandma left the room at five to start cooking for the hotel guests. I was always a light sleeper and had resented the fact that I had to sleep and might miss something. I never went back to sleep after she left the room. I became convinced that there was something under the bed; a monster of some sort. One morning I was sure I saw a big hairy paw reach up over the bed and just barely miss me. After a few days Grandma recognized my terror and allowed me to come down to the kitchen with her on the condition that I would be quiet. It was difficult, but I was quiet for those two hours from five to seven. I liked sitting in a corner watching her cook.

There were many things I enjoyed about the ten days I was there. We celebrated my sixth birthday in the hotel and I was presented with a frosted cake and many cards and a few gifts. Sadly, I missed my mother. We had always shared our birthdays together. My birthdays with Mother were simple and did not have the elegance and treats that I enjoyed at the hotel, but we were together and for part of that day she seemed happy. My birthday was the only time during my stay at the hotel that I became tearful about being away from her. When I asked why she couldn't come for my birthday, Grandma told me she had something very important to do that week and I would find out about it soon.

I didn't dwell on that issue because the next day a little girl named Norma, came to stay at the hotel with her parents. They arrived in the evening and I asked if she could play with me. Her mother said she was too tired from traveling, but Norma could play the next day. I was so excited to have a playmate. The next morning I had a hard time being quiet while Grandma cooked for the hotel. I waited impatiently for Norma to finish her breakfast with her parents, keeping her in sight and we made faces at each other when no one was watching. We both knew we were going to have a good time together.

There were some restrictions. We could not play in the lobby; we couldn't stay in either of our rooms, and we couldn't make very much noise. Neither of us had any toys with us. So we sat in the rocking chairs on the porch of the hotel in the weak February sun and there we invented, in our heads, an elaborate dollhouse. By the end of the day it had expanded into several houses in a miniature village. We imagined a school, a hospital, furniture, vehicles, gardens, pets, toys, clothes and food for our imaginary population. It was a day I will never forget. I wonder if she still remembers that day too. She left the next morning with her parents. We knew and accepted that we would never see each other again but I have never lost the fond memories of that day. For many years I played our game in my head whenever I was alone, bored or uncomfortable.

On my eleventh day of hotel living, the hotel clerk handed Grandma a note. Grandma read it and said, "You can go home today." She got my coat, hat and mittens and took me to the porch. "Just go up this hill; go past St. Joe's; keep going straight. After the sidewalk ends you can see your house across the field. Your mother will be waiting for you."

It was about a two mile walk and I was so eager to get home and see my mother that I ran most of the way. Shortly after I spied the house, I saw the door open and Mother standing in it waving to me. When I got to where I could hear her she said, with joy and excitement in her voice. "I have a present for you, a wonderful birthday present."

"What is it, what is it? A doll?"

"Oh, better than a doll, much better!"

She led me to the back of the house, through the curtain, and there in the middle of the bed was a beautiful little red-haired baby!

A real live baby...for me! "A baby sister!" I said with awe and wonder. For the first time in my little life, I cried for joy. Then I lay down beside her and examined her soft hair, her dear little head, nose, eyes, lips, arms, legs and every finger and toe. She was everything my heart longed for.

I told Mother, her name was Rose Marie. Mother told me it was Stephanie. I tried to convince Mother that she was wrong. This was Rose Marie; my imaginary playmate, incarnate. I told the neighbors and anyone who came to visit that her name was Rose Marie. By the second week, Mother capitulated, sent the birth certificate back and had the name changed from Stephanie to Rose Marie. I thought at the time I would always call her by the proper two-part name but eventually she became known as Rosie to most of the family and friends. "Rosie" suited her well. It matched her disposition perfectly.

I started reading to her the first day we met. I read to her every day for the next three or four years. She always listened with rapt attention and the reading session would quiet her in an instant. Gradually she began reading to me. There was never a time when she was taught to read. She simply assimilated it. She learned to read as she learned to walk, to talk, to feed herself, by watching me.

If earlier lights were shafts and glimmers, this was a sea of light.

The tension between Tom and me now was that we had one more person for whom to contend. She was the joy of our lives... separately.

CHAPTER 4

———— ✠ ————

Watertown Street

One warm September morning in 1939, Mother, Grandma, and Mrs. Woods, who had recently moved into Van Loan's big white house next door, were sitting outside the tarpaper shack where they had carried out a chair for Grandma. The other two were sitting on a bench made of a wide board supported by two log stumps. Their focus was on Rose Marie who was recovering from summer complaint, a flu-like illness, common to babies then. Each of the three women had a folk remedy they thought should be tried, but there was no tension or argument about it. They were exchanging ideas in a conversation that was soothing and simple.

Seemingly, out of nowhere, like a cloud cutting across the sun, a neighbor suddenly appeared with alarming news that Adolph Hitler, the dictator in Germany, had invaded Poland. So many new words and unfamiliar concepts for my six-year old brain to absorb. I had no idea what that news meant, but the stricken faces of the women told me that something very big and very serious had happened. The way they spit out the name "Hitler" and the anger they displayed when saying, "attacking a small country without provocation!" frightened me. Something had happened that profoundly changed the world and the course of history. I feared it would change our lives. Could Hitler come here?

For a long time, weeks growing into months, and even years, it seemed to me that the grown-ups talked of nothing but war. Anyone who had a radio had it tuned into news broadcasts all the time. Those who had no radios gathered around any wireless nearby. I grew tired and nervous as the adults talked war incessantly. "German" became a bad word to me. Also I had just learned the word "germ." They meant the same thing to me.

Rationing was imposed on all Americans. We had never had luxuries but somehow were made to feel further deprived by the prohibition of things we never had, such as pineapple. This indignity was fomented by wartime propaganda over the radio and in the daily papers. We were "doing without," bravely, they told us, because we were sharing our sacrifices with the soldiers who were out there on the front lines.

Rationing fascinated me. We were issued small booklets with different colored stamps that we had to redeem at the grocery store to buy almost all foods. In dry goods stores, other things were rationed, shoes among them. Strangely, even though we had never had more than one pair of shoes for each person in our family before The War, now owning only one pair was patriotic. Tires and gasoline were rationed. Rationing was a way that every American shared the burden of the war and played their part in what was known as The War Effort on the Home Front. I felt validated by the system as there was a separate ration stamp book for every person in a family. There was an official book with my name printed on it. I felt the whole family benefited from my stamps because I didn't eat as much as the adults, nor did I drive the car. Rationing also had a financial equalizing effect in that it was not only my family and other poor people who had to ration their basic necessities; the wealthy had the same constraints. It was years later that I learned about the black market. Those who had a luxurious life didn't suffer very much, I discovered.

The war went on far too long in my estimation. I had a bad case of war nerves. That is every time a bomber flew overhead I headed for a ditch or under furniture depending on where I was at the time. Rapid City Army Air Base was built in 1942, so there were many big planes flying over Rapid City then.

Dolores

During that time we moved from the little tarpaper shack on St. Patrick Street to Tom's house on Watertown Street in North Rapid. This was not a high class neighborhood. There were several basement houses. These were the remnant of construction that had started in the thirties and were abandoned in the depression due to lack of jobs, whereby the owners could have finished them. Now they were homes to the very poor. Next to Tom's house was a trailer house, which had some amenities, and a wonderful couple living in it, but, nevertheless, it was a trailer house. However I was glad to leave St. Patrick Street. I had never felt comfortable living just two doors from Van Loan.

Tom's house consisted of one large room where we ate, lived and slept. He built a bed for Rosie and me, a shallow wooden box holding a mattress. It was hinged, so in the daytime it folded up against the wall. At one end of the big room was a two burner kerosene stove, a counter for the water bucket, a small cupboard and a table. That was our kitchen. There was no plumbing. We pumped water from a well in the side yard. In the back yard was an outhouse. Although quite primitive, it was better than St. Patrick Street.

In the first week after we moved there, I met a girl named Bertha Dawson who lived about a block away. Her father was a newspaper man. He was the first man I knew who wore a suit and tie to work every day. Their house had two-stories, was painted a pale green and was the prettiest house I had ever seen. She had her own bedroom! Bertha was my first best friend. She showed me where the wild bluebells grew and initiated my lifelong love of wildflowers. Together we enjoyed playing with Rosie who was our living doll.

I started first grade at the Roosevelt school. What an exciting day that was for me! A real school! There were six grades, each in a separate room. In my class there were about thirty children. There was an inside lavatory. Milk was served to us mid-morning.

The school had an aroma that seemed to me to be the smell of wisdom and greatness. I loved being there.

The year of the first grade was a year of life-lasting lessons. There I came to experience exhilaration and disappointment, pride and humility.

Exhilaration came through my reading abilities. My first grade teacher, Miss Bloom, really seemed to love me. Once my mother and I met her at the grocery store and Miss Bloom told my mother that I was the best reader in the class. At home Mother told Tom, with great enthusiasm about that meeting and I felt my place in the family was elevated a notch.

Another thrilling aspect of that first year was my friend Anna Hovde, with whom I walked to school every day. I stopped at her house and walked with her the rest of the way. Her parents, immigrants from Norway, were learning the English language and American ways. They always talked to me and listened carefully to what I said. My first friends, Anna and Bertha were rosy-cheeked, plump little girls who, in my eyes had perfect lives. They shaped the positive side of my early childhood.

At the same time I carried a three-pronged pain. I missed my sisters. The pain of losing them was always just below the surface. I missed them and I imagined all the fun they were having without me. I imagined what we would be saying to each other. I imagined playing with them. Sometimes I feared I was losing my memory of them.

The second element of my pain was bearing the stigma of being a child of divorced parents, which also meant having a last name different from my mother's. At that time there were very few children of divorce. Whether it was true or not, I believed that I was the only one in my class who endured that dubious distinction. That is not to say there were not dysfunctional families; there were, but most people then chose to live it out rather than face the expense and stigma of divorce. We had been set free from one dysfunctional family and then Mother had married Tom. She was Mrs. Hudspeth and I was her daughter, Dolores Curry. For most of my childhood I knew not one other child who had a different name from her mother. A saving grace was having my little sister, Rosie, who was just crazy about me and I about her. I ardently wished that she and I had the same last name.

The third part of the tripartite pain was the lingering stigma of the incident with Van Loan. Even though it had occurred long ago, I still felt beneath every other little girl in the first grade. It felt to me as though it was visible. Other little girls, in their white starched pinafores might know, just by looking at me.

Family life was strange, as I look back on it. It did not seem strange to me at the time; it was just the way it was. Tom, my stepfather and I walked carefully around each other with no warmth between us. Competition for the affection of my mother and Rosie was a wall between us. There was an unassailable bond between Mother, Tom and Rosie. They would read the funnies in the daily newspaper and while they were doing that I would sneak a True Romance or True Confession magazine, take the flashlight and go into the closet to read. Granted, I didn't know exactly what I was reading but it was entertaining and titillating. I was a child who knew too much, and as I could not un-know it, I had an appetite to know more. The three of them would go out for rides in the car and I would opt to stay home and read. That was easier than not being able to enter their circle.

What happened in the winter of 1941 probably set in place a stance in my personality or unleashed one that had been lying dormant in my evolving character. The morning of that pivotal day was a typical winter day in Rapid City, cold and damp. I walked to school, stopping at Anna's house so we could walk together as we always did. Morning classes went on as if it were an ordinary day. Just before lunch a very strong wind came sweeping down from the North. A fast moving blizzard was upon us. The teacher took one look out the window and told the first graders to get into their coats, hats, mittens and overshoes; she was sure that our parents would come to get us before the blizzard got too fierce to get through.

One by one the children were taken home, usually by their fathers, some by car and others on foot. When Anna's father came to fetch her, he wanted to take me with them but I was holding out for Tom to come for me. Finally I was the last one in the room except for Miss Bloom who was looking out of the window as anxiously as I was, assessing the strength of the storm, and waiting for my rescue. It did not come. Finally I said, "I can do it by myself." I set out for home with a large measure of self-determination.

Of course I did make it and in a certain way, it made me. It set in place a fierce independence, a belief that I could do whatever was needed, by myself. That stance shaped and informed a great deal of my life thereafter. I never questioned why Tom did not come for me that day. Perhaps he knew I was able to do it and would be stronger and have more self-reliance by doing it myself. Of course, in the '40's in South Dakota, no one talked about such things as self-esteem or character; but they were there; as yet unnamed factors of life.

Throughout first grade I was the best reader in class and the weakest in arithmetic. At this point, my baby teeth had fallen out and were replaced by teeth far too big for my mouth, crooked and unattractive. I seldom smiled because I was self-conscious about them. My hair was straight and blond and raggedly cut. I was, in the vernacular of the time, "Skinny as a rail." My clothes were from Woolworth and not what most of the other children wore. In class I would look at other little girls and thoroughly believed that if only I had curly hair, straight teeth, rosy plump cheeks, clean ironed pinafores, a real father, a last name the same as my mother's, and no sordid experience in the past, then life would be good. I imagined that they all went to Sunday School every week. Most of all, I envied the innocence of the other little girls.

The last day of first grade I walked home pensively, pondering the long non-school days ahead. I was already missing Miss Bloom and Anna. Bertha, a year older than I, had found another best friend. As I got to our house I was still thinking about the summer ahead, and was standing on the end of the teeter-totter that Tom had put in the yard for Rosie and me. A big boy came running across the yard and jumped on the opposite end. Being much lighter than the boy, my body catapulted upward and came down with my full weight on my right arm, hand down and elbow locked. There was no pain at first, but my arm looked strange. I walked into the house to tell Mother.

She went quickly to a neighbor's to phone Tom, telling him to come at once because I had broken my arm. By the time he got there, the numbness had worn off and the pain was excruciating. The next thing I remember was waking up with a cast on my arm.

I have a dim memory of E.B. Hickman, bringing me an illustrated book of fairy tales. E.B., as she was called, was a woman who showed up occasionally in our lives. She was Tom's first wife, much older than he. She was, by our standards, a wealthy woman and her intrusions in our lives were always disruptive and unexpected. Why and how she showed up that day is a mystery to me, but I very much appreciated the book she brought, the first book I owned. Mother read it to me in the night when the pain from my broken arm was severe.

My main activity the rest of the summer was sitting on the stoop of one or the other of our two neighbors' houses, with the cast on my arm, talking for hours. What would a six year old and an adult find to talk about for so long? I wish I could remember.

One of the women, Mrs. Olson, had one of her legs amputated. I did small chores and enjoyed time with her and I know she enjoyed me. She had a refrigerator, electric toaster and a few other electrical appliances.

At home we had been connected to electricity for a short time and had only lights and a radio. I was still caught up in the wonder of being able to pull a chain and produce light. I also loved listening to Fibber McGee and Molly and Jack Benny on the radio, but those other appliances, the ones that Mrs. Olson had, seemed to be far out of reach for my family.

Near the end of the summer, the cast was removed and the arm looked very strange...bent at an odd angle. I was directed by the doctor to carry a bucket of sand around for the next few weeks and he said the arm would straighten itself before school started.

During those weeks of walking and carrying the bucket of sand, I had time to contemplate the end of summer and going back to school. I was worried about the second grade arithmetic. I was so frustrated and humiliated by that subject in first grade. Also, I dreaded facing another year of embarrassment from having a different last name than my mother. Again I would be on guard lest one of those innocent little girls discovered the source of my shame.

Mother took me downtown to do back-to school shopping. This was new experience for me. I got a new dress, of better quality than usual, shoes, and a pencil box, all from Woolworths. I loved the smell of those new things, even the pencil box. I was somewhat reconciled to the idea of going back to school. Then one day before the new school year started, Mother said she had something important to tell me. Her voice was serious. "How would you like to go to Colorado to live?" she asked me.

"Would it be warmer or colder there?" I asked. She said it would probably be warmer.

Mother told me that we would have a big house with a yard, like Bertha's, but even bigger. Rosie and I would have our own bedroom. I would take piano lessons. A new life was unfolding in my mind. My life would be like the lives of the little girls I envied. I asked Mother if I could change my last name so it would be the same as hers. She said she could not think of a single reason why I could not do that! There *was* a reason, but neither of us knew it yet.

A few days later, we took off with high anticipation in Tom's tightly packed Packard coupe, Rosie and I in the rumble seat. When we wanted to sleep, one of us climbed onto the little shelf under the back window and the other stretched out on the narrow seat.

We went across Wyoming on a long hot day in August. We stayed overnight in Rock Springs with Tom's stepdaughter, Josephine, the daughter EB had before she and Tom were married. She was as old as my mother. Tom and Josephine talked about the job he was going to do in Colorado with his son, Dan, the child he and EB had together. Often, I listened in on the adults' conversations but this time I was distracted by imagining our new home.

My first glimpse of Colorado, through the back window of the Packard was not what I expected. I had been asleep and awoke abruptly from my perch above the back seat, because we had suddenly stopped. I was disoriented, sleepily coming out of a dream about a bedroom of my own. What I saw was a solid wall, which turned out to be snow; deep, wet, cold snow. The car was stopped in a narrow mountain pass in the Rocky Mountains. Mother told me we were in a blizzard and could not go any further that night. We would sleep in the car. I wondered about the warmer Colorado we had talked of back in South Dakota. I did not sleep again that long night. At daybreak a snowplow appeared, and we followed it through the pass and arrived in Black Hawk, our new home. The snow had disappeared and it was a summer day. The abrupt shift in the weather unsettled me. Colorado weather seemed an untrustworthy omen to me.

CHAPTER 5

Colorado

After awakening in the darkness in the rumble seat of Tom's Packard coupe, bleary-eyed and hemmed in by a wall of snow, the foreboding I felt that first night was unmistakable. Anxious to discover what lay beyond the unknown in this new and different place, we set about getting oriented and locating our temporary home.

First we went to the home of Tom's son, Dan and his family who lived in a large trailer house that Tom had built back in Rapid City. There I met Dan's son, Jackie, just a few months younger than I. Immediately I sensed that we would become close friends. I was drawn to this pale, thin little boy who had more toys than I had ever seen. I noticed that he was quite attached to his mother, Ulah. She eyed me warily, as if I might beguile him and spirit him away from her.

Next we went to see our house. I was enchanted. It had a second story, and many, many rooms. It had a yard and a lawn, burnt yellow from the August sun, but a lawn, nevertheless. There was an old upright piano in the living room. To me it was beautiful. I could see myself making music from its smooth ivory keys. The bedroom that Rosie and I would share seemed huge. Yes, indeed! This would be a different life from that in South Dakota.

The crew who were to work with Tom arrived that evening. I then began to understand what we were doing there. Tom had bid on the job of supervising a crew to build a road between Idaho Springs and Golden, Colorado. Tom was basically a business man and a carpenter, and I believe he must have been surprised to have been granted the contract. He was a competent man and had the confidence and integrity to honor his contracts, so he hired a crew that had the skills and experience to build a road. He trusted Dan's skill and maturity implicitly; enough to appoint him foreman on the job. The crew would live in our house and mother would cook for them and do their laundry.

The first of the crew to arrive was Jumbo, named for his size. He was by far the largest man I had ever seen. As if to offset the threat of his size, he was extremely kind and gentle, a friendly giant. Shortly thereafter a man named Ross joined the group. He looked small beside Jumbo, and he had a teasing manner. I was uneasy with him right away. It seemed that he never took his eyes off me and that made me squirm under my clothes. My mind went back to Van Loan. Ever since his violation of me, I had feared almost every man I encountered.

There was one more man on the crew but I remember nothing about him. I do not remember where they slept or very much about them at all. I recall that I felt uneasiness about them sleeping in our house. I did not spend much time in the house when the men were there. In memory I did not spend much time in the house at all, especially during this last month before school was to start. Most of the time I was playing with Jackie, far away from the house.

Even though Jackie's mother seemed wary of me, she was willing to let him play with me, unsupervised, for hours at a time. That was a time when children were free. We left our homes in the morning and no one called us back. We went home when we got hungry. People believed that all the children would be safe and that everyone in town would watch out for their well-being and safety. We had precious time to play before the school year started. So we explored the town, even the under-belly of it.

The town of Black Hawk was built in a narrow valley between two high mountains. Houses were constructed along streets and perched precariously on the hillsides above. A stream called "The

Flume," covered with a sturdy wooden boardwalk ran under the middle of the town. Jackie and I searched until we found the entrance at the higher elevation of town where the stream started and flowed through the rocks about five feet below the sidewalk. You could enter that place, climb down a rocky wall and scamper under the sidewalk on a narrow ledge of rock beside The Flume. The only light was from the cracks in the wooden sidewalk above. Down there it was damp, dark, cool and enchantingly dangerous. We would make little sailboats out of leaves and twigs and follow them down the stream from the upper end of town to the lower end where it met a larger faster flowing stream. When we reached the lower end we would climb the rocks, out of the dank, and sit in the warm sunshine on a brick wall and watch the confluence of the two streams, sometimes getting to the wall in time to watch our sailboats go on sailing down the larger river. Ever since that magical time, I've been fascinated by a confluence of waters, and can watch it for hours. I even love the word "confluence."

As fate would have it, some adult realized what we were doing during those hours when we were unaccounted for, and realized the strong possibility that we could slip off the narrow rocky path and be swept into the fast flowing rapids. To make matters worse, this flume carried the potentially dangerous waste from the mines upstream. No one knew for certain that they were dangerous but there was some concern about it. So our adventures were brought to an abrupt halt before we met the potential disaster of drowning or being poisoned by the chemical run-off. I've never regretted the time we had there in the underground channel.

Undeterred by the flume misadventure, Jackie and I continued to pursue new frontiers and challenges. Dan and Ulah, Jackie's parents, thought that since I was six months older, I was responsible for him. Mother had always given me a free rein and Ulah enjoyed the relief from constant mothering. So we were still able to run about town, exploring and enjoying life.

Once when we went beyond the upper limit of town, farther than we had ever gone before, we came to a magnificent mansion surrounded by an impenetrable white metal fence. It was exquisitely landscaped with a broad sweeping lawn bordered by a variety of flowering shrubs. While we were taking it in, we saw a child, a beautiful little boy in a white sailor suit, younger than either of us. He came running eagerly over to the fence and we talked with him a while. He had every toy imaginable. He even had a little red car run by a battery so he could actually drive it. We found out that his name was Gerald Burlingham Montgomery and he was not allowed to, and regrettably, could not get out of his yard. Also he was not supposed to talk to anyone. Very soon his nanny, a severe looking women in a nurse's uniform came to rescue him from the street urchins, as she called us. We were not diminished by her assessment. We felt sorry for poor little Gerald Burlingham Montgomery, and exulted in our freedom.

We decided one day that it was time for me to learn to ride a bicycle. Jackie had a two-wheeler and had not ridden much since I arrived because we pursued our adventures on foot and besides, there was only one bicycle. We imagined that somehow, if I learned to ride we would find another bicycle and then we could share the thrill of racing down Main Street faster than the wind.

In the middle of town was a gas station owned by a mechanic named Blackie. We had come to know him quite well and liked to sit on his stoop and talk with him about whatever occurred to us. He said he had just the right setup for me to learn to ride the bicycle. There was a flat driveway beside his shop, at a right angle to the steeply sloping main street. I could get started on that, and when I got my balance I could turn up the street until I was confident enough to reverse the direction. That was the plan. After a few practice runs on the flat driveway I steered the bicycle up the street, went a few feet, and then, with an overdose of self-confidence and bravado, I turned down the street. My ride started pleasantly, but in seconds gravity took over and I was flying down the street much faster than the wind! I realized that I didn't know how to stop! None of my training sessions included a brake lesson. In about two minutes I could see the end of the street and a brick wall coming toward me at an alarming speed. Somehow I managed to jump off and push the bike away from me before we met the wall. Both the bicycle and I were a bit damaged but I was more exhilarated that hurt. Faster than the wind! It took my breath away and gave me something too wonderful to name!

My mother was quite happy in that home in Colorado. For the first time in her life, she had an unlimited budget to run the house. We had milk delivered, and even better, a bakery wagon that came by a few times a week. Imagine, sumptuous pastries brought right to our doorstep! She cooked bounteous meals for the crew every morning and night, and she packed hearty lunches for them too. I helped in the kitchen in the morning and at night, but in the daytime, I was free. Mother had time to enjoy Rose Marie as she had never had with her other daughters. I watched my mother shed her thin, ragged self and transform into a round, beautiful, happy woman.

We went to Denver one day and she bought me a dress, not like the ones from Woolworth's that I had worn at my old school. This was like the ones the beautiful little girls wore for the first day of school. She also arranged for me to start piano lessons. The piano teacher, coincidentally, was to be my second grade teacher, and she owned the house we lived in. That was the beginning of the troubles.

Where to start? They are jumbled up in my memory in no sequential order. Each of the troubles taught me an important lesson. I've come to believe that is the use of troubles.

Let's start with piano lessons. They must have come before the other troubles because I had the first lesson just a few days before school started. It was going to be at my teacher's house. Can you imagine my enthusiasm! It was huge. I was imagining that I would be producing music that fell from my fingers and trickled out like a waterfall. I was imagining my teacher would be someone like Miss Bloom, my beautiful beloved first grade teacher. However, in sharp contrast, this person turned out to be ugly, big and scary. I did not reserve a place for her name in my memory bank, so I will refer to her as Mrs. Schtrume. She was stern and imposing. Before we started the piano lesson she asked if my mother was taking good care of the carpets in the house. How embarrassing! I did not know what carpets were. It was not yet a word in my vocabulary. I said I thought so. She asked if the workmen took off their shoes when they came in the house. I knew the right answer to her question was "yes," so that was my reply, even though I had never noticed if they did or not. Her questions made me nervous. I knew Mother was happy in that house and wanted to continue to live there, but what if those things called carpets were not kept up to Mrs. Schtrume's standards? What then? Should I tell Mother about the questions or keep them to myself? I decided to hold on to it for a while.

The piano lesson began: "Hold your hands just so. If you let them get out of the proper position, I will tap them with this ruler." We began with some scales. We continued them for most of an hour. These lessons were not going to be fun. They were going to be about the discipline of music. At the end of the lesson she said, "The next lesson will be at your house." My heart sank.

My house! She had let me know at the beginning of the lesson that it was, in fact, her house and that she was letting us inhabit it. I felt the power differential between being a home owner and a tenant. It was a long and tedious hour until the piano lesson ended. Other lessons were forthcoming.

Soon it was the first day of school. The new dress and shoes, the prospect of many new children I would meet and make friends with, did not blunt the apprehension of dealing with Mrs. Schtrume again. I was right! School was no more fun than the piano lesson.

It was immediately apparent to me that the Colorado schools were way ahead of those in South Dakota..

I could read as well as anybody, but the arithmetic! They were adding up columns of numbers! "What is a column?" I wondered, but was too embarrassed to ask. I had barely mastered basic addition and subtraction facts. On the third day I realized that the answers to the arithmetic problems were in the back of the book. I was sitting in the back of the room and in desperation, having no idea of how you added up all those numbers; I went to the back of the book for answers. I was furtively matching up the numbered answers with the problems when I looked up and saw that Mrs. Schtrume's eyes were fastened on me.

I felt a wave of heat course through my body. My stomach sank to my knees, which had turned to jelly. I raised my hand, pointing one finger up which meant that I needed to use the lavatory. Without changing expression she nodded permission. I quickly ran to the lavatory, which was a scary place for me, very unlike the one in South Dakota. This one had wooden seats, over a deep hole in the ground. You could not even see the bottom of it. But it was necessary for me to sit there immediately. Then I have no idea why I felt that dropping the entire container of toilet paper, piece by piece down the hole was somehow a purgation of the terrible thing I had done. Was I killing time, avoiding going back to the schoolroom, or, symbolically throwing my terrible sin down the hole?

After a while a girl from third grade came to get me. Mired in deep humiliation, I went back to the class room and slunk into my seat. Mrs. Schtrume said, after I was back in my seat, "Let's have Dolores read something to the class," and she put a book in my hands. The book was as comforting to me as the assurance a beloved dog can give a person when you know you don't deserve such acceptance. I regained some measure of dignity through exercising my considerable gift of reading. To her credit, Mrs. Schtrume did not mention my transgression to me.

I learned three important life lessons that day: that trying to cover up unknowing is never worth the humiliation of cheating and being caught; that it is not easy to get rid of guilt, and no hole is deep enough to bury it in. The most important lesson...that even people you do not like, such as Mrs. Schtrume, may have an awareness and kindness that you never expected. That was my first conscious encounter with Grace.

The house in which we lived became less attractive after Mrs. Schtrume came to give me my next piano lesson. Mother was not happy with the arrangement. I'm sure she felt that Mrs. Schtrume was spying on us and assessing the care of the house. The day after my piano lesson in the house, the carpets were covered with flattened cardboard boxes. The house also came to feel less safe after one night when the plaster ceiling came crashing down onto the bed where Rosie and I were sleeping. Rosie went into Mother and Tom's room to sleep the rest of the night but I was in the room alone with remnants of fear. I felt as I had when I stayed with Grandma in the Garlik Hotel, years before.

There were more lessons to come, the hardest of all the Colorado lessons. It happened like this: Jackie and I had continued our friendship, playing after school and on Saturdays, exuberantly exploring every new avenue the world offered us. We were still having splendid times exploring the town, and playing the way six and seven year olds do.

One day we were playing house, in a protected, secluded corner of the yard. We assigned roles. He would be the father and I would be the mother. Thanks to the education that I had from my cousin Dorothy when I was about four or five, I knew what mothers and fathers did, and was embarrassed to know so much. But I got carried away when explaining it to Jackie and we began some childish exploration of a new and different kind. In the midst of this exploration, who should come bursting upon the scene but Ulah, Jackie's mother! She was furious. She told me I was a little whore, a new word for me, but I knew it wasn't a good word. She called me a few more names and said Jackie could never play with me again! The prospect of this was devastating! I was humiliated beyond what I thought I could bear. And so sad, so very sad! The end of playing!

Had it ended there it still would have stayed with me for the rest of my life, but it didn't end. The next day when I arrived at school, the children in the playground began a chant: "Curry Hudspeth, Curry Hudspeth," they taunted over and over again. Jackie had betrayed me. He was the only one who knew that I was using my mother's last name and that mine was really Curry. I was more humiliated than the day before! I ran home and sobbed in my mother's arms for hours.

The lessons from that day were profound. I can condense them into a few words but the enormity of the degradation was beyond any words. I learned that being an impostor to your true self is something that will squelch your spirit, will sap the joy from your life, and that you can never get away with it. If not betrayed by someone else, perhaps even your best friend, you betray your own soul. I could never again be anyone but myself, a lesson that life honed to a fine point in the years to follow. I reclaimed my own name, and was known as Dolores Curry for the rest of my school days. I gave up my name twice in my adult life but reclaimed it in my early 50's and kept it to the end of my days.

That was the end of summer and what a long winter ensued. I had no friends at school. Piano lessons ceased. School was almost unbearable. I retreated into reading. Mother must have known my pain and gave me special time and attention. Once we walked up the boardwalk, over the flume where Jackie and I had played, and came to the town of Central City. There was an opera house there and she said that on a certain afternoon we would go there to hear some music. The little waning flame of my spirit flared up in a burst of warmth at that prospect. When the day came and we attended the *Grand 'Ole Opry* I was thrilled. It was the reconnection to the music I had known in my early childhood in the Black Hills. The love of music sustained me then and has ever since.

Another time, Mother and I poured over the Montgomery Ward catalog and picked out a dress for me to wear in the school Christmas program. It was blue taffeta with a pleated skirt, a little cluster of flowers at the neck. It was a very special dress. She let me fill out the order blank. Every day I would come home from school waiting for the package to arrive. Even into my old age my spirit is kindled by Old Time Music, by blue dresses, and by ordering things from catalogs.

After the Betrayal, in the springtime, Aunt Chrystal came to visit us. Aunt Chrystal was my mother's aunt, someone that every child should have in her life. Her history tells something of her character. She had been married early to a man that no one of my generation ever met. She and he had gone to San Francisco in the early 1900's. They had been there during the Great San Francisco earthquake and fire. Family stories tell that Aunt Chrystal came back to South Dakota as a nurse, but without her husband whom she referred to as Mr. Minnick. No one ever knew or told me what happened to Mr. Minnick, but he never came up in the family conversations again. Aunt Chrystal moved to Oregon City and began her lifelong career as a nurse. When she was hired at the hospital, she stated her age as ten years younger than her actual age because she knew she would want to work more years than the policy of the hospital would allow. She was the head nurse at that hospital for many years. I used to write letters to her partly because I loved the appearance of her address on the envelope:

Chrystal Minnick, Head Nurse
Oregon City Hospital
Oregon City
Oregon

She was a devout Catholic and when she came to visit in Colorado, she brought me a little silver cross, which I cherished. Better than that, she brought a spirit of adventure. We went out every day exploring the mountains that rose up around the little town. We found mine-shafts, gooseberries, abandoned shacks, animal skeletons and more. She found everything interesting. We laughed and played; she was more fun than Jackie, and her visit eased the shame and humiliation I had suffered through the winter. Mother was exhausted by Aunt Chrystal's energy by the time her visit was over. I was energized. She left me with a little autograph book in which she had written the first entry:

There is so much Good in the worst of us;
And so much Bad in the best of us,
That it doesn't behoove any of us,
To talk about the rest of us.

Before the year was over we left Colorado and headed back to South Dakota. No one explained why we left when we did, but there was some disagreement between Tom and Dan, about the road project.

On the way to Rapid City we stopped to visit Aunt Mary who had recently married Uncle Marvin. They, along with my favorite cousin, Dorothy, lived in a little mining town named Trojan, near Lead SD. It was decided that I would stay with them until Mother, Tom and Rosie got settled again in Rapid City. This was a continuation of my multifamily growing-up.

It was not surprising that Aunt Mary would be married again; most people expected it would be within a short time after Oliver's untimely death. She remained single for about six years and was courted by several unmarried farmers, ranchers and cowboys who lived on the prairie. Once, Roland Anderson danced every dance with her at the Farmers Union dance. Then he asked her to eat dinner with him. Roland was a good dancer but not much of a talker. He was a sheepherder so his daily life was very quiet except for the sound of the bleating sheep and the wind in the grass. It was almost as if he had forgotten how to talk. After the fairly silent dinner together, he asked Mary if he could take her home, to the house where she was boarding. On the way there he stopped by a little bridge. They sat in silence for a long time. Then he blurted out, "Mary, would you marry me?"

She thought about it for a few moments and said, "Yes, Roland, I would."

The silence dropped like a thud without sound. Several minutes went by. Not being able to bear the weight of the silence any longer, she said, "Roland, why don't you say something?"

He answered, in a labored whisper, "I think I might have said too much already."

She paused but a moment and answered, "Well, let's just call the whole thing off."

All he could manage was a strangled, "Ok."

He took her home and never asked her to dance again...that is until the wedding dance when Aunt Mary married Uncle Marvin, Roland's older brother. Aunt Mary, Uncle Marvin and Dorothy now lived in a little mining town named Trojan, near Lead South Dakota.

I was enrolled in the Trojan School for a while and regained some confidence in my academic strength. I could read far above grade level, and was closer to the acceptable level in arithmetic than ever before. Aunt Mary, the teacher *par excellence,* was always there and interested in what I was learning. Dorothy and I played school at home, which was a powerful remedial education for me. When we played, she was always the teacher and I played the role of various children at many levels of learning.

Often, today, in our sanitized, safety conscious, child-protective world, I remember scenes from my childhood and marvel and wonder how we survived. One such powerful memory, which still comes up in dreams repeatedly, is a game we used to play at lunch time. Perhaps the teachers needed a break and felt justified in sending all of us, from grade one through eight to the upper floor of the building to entertain ourselves from the time we finished eating our packed lunches to when classes began again...probably thirty to forty-five minutes. I have no idea how many children there were, but enough to make a large circle sitting on the floor. We would sit in the circle, while one of the big boys sat next to the electrical outlet. He had rigged up a game wherein at his signal we would all hold hands and would all get an electrical shock! Then we would get silly and laugh like drunken sailors. Perhaps we were on to the idea of getting high...so young...so early in the scheme of things. I don't remember how it ended, but somehow, without disaster.

Disaster and danger hovered around my life, tempered by safety nets and loving parent figures. Aunt Mary was important in my life and her marriage to Uncle Marvin was an expansion of her influence. He was a very large man, Norwegian, with a big smile and a good nature. He liked to laugh, and in many ways was childlike, and most surprising to me, he liked me...no, he loved me, and I was not afraid of him. I thoroughly enjoyed my time with them in Trojan. I spent every school vacation for many years with Aunt Mary and Uncle Marvin. They lived in Trojan a short while and then moved to the Hereford Flat, not far from where Aunt Mary and Uncle Oliver had lived about six years before.

I stayed with them in Trojan a month or so until Mother, Rosie and Tom got settled in at Tom's house on Watertown St. When I got back to Rapid City, I remember feeling that I was home again. Colorado had been a strange and foreign place and my time there was over, blessedly over. However, I carried more of Colorado in my emotional baggage than I realized.

I went home as Dolores Curry and tried, for the rest of my days, to be true to that person.

CHAPTER 6

Montana

It was the darkest night I had ever seen in my entire life. However, my life had spanned only nine years thus far. I would see darker nights later on. On this moonless night in June I had a very narrow perspective on life, both in time and in geography. Here we were in Idaho. Mother and four of her five daughters, walking down a highway in the middle of the night.

Just a half hour before, I had been asleep on a scratchy seat on a train when my mother, in an anxious voice, was telling me, "Wake up! Now! We have to get off the train, right now. We have to find a place to stay."

Awkwardly, the five of us tumbled down the steps of the train and here we were, stumbling along the dark gravel highway. The only thing that kept us together was Mary Lou's white blouse showing up in the faint starlight. Also, the white of the cast on my arm was visible in the dark night. I had broken my right elbow again, as I had three years before, when I was six. As our eyes became accustomed to the dark, we began to see each other, so we could follow Mother on the narrow shoulder of the road.

Suddenly, a much brighter light, an elongated beam, swept across the sky, like nothing I had ever seen. In a panic, I sputtered, "What was that?" In a matter-of-fact way, Mary Lou informed me that it was a searchlight. With that information I became acutely alert and the events of the late afternoon and early part of the night came back to me in a rush.

Search lights! Of course, I reasoned, they were looking for us. As the beacon swept across the sky for the second time, I headed for the ditch and told the other four, "Get down!"

They were annoyed with me and one of them said, "What's the matter with you? Get up out of there! We have to stay together!" I was puzzled. Didn't they care if we were found...after all we had been through?" Sometimes the world can be bewildering to a nine year old. I began to sob with frustration and fear.

Finally, Mother realized what was going on in my mixed-up little head and she stopped and held me close, explaining that the searchlights were not looking for us. They were from an airbase nearby and were scanning for enemy planes in the sky. This did not assuage my fears. I had a bad case of war nerves, since the Japanese bombed Pearl Harbor, and the grown-ups in my life talked of nothing else. From the airbase outside of Rapid City, big bombers landed and took off regularly, but I never got over it. It had been going on for a couple of years but still I ran and hid under furniture every time they went over. If I heard them when I was walking home from school, I headed for the ditch, just as I did on this strange night in Idaho. As Mother held me, some partial rationality returned and I remembered the events that led us to this point.

A week before, Mother, Rosie and I took a Greyhound bus to visit Bobbie, Mary Lou and Kitty in Dillon, Montana, where they lived with Bob and Margaret. Tom went along with this plan, probably because he knew Mother was determined to carry it out, no matter what. He also knew how much she missed her children, and he loved her and thought it would make her happy. He gave her money for the fare, and a little spending money, promising to send more in a couple of weeks for the return tickets.

We left Rapid City in the early evening, slept overnight on the bus and arrived in Dillon shortly after noon the next day. Upon our arrival, Mother asked the station master for directions to the grade school. We walked there, and Mother told the secretary at the school office that we wanted to see the Curry girls; that she was their mother and, with a nod to us, we were their sisters. Looking back, it is interesting to note the innocence and trust that prevailed in 1942. No one asked for proof or for papers. We did not expect that they would. People believed each other.

The secretary sent a student to bring my sisters to us. Kitty and Mary Lou came running down the hall and we hugged, laughed, cried and covered each other with kisses. The first words out of each of their mouths were, "Take us back with you! Take us back! Oh, Please, take us back!"

The office staff witnessing this didn't hesitate in excusing them for the rest of the day. Mother asked if they could have the next day off, and after the secretary spoke with the principal, she said they could have off the next three days, the last days of the school year. Next, we went to the high school where Bobbie attended. The joyous reunion scene was repeated.

We found a park nearby and sat under the trees where the girls told of their life with Bob and Margaret. They lamented Margaret's strict discipline. When Kitty wet the bed, she was forced to wash her sheets by hand, after Margaret rubbed Kitty's face with the dirty sheets. Mary Lou told us how she tried to be invisible, as quiet as a mouse, to avoid being noticed at all. Bobbie fared somewhat better as she was older and had a part time job in a dime store, and was not at the house as much as the other two. Bobbie could always stand up for herself. She had the confidence that came with her seniority. They all complained of the terrible fights between Bob and Margaret. Bob would get drunk and become very mean to everyone in his path.

From that moment on, the plan was to get out of there all together, and we would get back to Rapid City, somehow. There was considerable planning, plotting and conjecture going on among Mother and the three older girls. I was not in on that as someone had to watch Rosie, and that someone would, of course, be me.

The first night in Montana we stayed in Bob and Margaret's log house. I had seen pictures of this house that Bob had built for them, and I had daydreamed of how sweet it would be to live there. That changed abruptly after the nightmare of that first night in Dillon. I can't imagine how anyone could think it possible for all of us to stay there together. Some things are too complicated for a nine year old to figure out.

What happened was what *had* to happen, considering the cast of characters. Bob had gone out, which left in the little log house, Mother and her five daughters, and Margaret, the proverbial one who had broken up Mother's marriage and who was now the wicked stepmother.

The mood at the evening meal was strained. We were getting ready for bed when the pent up fury bubbled to the surface. Bobbie's nightgown was missing a button and Mother asked for a needle and thread so she could sew it on. Margaret was incensed by this request, and a furious argument broke out between them. They were spitting out words. "She's my daughter, I will do it." Margaret yelled, "It's my house! I will do it."

Terrified by what I expected to happen next, I called out loudly, "I have to go to the toilet!" There was no indoor plumbing, and my arm was in a cast so I definitely needed help. Bobbie offered to take me, but Mother was the one I wanted. That eased some of the tension in the house. Mother and I went out, and I stalled as long as possible. Bobbie slipped out and went to a neighbor, who got Bob out of a local bar and brought him home. Fortunately he was not totally drunk, and came quickly to settle the fracas, preventing the breakout of a physical fight. We all settled down and slept for the night. I did not sleep soundly that bizarre night. It felt as if we were on the brink of disaster.

The next day Bob rented a little shack less than a block away, for Mother and Rosie. He said I could stay in the log house with my sisters, but I did not want to stay there another night. Our few days in that little shack were pleasant, not because of the amenities...there were none. No furniture, no plumbing or electricity, but we got by. It was somewhat like camping out. My sisters came over every day and the first thing we did was to pick grass and greens for the rabbits that they kept in pens in their yard. They were not pets, but Bob's latest commercial venture. Then we had most of the day to talk and do whatever we pleased. We made peanut butter sandwiches and picked apples and went to the park for picnics and to play there the rest of the day.

In the cool shade of the park, we formulated a plan for our escape. Sometime soon, when both Bob and Margaret were busy, we would make a break and leave Dillon together on the bus.

The opportunity came very soon. Bob and Margaret left one afternoon to go up into the mountains to visit friends, and they would be gone overnight. Shortly after they drove away, Mother and all of us except Bobbie went to the bus station. The bus going toward Rapid City did not leave until the next morning, too late for a safe getaway. However, we could escape by train that evening. We needed to leave Montana as soon as possible, as Bob's custody rights ended at the state line. The only train leaving that night was going in the opposite direction, but Mother was confident that something would work out once she had custody of her own children. So we took the train to Spencer, Idaho. Most of us anyway. Bobbie did not make it to the station in time. Mary Lou had gone that afternoon to the store where Bobbie worked, to tell her of the plan, and that there was a bus leaving Dillon for Spencer at midnight, in case she missed the train. I fell asleep immediately as the train chugged out of Dillon.

I woke up completely disoriented. We were getting off the train at Spencer. As we walked down the aisle of the train there was nothing you could see from the windows that indicated there was any town there at all. Mother asked the conductor how far it was to town from where we were getting off. He said there was a gas station about a mile up the road and pointed the direction we were to follow. We walked quite a long distance, in the dark, with the searchlights overhead and eventually came to a darkened gas station.

Mother knocked repeatedly on the door until the sleepy owner responded. He lived in a room above, and was wary about coming down in the middle of the night to answer the door. He was shocked to see a woman and four girls at his door at midnight. She told him of her dilemma, and of how she thought she might get a job in Spencer, perhaps as a waitress, until she could earn enough money to get to South Dakota, or even to Utah where her father lived. He informed her that there were no jobs in Spencer. Here, in the gas station was the post office and there was nothing else. This was it. This was Spencer.

Mother asked if she could make a collect phone call and he cautiously allowed it. She reached her father, Jay Michelson, in Ogden, Utah and succinctly told him her complicated story. Grandpa spoke with the gas station owner and said he would wire money by Western Union in the morning, if the station owner would give us enough cash to get on the bus, which would take us to Ogden. Perhaps, because the station owner could not imagine putting us up in the station indefinitely, he agreed to that plan and we slept the rest of the night on blankets on the concrete floor of the garage.

After a long sleepless night Mother arose, fretting about Bobbie, but decided we would go on anyway, hoping she would find us. Miraculously, when we boarded the bus, there was Bobbie. In the midst of our laughing, hugging and kissing, the passengers applauded.

Grandpa was there to meet us when we arrived at the Greyhound station in Ogden. He guided us to the city bus stop from which we all rode to his house on Kiesel Avenue, a couple of miles away.

City busses were a novelty to all of us and we thought it a marvel-ous way to travel.

The Ogden City bus stopped a block from Grandpa's house and our motley crew walked to the house. I loved the house and yard there. It was surrounded by gardens, both vegetable and flower, mostly roses.

Grandpa, after he and Hattie divorced, had travelled exten-sively around the West, working as a carpenter and handyman. In Ogden he had met and married Ruth, a tiny woman from England. She was the first person I had ever met who had an English accent. My sisters and I were amused by her, and encouraged her to talk to us. She and Grandpa had two sons, Louie and Jimmy. They were both younger than I. Louie was a baby and it was fun for me to wheel him in his carriage and tell people that this was my little uncle.

For Grandpa, it must have been strange to have so many fe-males in his house, but he never seemed to mind. I thoroughly enjoyed being there. Most especially, I took delight in the gardens. He took us all to the ice cream store Being with my sisters, all of them, in one place, safe at last, made me feel whole again. I had felt a hole in my heart since they were taken away seven years before.

We were in Ogden about a week when Tom wired Mother money and told her to come home. He missed her and Rosie. I did not hear his reaction when she told him there would be three more than he expected. Her daughters were all coming home. Whatever his reac-tion was, we all went to Rapid City on the Greyhound.

We walked up North Street about two miles from the bus sta-tion to the house on Watertown Street; the house with one large room, a kitchen the size of a closet, and a garage with a dirt floor. Fortunately, it was summertime and we could quite comfortably sleep on mattresses on the floor of the garage. Tom came home that night to find a deluge of females in his house.

We enjoyed a few weeks of playing as children do. It was great for me to play with my sisters. We had very few toys or games, but we had each other and we were imaginative and creative. We captured a few tadpoles from the creek and gave them each a name; very poetic names: Robert Louis Stevenson, James Whitcomb Riley, Tom Sawyer and Popacotypetal. When we found Popycotypetal dead we conducted an elaborate funeral for her. We marched in a processional where we sang the popular song for which she was named, and buried her in a decorated matchbox. We released her siblings in the creek in her honor. Those glorious days of innocent childhood play lasted only a little while.

As fall approached, our reassembled, fragile family system began to change. Mary Lou was starting high school and wanted to get a job and earn her own money. Mother found a job for her helping a friend take care of her children in exchange for room, board and a small salary. Bobbie stayed on Watertown Street with the rest of us for less than a week after which she found a job downtown and was living elsewhere. She was paying her own way.

That left Kitty, Rosie and me at home with Tom and Mother. Tom was building trailer houses in our yard and Rosie spent most of her waking hours with him, pounding nails into boards with her own little hammer.

So, it came down to Kitty and me playing together. At the beginning we often argued, asserting our rights with one another. I soon realized that I would never win an argument or a game with her. Kitty was a strong character. That was the only way she could have withstood the abuse she suffered under Margaret. I came to an agreement with myself that I would never contend with her. When a disagreement came up, I would say nothing, except to myself. I would say to myself, "I know that I am right, and that is all that matters, to me." We got along smoothly thereafter.

After a few months on Watertown Street, we moved to a nicer house on New York Street. We had a bedroom for the four girls, and a living room. We enjoyed a few more months of sisterhood there. Kitty and I converted an abandoned chicken house on our property into a playhouse. We spent about half of our free time there, fixing it up with whatever we could find to use as furnishings. When we were not in the chicken coop, we were playing in the creek that ran through New York Street Park.

Fifth grade was in a large public school in Rapid City. I was a mediocre student and missed large blocks of school due to various illnesses. My tonsils were removed and an appendectomy was performed that same year.

Appendicitis carried important side effects for me. I became quite ill, complained of pains in my stomach. Mother allowed me to stay home and after the fourth day took me to Dr. Dawley. He said, "She has appendicitis and should have surgery."

There was no such thing as medical or health insurance. Mother had little money of her own and could not figure out who would pay for the operation. So she told the doctor she would have to think about it. He warned her that it was serious, and if I should vomit a green substance she should take me to the hospital emergency room immediately. I vomited the following day and was admitted to the hospital.

Before starting the surgery, the hospital wanted to know about the financial arrangements. The bill would be one-hundred-fifty dollars. Bobbie called our father, and he said that he would pay, only if I would come and live with him when I was well. Mother said that was not possible. Tom would not pay because he felt it was Bob's responsibility. Finally mother made an arrangement with Dr. Dawley. She would clean his offices until the debt was paid.

The operation was successful. I stayed in the hospital for ten days. Both Dr. Dawley and his partner, Dr. Kegaries, came to visit me every day, and we talked together. I discovered that they attended the Congregational Church in Rapid City. When I was well enough to attend church, I went there. Mother seemed to recognize that even though she maintained her Catholicism, I was going to be an independent thinker about my spiritual life. We did not discuss this; it was an unspoken agreement. I attended that church throughout fifth grade. Most of the time alone; once or twice Rosie and Mother joined me.

The summer after fifth grade, Mother went to the Black Hills Teachers College in Spearfish to obtain an emergency teaching certificate. Teachers in the country schools were scarce and one could teach after one successful summer semester. Mother was working on her high school diploma from the American correspondence school and thought she was ineligible but Aunt Mary persuaded her to try. How pleased she was when she achieved the highest score of all the applicants on the vocabulary test, an entrance requirement of the program. Rosie and I went with her to Spearfish, where she rented a one room tourist cabin. We went to the lab school under the tutelage of college students practicing their teaching skills. It was a rich learning environment and both of us learned and enjoyed the entire experience.

Once my class went on a field trip to Iron Mountain, just outside Spearfish. We collected samples of the local flora. We found some cacti among them. While others wondered what they tasted like, and wondered if they were edible, I decided to try. I never learned what they were, but I hallucinated and felt euphoric, and then became quite ill. Nothing more came of the incident, but I never forgot it, and never again experimented with strange flora... a good lesson to learn before high school and all that was to follow.

After our lab school was over, there were still a few weeks of summer school for Mother to finish her course at the college. For the rest of the summer I joined Mary Lou and Kitty who were out at Aunt Mary and Uncle Marvin's farm.

My family firmly believed that children on farms were healthier than those living in town. Mary Lou and Kitty thrived on the farm that summer, and became tan and strong. They worked at the chores as well as shocking the sheaves of wheat and corn. The chores were getting the cows into the barnyard in the evening, and milking them, feeding the animals, chopping wood, keeping the water tanks for the animals full. "Chores" were the outdoor tasks that kept the farm running. Shocking the grain was part of "harvesting," and was separate from the chores. Harvesting had to do with income of the farm.

I was kept in the house to help Aunt Mary, as I was thought to be fragile. We worked in the kitchen and garden to provide meals for the workers. We also canned vegetables, fruit and meat. We separated the milk from the cream, churned butter, and baked the bread. We did the laundry once a week in a wringer washer, hung the wash out on the clothes line, and ironed them with flatirons heated on the kitchen stove. No matter that the temperature hovered around a hundred degrees; we kept the kitchen stove going all the time, as most of the household chores demanded a working fire.

We all loved being on the farm...always busy and feeling productive. Every day after the noon meal, which we called dinner, there was a rest period. The men and outdoor workers leaned against the shady side of the house, talked awhile, and fell asleep.

Inside, Aunt Mary and I sat at the dining room table after we had washed the dishes and put them away. We got out her books... mostly poetry. We read the poems and other works of Hawthorn, Longfellow, Keats, Wordsworth, Oliver Holmes, and Tennyson. We read them aloud to each other. My love of poetry never left me. The hot, labor intensive, yet healing and restful summer days on the prairie ended, and we went back to the city. The poetry echoed in my head forever.

I loved the summer on the farm. However, when it was time to start school, I was still very thin and frail. I reluctantly entered the sixth grade in the same public school in Rapid City. I was falling behind in arithmetic and losing confidence in my reading skills. By the end of September, I had been ill three times and had missed many days of school in the first six weeks. My grades were not good.

One day I came home from school in tears. Mother tried to comfort me, but I cried for a long time until I could talk about it. I told her how I loved being on the farm and how happy I had been out there. I told her I was afraid I was going to fail, and if I did, I could not bear the humiliation. This touched a chord in Mother, remembering her own failure in eighth grade. I felt a shiver go through her. She doubled her effort to find a way to save me from what she had gone through. I wanted to go back to the farm, but that was not an option. Aunt Mary and Uncle Marvin were just getting started and could not take on another person for the winter.

Slowly it dawned on her. There was another farm in our family...a well-established farm, where the girls in that family had grown up to be healthy, successful career woman. Immediately, she wrote to her Aunt Mabel, in Miller SD and asked if I could stay there for the school year. In four days we received an answer, and plans were underway for this new adventure. Mother was sure I would thrive there. Aunt Mabel was Grandma's sister, so I was confident that it would be all right. I went eagerly, looking forward to an opportunity for a successful school year. Miller was across the state in Hand County, three hundred miles away. I would be going by train on an overnight trip, by myself. I was more than ready for this bit of independence and adventure.

CHAPTER 7

━━━━ ❧ ━━━━

Miller SD

"Very grown-up" was my assessment of myself as the Chicago & Northwestern passenger train carried me out of Rapid City, across the prairie eastward on a Saturday evening in early September, 1944. I remember the train stopping in the towns of New Underwood, Wasta, Wall, Murdo and Pierre, all towns I recognized. I watched with fascination as the landscape gradually changed from the rolling prairie terrain to the river breaks where it became more rugged, and after the Missouri River the land gradually flattened out into lush farmland. It became dark and the sound of the train wheels clicking on the track transported me into a sound sleep. Occasionally I would almost awaken as the porter called out names of towns I did not recognize...."Blunt!" "Harrold!" "Holabird!"

The next thing I knew a porter was bending over me saying, "Your stop is coming up, young lady." I opened my eyes, peered out the dust-coated window and saw the dawn of a cold, grey day. Through the train window I saw a town that looked strange and interesting to me. It was neat and clean and at the same time, bleak and lifeless. Next to the tracks was the grain elevator, a familiar sight in many of the towns I had seen the night before. Somehow, this one was different. I shook off the uneasiness, grasped my suitcase and staggered down the aisle as the train lurched to a stop.

As I stepped down to the platform, I saw coming toward me three people, two of whom I recognized from pictures I had been shown at home back in Rapid City. They were Aunt Mabel, a short, stout woman who looked like Grandma, except for her roundness. The second one I recognized was Elaine, who was to be my teacher this school year. Elaine was Aunt Mabel and Uncle John's youngest daughter and had just attained her Normal Certificate to teach in a county school. She was nineteen and lived at home. The third person in the reception party was Uncle John, as round as Aunt Mabel, and a complete stranger to me.

The two women were politely smiling, albeit without much warmth. Uncle John's face was unreadable. Silently he took my suit case and carried it to the car. As we drove away from the railroad station I observed they were more reserved than my family in Rapid City.

"While we're in town," Aunt Mabel said, "we should go see Doris." From conversations at home, I knew that Doris was their oldest daughter who lived in the town of Miller.

I was impressed by the spacious and elegantly furnished home of Doris and her husband, Harry. He was not there that morning and I seldom saw him nor knew anything about him, such as where he worked or why he was gone so much of the time. On that first morning I perceived that Doris was warmer to me in her welcome than the rest of the family had been. Perhaps she was more at ease around younger people as she was secretary at the local school. She introduced me to Toll House cookies which she had just taken out of the oven and they were the most luscious food I had ever put into my mouth. I had one, thinking that was what was allowed, but she encouraged me to have as many as I wanted. I left her house staggered by the abundance of what I had just partaken. This was the beginning of a food feast that would last for months.

As we drove the fifteen miles from Miller to the farm, I could see the difference between these eastern farms and the ones on the prairie. The houses and barns were larger and well maintained. There was a tidiness to the landscape which contrasted to the prairie which sprawled untamed and immensely free, spreading out as far as your eyes could see.

When we reach the Gaudig farm, where I would live for a school year, I could see that it was more prosperous and larger than any farm I knew. I saw equipment in the yard my Uncle Marvin would love to have. Holding sway over the farmyard was a tall windmill constantly turning in the wind, emitting a musical squeak with each turn. It pumped a steady stream of water into three troughs: the lower one having a pipe that carried water down to the garden area. There was a huge barn, around which were many cows, and a large pig pen, filled with squealing pigs of all sizes. About a hundred chickens, mixed in with a sprinkling of turkeys, roamed freely in the yard. Only two horses were kept on the farm: Trixie, a thin, swayback, thirty-year-old horse which, I was told, my mother had ridden. The second was Sparky, a little black-and-white horse that belonged to Elaine.

We entered the large farmhouse into a huge, warm, well-appointed kitchen, obviously the heart of the home. There I met Ethel, another daughter of Aunt Mabel and Uncle John. Ethel was two or three years older than Elaine. Her husband, Jay, was in the Marines on active duty somewhere in the Pacific Ocean. She lived at home with her six-week-old baby boy, Neil, who had not yet met his father. This was to be my family for the rest of the school year....Aunt Mabel, Uncle John, Elaine, Ethel, and the baby Neil.

I was shown to my room! The first time I ever had a room of my own. It was a small room with a window from which I could look out into the farmyard and keep an eye on the old horse, Trixie. That pleased me. I unpacked my suitcase and put my few belongings in the empty dresser. There was also a bed and chair in the room. I felt very privileged to call this my own space.

After a little while of enjoying the idea of having my own room, I went outside to look around. I walked to the pasture where Trixie was kept. She came to me and let me know she wanted to be petted. Her warm muzzle and soulful dark eyes endeared her to me. I stayed with her quite a while until Uncle John, who had been watching quietly from a little distance away, called me and told me it would be my job to feed her morning and night. He showed me where her feed was kept and told me to mix it with warm water which he had brought from the house. She had no teeth to chew grass or whole grain so she ate the mush, made especially for her. This was my first assignment: feeding Trixie her warm mush morning and night. I was glad to have something to do. It made me feel useful and part of the farm. I had a glimmer into the character of Uncle John. Although he seemed stern and serious, he had a kind nature, and was someone I need not fear.

After a while I was called into dinner. What a sumptuous dinner it was! There were two roast pheasants, potatoes, carrots, and onions and turnips that had been roasted with the birds, with a delicious, savory stuffing inside. There was a fruit sauce, cooked greens, pickled beets, corn, hot rolls and other things I do not remember. Of course there was dessert...always there would be dessert...cakes, pies, cookies, puddings, cream puffs and things I had never seen or imagined in my dreams. Dessert that night was chocolate cake with a buttery icing. This was Sunday dinner but the dinners that followed were nearly as sumptuous. Hand County was in the heart of the pheasant country and every morning during the season the young men in the family would go out and shoot the legal limit, take the birds to a freezer in town, where they were accessible to anyone in the family to pick up. We were never out of pheasant. We also had many other types of wild game as well as the beef, pork, chicken and turkey from the farm.

The first Sunday afternoon we went to visit Uncle John and Aunt Mabel's son, Lester, who lived on a farm a couple of miles away. Lester and his wife, Thelma, had two little girls, Betty Jean and Loretta. I loved playing with them and knew exactly how to play with them because they were nearly the same age as Rosie, whom I was starting to miss. There was another son, Elbert, and his wife, who lived a little further away and whom I met later on.

That first day I met Dean Huisman, who was Elaine's boyfriend. These three men, Lester, Elbert and Dean, were friends and the ones who kept the family furnished with game.

When we got back to our farm, Uncle John gave me a quart can and told me we were going out to milk the cows. A short time after he started milking the first cow, he motioned for me to come closer and let me know that he wanted to squirt the milk into the can. When it was nearly full he told me to drink it. I was reluctant, thinking that warm milk was not a great idea, but I dared not oppose him. In a moment I realized that it tasted very good and drank it all. This was the start of a ritual that would take place every night at milking time...drinking a quart of milk fresh from the cow; milk so rich that that they would separate off half the cream and it would still meet the market standards for whole milk. After the milking, we went to the house for supper; leftovers from dinner; a generous meal, with dessert.

The next day was my first day in a country school...except for the few days in that country school when I was four years old. My teacher, Elaine, and I started out for school at the same time, she on her horse and I walking beside to the end of the driveway. From there she pointed out the way and then rode on ahead, while I walked on alone. Elaine, being the teacher, needed to be there before her students. The exception to this was that the oldest student could come in early and start the fire in the potbellied stove which sat in the back of the room. In this school, that would be Charlotte, who would become my best friend.

Elaine, on her pony was soon out of sight, and off I went through some cattails by a little bridge. Never before had I seen or smelled cattails and I liked the smoky odor they emitted. Up out of the swampy area, and on to the second mile marker, where I turned left and walked one more mile. I could see the little white frame school building most of the way but it seemed like a long walk. Before the year was over it became an easy walk, and I learned to see the wonder of nature around me as the seasons changed from fall to winter and back to spring.

There were eight students in this school: two second graders, two fourth graders, three sixth graders and one eighth grader. I was excited to be there and eager to meet my schoolmates. In my sixth grade class was Mary Johnson, a round-cheeked, Norwegian girl who reminded me of my first school friend, Anna. The other sixth-grader was a quiet, thin dark haired girl, Francis. I loved everything about that little school. It was like a family. I was welcomed and accepted from the first moment on.

School was never dull or boring and the work was never too hard. Arithmetic was my weakest subject, but even in that I could make good grades and meet the standards the county sent out to assess the progress of the children in the country schools. In my sixth grade class, each of us progressed in our own level in the core subjects; reading, spelling, language and arithmetic. Social studies, music and art were subjects the entire school worked on through educational projects. Everybody participated at their level, working toward a culminating event that belonged to all. At the end of a project the school invited the entire community to a program to view the results of our work. We answered questions from the parents, or others in attendance. Other times, our culminating event was a class trip to another country school or to a business in town. I remember having a guided tour of the dairy where our milk was processed and prepared for market. Another time our art projects were entered in the State Fair in Huron. I won blue and red ribbons for pencil drawings I entered. The one I liked best was of a little fishing shack with a boat pulled alongside, next to a body of water. The ribbons were a source of pride for me and won a few words of praise from Uncle John. Gradually I was regaining the academic confidence I had as a first grader.

Every afternoon when I got home from school, I played with baby Neil and rejoiced in his milestones...his first tooth, his first steps, his first words. We did not have homework then. Farm children had too many chores to do in the evening after school. My first chore was to feed Trixie. Feeding her and caring for her was an act of mercy and love. I loved that she depended on me and met me at the fence and nuzzled my hand. I loved the fact that she had carried my mother on her back. Once, with Uncle John's help, I got up on her back, but she was too bony to be comfortable and too thin to carry a saddle. She was an old lady and needed care and comfort which I was happy to give her.

One of my other chores was to "slop" the pigs. That meant that I carried out a pail of kitchen waste to the pigpen and called out, "Sooey! Sooey! Sooey". They came running to get that treat, slobbering and snorting in their piggish way. It always made me laugh. I also helped feed the chickens and gather the eggs.

The windmill pumped the water from a deep well to the surface, into a water trough and we scooped buckets from the trough for cooking, drinking and washing up. Bringing in the water was everybody's chore and there was a constant movement of people from the water trough to the house.

There were always chores in the kitchen. We washed and dried the dishes after each meal. We cleaned the apparatus of the separator, a contraption that used centrifugal force to separate the milk from the cream. That was a big job, because the separator had many parts, and they had to be cleaned meticulously. We washed the glass chimneys for the kerosene lamps, we swept the floors, we prepared nuts for Aunt Mabel's scrumptious desserts; we sorted beans and shelled peas. I came too late in the year for the canning of food for winter, but appreciated the bounty that the summer gardens had produced and the family had laboriously preserved. I had little time to be homesick.

The feeling I had when the small contingent of the family met me at the train---the feeling that they were not as warm and comfortable as my West-river family was soon dissipated. They included me in their busy farm life as naturally as if I were their own daughter.

One day, Uncle John told Ethel and Elaine to take me to town and get me whatever clothing I needed. I was overwhelmed! This was not a trip to Woolworth but to a fine clothing store where a clerk helped us and brought things to me in the dressing room and spoke of alterations. I had never heard that word before. I came back to the farm with a tan camel hair coat, a brown corduroy dress, shoes for special occasions, skirts, blouses, flannel lined long pants, and sweaters for the cold weather which would soon set in. Also, a pair of sturdy, serviceable shoes for school, boots for wet weather, and the most elegant underwear I had ever seen. Never had I imagined that I would have clothing such as this.

Trips to town were always punctuated with a visit to Doris and Harry's house....Doris of Toll House cookie memory. She always welcomed me warmly and had a delicious treat for me. I was presented with a prune whip at Doris's house, which I first resisted but upon allowing myself to taste it, found it to be exotic and delicious. She never failed, her treats were always that....a real treat!

Next to Doris and Harry's home was the family who had a boy, Gary. I remember him well. He was becoming a teen-ager and flirted with me. That pleased and scared me at the same time. However, I will never forget him and his assessment of me, after the family decided I needed some dental attention.

My second teeth had come in crooked, and misaligned. I seldom smiled without my hand over my mouth because I was self-conscious about it. The dentist said that my teeth were too big for my gums and that some would have to come out. He extracted one on each side of the top row of teeth. After the extraction, I was taken to Doris's house to recover. I slept there most of the afternoon and woke up shortly before she came home from work. I went outside and across the fence was Gary in his yard. He told me to smile without my hand over my mouth and he said, "You will really be pretty when your mouth heals up." I was eleven years old and it was the first time I had ever heard or thought of myself as being pretty. That incident, that remark, ushered in a vanity that I carried for better or worse for the rest of my life.

At Christmas time, Rosie and Mother came on the train to see me perform in the Christmas program. The next morning we three got back on the train chugging West-river, to spend the holiday together in Rapid City. It was wonderful to be home again...with some exceptions. We lived on Omaha Street then. Our house had a rented apartment in the front, and our dwelling in the back of the house. Behind that was the trailer house in the back yard where the overflow of the family stayed periodically. I stayed in the house and shared a tiny room with Rosie.

Our fragile family constellation had changed while I was East River. Mother was taking care of two children, a boy named Skippy to whom Rosie was very attached, and his older sister, Mary. Those children were at our house most of the time. My sister, Kitty, had gone to Dillon with her dad...*my* dad, too, but not so firmly as he was *her* dad. I did not expect to see her this Christmas. As a surprise, she was brought to South Dakota by her dad for the holiday. She was thirteen and beautiful, and I was awed by her.

Bobbie had married Jack and they had a baby boy, Jackie. Mary Lou married Lawrence and had her baby Michele. Both of those sisters were so enthralled by their babies that we had little time together. I loved playing with Jackie and Michele and compared them to Neil, Ethel's baby, at Aunt Mabel and Uncle John's house. It was a rarity to have all my sisters at home for Christmas. Mary Lou, Kitty and the baby stayed in the trailer.

What I remember most clearly about that Christmas was that my older sisters had a camaraderie developed from their years together in Montana, while I was in South Dakota. I desperately wanted to be part of their lives, to understand their banter and jokes, but I was on the outside looking in. One of them remarked, on seeing my new clothes, "Oh, she is one of the Gaudig girls, now." That remark cut me to the core. I so much wanted to be one of them, one of the Curry girls. I felt I was one of them....they just didn't know it.

I remember Mother taking us to a photographer and having our picture taken together. It is a sad picture as the unthinking photographer put Rosie, my shining star, off to the side of the picture, apart from the rest of us. Oh! How I longed for a cohesive family.

After Christmas, I went back by train, across the prairie, across the Missouri, and then into the farmland of eastern South Dakota, to take my place in my family of the year, the Gaudigs.

When I got there I immediately looked for my old horse, Trixie. Uncle John told me she had run away and they couldn't find her. I believed him or pretended that I did. It was easier than allowing the realization that the thirty year old horse had died or been "put down" as they euphemistically called it. I felt the loss and wondered why they didn't look for her.

There in Hand County, in that family, attending that little school I came into a realization that I was not stupid or inconsequential. Lonely perhaps, but not inconsequential. I also learned to adapt to the conditions of life as they were presented to me. I learned that home was something I could carry around inside. I learned that sadness, disappointment and even loneliness were temporary conditions; I did not need to carry them with me. After losing important things, such as Trixie, life goes on, and I still had the memory which was sweet and real. I learned that family was something that I would keep on building. I also suspected that each family was unique. There would be no such thing as a perfect family.

In February there was a predictable blizzard that caused school to be closed for a week. Being cooped up in the house for a week was considerably boring. I missed going out to feed Trixie. I missed stopping at the Johnson's house on my way to school. During that week I read Uncle John's entire collection of Jack London books, which earned his respect for me. He was not a man who could easily speak his feelings. Now he included me in conversations and in a thoughtful manner, answered any questions I asked. He asked me what we were learning in school and wanted to see my report cards.

Stopping at the Johnson home to walk the rest of the way with Mary was a joy. A rollicking good time was always going as they joked and teased one another. Mrs. Johnson loved to laugh and to make others laugh with her. There were six children in the family ranging in age between eleven and sixteen. That was what my family would be like when I grew up, I promised myself. At least, something like that. There, in that steamy hot kitchen, I developed my first crush on a boy, Warren, Mary's brother, a young teenager. The crush consisted on making eye contact and flirting a little. A new awareness was awakening in me.

In April our school went on a field trip to a farm where we gathered milkweed pods, stuffing them into large bags which were taken to town and sent off to be made into parachutes for the Air Force. This was our contribution for the War Effort. We felt a surge of self-satisfied patriotism. While we were in the field a truck pulled over by the side of the road, and honked the horn repeatedly. We all ran over to the truck, and the driver gravely delivered the news that Franklin Roosevelt had died of a stroke the evening before. We were profoundly shocked. He had been our President for all our lives. My mother had always spoken highly of him and credited his programs of getting us through the depression of the 30's. At the table that night I realized that Uncle John and Aunt Mabel did not share those feelings. That was my introduction to partisan politics and their power over and between people. Hearing the sharpness in their voices and the few deprecatory remarks, I did not want to pursue any further conversation about the death of my President.

The school year ended with a community picnic at the school grounds, where we had an exhibit of our art work and projects for the year, and awards were given. It had been a successful year for me. As my mother had expected, when she sent me to the farm, I became strong and healthy. What no one could have predicted, I also attained a measure of self-esteem and and self- assuredness, that would serve me well the rest of my life.

By June I was back on the prairie with Aunt Mary and Uncle Marvin to spend the summer. It was a glorious summer. Dorothy was home. Aunt and Uncle Marvin's little boy, Jimmy Dale was a toddler. Kitty was there for part of the summer. After my lonely winter I was tired of being the only child. It was exciting and stimulating for me to have so many people around. We worked, laughed and reveled in the company of each other.

Uncle Marvin and I were always the first to rise in the morning. I would go to the chicken coop to gather the eggs and he would do chores at the barn. We would meet at breakfast and tell each other stories; mine from the egg gathering, his from something that happened in the barnyard. Those stories always made us laugh. That was the summer he gave me the name "Sunshine." I was clearly his favorite girl and that was heady for me. No man in my entire existence had ever put me first.

When threshing time came, there were hired hands, boys who would come out from town for a couple of weeks to help with the extra work of threshing the wheat and bringing in the hay. Kitty fell in love with a handsome boy named Johnny, and I fell in love with her love affair. A love affair meant that the lovers danced most of the dances together at the Farmers' Union dance and ate supper together. That was it.

Every other week the whole family and the hired hands would go to the Farmers' Union meeting, which were always followed by a dance. Oh, how we loved those dances! Usually the Haley family was the band. We loved their music, and their family. I determined that I wanted a family like that when I grew up. I was still considered a child and therefore danced only with Uncle Marvin and his brother, Uncle Roland. Maybe I was still a child but I certainly could feel the stirrings of adolescence creeping up on me. Soon, I knew, I would be dancing with one of those cowboys or hired hands. I got a thrill out of watching Kitty. She was so pretty! As the young men watched her every move, she blossomed under their appreciative eyes.

Most of my duties were in the house with Aunt Mary but occasionally Dorothy and I were allowed to ride horses over to the Hereford Store to get the mail which was delivered twice a week. Dorothy always rode Dan, a sleek black frisky little horse. I rode Toots, an old work horse who plodded along and needed a firm prodding to make her trot or gallop. Uncle Marvin thought it was safer for me to ride her. One day I pleaded with Dorothy to let me ride Dan. We were out of sight of the house so we thought no one would know. The one who knew and sensed my incompetence was the horse, Dan. No sooner had I mounted him than he reared up and shook me off like a rag doll. Fortunately, only my dignity was injured. We got back on our respective horses and rode on to the Hereford Store.

A week later, Dolph Behrent was helping with the harvest and we were all at the dinner table. He winked at me and said, "How'd you like the ride on that little black horse?" I had to confess and bear a rebuke, albeit, mild and loving from Uncle Marvin. No rancor could mar that summer. I felt as if Uncle Marvin's Sunshine could do no wrong.

As wonderful as that summer was, I learned, in less than one quarter of a hour, the major downside of farming. The crops were growing, the wheat had been partially harvested and the cornfield was lush with the tassels beginning to form. It started out to be a beautiful day and continued to be so until about midafternoon. Clouds formed quickly and soon were dark and full. We always welcomed rain and gathered in front of the house to watch and to smell the aroma, to feel the electrical charge in the air that comes before the rain. First came the thunder, then with a shudder, the clouds seemed to open up and hurl down hailstones, some the size of tennis balls, and you could see the crops in the fields flatten under the assault. It lasted only five minutes. Aunt Mary and Uncle Marvin retreated to the bedroom and shut the door. The door was not thick enough to muffle the sounds of his sobs and her practical comforting.

This happened to many farmers on the prairie. Not many were prosperous enough to have hail insurance. Some, like Aunt Mary and Uncle Marvin had a second income....Aunt Mary's teaching salary. This would see them through the winter, but provide nothing for improvement or even maintenance of the farm. In many cases, the farmer went to the Black Hills and worked in the gold mines for the winter. That was a grim prospect. He lived in a boarding house in the mining town and his wife and children feebly maintained the farm for the winter.

After the hail storm the conversations at our farm were subdued and serious. Aunt Mary always practical and accepting, imparted confidence that they would get through this. She had been through worse.

As summer was about to collide with autumn Kitty and I returned to Rapid City. Back on Omaha Street, Kitty became bored and missed her dad. She wanted to go back to Montana. I do not remember any discussion of this. Kitty was a strong-willed child and no one, not her mother or her father could withhold what she wanted. Arrangements were made by mail; Bob wrote that he would be in Rapid City in a week to take Kitty to Montana.

When Bob arrived in Rapid City, Kitty and I were to meet him somewhere other than at Mother's house. She never wanted to see him again. I went with Kitty to meet him and to say goodbye to her. We walked a few blocks from our house to a lumber yard where we Bob was waiting for us. We were surprised to see our Grandpa Curry in the car. For about fifty years Grandpa Curry had managed the train station at Tilford, a small town about twenty miles north of Rapid City. I had met him only a few times in my life, and had not seen him since I was seven when Mother, Tom, Rosie and I went to offer our condolences upon the death of his wife, Grandma Elizabeth Curry. The train station in Tilford had recently closed and Grandpa Curry was going to Montana with Bob and Kitty.

Before they left for Montana, Bob had a family photo taken at a studio. It is an important picture in that it is the only picture of Bob with his four daughters. Also in the picture was his son-in-law, Jack, his grandchildren, Michele and Jackie and his father, Lou Curry.

For me it was important because it was a good picture of my Curry sisters and my father, and it was that picture that made me realize how much I had grown up that year. In our family pictures collection, there is a snapshot of me taken just before I left for Miller in which I appeared gaunt and pale, my arms like sticks hanging by my side. At the time of this picture, before my experience in Miller, I weighed sixty pounds. Ten months later, in this new photo, I was a robust, budding, almost teenager. Life on the farms had yielded a fifty-five pound weight gain for me. Uncle John and Uncle Marvin must have been proud.

The winter on the farm in Hand County and the summer on the farm at Hereford had given me something far greater than physical health. I now had self-esteem and confidence and saw myself as a competent player in this game of life.

CHAPTER 8

Hereford

It was about ten days before school was to start. I was seriously dreading it. I would be going back to the Rapid City School system where I had started sixth grade and performed so miserably. Little did I know that my rescue was near at hand. It should not have been a surprise that it came through Aunt Mary. She was shopping in town and of course came to our house to catch up on the news. Mother, Aunt Mary, and I sat at the kitchen table sharing a pitcher of lemonade, talking about our lives and friends. Mother was excited because this was going to be her first year of teaching. Her school was in Cleghorn Canyon ten miles south of Rapid City. They talked about that at some length. When that subject had been exhausted, there was a lull in the conversation until Aunt Mary said, as if were the most normal thing in the world, "The morning after you left the farm, Dolores, Marvin sat down at the breakfast table and cried. I asked what was the matter and he said, 'I can't eat breakfast without my Sunshine.'"

I cannot convey the magnitude of that statement for me. Someone cried, someone loved me that much! Oh, I knew that Mother, Grandma and Rosie loved me, but this was a man who was not even technically related to me. And it was a man...not a man like Van Loan, the molester of my early childhood. Uncle Marvin would never molest me and would crush like an ant anyone who even thought about it.

After taking that in, I exclaimed, "Why, I could go to school out there, at Hereford this year!" I did not ask Mother or Aunt

Mary if it was all right...it seemed so clear that this was the solution to my angst about school and to Uncle Marvin's sadness. I can't recall the slightest glimmer of opposition to my idea. It was a *fait accompli*. I could hardly contain my excitement. I would be going to the Lodge School, two miles from the house. This would be in a building that my Grandfather Michelson had built in the 1920's. I would be back in a country school like the one in which I had such a great experience the year before. I could hardly wait until school started.

Aunt Mary made some inquiries and found that I would be the only seventh grader and there were no eighth graders, so I would hold an honored place, the most senior student in the school. That meant that I had to be there early and set up the schoolroom. Early in the year that meant putting the date on the blackboard and writing anything special about the day: whose birthday it was, who might be visiting that day, what holiday we were preparing for, and what we would do about it on this particular day. By the end of September I would be starting the fire in the potbellied stove. I felt important and very eager to get started.

Aunt Mary was going to be teaching at the McNenny School, about three miles in the opposite direction. Most days she rode the frisky little horse, Dan, across the gullies and rolling hills leading down to the Belle Fourche River. By riding cross country, her trip was three miles instead of the five it would have been by the road. I offered to do many of the morning chores to make life easier for her.

The first day of school was glorious...one of those warm, clear September days, which you knew was one of the few left. I got up early and enthusiastically gathered the eggs, fed the chickens, and started breakfast while Aunt Mary and Uncle Marvin milked the cows. Jimmy Dale was two years old then, and I eagerly got him up, dressed and ready for the day. The four of us ate breakfast together. Although we each had plans and schedules for the day we always sat down together and had stories or concerns to talk about as we ate our hot breakfast together. Dorothy was now in High School and went to New Underwood, twenty-three miles south of home where she stayed in a dormitory, as did all the prairie children who went to high school. Sometimes she was home for the weekend but more often had activities of school or had to stay in New Underwood as the dirt road between was impassable.

After Aunt Mary left for school, I washed and dried the breakfast dishes. The dishwashing area was at a table under a window looking out to the West. Dishes were washed in a dishpan and rinsed in hot water from the reservoir, a tank attached to the end of the cook-stove, which kept hot water available for use at any time. As I did my tasks there at that window, it never seemed like work to me. I listened to Arthur Godfrey on the battery-operated radio, and watched Aunt Mary riding over the hills and gullies. On a clear day I could see Bear Butte, about forty miles away. Those images: Aunt Mary riding across the breaks, Bear Butte, the prairie sentinel, and the day emerging as the sun moved over it, became like ritual, a liturgy for me...in a certain way, a prayer.

One exceptionally beautifully day in September, early in the school year, perhaps only a week after the beginning of school I was walking home from school, facing west, and in a dreamlike way focusing on Bear Butte, a volcanic cone that rises up out of the prairie and has been the site of worship for the Plains Indians longer than history can trace. I remember so clearly, on that day, stopping to talk to a horse that trotted over to the edge of a field. After that visit, I walked on toward our farmyard. Suddenly I was unable to go on. I was not in pain, I was not tired. I was simply stopped, silenced. I breathed deeply and fell or was gently pushed to the ground. I was filled with a great, peaceful, expansive presence. Something told me to hold on to this moment for the rest of my life because it was important. I felt as if I knew *everything!* I had no words for what it was that I knew. It was as if I had grasped the ultimate truth right then. I can still remember the feeling of the warm dirt under me, the sun on my body, the quality of the air I was breathing, the fabric of my dress. After a few moments I got up and continued my walk home. I did not speak of this incident, because I had no words to tell of it that would make any sense to someone else. However, I have held in my heart for my entire life.

The Lodge School fulfilled all that I had hoped for. My teacher, Shirley Horton, was twenty years old and was very enthusiastic about teaching. She was an excellent organizer and teacher and managed her eight charges very well. There were no other students close to my age. The other seven were all under ten years old. I was allowed to call her Shirley, and she engaged me in everything the county schools had to offer. She entered me in spelling contests at county and regional levels where I won ribbons. She also got me enrolled in the Young Citizens League, a character-building program promoting community involvement, knowledge of the essentials of government at every level, and how our little township fit into the larger picture. Through those events I got to know other children throughout the region. The Farmer's Union meetings became exciting. I had some knowledge of what they were about; also it was a good chance for me to see my new best friend, Darla, a student in Aunt Mary's school. We remained friends into high school and in our early days of marriage.

I always arrived at school early to perform my duties. Very soon cold weather set in and I had to get the fire started. I felt responsible for those younger children, and I did not want any of them to suffer the bitter cold of the South Dakota winter one moment longer than necessary. Often by midmorning the room would be aromatic with our lunch, a hot soup containing vegetables, meat, broth and other ingredients that each child had brought from home, boiling away on the top of the stove. Sometimes there were potatoes baking in the coals at the bottom of the stove. I have only pleasant memories of that year of school. Among them are the fervent patriotism fostered by the Young Citizen's League, preparation for spelling contests, celebrations of each holiday with contributions from each child and their family, and especially the close friendship with my teacher, Shirley.

At home we had a busy schedule but were never too busy to enjoy the company of one another. Aunt Mary and I would sit at the dining room table in the evening and go over spelling words or read poetry. Uncle Marvin who had meager formal schooling, read very little. However, because he loved horses, he wanted to read the book, *Smokey, The Cowhorse* by Will James. Each night for several weeks he laboriously read a few pages. One night, Aunt Mary looked over to where he was reading by the lamp and noticed that tears were running down his cheeks. "Why, Marvin! What is the matter?" she exclaimed.

With a heaving sob he answered, "Some sunna-a-bitch is gonna kill Smokey." She did not laugh or ridicule him in any way but offered him comfort and understanding. I admired their relationship. She was wise and educated and had easily talked with senators and the governor; he was simple, with no sophistication or guile, and they got along perfectly, with love and respect for each other.

Sometimes in the evening after supper we worked on our baskets for an upcoming Box Social. This was an event held in conjunction with the Farmers' Union meeting. The dance would start after the meeting, and after the dance the Social began. For that, each woman of the community brought a decorated box, filled with a delicious supper for two, and kept it hidden from the men in their family. No men were to know who made any certain box. Late in the evening, when the dancers were exhausted, and the music had worn out the musicians, the Social would begin. Intrigue surrounded the presentation of the decorated boxes. They were sold to the highest bidder by an auctioneer who was usually a good entertainer. Sometimes it would be Francis Haley, always a treat as he was a professional auctioneer, as well as a rodeo announcer.

The boxes were bid upon and each man ate dinner with the woman upon whose basket he won. The proceeds from these events went to whatever cause the Farmers' Union was promoting at the time. Sometimes it was to help out one of the farmers who had an unfortunate incident, such as a barn fire, or an illness. There were several other events to raise money for the farmers in need, but my favorite was the Box Social.

The biggest and most important school event of the year was the Christmas Program. We spent many hours practicing our presentation and decorating the little school room. I had a huge part in the program, being the stage manager, and was quite inflated with my own importance. It was a fitting role for the oldest student in the school and I took it seriously. The program would be on the Saturday night before Christmas; after that we would be off school for two weeks and I intended to spend it in Rapid City with Mother, Tom, and Rosie.

That Saturday was a long day, waiting for the excitement of the evening. It was a cold day, but we were not in the least disheartened by it. We were used to it. Immediately after an early supper, we began to get ready. Dorothy was home from high school and that made the day even more special and exciting. Out there on the farm, every family member took a bath once a week: every Saturday. Everyone else had taken a bath earlier in the day; I was the last. Taking a bath out there on the farm was nothing at all like taking a bath in town, and even less like it is in modern times. We had no indoor plumbing, therefore no bathroom. In the winter we took baths in the kitchen, where it was warm. We had to get a big galvanized tub into the house from where it hung on a nail outside...it would have taken up too much room inside the little house.

That night it was even colder than it had been during the day. When I got the tub into the kitchen the tub had to warm up for about fifteen minutes so that it did not chill the water that I would put into it for my bath. After the tub was warm enough, I put water from the reservoir into it to a depth of about four inches, and washed myself all over.

It was a hurried bath, after which I dried off, got dressed and slid the tub along the floor and out the door, because with the water in it, the tub was too heavy for me to lift. I emptied the water on the ground and hung the tub on its hook on the side of the house, looking forward to the warmth of the oil stove in the living room. In the short moment while I was hanging the tub and turning to go into the house, the bath water had frozen and become a slippery ribbon of ice. I slid down that ribbon and landed on my right hand with my elbow locked. Just as it had when I was six years old and nine years old, my elbow shattered. I heard the crunch. Somehow, I got myself upright and slithered into the house and sidled up almost behind the stove in the living room, trying to hide. Aunt Mary and Dorothy both looked at me and one of them said, "What happened? You're white as a sheet!"

Next, Dorothy said, "You've broken your arm again. Now we can't go to the school program."

I cried, "I have to go to the program. I'm the announcer, the stage manager. I have the biggest part in it, I have to go."

Aunt Mary, in her calm and resolute way said, "Dolores, no one is indispensable. We'll find someone to take you to town and the rest of us will go to the program.

We all piled into the car and drove to Dolph's farm about a mile and a half away. Aunt Mary asked him if he could take me to the Rapid City Hospital and have someone get my mother. He agreed to do so and the rest of the family left to go to the Christmas program. I was bundled up into Dolph's car and we were off to Rapid City forty-five miles away.

It was a long way to town with my throbbing arm and my deep disappointment. Oh, how I wanted to be at the school program. After a while the pain subsided as my arm had become numb. Dolph had no children and was not tuned to the sensitivity of a child such as myself. All the way to Rapid City he told stories of horses he had to shoot because they had a broken bone, and other stories of people who had amputations from farm accidents. I was numb all over by the time we reached the St. John's hospital in Rapid City.

Once we arrived at the hospital Dolph came in briefly to give a note to someone at the receiving desk and then he left to go back to the farm as it was quite late in the night. He had to attend to his livestock in a few hours. I waited at the hospital in the lobby for quite a while. The attending doctor said he could do nothing until my mother was present. I do not know how she was found. We did not have a phone in the house at this time. Occasionally a nun would stop by to see how I was doing and assure me that my mother would be there soon.

After what seemed an unbearably long time Mother arrived and gave her permission for the doctor to treat me. He began the examination of my arm by attempting to straighten it. Immediately, I lost consciousness, and was told later, that my mother did the same. When I awoke in the hospital bed in the dark, I could not feel my arm and was sure it had been amputated. I screamed, and a nurse, who was also a nun, came to my bedside, comforted me and assured me that it was because my arm was in a cast that I could not feel it. She told me that my mother had stayed most of the night but had to go home for a little while and would soon be back and that I could go home later in the day.

I spent the rest of the Christmas holiday in Rapid City with Mother, Tom and Rosie. I remember so very little of it that I believe I must have been in shock for several days. Rosie tells me that we had a wonderful Christmas dinner; that both of my older sisters, Bobbie and Mary Lou were there for Christmas dinner along with their husbands, Jack and Lawrence, and the babies, Jackie and Michele.

After that holiday I went back to Hereford and back to school. The program had gone on without me; I digested the truths that

I had learned. First, no one is indispensable; second, life goes on beyond disappointment.

In the spring the Farmers' Union Women's Auxiliary had decided to do a three-act play, involving people from the entire township. Mrs. McNenny, the mother of the children in Aunt Mary's school, had experience in the drama department of her college in the eastern part of the state. The play, *There Goes The Bride,* was her vision; she was the producer and director. Several adults and a few children auditioned for parts. I landed a fairly substantial role in the play.

I am sure that the main purpose of this endeavor was to forge a greater alliance between the individual farmers for very practical purposes. The stronger the Union, the greater was their bargaining power when it came time to sell their crops and produce.

The McNennys were a community-spirited, politically progressive family. About ten years later, their son, Kenneth who had been Aunt Mary's student became a senator in the State legislature. The McNennys knew that in the production of this play, large group of farmers and their families would be meeting once a week for a couple of months. Friendships would be forged; information and ideas would be exchanged. The play had a much larger purpose than what it presented to me.

For me, the play itself was the most important thing with which I had ever been involved. For me, it ushered in a lifelong love of staged drama and all aspects of theater. It also was the site of my first puppy love. A young student, Ray Aga, a year older than I, sang during the intermission. He had the most beautiful voice I had ever heard and I was completely smitten. I still remember the song, *It Was Only A Paper Moon.* I mooned over that boy for weeks afterward.

To celebrate the end of our school year, we had an elaborate picnic down by the Belle Fourche River. All the schools in the district would celebrate together. Wonderful food appeared as the families arrived. Large slabs of ice, taken from the river in early spring and preserved in underground ice houses were brought, broken and used in the ice cream freezers which we all took turns churning, until the delicious custard turned into the frozen treat. Never was there a more appreciated dessert than the ice cream the community produced that warm day by the river. People lined up, women first, then children and finally the men. After the meal, and luscious dessert, came the games. Some played soft ball, some tossed horse shoes and many just sat in the sunshine and watched. What a memorable festive day it was!

The next day while packing my things to go back to Rapid City I was listening to the local radio station. Every Saturday morning there was a program that took requests for songs dedicated to named individuals, usually to celebrate a birthday, anniversary or notable achievement. I heard my name, and realized that a song, *The Red River Valley*, was being dedicated to me. I was thrilled. As the morning went on there were several more songs dedicated to me, commenting on my departure from the community. Several times the song was *You Are My Sunshine*, thanks to Uncle Marvin and his nickname for me. From the thrill of hearing my name so many times on the radio that day I was deeply moved by the kindness and love the Hereford Community showered upon me.

Over the summer that followed, I divided my time between Hereford and Rapid City. There was always work and play at the farm, and in town I got to spend time with Rosie and the babies, Jackie and Michele, as well as with my older sisters. Kitty was back in Montana.

Weighing heavily on my mind was where I would be going to school the next year. It would be my last year of grade school, and I would be getting ready for high school. I was becoming a teenager and wanted to be with more people my own age. That pulled me toward going to the school in town. On the other hand, my academic success and community involvement drew me in the direction of going again to a country school.

From my experience I was beginning to learn about "Trusting the Process." For every dilemma there was an answer, and one simply had to wait for it to become apparent.

Around the middle of August, Mother was hired to teach a country school nearby. That meant that I could attend her country school and live at home in Rapid City. I knew there were people my age nearby, and I could make friends and spend time with them after school. I knew there was a teen center in downtown Rapid City. All those factors contributed to my decision. When the answer was clear in my mind it seemed so easy. I could have it both ways...the country school experience where Mother was teaching and the social life of a teenager in town. Ah! Trusting the Process!

CHAPTER 9

Pennington County & New Mexico

This was truly going to be the year I transitioned out of childhood into adulthood, albeit young adulthood.

A few days before school was to start, Mother, Rosie, and I drove out to the school to see how long the drive would take. On that clear September day it was about an hour's drive from Rapid City. We knew with certainty that would not be the case during the winter when the predictable blizzards would cover every road with drifts of blowing snow. Such was a South Dakota winter.

The schoolhouse was an ordinary small white clapboard building standing in the middle of a large, unadorned, stark yard with yellow hip high grass swaying in the ever present wind. There was a swing set, a seesaw and, at the far edge of the yard, two outhouses. The nearest dwelling was a mile away.

Mother, Rosie, and I readied the room for the classes that would soon start, placing the desks in clusters according to the grades of the students who would be grouped in them. From a roster of pupils, who would be attending, and the grade and age of each student, we could see that I would have no class mates...a span of four years between me and the student closest to my age. Pondering that fact, I realized, like so many things I had already learned, there was more than one angle to it. On one hand, I would have complete autonomy, with no one to compete against or to distract me. On the other hand, I would have no peer with whom to socialize. However, I had made the choice to attend a country school, so I accepted it, just as it was.

I put those thoughts away and set about making the room warm and welcoming for the students who would arrive the next Monday morning. We put posters around the room and decorated it with whatever colorful artifacts we could find that had been left by former students and teachers.

On the first day of school, as the other six students arrived and took their seats, they immediately began to assert their personalities. As their strengths and weaknesses emerged, Mother and I could both see that she was going to have her hands full with the six children in the lower classes. Rosie was a fast and eager learner and would not take a big portion of Mother's energy. But the other six...that was another story.

Mother got them busy with their lessons and called me to her desk. She had in her hand a large, thick book, which was the eighth-grade curriculum, sent out by the Meade County Education office. It contained all that was expected of eighth grade students, together with sequence and teaching methodology. This was the proscribed way of preparing students for high school. There were enrichment activities for students who could meet greater challenges.

Mother put the tome in my hands and said, "Dolores, this is what the other Meade County students will be learning in preparation for high school next year. Follow this curriculum as well as you can and you will know what most of them will know. I will have very little time to help you but if you get stuck, we will see where we can find help. Every six weeks the county will send out tests in every subject. You can do them on your own, and I will send them in."

I welcomed the challenge. I dived into it with the enthusiasm of a hungry animal in pursuit of its prey. With no distractions, I had time to do every lesson thoroughly and methodically. One time I needed help in figuring out how to find and work with the square root of numbers. Mother and I worked together, but it was only with the help of Aunt Mary, on one of her trips to town, that I got through it well enough to pass the six weeks exam. Arithmetic was never my strong suit. I could learn it well enough to pass tests but it was not knowledge that stayed with me. Too many permutations, combinations, arrangements and rules for those ten digits! Then arbitrary symbols were added! My brain was not configured to deal with numbers and symbols. Give me words any day! Words were sweet to me. English, spelling, social studies, science, art, and music; those were my bliss.

In town, near our house on Omaha Street, I found a couple of friends, the Olmstead sisters, Cora and Doris. How we met is lost in memory but the times we had together, crossing the threshold of adolescence, are as sharp in my memory as the cold winter nights in Rapid City. The city council had wisely decided that the young people needed somewhere to gather and sponsored a teen center, where we could go to socialize, listen to music, and dance.

It was there that I had my second love affair. A group of boys from Sturgis began coming to Rapid to visit our teen center. One of them was a tall thin, cerebral sort of a boy. His father was superintendent of the elementary school in Sturgis. I don't remember how we became acquainted or how we decided that we were a couple. I don't remember what we talked about or how we spent time together. I do remember that when he kissed me one night, that was it...the end of it. Perhaps I was frightened. Perhaps I felt confused or threatened. Whatever, I did not want to go further in that direction. Perhaps if he had recited poetry or taken me to a play, it might have gone on. This was physical. It was not to be... not then.

When Christmas vacation was over, I started some serious study preparing for the State Spelling Contest. Every available moment I had was given over to spell words that someone dictated to me; often that someone was Rosie, because she always finished her work ahead of the other students in her grade. I spelled them orally or wrote them until I had gone through the entire list of words used in previous years at the state contest.

Through the spring there were various eliminations...at different levels; the district, county, and region. In each I advanced to the next step. Finally, I received official word; I would be going to the State Fair! It was a big event for me...across the state... three nights in a dormitory on the fairgrounds, and tickets for the food concessions there. The anticipation of the contests was very exciting. It was a point of particular interest that there were three contestants from Meade County going to the finals, and all were named Dolores, with several variations in the spelling. Here we were: the Scandinavian derivatives of that exotic Spanish movie star, Dolores Del Rio from 1933. We met Mr. Peregrine, the superintendent of Meade county schools, early in the morning at the court house and he drove us across the state. What an exciting trip...eating in a restaurant on the way, the anticipation of the fair... the company of the other Doloreses. So much to take in!

The oral spelling contest was held on the first day and the written on the second. I was first runner-up to the oral championship, that is, second place. That was good enough for me. I went down on *relativity*. I put an "e" where the "a" should have been. Still, I felt victorious.

The next morning the written contest was held and we had to wait until mid-afternoon to get the results. I placed lower than second, and I never remembered what place that was. However, Rosie never forgot. Sixty years later, she told me it was third place. Numbers did not mean much to me. Whatever I did, when it was about numbers, she remembered for me. Actually, she remembered everything for me, numbers and otherwise.

School was out. The spelling contest was over. What surprises were in store for me this summer? The answer came by way of a letter from my sister Bobbie in Roswell New Mexico. Before I went to Miller, she had married Jack Thomas, an airman stationed at the base in Rapid City. They now had two little children, Jackie and Cleanne. Bobbie needed a baby-sitter for the summer. I was the perfect candidate, willing and able...no, more than that, I was eager and enthusiastic.

This was yet another culture for me to explore...the life of a young military family and another adventure in a place I had never been! Furthermore, I would have time with Bobbie, whom I felt I hardly knew. I was interested to see how she and other military families lived. I knew it would be different that the sub-cultures I had already experienced...but different, in what way? I wanted to experience it.

It was a long bus ride from Rapid City to Roswell, at least twenty-four hours; maybe more. I boarded the bus in the morning, rode through the day and slept through the night awakening to see the landscape of the Southwest out the window. I watched with hypnotic fascination as the sand dunes and mesas glided past the bus windows like the backdrop of a western movie. I arrived in Roswell late in the day and Jack picked me up at the station. The babies were already in bed at home with Bobbie.

Bobbie and Jack had a small house. Where I slept and where we ate, or anything at all about the interior of the house, never found a place in my memory. My main interest was in the babies: Jackie, about two years old and Cleanne, close to nine months. They were adorable; caring for them and playing with them, were my main pursuits and my joy.

Bobbie and Jack lived in the midst of an off-base housing development for military families. It was utilitarian, far from elegant. One sensory memory that stayed with me was the aromas of the cooking coming from the houses in the evening. These young families came from everywhere in the United States and brought their own food culture with them. Jack was from Tennessee and he specialized in curried dishes. This was foreign to my background, but he was such a good cook that I loved it. It was many years before I discovered what it was that made his food taste and smell so wonderful.

The main interest of the young airmen was cars. In the front of every house was a car. In the evenings and weekends, was a young man polishing it, or checking under the hood or under the chassis.

The wives were busy with the babies. The "pill" was years from being invented so there were a multitude of little ones. I don't know what the young wives did every afternoon, but I watched their babies while they were gone. I had anywhere from four to eight babies and toddlers every weekday. This was in pre-television days. I played with those little ones all afternoon. I changed many, many cloth diapers. I do not remember being distressed by any of it. I felt useful, grown-up, responsible, and needed.

I remember one adventure that happened when, after supper, I said I wanted to go for a walk by myself. I needed to explore my surroundings. Jack insisted I take the family dog, Toby, with me for safety, and in case I got lost. Soon after I left the house, I noticed that not one word I was hearing was in a language I understood. I also noticed it was getting dark and I was not sure of how to get home. I was being stared at and talked about in a foreign language. As fear gripped me, the dog seemed to sense it and moved closer to my side. I was extremely grateful for Toby and the feeling of safety and comfort he gave me. He led me back to the military housing area and I had a new respect for my canine friend. Now I understood why people so loved their dogs.

When my time in Roswell was over, a few weeks before high school was to start, I boarded the Greyhound for the trip home. The trip included a three-hour layover in Santa Fe. The layover began about nine o'clock at night. I found a vacant bench in the terminal and stretched out, immediately falling into a deep sleep. I was awakened by a policeman shaking my shoulder. He asked why

I was there. I told him my perfectly logical and respectable story, but he was skeptical. He thought I was running away from home.

Fortunately, by then we had a phone in our house in Rapid City. I told him I would call my mother and he could talk with her. I used my baby-sitting money for the pay-phone and reached her quickly. There was fear in her voice as she answered a call from me in the middle of the night. I assured her I was all right and handed the phone to the officer. He asked her to describe me and tell him where I was coming from and where I was going. After a while he accepted that I was who I said I was and that I was going where I said I was going. The expressions on his face and the tone of his voice told me he thoroughly disapproved of her allowing me to travel alone. After the call he told me to go back to sleep and he would see that I would be safely on the next bus going north.

Looking back, I know that I have been provided with angels all along the way.

CHAPTER 10

Sturgis & Montana

On the long bus ride home I had time to devise a plan for high school. Arriving home on Omaha Street I eagerly told Mother my plan while unpacking. I told her that since I had attended school in Pennington, Hand, and Meade Counties in the past three years, I had the experience to assess the best place for me to attend high school. I knew that among my options, Meade County had the highest educational standards and that I would get the best education at Sturgis High School.

Mother appreciated the logic of my stance, but pointed out that we lived in Rapid City and asked how I proposed to get to Sturgis every day. It was thirty miles away. I said, "I will find a family where I can work for my room and board, and go from there." Mother offered no objection. She was preoccupied be-cause she had not yet been offered a teaching position.

One morning in late August she said, "Do you want to go to Sturgis today and see if you can find a job and a place to live? I could take you there and while you look for a job, I could go to the superintendent's office and apply in person for a position in Meade County." I was delighted at this plan. Mother, Rosie and I were ready in about fifteen minutes, and drove the thirty miles in high spirits.

When we got to Sturgis Mother dropped me off at the Sturgis Tribune and I went in to check out the want-ads in the back section of the paper. The first job listing I found was at a new bakery, just down the street from the tribune office. With great expectation and a positive attitude, I entered the bakery and found a young Finnish couple, Eric and Maarta Kerttu, who spoke just enough English to get by. They had recently bought the building and a minimum amount of equipment to get started in the bakery business in Sturgis. I showed them the ad and they understood that I wanted to fill the position for which they advertised. In unison, they said, "Yes, yes!" Maarta, had a slightly better grasp of the language and asked, "Start Monday?" It took several attempts on my part but she came to understand that I also needed a place to stay. She excused herself and went in the back to confer with Eric, and came back saying, "In our house, in basement." With gestures and words I realized that she wanted me to go with her to see it. Their house was not far from the middle of town and even closer to the school; just one short block. It was perfectly acceptable to me...a large room in the basement, with some boxes along one wall, a small single bed and dresser opposite, and lots of floor space. Within an hour, I had a job and a place to live, and went back to the corner of the Tribune where Mother had said she would pick me up. I waited about fifteen minutes until she came for me.

We were both excited. I wanted to tell her all about my success and she, too had something to tell. She had not found a school but had found a house, a red house, for sale that thought Tom might be interested in buying. She said she would work on that. In the meantime my plan to live with and work for the Kerttu's seemed to be reasonable.

Mother took me back to Sturgis the next Sunday night and I moved into my basement room. My, but I felt grown-up! I unpacked my few things and found a clothesline in the basement on which to hang my clothes. I had a small dinner with the Kerttu's upstairs and we began a very amicable arrangement which lasted through my first year of high school. Our plan was that I would work in the morning before school an hour in the morning, an hour between noon and one, and from four to six in the evening. I would be charged no rent and would get a small salary and my tips.

When school started, I went to the office and asked to speak with the superintendent, Mr. Grunwald. I asked him if I could be excused a half hour before lunch to go work at the bakery for their lunch hour, a time when they served a light lunch and savory, hot-out-of-the oven pastries. That was when I made my tips which provided me with spending money. Mr. Grunwald was agreeable, with the caveat that I must keep my grades above a C.

Mother was without a job for a few months, and was finally offered a school at White Owl, a small dot on the map, eighty-five northwest of Rapid City and fifty-eight miles east of Sturgis. The young teacher, who started there, found it too isolated and departed suddenly. The White Owl school board was happy to find Mother and she reciprocated their feelings. At that point Tom came with her to Sturgis and looked at the house and began the process of buying it.

I started high school and loved every minute. I joined every club and took part in every extracurricular activity possible. I rented a flute, played in the band, sang in two choruses, and was on the school newspaper staff. I was in the drama club and in the speech club. Somehow, I managed to do it all. I could work it all in and keep my job at the bakery.

In a few weeks Tom bought the red house in Sturgis where he, Mother and Rosie moved in and began their life in Sturgis, which was to last for a half a century. Mother started out commuting to White Owl and took Rosie with her.However, the daily commute from Sturgis to White Owl was too far, especially with winter coming. She began to stay in the school house during the week and came home on weekends. She and Rosie had a rollaway bed, a cook stove that also heated the school and not very much else. The plan then was that I give up my basement room, and stay in the red house and cook and keep house for Tom. By this time Tom had bought a card shop on Main Street so we were seldom at the house at the same time.

That worked for about a week and a half. The school part was great, but somehow, the home situation did not feel right. So I went back to my original plan and moved back into the basement apartment where I lived for the rest of my freshman year.

Every Sunday I went home to the red house for dinner. Mother and Rosie came home on Friday night for the weekend and I stayed with them until they left for the long drive to White Owl. During the week I was so busy with school and my job that I had little time to miss them. I know Rosie missed me.

As the season was turning from fall to winter, I worried about their isolation. I thought they needed a radio and searched the stores in Sturgis for a battery-operated radio I could buy for them. I believed they needed news from outside and even more acutely they needed weather reports. On the prairie, blizzards were a serious matter and one needed to be forewarned. I found a second hand radio at the Lushbough Hardware Store in Sturgis. When I found that it didn't work, I took it back to the store and they repaired it for me. Finally they were connected to the rest of the world. I felt better knowing Rosie and Mother had news from the outside world. I was becoming more and more self-sufficient and independent.

One aspect of my emerging self was that I was became aware of an unabated spiritual hunger. I knew that somewhere, some place, something would feed this empty space. I contemplated Catholicism but was angry with the church because of their treatment of my mother. I tried the Presbyterian Church because they had a large choir and it was the church of many of my classmates. I went there a few months but my hunger was not appeased. I tried the Lutheran Church because the most intelligent and talented girl in the high school went there. That church did not touch the hunger in me at all. It felt just too sweet and I felt that was only half of what

I was seeking. Perhaps if I had given it more time, but "perhapses" and "might-have-beens" along with "what-ifs" are like fairy tales... interesting, but not very useful. I decided to wait, patiently wait, until something moved in me or pulled me in. I believed that an elusive force would find a spiritual home for me. I trusted that would happen. Again, Trusting the process.

I had no special boyfriend in most of the first year of high school. My life was taken up with work, studies and extracurricular activities. Oh, I was looking, and was looked at, but school was much more interesting. However, as spring emerged, this changed. It was a beautiful April day, the first one where a person did not need a coat, and the sun was warm on my bare arms. A few of my girlfriends and I were walking along Main Street and at the far end of the street we came to a lumber yard. We hopped from one pile of lumber to another and enjoyed this playfulness. How great it was to be unencumbered by coats and boots, and to be spontaneous and freely ourselves. In the midst of this exuberance, we were interrupted by a car full of teen-age boys, which pulled up alongside the curb. One of them stepped out of the car and asked, "What does a person do on a Sunday afternoon in Sturgis?"

We asked where they were from, and were told that they came from Newell, a small town about forty miles north of Sturgis. We then asked, "What do you do in Newell on any afternoon?" This started conversations which led to more questions, answers and observations until we were acquainted.

One of the boys was especially interesting to me and apparently he was interested in me too. We moved apart from the others and talked until the sun was low in the sky. We were reluctant to stop talking. Too soon the driver said he had to get the car home to Newell before dark.

Before they left, the boy with whom I was talking, gave me his address and I gave him mine. He was a star basketball player on his high school team. We agreed to write to each other. So this boy, whose name was Bob, coincidentally, the same as my father's name, became my romantic interest. It was safe and consumed so little time... a letter each week, meeting at a basketball game, or intra-school events, perhaps a public dance. Because we were most often inaccessible to each other, our relationship did not infringe on any of my school events. Our letters were sweet and endearing, and when we did see each other, they filled the void of loneliness. We could make each other laugh and were great companions when together. Our long-distance affair satisfied my need to be wanted. It also kept other would-be-suitors at a safe distance.

Near the end of the school year an outbreak of a disease about which we knew nothing, engulfed Sturgis and many other places in the United States. It was polio! The infection was rampant in our little town. School was declared over for the year. There would be no graduation ceremony. Large gatherings were banned. It was an eerie town for a couple of weeks. During that time I suffered a migraine headache, the first of many. It was frightening. Mother panicked, believing it was polio. Aunt Mary was there and with her wisdom and self-control calmed her hysterical sister. The migraine lasted a couple of days and then passed, recurring many times throughout my life. However, many of the children in Sturgis were not that fortunate. Polio left one child dead. Several carried the effects of polio for the rest of their lives.

After the polio crises, I thought that I should get to know my father in Montana and perhaps even spend the entire summer there. I wrote to him saying I would come to Montana for a visit if he wanted. Kitty was now in Rapid City living with Dorothy. It seemed to be a good time to go to Montana because there would be no competition with Kitty for Bob's time and attention.

Another factor in my decision was that I felt I needed to break away from Mother. No mother could have been less demanding or less controlling than mine. Nevertheless, I felt the primordial urge to separate from her.

When I proposed to go to Montana, I left it open-ended, not revealing to either Mother or Bob when I intended to return. I was paying my own way with money I earned. I had enough bus fare for plan B, which was Portland, Oregon, where Mary Lou lived with her husband, Royal, and her toddler, Michele. I would go there if it did not work out in Montana.

Boarding the Jackrabbit Bus at Sturgis in the afternoon, changing busses in Newcastle Wyoming, talking with strangers, carried me from the familiar to the unknown. I watched the landscape and the light change as the afternoon faded into evening. Darkness fell and I slept soundly, waking when the driver announced we would arrive in Butte in fifteen minutes.

When I stepped off the bus, Bob was there to meet me. I felt a rush of affection for him. He was handsome; his eyes twinkled and he made jokes about everything. He seemed lighthearted and good-natured to me. He took me out to breakfast in Butte, a strange town with a cone-shaped mountain in the middle of Main Street, which Daddy (now, for the first time in my life, I could call him Daddy, just as my sisters did) told me was a copper slag mountain. We went into a restaurant that had dollar-hots on the menu. I ordered them and smothered the little pancakes in maple syrup and a lavish amount of butter. When Daddy paid for breakfast with silver dollars from a leather pouch hanging off his belt, I was amused and intrigued.

We drove to Dillon where he lived in the log house with Margaret and their little girl, Shirley, who was a year younger than Rosie. When we arrived at the house, I was intrigued by the realization that I was in the house where my sisters had lived for so many years.

Margaret was a good housekeeper. The house was neat, but lacked warmth. She asked me many questions about my life. In a very short time, I did not want to answer any more of her questions as they seemed intrusive. I asked Daddy if he would show me where he worked. He was eager to do that and took me to his shop near the house. He told me he was the best mechanic in Montana. I was impressed. He seemed very capable.

Early the next morning after breakfast Daddy and I went to a grocery store where he bought a large bag of groceries and a box of potatoes. We were going up into the high mountains to see some of his friends. We drove a long while, probably about three hours, before we came to a little cafe, bar and gas station, all in one building. I was glad for the stop. For three hours he had been talking without ceasing. I got lost in the stories, which were convoluted and sometimes funny. But there were so many, and they were so long; I was ready for a diversion.

Daddy and the bartender, Roy, were obviously good friends. They greeted each other with coarse language, hitting each other hard on the back, and calling each other names I would never have said out loud. These are things Montana men do, I told myself. I was hungry and thirsty and my rose-colored glasses were clearing up. Daddy was showing off for me, conversely he was showing me off for his friend. "Isn't she a pretty little thing? She is going to be a real looker." And more remarks along that line. I felt as though I was being graded, weighed, and assessed for market; not a good feeling!

Together they started cajoling me into having a drink, a gin fizz is what they decided would be good for me. I was stunned. I was fifteen, had never had a drink, never wanted one; had decided long ago that I wanted to get through high school before I ever tried alcohol or cigarettes. I had seen enough to know that it was not the way I wanted to go.

"C'mon, it will loosen you up. It will be fun," they pressured. It became an impasse between us.

I began to get angry, and as was my *modus operandi*, I went quietly inside myself. Bob ordered lunch for me, and I pushed the food around the plate in silence. The lump in my throat, made of self-righteous indignation, and disappointment, left room for nothing else. I got up and got a glass of water for myself, not trusting either of them to get water for me. When he finished eating, Bob and I got back in the car and continued up the mountain.

It was a silent drive. Occasionally Bob would point out a landmark or a wild animal and I would murmur something to acknowledge I had heard, but also indicated that I was not going to interact. Once he said, "I didn't expect that you would be so much like your mother."

I answered, "You should have."

We were on such a narrow and treacherous trail I feared we would never get back. When I was about to ask where we were, we entered a clearing in the woods. In that space was a long log house, a large picnic table outside, a water pump, a fire pit, several dogs and several quiet, shy children of various ages. They were barefoot and in tattered clothing.

A woman came running from the house and as Bob got out of the car, she hugged him and greeted him warmly. Soon there were some grown men, greeting him in a friendly way. They spoke in a dialect so foreign that I could make out only a few words. Apparently, they were good friends with Bob and held him in high esteem.

When I got out of the car, Bob said, "This is my daughter, Dolores."

The older woman, held me at arm's length, looked at me intently and said something to Bob that I could not understand. She called one of the girls to her and said something I took to mean that the girl should befriend me. The girl motioned for me to follow her as she led me into the house. It was a very primitive dwelling. At first I could barely see, as it was illuminated only by the light from three small windows.

There wasn't one piece of furniture that had been purchased. Everything was hewn out of log or stone. There were a couple of spaces on each end of the building that were partitioned off, probably sleeping spaces. A huge fireplace was festooned with several bunches of drying green bundles which emitted appealing aromas. There were shelves with tools, a few kitchen utensils, and plates of pewter and mugs made of wood. One piece stood out from the rest. It was a bone china cup with gilt edges, painted with tiny roses in a garland around the perimeter of gold. I seemed incongruous in that plain simple room. I knew there was story to it but could not understand the dialect well enough to ask the questions in my mind.

The girl led me back outside and took me to a nest of kittens. She seemed to know that most girls would warm up to such a treasure. I held and played with the kittens for a long time. Then she led me to a swing hanging from a tree branch very high above. When I sat in the swing and she pushed me into the air, I swung out over the edge of the clearing and could see below a valley, so far below that it took my breath away. I had never been so far above the ground.

Bob had unloaded the car and taken the groceries over to the table where they were set out with grunts and gestures of appreciation. I could see that they seldom had store-bought food. Some of the men started a fire in a pit where many fires had been before. Others went to the cellar in the side of a rise in the land, and brought out a haunch of an animal, and with great expertise, threaded it onto a spit over the fire. About every fifteen minutes someone would turn the handle at the end of the spit to roast another side of the animal. From a well, the children fetched water and filled pots hanging over the fire. Everybody, with one exception, seemed to know what to do. That was me. I was watching and taking it in as if it were a play in which I had no part.

After a while the mother brought from the house the pewter plates and started to organize the table for a meal. Everyone picked up a plate and stood in line near the fire. The mother ladled vegetables from the pots and the father cut slabs of meat from the roasting haunch over the fire.

By then, I had relaxed enough to get over my anger at Bob and became very interested in this family and what was happening right before my eyes. Also I was very hungry, having not eaten since early morning. I sat with the girl who had taken me to the kittens and the swing...who had been assigned to entertain me. By now, I felt I was in the scene, not merely observing it.

Now I understood some of the dialect. The mother sat down beside me and pointed to Bob. She told me in this strange tongue, "When we had the sickness, Bob bring us medicine." She went on to say, "Always he help us, and he bring us food."

After an hour or so of feasting and jesting, the men, who had been taking swallows from jugs, were laughing and enjoying themselves immensely. They brought out some primitive instruments; flutes carved from wood, a washboard, wooden spoons which clapped together, a washtub to which a broomstick had been affixed with a rope stretched tightly so that it sounded like a bass fiddle, a skin drum, a banjo and, incongruently, a very good guitar. The mother turned to me and said, with a broad smile on her face, "Bob, he bring us food and he bring us music!"

I fell under the trance of the music. It was all that music could be...it filled the trees from which I had swung. It filled the valley over which I had swayed. It filled me until tears welled in my eyes. It went on and on for hours and then began to slow in tempo, soften in tone, and finally faded away in whispers.

We gathered again at the long wooden table. Mugs were brought out and set by a large metal pitcher filled with a hot drink made from chicory and sweetened with molasses. One of the older girls filled each mug with the steaming aromatic drink. However, when she reached me, the mother said, "Oh, get her the cup. This is Bob's daughter!" The girl went in the house and carefully carried it to me. She placed in front of me the bone china cup with the garland of roses around the gold rim. I was speechless. I had received a unearned honor. I was a confused princess for that hour.

I could not help but remember Aunt Chrystal's autograph book in which she had written that piece about the good in the worst of us and the bad in the best of us. It was good, I knew, to have seen this side of my father, Bob Curry. I had been given that insight and for this night could hold it securely. I hoped to remember it the rest of my life.

Still, given all that had happened I did not want to live with him and Margaret. I had the fare to take me to Portland.

CHAPTER 11

Portland

I was in a reflective mood that night, pondering all that I had experienced in just one day. First, driving off in the morning with rose-colored glasses looking at this man who was my father and whom I wanted to see that way...a caring, fun-loving, decent human being. In just a few short hours those blinders fell away and I saw a crude, coarse, insensitive ruffian with whom I wanted no relationship at all. Then came the complex feelings I had when I saw the better side of this man; generous and compassionate to a poor family in the mountains. It was too much for me to stick around and see the outcome of this scenario that involved me and Bob...or do I want to call him Daddy, as my sisters do? I was surprised that he did not give me any argument when I told him that I would be leaving in the morning, for Portland. He simply said, "We'll have to get up early."

The Greyhound left at six in the morning and I was on it. Leaving Dillon and Bob Curry was not as hard as I thought it was going to be. I slept on the bus until late afternoon, when I realized we were driving through the most magnificent mountains I had ever seen, along the Columbia River Gorge. I was mesmerized by the beauty of it and watched out the window in a trance until dark. I slept again and woke up only when the driver called out, "Portland! Portland Oregon!" Even through my sleepy eyes I could see that the Portland bus Station was way more modern and streamlined than Rapid City or Butte's. Mary Lou's husband, Royal, and his friend met me at the station. We drove on to Oregon City and stopped to get ice-cream to celebrate my arrival. Mary Lou was elated and fussed over me, making sure I felt welcomed and comfortable. The toddler, Michele, whom I had not seen since she was a baby, was asleep and they would not hear of awakening her even though I pleaded. We ate the ice-cream...lemon custard it was, with chocolate syrup over it. I believed that was the most tantalizing taste combination I had ever experienced.

I slept well and awoke in the morning, noticing a different quality of air than I had ever experienced. It was warm and *humid*, a word I did not recall using in South Dakota.

Ah! Portland in early June! I had not seen such a beautiful city in all my travels, thus far. We didn't drive into the middle of the city that day because of congestion due to the Rose Festival Parade. We got a good place near the Burnside Bridge from which to watch it. The lushness of pinks, reds, oranges, yellows was spectacular! Every color I could imagine captured in the petals of a million roses. The aroma was intoxicating and the music of the Rose Parade brought me to tears! There were more than a thousand floats all decorated with real roses...no crepe paper allowed here!

The parade was held a week after there had been a terrible flood in Vanport City near Portland. The habitable space in that town was wiped out, and many of its citizens found refuge in Portland. More tears for me when the Vanport float went by bearing the banner, "For us a Rose, In Portland grows." The people of Vanport people were expressing their gratitude for the generosity that the people of Portland had shown in the aftermath of the flood. I felt the power of civic compassion.

After the parade we went back to their house and enjoyed the holiday together. In Portland the time of the Rose Festival is as important as any other holiday of the year. Perhaps more so, because the long winter and spring rains have ceased, and that alone is worth celebrating. Michele, my first niece, now two and a half, was a source of delight for all of us. For many hours we simply watched her play. Those first few days in Portland were joyous. There was the sheer joy of being with my sisters. Kitty lived with Mary Lou and Royal in Oregon City and she worked at a restaurant in Portland. She was out of the house most of the time but there enough to be a part of the family. They all made me feel loved and welcome.

They took me to the ocean, my first glimpse of that majestic wonder. To someone raised on the dry Dakota plains, it was beyond superlatives. It took my breath away and left me speechless! It put the world in a different perspective. I would hereinafter regard the planet differently. It seemed that this was the lungs of the earth; it breathed in every morning and out in the evening. Even the moon was held in its spell. This was the one true thing, and everything else was inconsequential in contrast to this eternal wonder.

On my third day, both Mary Lou and Royal went back to work, and I saw another side of their life together. They both worked hard for little pay; Mary Lou as a waitress, and Royal as a cab driver. They were poor and strived to live with dignity. Until I arrived, Mary Lou worked in the daytime; Royal stayed with Michele, and went to work when Mary Lou got home in the late afternoon. Now Royal could work longer hours and I could be with Michele in the daytime. That was a treat for me. I loved taking care of her. However, that lasted for only a couple of weeks.

Royal, a sometimes taxi driver, was often out of work. I learned later that he had an alcohol problem. He was a binge drinker, so for the periods between the drinking, he was a kind and understanding man. The first time I witnessed the other side, it was devastating. I saw this kind, sweet man turn surly and frightening. I wanted to place a great distance between us and I also wanted to take Michele with me. On this day, Mary Lou was at work and I was in the house with Royal and Michele. He became irrationally angry at some trivial thing, and shouted at the toddler and spanked her. I grabbed her up in my arms and fled to a neighbor's house and stayed there until Mary Lou came home. By the time she arrived, he had sobered up and was contrite. However, I never again felt comfortable with him.

One day Kitty was off work and stayed home all day. Seldom did it happen that everybody was at home at the same time. It was a hot humid day and perhaps there were just too many bodies in the small house. I did not see it coming but suddenly a huge verbal fight erupted between Mary Lou and Kitty. I detested such confrontations, and stayed out of earshot through most of it. No matter that it was hot and humid outside; it was better than the heated argument going on inside. I waited it out. The end result was that Kitty would move her things out, and live elsewhere.

Kitty came to me and confided that she had no place to go and could think of nothing except to a downtown hotel close to her job. Royal had been her source of transportation before this. She entreated me to go with her and Kitty was very persuasive. She pointed out that Mary Lou had Royal, for better and for worse, but she was not alone. Kitty would be all alone if I did not go with her. So we moved into a room at a hotel in Portland, not a luxury hotel, but clean and safe. Kitty was seventeen; I was fifteen. I thought I could get a job downtown as I had worked in Sturgis and had a letter of recommendation from my employers at the bakery.

It came as a surprise to me that jobs were hard to find in Portland. Most of the waitress jobs were taken by students who had started as soon as school was out, or by people from Vanport who had been affected by the flood a few weeks earlier.

I applied everywhere within walking distance and found nothing. For a few days, I explored Portland, walking around parks still abounding with roses. I went to museums and the library. Every day Kitty would ask me if I needed any money, and I would say, "Oh, I could use a dollar or so." She would give it to me, never realizing that I had nothing else. I never wanted to tell anyone that I did not have money. I felt it shameful to me. I would take that dollar, and in 1948, one could eat on a dollar a day. I would buy a bowl of cereal for breakfast, and a Mars candy bar and a glass of milk later in the day. Sometimes Kitty and I would go out for dinner, and occasionally, Royal would pick me up and take me back to their house for a meal. I wasn't starving.

Kitty was very busy with her work and falling in love with the love of her life. She met Jimmy Tyler, and immediately they were lost to the world in their love for each other. They began their sixty years of marriage within a few months of their first meeting.

I knew it was time for me to leave, but I still had no bus fare to get back to South Dakota and was not going to ask either Mary Lou or Kitty for it. One day I used my food money for bus fare to get to the outskirts of Portland where there was a drive-in restaurant. My reasoning was that I liked bus rides, and just maybe, they would hire me, and then I would have money to get back to Sturgis.

There was only a month of summer left and that is how long it would take to save the amount of money I needed. The drive-in was an interesting place. The waitresses were called carhops and roller-skated out to the cars to deliver orders. I had not roller-skated since I was nine and had broken my arm. But I convinced them that I could do it, and they hired me. In a couple of days, full of confidence, I was skating out to the cars; only once spilling a milkshake on a customer.

There was a dishwasher there, a boy named George, who was about a year older than I. He developed a serious crush on me the first day I worked there. Every day he asked if he could take me to a movie or if he could ride with me on the bus to my home. I did not want to be in a dark theater with him and I did not want him to know where I lived. However, when he asked me to go with him to Jantzen Beach, a popular amusement park, I said yes. I reasoned that there would be many other people around, and it might be fun. I had not had very much fun that summer, as I had no peers there. We were going to leave from work, and he had his father's car that day and drove to Jantzen Beach. I intended to take a city bus home, but when I inquired at the gate, I was told there were no busses going back into the downtown area at night. All through the evening I was uneasy that he would drive me home, and find out where I lived. I was relieved when he dropped me off at the hotel with no remarks or suggestion that he would walk me to the door.

I still had two weeks to work and was sorry we worked at the same place. He never let up nor missed an opportunity to say something about his everlasting love for me. I gave him no encouragement whatsoever and tried to ignore him, never making eye contact, nor getting into a conversation with him. It was a long two weeks, but I had to stay there until I had the bus fare to go home.

A couple of days before I was to leave, George asked if he could have my picture taken at a studio in Portland. My vanity won out over my wisdom and I met him at the studio and had my picture taken. It was an enhanced glamour picture taken with a gauzy finish, and was very flattering. I had a small copy, but he had a huge one and carried it in a big artist's portfolio and, to my embarrassment, showed it to everyone at work. I wished I had never allowed the picture to be taken.

At last I had the fare to get back to Sturgis, and arrived on a Saturday just in time to start school on Monday. Strange how that has worked out for me in exactly the same way, over and over again, throughout my life. I always had the fare to go somewhere else, and always just in time.

CHAPTER 12

El Paso

What a joy to get back to Sturgis in September; the trees were turning the brilliant colors of fall; the air was crisp and clean, and I was home and felt at home. I started my sophomore year immediately and slipped back into it as easily as slipping into a comfortable bath. It enveloped me. On the first day I registered for speech club, drama, debate, and journalism. I was appointed editor of the school paper, *The Bear Butte Breezes*. I also settled comfortably into all my former music activities: band, mixed chorus, *a capella* choir, and glee club. I knew it was going to be a productive and fulfilling year.

Mother and Rosie were staying during the week out at the Elk Creek School and were in town on weekends. In bad weather, they stayed with families near the school. I found a boarding house for girls whose parents lived too far out of town for a reasonable commute. It was home to eight high school girls ranging in age from fourteen to nineteen. We had two large dormitory style rooms on the third floor. My school activities were the most important thing in the world for me; where I lived was unimportant. I went to the red house every Sunday to spend the day with Mother, Rosie and Tom.

Coinciding with finding a place to live was finding a job. It was much easier than I thought it would be. The bakery had been sold to a young couple, Shorty and Jennie Weimer, and it seemed they were managing it quite well between the two of them. I went in to apply for a job, just in case they could use some additional help, and got there on the day that Jennie realized she was pregnant. They were delighted to have someone who had some experience at the bakery and who could be there in the morning, and for the lunch crowd and would ease some of the burden on Jennie. It was a great arrangement for all of us.

My boyfriend Bob and I got back together about a week after I got back. He was still as active in his school as I was in mine but we managed to see each other as often as our schedules and budgets would allow. We always wrote a letter a week to each other and very sweet letters they were. We managed a date about once a month. His school was smaller than mine so our athletic events were in different leagues. I never saw him play basketball but knew he was good at it. My schedule did not leave time for an everyday connection and neither did his, so this was a satisfactory arrangement for both of us. I never felt that I was missing out on anything. My life was full and rich.

It seemed to me the September and October of '49 were bathed in sunshine and success. I remember colors from that year very clearly. A fashion fad must have dictated that the girls wear autumn colors; burnished gold, sunflower yellow, and coppery orange sweaters, aligning perfectly with the trees in their fall mode.

Our English teacher, Miss Phelps, a recent graduate from Brookings College in the eastern part of the state, taught us to be aware of what was going on around us...to use our senses and examine our reactions to them. Every morning, she had us write for ten minutes at the beginning of the class, prompted by a phrase she had written on the blackboard. What a way to start the day! I remember thinking, "I will always do this."

Life was as good as it could be; I had a place to live, a job I liked, and a school year that promised to be satisfying and productive. Was it too good to be true? I didn't think so until a storm cloud hit and produced a tempest that would last for a very long time.

Sometime in October, during football season, before the first snowfall, I was in study hall, when I was called into the superintendent's office. I wasn't worried. I was in good standing with him and all the staff, because of the editorship of the paper and because it was a small school where you knew where you stood. On the way to the office, I asked casually, "What does he want?"

"Well... he drew out the word... there is a stranger who wants to see you." Still not alarmed, I thought of Bob Curry. He might have come to see me. He would do something like that.

When I reached the office, the bottom dropped out of my stomach and the blood rushed to my head. There was George! I blinked. I must be hallucinating! But there he was: the dishwasher from Portland! I could hardly comprehend what was going on. Mr, Grunwald, the superintendent, said, "Is this someone you know, Dolores?"

I said, "Yes, but I do not want to see him." I rushed from the office to the lavatory and vomited.

After a while, someone from the office came to get me and told me that Mr. Grunwald said we needed to talk about this. I went back to the office; George was not in the room. Mr. Grunwald motioned for me to sit across the desk from him and he asked me to tell him what was going on. I was very embarrassed. I knew this looked like so much more than it was. I told him that we had but one date and that it meant nothing to me. Mr. Grunwald said, "But it means a great deal to the young man." He went on to say I owed the young man at least a meeting to discuss it with him.

George was ushered into the room and Mr. Grunwald left us alone. I told George very clearly that I did not want to see him, did not want him in Sturgis, and that he had to go back to Portland. He told me that he would not go back. He had to see me, he said, even if I would not go out with him. He said, "You will change your mind, when you see how much I love you." I nearly vomited again.

It was now time for me to go to the bakery to serve the lunch crowd. I told him I had to go to work. He said he would walk me there. I told him firmly that he could not do that and he said, "Then I will follow you." I was agitated and shaky when I got to the bakery and quickly told Jennie that she should not allow him to come inside the bakery. She could see how upset I was, and called Lil, who was not a large man but had a commanding manner. Lil ordered George to stay outside. I was thankful for their protection. I had found a sanctuary.

The days that followed were nightmarish, the nights positively bizarre. I received a letter from George's parents, which they had sent to the superintendent who had given it to me. In the letter, the parents implored me to let their boy come home! I answered the letter and told them that I, more than anyone, wanted George to return home. Thinking that perhaps the letter from his parents would persuade him to go home, I asked one of the boys at school who had befriended George, to give the letter to him. Still, he stayed in Sturgis.

George was taken into the home of the football coach. He enrolled in school, my school! I was furious. He played football and was a good player. As editor of the paper and sports editor, I had to report his successes. Playing football and being good at it made him a hero in the high school and in the town as well. Soon it felt to me as if I were being shunned by other students, especially the boys. These boys had been my friends. We were on debate teams, committees, music classes and plays together. Now they seemed to feel I was doing George a disservice. And George! Whenever he was not at football practice, he was following me.

When Mother was home for the weekend, I told her the whole story. She contacted the police. They tried to assure her that he was harmless, a good football player who was just a teenager in love, but not a threat to me. We felt he was a threat.

After dark he would walk by the boarding house where I lived. It was a corner house and my bed was in the corner of the third floor. He wore cleats on his shoes and night after night I would hear those cleats; twenty steps in one direction, turn around, twenty steps in the other, over and over, night after night. Mother went to the police the next weekend. They said that since he had never tried to enter the house there was nothing they could do. They also suggested obliquely, that her daughter might be playing a part in this, giving him some encouragement perhaps.

The situation began to wear upon me. Fall had turned to winter and there was no sunshine in Sturgis. Even my extracurricular activities at school lost their luster for me. Mother and I had long talks about the situation on Sundays when I was at the red house for dinner. I believe it was Mother's idea, but she brought it up in such a way that I could think it was mine.

Mother's sister, Edith, was married to Bill Waterson, who worked in El Paso, Texas, with the Border Patrol for the US Government. They had prospered in El Paso and had four children: Mary, in her first year of college, Mildred, a senior in high school, Marlene, a freshman and Billy, in sixth grade. Uncle Bill had told Mother that he would send me to college if I came there to live with them. She had not told me until now, when she knew I needed a safe haven. The situation in Sturgis had become intolerable for me, with George sapping the joy out of my life, and smearing my reputation. I agreed to go to El Paso at the end of the semester.

In January there was a blizzard that was noteworthy even in this land where blizzards were common. I remember going downstairs in the morning, and finding it pitch dark. Then I realized that the snow was above the windows. The snow was piled up to the rafters of the first floor of the house. Fortunately the blizzard was a diversion from the specter of George stalking me.

I helped Jennie and Shorty dig out the bakery. It was one of the first eating places in town to reopen after the storm and business was brisk. Since school was closed I worked at the bakery until things got back to normal. After the snow was cleared away, the sidewalk bare again, the sounds of the footsteps around my house resumed. He was never going to give it up. I was eager to get out of there. I was in emotional torment and needed to be where I could find a measure of peace.

The day after the semester ended I was on the bus to El Paso. As the bus headed south, it seemed that I had been granted a reprieve from an undeserved sentence. I slept most of the way to El Paso and woke on the morning of the second day to warmth and sunshine. I began to get a glimmer that this might be more than deliverance; it might be a new adventure.

Aunt Edith and Uncle Bill met me at the bus station. She laughed and said they could not all come or there would be no room for me in the car. It was apparent that they liked me and that Aunt Edith and Uncle Bill saw a great future for me in El Paso.

Theirs was a big, modern house; the best I had lived in up to this point in my life. Marlene shared her bedroom with me and there was plenty of room for everyone in that house. As I was unpacking my belongings, Mary was entertaining some college friends she had invited to come and meet me. We played games and listened to music, ate potato chips and each one had a bottle of pop. This was going to be a new adventure for me.

Phil, a tall handsome college boy asked me to go to a movie the next Saturday night. I asked Mary, "Do you think it would be all right with your mother and dad if I went to a movie with Phil?" I was checking out my parameters. This was a new experience for me. I didn't want to spoil it. I had made my own decisions for many years, but somehow, this situation felt protective and kind. She said I would have to ask Uncle Bill. He had the final word on that issue. He gave me permission to go out with this young man, and outlined the conditions which had to be met.

My second day, we went to church at St. Clements, in the middle of downtown El Paso. I had never given up my quest for a spiritual home and this felt comfortable for me right from the first few minutes. Could this be it be the place that would satisfy my hunger?

It was an Episcopal church, a denomination I knew very little about. The Episcopal Church in Sturgis was so small that it had never drawn my attention. This one seemed to be a good fit for me. It was like the Catholic church I attended when I was five years old, and it brought back those memories. My cousins sang in the choir; by the second week I was singing in the choir, too. Several members of the church were professors at Texas Western University located in El Paso. I liked to listen in on their conversations about theology. I understood little of what they were talking about, but I wanted to understand it and be able to talk of it myself. I desired to explore the unknowable and felt that this was where that could happen.

My life was again on an even keel and I was basking in it. Marlene, the cousin closest to my age, and I became good friends. We laughed together and had earnest conversations as we drifted off to sleep in the same bedroom. She filled the place of my missing sisters...almost.

Just as all the children in the family, I had chores to do. For this we were paid. It seemed like free money to me. I had been working for my own money for more than two years. Here in El Paso I also took a few baby-sitting jobs. This was even more money that felt just too easy to attain! The Waterson girls and I shopped and spent money every weekend. We bought clothes and jewelry and makeup and other trifles that caught our fancy. It seemed almost decadent to me, but not so much that I did not enjoy it.

We lived within walking distance of the school and all of us went home for lunch every day. Our lunch times were staggered so when I was home for lunch, I was the only one of the children there for that hour. Aunt Edith and I visited and got to know each other well. I remember helping her make fig newtons one day on my lunch hour. They were made from figs that came from a tree in our yard and that was a great novelty for me. It seemed to me that she and I were becoming friends as well as relatives.

We girls had movie dates with the college boys and that was fun and not threatening in any way. Uncle Bill had some rules that had to be met concerning those dates. The boys had to come in the house and talk with him when they picked us up, and they had to get us home on time and come in the house when we got there. Uncle Bill would be waiting inside. It was a pleasant and safe way to be a teenager.

We were all active in the church and were driven to choir practice every Wednesday night, and attended services on Sunday. That spring the church choir produced a musical comedy as a fund-raiser for a worthy cause. It was a parody on *The Barber of Seville* and was delightful. I felt honored to have a part in it.

At school I was playing in the band, had joined the modern dance group, and the speech club. It was a school ten times the size of Sturgis and I never felt as confidant there as I did in Sturgis. Uncle Bill was always interested in what I was doing. He was interested in the education of all his children, and we talked about school at the dinner table every evening. He treated me as one of his own.

I didn't see it coming, but perhaps could have if I had been looking for signals or if I had known human nature better. Aunt Edith was fiercely proud, protective and loyal to her own children. One evening after I had won an oratory prize and been given recognition in the school paper, Uncle Bill saw the article. At the dinner table he commented on how he thought it was remarkable that I came from such a small school and was making a name for myself in El Paso High. That was too much for Aunt Edith. She burst out, "If it were one of your own children, you wouldn't have even noticed!" She left the table in tears.

That was in April, just before Easter, but the atmosphere at home became as cold as winter. After that it seemed I could do nothing right. Marlene and I were no longer allowed to be alone together, which was very hard for me. Marlene was my best friend.

I was puzzled and anxious over what to do next. The only thing I could think of was to return to South Dakota. But, "What about George?" I asked myself. I pondered the question and decided that whatever happened, I was stronger now and could deal with it. It would be no worse than it was here.

It took some courage to tell Uncle Bill and Aunt Edith of my decision, but they accepted it without comment or argument. They perceived the same thing that I did...my living there was not working out. After I told them I was going, the tension eased and we got along reasonably well for those last six weeks. Soon I was on my way home, with one more major life lesson: Awards and success do not come without a price. That price I was willing to pay.

When I got back to Sturgis, I took care of my first worry immediately. I called a friend who would know; a boy who was in most of the same organizations as I. He told me that George, along with about eighty percent of the boys over eighteen years of age, had gone off to the National Guard Camp to be prepared for the Korean Conflict. Whereas that was rather devastating news... most of our young men were gone; for me, it was a relief. I could breathe again.

Bob, my boyfriend from Newell, and I kept up correspondence while I was in El Paso and we took up our relationship where we had left off. He, too, was relieved that George was out of my life. Bob and I had a few dates, to movies and dances, but he could not afford to make the trip often.

I did not yet have a job in Sturgis and before I could look for one, my cousin Dorothy needed someone to care for her young son, LaVern. Because Dorothy was my favorite cousin, and almost my favorite person, I wanted to help her in any way I could. LaVern was two years old and a most adorable little boy. I was eager to take care of him and would have done it for no pay at all, but she insisted on paying me.

I loved that little boy and he loved me. Every day I would dress him up and take him downtown. We would go to the bakery where he would play with his toy car and I would have coffee with the Weimers. He called me "Mama,." With his blond hair and blue eyes, one could have easily believed he was my child. It raised a few eyebrows in town, but it amused me. It was liberation from being controlled by what other people thought of me. Freedom was mine as long as I was true to myself.

I started going to St. Thomas, the Episcopal church in Sturgis. It was very different from the cosmopolitan St. Clement's of El Paso. There were seldom more than ten people in the congregation. It was summer and there were no activities; no choir or youth group. I went to a service every Sunday morning, sang the hymns, listened to the sermons, and left without speaking to anyone. I was trying it on, but not yet buying it.

In the middle of the summer, Kitty and her baby, Connie, came to visit us in South Dakota. Kitty and Jimmy had married shortly after I left Portland the year before and had this beautiful baby girl. In a family of towheads, she broke the mold and had light brown hair with a soft curl to it. Kitty and I had a good time with the Connie and LaVern. We had never played dolls together enough as children and this filled that void.

Her visit was not long enough to satisfy our desire to be together, and she begged me to return to Portland with her. I talked with Mother, who did not like the idea at all. She said, I had been gone most of the winter and it was unreasonable for me go away again so soon. Also there was the concern about LaVern. I convinced her that she could take care of him as well or better than I, and she could use the extra income.

I also reminded her that if I went to Portland, I would not have to deal with George when National Guard Camp was over. She never totally agreed, but that part of my reasoning began to soften her opposition. Also, she knew it was useless to argue with me once I had made up my mind to go somewhere. By now, the "going fever" had a firm hold on me.

CHAPTER 13

Portland Revisited

Kitty, Connie and I were off to Portland by Greyhound bus. Traveling with a baby and an older sister was not quite as easy as traveling alone, but certainly not the most difficult thing I had ever done. Kitty and I always laughed a lot when we were together, so the trip went by quickly. Jimmy, Kitty's husband, met us at the bus station and their love was visibly passionate when they embraced each other after a ten day separation.

This little family, Kitty, Jimmy, and Connie, lived in a small apartment where I slept on the sofa in the living room. The same degree of passion in their love for each other was present in daily life and often erupted in quarrels, which disturbed me but seemed to be quite ordinary and acceptable to them. Another way of relating, I told myself. Whereas the quarreling frightened me, I also came to see that theirs was an honest relationship with no artifice at all. In a way I envied that. Every emotion was out there to be experienced; I had learned to curb my own emotions and could not unlearn it.

I quickly found a job at a midtown restaurant within walking distance of the house. Kitty and Jimmy, especially Jimmy, were very protective of me that summer. Jimmy had a younger sister and he had always been her protector. He seemed to feel that he had to take care of me in the same way. It was a difficult situation. They were only a few years older than I, and were not my parents. I was feeling quite grown-up and had become independent. Challenged

137

by their protective attitude, I took chances that could have landed me in serious trouble. Only by a slim margin was calamity averted.

One day a handsome, well-dressed, young man drove up to the curb outside the restaurant in a chartreuse convertible. I couldn't help but notice that he was noticing me through the plate glass window. After a while he came in and sat at the counter and ordered a cup of coffee. I could see he came in with the sole purpose of meeting me. I was responding because he was successfully flattering me. He had an easy way of talking, half joking, half serious and he seemed to be intelligent and was well-spoken. He ordered a lunch and stayed around for a long time, eating it and engaging me in conversation. It was a slow afternoon in the restaurant, so I lingered around where he was sitting at the counter and allowed myself to be pulled into his orbit. He stayed until it was time for me to leave and then asked me if I needed a ride home. I took him up on the offer. He was the perfect gentleman, politely dropped me off at the apartment and drove away.

The next day he showed up at the restaurant at about the same time. This time he led the conversation toward my work and my plans for the rest of my life. Did I really want to be waitressing forever, he asked. I assured him that I planned to do other things when I got out of high school. He said he knew I was too smart to stay in a job like this, and he could offer me a better job right away. By the end of the summer, he said, I could be driving a car as classy as his.

He said he would wait for me after work and take me to meet the people who could make this possible. I know it sounds incredible that I could be so naive, but I agreed. He took me to a hotel where an older woman and man told me about the business, which was to go with them from town to town selling magazine subscriptions. They knew the right places to go, where the market was right, they said. They told me that in no time I would be making great money. They showed me pictures and testimonies of people who had done this. The greatest pull of their sales pitch was going to other cities. I said I would let them know the next day.

The handsome young man took me home. I pondered my decision alone for a few hours that evening and finally decided to tell Kitty and Jim about it. They, predictably, and in unison, exploded! "You absolutely cannot do that! Don't you know that these are the kind of people who recruit girls such as you and make sex-slaves of them? Is this what you want to do for the rest of your life?"

By the time they had finished I was admonished and frightened. At this point I wondered how to get out of the situation. I didn't get much sleep that night.

The next day Jim had to go to work and Kitty had to stay at home with the baby, so I set off for work, walking alone. As I reached an alley, a big black car pulled up blocking my way, and a woman rolled down the window and told me to get in. I ran around the back of the car and was able to get to the restaurant before they could get the car turned around or go around the block. When I got to work I had to tell the people I worked with what had happened and asked them to prevent those people from coming into the restaurant.

The people in the black car did not show up, nor did the handsome young man ever again.

In the newspaper that evening Jim read that the police were on the trail of a white slavery ring purported to be in the Portland area. I had narrowly escaped disaster. One more lifesaving lesson for me.

During that summer of 1950, the Korean Conflict had become outright war and the country was preparing our young men to go to war. One of Jim's friends, Harold, was in the National Guard. He was called into active duty with just two weeks to get his affairs in order. Harold had been working at Sears since his high school graduation two years before. Sears had given him a severance pay and he decided he wanted to spend that bonus with me before he left the country. He was certain that he would not return. We did not even pretend to be "in love." He simply wanted to have a good time and share it with someone before he left for the war. He had no family in the area. It seemed safe enough to me, and Jim and Kitty approved of this plan.

Harold took me to high-class restaurants around Portland, unlike any I had ever seen. I remember my confusion when I was brought a finger bowl and warm towel as we ate king crab in an elegant restaurant overlooking the city of Portland, where you could see all five bridges spanning the Columbia and Willamette rivers. He took me to Jantzen Beach to see Louie Prima, my first and most impressive music date. We went to every movie worth seeing...we did everything we could do in the two weeks before his deployment.

It was a gentle and sweet time for both of us. He respected me and I felt a tender sadness for him. It seemed that I was all he had, and I had so little to give... companionship, conversation and laughter were the sum total of my offer. Perhaps the *joie de vivre* was exactly what he needed. I am sure he spent his entire severance pay. He bought me some gifts which I told him to return. I accepted only the gift of flowers. I could not accept the angora sweater or the expensive jewelry. That would have given the wrong impression, because at that time such gifts were appropriate only if the couple were engaged.

After the two weeks, Harold left to join his company to prepare for going to Korea. I boarded the bus for Sturgis, and went home to start my junior year of high school.

CHAPTER 14

Home Again in Sturgis

The buses I took around the West, most often dropped me off at my destination after dark. This was no exception; I arrived in Sturgis quite late in the evening, but Mother and Rosie were there to meet me. I wasn't sure they would, because of Mother's resistance to my leaving in June. We went back to the red house and talked long into the night. We talked of my adventures in Portland and of their summer in Sturgis. Also, at the top of everybody's mind was the beginning of the school year four days away.

The next day, I walked over to Cora Standley's and we reconnected which felt good to me. She was a loyal friend, who had never questioned my going away or coming back. She was a rock; a touchstone to which I could return. She forgot to mention to me that most of the young men in town had gone with the National Guard to enter the Korean Conflict. This was glaringly apparent when school started and the male population was sparse. Most of the senior boys were gone as well as some of the older juniors. It seemed so unnatural to have so few young men in town...as if notes were missing from a common chord, colors missing from the color wheel.

Our activities at school were strangely lopsided as to gender. Many of the senior girls dated junior boys. The boys who did not go with the National Guard always made sure we knew why they were not going. There was a degree of guilt about not being in the war, protecting our country. In reality, our boys were protecting an ideology. It was the first armed conflict of the Cold War which was

141

between the ideologies of the governments of the United States and Russia, being fought on the Korean Peninsula. But we were merely high school students and few of us understood this war at all. For me, there was a measure of relief that George was out of my life. He had gone with the Sturgis National Guard.

There were several distinct groups of students in Sturgis High School. The most desirable, for me, were those who had gone to school together since first grade and lived in the same house or neighborhood all of their lives. Next were the farm kids, who were loosely connected by the lives they had lived and activities that brought them together, rodeos, the stock yards, and the events that connected the rural schools. Each group had a common language. Some who lived close to town commuted together and thereby formed close friendships. Then there were the others, not connected to anything at all except they were going to school in Sturgis for various reasons.

I did not fit exclusively into any of the groups. I had friends and something in common to someone in every group. I remained friends with country children who came into town for high school. I lived in various places in town throughout high school. I had friends of differing backgrounds because of the many activities in which I was involved.

Jocelyn Spencer was a girl whom I had known since early childhood. Her father had been in the lumber business and knew my father, Bob Curry, through his sawmill in the Black Hills. Her mother and mine had kept a friendship alive for twenty years and Jocelyn and I were very happy to find each other when we entered high school. She had not been in Sturgis very long when I arrived.

Another close and abiding friend was Cora, usually the first one I visited when I returned from a trip. She lived not far from the red house. When I started high school as a freshman and went home for Sunday dinners, I would often go to her house for a visit. Cora was a serious, studious girl, with a quirky sense of humor. I was slightly envious of her solid sense of self and her wonderful tightly knit family. My family was so different and my sense of self was on shaky ground.

Teresa, who was to become my lifelong friend, connected with me in our sophomore year and we remained friends forever. She was one of the people I contacted as soon as school started. Her parents operated a farm on the prairie and also owned a house in town on Willard Street. That house became part of my life and story. The first time I saw her after I returned to Sturgis we connected and had our own private jokes and were immediately totally at ease, open and free with each other. Right away she asked me if I could live with her in the apartment in the back of her father's house in town and right away I said "Yes! Yes!"

Her father was pleased to have someone living with her so he charged me no rent. I was delighted to accept the offer. We lived in a tiny efficiency apartment at the back of the house; one big room, with a double bed in the corner, one dresser on each side of the room, and a table in the middle. In back of that was a tiny kitchen with a kerosene stove and directly off that was a shower and an indoor commode. The shower was a luxury for me...I had not had that since El Paso. In the main part of the house lived a lawyer, Mr. Kerper, his wife and two small children.

After school started, we learned that Mr. Kerper, needed secretarial help at his Main Street law office. Teresa, who was pursuing a business curriculum, applied for the job. He accepted her immediately and she worked for him for the last two years of school, on a work-release program that was offered by the school. I found that the city was looking for someone to transcribe the city ordinances into a new format and I applied for and was hired to do that job.

As Mr. Kerper was the city solicitor, I worked from his office. Teresa, as his secretary was in the same building. Our offices were in separate rooms with a thin partition between. We were both employed there in the afternoons for our junior year of high school. She continued working there for our senior year. We earned some credits toward our graduating requirement and had spending money from our salaries. We helped each other in every way possible. When she was learning shorthand, and taking dictation, I was working in the adjoining room, so I listened in and took notes in case she missed anything. Working together and living together we became closer than sisters, and we had wonderful adventures together.

We had our little love affairs…mine, the long distance affair with Bob, the boy from Newell, and she with Francis, a year ahead of us in school. It was an innocent time. Sex was dangerous territory, and often the end of the road for young women, as far as education was concerned in those years before the invention and acceptance of birth control. If a girl became pregnant, she was excluded from school. No exceptions! As for Teresa and me…we had plans, and sexual activity did not fit in with them. We had an unspoken taboo on ever having one of our boyfriends in the apartment. All of that did not prevent us from talking about sex at length and telling bawdy jokes to each other.

We had such a good time living there, feeling increasingly grown-up. Neither of us had any adult supervision. Sometimes she went home for the weekend and I almost always went to the red house to spend Sunday afternoon with Mother, Rosie and Tom. Both Teresa and I were given excuses from our parents to have on hand in case we needed them. It was in this form: *Dolores (Teresa) was not in school on (date) as she was ill.* We each had a dozen of them and never, ever used them. We were in excellent health and had no reason not to go to school. Neither of us was tempted by cigarettes or alcohol. We charged our groceries on her father's account at the local grocery store, and would not have wanted him to see anything like that on the bill. Furthermore, we were not going to use our hard earned money for such frivolous things. I had agreed to pay Teresa's father my share of the grocery bill after the school year when I would be working full time.

One night we were at the local drug store having a soda, and heard of a robbery on a farm outside of Sturgis. The city and county law officers were on the way out there, with sirens shrieking. Teresa feared that it might be on her father's farm and was frightened. Some boys we didn't know very well, who happened to be in the drug store, overheard our conversation, and offered to take us there in their car, to investigate. It turned out not to be at her father's farm, and the boys brought us home safely. Teresa worried for the next couple of weeks that her father would find out that we had gone for a ride in a car with "boys." That was the most delinquent act we ever did in that innocent time together.

We ate quite well, and with our little two burner kerosene stove, managed to make what we thought were elegant meals. We had some dinners to which we invited other friends. Once I invited Katy Phelps, the young English teacher.

After the school year was well underway, I noticed on my walk to the red house, that the Episcopal Church had more activity than I had noticed before. I found that there were a few high school students who went there. I started to attend. I didn't talk with anyone, just went in, sat in the back, did not take communion, and left before anyone else. By Christmas time I was familiar with the liturgy and began to talk with the few students from school who were attending there. Soon I was talking with one of the elders. I asked her how one goes about becoming confirmed and thereby eligible to take communion. She arranged for me to meet the priest. That was the first step.

In a few days I got a letter from Father Biller, saying he could meet me the next Friday at my house. I asked Mrs. Kerper if I could meet with him in the living room of the main house rather than in our small apartment where the bed took up half the living space. I eagerly awaited Father Biller the next Friday.

He introduced himself and said I could call him Father Biller, putting me at ease immediately. He was a supply priest to Sturgis, Deadwood and the Pine Ridge Reservation. A supply priest in the Episcopal Church is one who serves a church when the regular priest, the Rector, is not available. In this case, Father Biller had served as a supply priest for these three parishes for several years, similar to the circuit riders of a former era in the West. The difference was mainly that Father Biller drove an automobile instead of making the run by horseback.

He suggested that we arrange to meet every Friday, as he went to the Pine Ridge Reservation on that day, and could easily stop to see me on the way. He would leave with me a booklet titled, *Forward Day by Day.* In it were assigned readings from the Old Testament, the Gospels, a Psalm and an Epistle, for each day. There was a reflection on one of the above readings. I was to read the daily readings and reflections and write any thoughts, feelings, inspirations, or questions I had concerning what I had read. When he came to the house on Friday, we would discuss the material. I felt it was a good way to get ready to become a member of a church. I never felt my questions were too trivial, or that I was expected to know more. Father Biller led me into a deeper understanding of what we can know and of an appreciation for the mysteries of God, *i.e.* the unknowable. There were no tests... only an accumulation of knowledge. It was next step, and an important one, of my spiritual quest.

We kept this schedule for eight weeks, when the Bishop, Conrad Gesner, came to St. Thomas Church in Sturgis for his annual visit. There had been no confirmands at St. Thomas for several years. This was an exciting event for me and for the church. There were few members in the church and most became involved in my confirmation. One woman, a fine seamstress, made a dress for me of white organdy. She and I shopped at JC Penneys for the material and pattern, for which she paid the entire bill. Another baked a tiered cake. The Lindstrom family arranged for their son, Bob, an accomplished vocalist to come home from college to sing a solo for the ceremony. I was nearly overwhelmed at the importance the event was taking on.

On the Sunday of the confirmation, I had been prepared for the general outline of the service, but not prepared for the emotional impact of it. I was seated in the front row of the church with two women who were my sponsors. When the appointed time came in the service, I was called up to the altar rail where Bishop Gesner put his hands on my head and said the 1928 version of the following prayer, "Defend, O Lord, your servant Dolores with your heavenly grace, that she may continue yours for ever, and daily increase in your Holy Spirit more and more, until she comes to your everlasting kingdom." I truly felt something profound was happening. It was similar, but not exactly the same as the feeling I had when I was thirteen and was walking home from school at Hereford, facing Bear Butte and had that powerful spiritual experience. I felt truly blessed and anointed and other things too intense for words.

When I turned to walk back to take my place in the front, I saw my mother and Rosie sitting in the back of the church! I was very moved. Mother, with her strong Catholic roots, had come to witness and to tacitly support this action of mine, which I had taken independently. I had not discussed it with her, only telling her when it would happen. I had hoped, but not expected, that she would be there. And Rosie! How appropriate that she should be there... the one person who brought light into my life, eleven years before. In addition to those two important people was one more...a Native American friend of Father Biller, from the Pine Ridge Reservation, sitting in the back row. I had never seen a Native American in a white church before. I felt this would have meaning in my life later on. Far surpassing anything else that happened was that I had a church home. At last, I belonged to a church!

The church and many events connected with it became a part of my life. The rest of it was school and the extracurricular activities, my work at the law office, Sunday dinners in the red house, visits to Aunt Mary and Uncle Marvin's farm, and dances on Saturday nights.

Those dances were the times when I would connect with Bob, the love of my life, so far.

At one of those dances I came into an awareness of the transitory nature of life and recognizing that, also became aware of the preciousness of life.

The dance that night was in an upstairs hall in Whitewood, a small town six miles north of Sturgis. We went in high spirits. The Haley family was playing and we considered them to be the best band around. The floor was crowded by people of all ages from twelve to seventy-five. Our group of teenagers hung out together in a cluster between dances.. The music was hot and we were swing dancing and jitterbugging.

Several young people from Newell were there, including my boyfriend, Bob. When the fateful event happened I had been dancing with Bob's friend Marion. Marion was telling me that he had been drinking quite a bit over the winter and last week had decided to give it up. He told me it was the first time he had ever danced sober and said it was hard to do it without a drink, but he was going to do it. The dance was over and he was saying, "It just costs too much and isn't good for me anyway." He walked me back to the cluster of teenagers.

We were near the staircase, and as Marion said those words, another boy overheard, tapped him on the chest, not very hard, saying, "Yeah, I'll believe that when I see it." Marion threw his head back as if to answer, but lost his balance and went tumbling down the staircase. His neck was broken and he was dead by the time the ambulance arrived.

I remember nothing until the next day, when Mother was taking me out to Aunt Mary and Uncle Marvin's for dinner. When we arrived, she told Aunt Mary that I was in shock, and as she said that, the memory of the night before returned. It came flooding back and I told of the event just as I recalled it, to Aunt Mary. She said very few words, but sat with me in a healing silence for a long time.

Fortunately school was so absorbing that I got back to it on Monday morning and immersed myself in all that was going on. But that night at the dance in Whitewood, affected my outlook on life in a profound way.

At school we started every day with band practice. Unless there was a large amount of snow or the temperature was below thirty degrees, we marched outside. Otherwise, we were in the gym, practicing intricate maneuvers to perform at the halftime of games or were preparing for a concert. We had two bands, one was The Band, which was both a marching and concert band. The other was a dance band, in which I wanted to play but could not fit the practices into my schedule. Furthermore, it was an all-male band, and I was not yet ready to break the gender barrier.

Almost as enjoyable as the band, was the journalism group. This was considered an extracurricular activity; that is, we gained no credits towards graduation nor were there grades. However, editing and publishing the *Bear Butte Breezes* was the most educational of all the things I did at school. We published a newspaper monthly and worked on the *Mato Paha*, our yearbook. I did much of the writing, assigning articles, editing them and overseeing the layout and printing of the *Bear Butte Breezes*.

In Sturgis there was an old newspaper, *The Black Hills Press*; owned, operated, written, printed and published by a man known to us as Scottie. He was a man who passionately loved every aspect of the newspaper business as he knew it. He eagerly took on the high school students and taught them everything he could in the time they were given to work there in his establishment. He taught me layout techniques and linotyping. He could not afford to hire anyone in his small operation. However, I learned enough from him that when school was out after my junior year, I applied at the office of the *Sturgis Tribune*, was hired on the spot and worked there for the rest of my school days.

Going back to my junior year, one of the highlights was the class play. It was a big event of the year and the drama club along with the English class read many scripts and discussed them at length before choosing one to produce. Boldly, we chose Thornton Wilder's *Our Town*. Although this play had first been produced when I was five years old, it was a totally new concept in Sturgis. The sparse stage sets, the interaction between the stage manager and the audience, and the sad ending, were not the common fare of plays in our town. "People wanted a *play*, not a cerebral *work* of profound concepts," was the argument against *Our Town*. The opposing view won the argument by proposing that Sturgis had minds every bit as sophisticated as those in Boston and New York where the play had been a huge success. Furthermore, it had been rejected by Russia, our enemy in the Cold War. The winning argument posited was that Sturgis was more open minded than Russia. Thus, it was chosen as the play of the year.

Naturally, I wanted a part, not just any part; I wanted to play Emily. It happened that the tryouts were on a day when many of the possible Emilys were away at some other event. The readings for the parts were conducted during English class. When Mrs. Anderson asked who wanted to read the part of Emily, my hand shot up! As I was reading lines I came to the place where Emily is pleading with the Stage Manager to let her come back to experience life again. He reluctantly grants her just one day. One of the other post-life characters admonishes Emily to choose an ordinary day because even that will be too much to bear. Emily pleads, "Oh, please let me come back on my birthday, February 11th, oh, please!"

As I read the lines, I blurted out, "That is *my* birthday. February 11th is my birthday; really it is!"

Mrs. Anderson said, "Well, it would seem the part is for you." The class applauded. No one else even tried out for the part. Rosie helped me learn the lines on the weekends when I went to the red house. Reading, acting and saying the words of wisdom that Thornton Wilder has embedded in the play became part of me. It was a pure gift, a gift that never wore out nor got lost.

Those years were so amazing and wonderful and heart-building as well as heartbreaking. And I lived them with zest and earnestness as if I were building a ship that would endure the rest of my life and beyond.

There were uncanny similarities between Teresa and me. We could talk in a shorthand language because each of us could start a thought and the other could finish it. Trying to keep our separate identities, we went to separate towns to buy our winter coats. She went to Rapid City and I went to Deadwood. When we got home and took our long maroon coats out of the boxes, they were almost identical. We laughed about it and wore them with delight.

The same thing happened with our beautiful white eyelet gowns for the Junior/Senior prom; we tried to be individuals but came home with nearly the same gown. We were both excited about the prom. Both of us were on the committee that arranged for speakers and entertainment at the banquet preceding the dance. All through the banquet, I was watching for Bob. He was to come from Newell and expected to arrive about nine, after the dinner and before the dance. I was anticipating this as all of my friends had heard of him. "Her phantom boyfriend," they called him because few of them had met him. I wanted my school friends to see him and I wanted him to see me in my element. However, he was not there at the end of the dinner. He was not there at the beginning of the dance.

We lived only a block from the school so I walked home, telling Teresa to send him over when he arrived, but I knew that he was not going to show up; somehow I just knew. I sat on the steps of the apartment, listening to the music from the school auditorium and sobbed for hours like the school girl I was. For days afterwards, I waited anxiously for word from Bob. I could have worried that he had been in an accident, but somehow, I knew that was not the case. Finally, after about a week I got a letter from with the return address of Oxnard, California. He had enlisted in the Coast Guard and said in the letter that he just didn't know how to tell me. I forgave him easily and we resumed our paper love affair.

That was near the end of our junior year and then the summer vacation began. Teresa went out to the farm for the summer and I moved to the red house. I started work at the *Sturgis Tribune* immediately. Oh, how I loved that job! I proofread and edited articles that came in from the farm and ranch land outside of Sturgis. I linotyped several hours a day, and did whatever was needed at this family operation. Being a part of it was thrilling for me. It felt solid and right that I should be there. I was earning more money than I had ever earned before and was able to pay Teresa's father for my share of the grocery bill, as I had promised. I stayed with the Tribune for the rest of my days in Sturgis.

When school started in 1950 Teresa and I resumed our living at the apartment on Willard St. We shopped at the local grocery store for all our food except the produce she brought from the farm. I was uneasy about how I was going to pay her father for my share after this year, but we continued charging, and eating rather well. The senior year was expensive, with senior pictures, class rings, and school clothes. I never had any money left at the end of the month. Everything was paid for with cash; we had never heard of credit cards and did not have bank accounts. In the high school curriculum was a course titled "Home Economics," but I firmly believe Teresa and I learned far more about home economics than we would have in the class at the high school.

We enjoyed shopping for groceries and cooking for each other. One day when shopping, we were at the meat counter pondering what to buy for our supper, when one of the clerks behind the counter addressed me, saying, "I understand your stepfather is quite a gambler." I was stunned by the blunt, inappropriate remark and remained silent for a moment to gather my wits. She filled that moment, asking, "Is that true?"

I answered, "I really don't know. I never thought it was any of my business."

That conversation was overheard by another clerk who was amused by it and told several other people. Sturgis is a small town and it soon came back to my mother, who told the story to Tom. I believe that was the point where Tom began to respect me as a real person. We began to talk with each other on Sundays when I was home. Tom was by nature, a quiet, reflective man, so the talks were not animated and extensive but they were an exchange of ideas between equals.

There were so many high points of the senior year that I could not possibly remember all of them but others are engraved in my memory so deeply I can never forget them. For example: playing a flute solo in a dramatic production, being on the debate team which won a tournament so important that a caravan of cars met us and accompanied us into the high school, just as they did for a major athletic victory; a group of my friends having a surprise 18th birthday party for me; being inducted into the Thespian Society; finishing the yearbook. On and on, one productive day after another.

Our high school basketball team, The Sturgis Scoopers was from the smallest school in the State A conference. If we had three fewer students we would not have qualified. However, we had a phenomenal basketball team that year and ended up going to the finals in Sioux Falls, across the state. I simply did not have enough money to get there, but Mother and Tom reluctantly gave me half, and I was able to do the rest with my earnings. Their reluctance was that they did not follow sports nor see the value of spending so much money on an unimportant event. I was covering the it for both the school paper and the Tribune, but neither of those offered compensation. During the tournament I was given the privilege of staying in a college dormitory in Sioux Falls; that of Augustana College. I was awed by the college. The campus was beautiful, Grecian in design. The halls were long, white and had molded garlands around the top border. They seemed to me to reek of knowledge and grace. I had the faintest stirrings of attending a college such as this.

Our basketball team was triumphant, becoming the championship of the state that year! Our little school of Sturgis! We went home in high spirits! The experience of the tournament was great, but the experience of Augustana was enduring and pervasive. However, Black Hills Teacher's College was a fine college and I would have been satisfied to go there. I scheduled a meeting to talk about college with Mr. Grunwald, the superintendent of the school. He told me that there were scholarships available for students such as myself, and that I had a good chance of being granted one of them. Then he asked me if I had considered any colleges, and I surprised myself by saying, "Well, I did like Augustana when I was there for the basketball tournament." He seemed to think this was not an outrageous consideration and helped me fill out the application for a scholarship at Augustana.

A few weeks later our debate team was debating in Lead, a mining town north of Sturgis, and in the audience were some representatives from Augustana. After the debate they asked if they could interview me, which I heartily accepted. They asked several questions about subjects in which I excelled, about extra-curricular activities, and careers I had considered for my future. Three weeks later I got a letter from Augustana College telling me that I was a recipient of a full academic scholarship, which would be for the full four years providing I maintained a 3.0 grade average. I was nearly intoxicated with joy! By graduation, I was positively exultant!

It was all so dazzling...that time surrounding graduation! I had never anticipated how glorious it would be. I was the first of the Curry girls to graduate from high school. I was also the first of Aunt Mary's progeny...yes, I know that technically, I was not her direct progeny but she was such an important part of my life we both felt a direct line between us. Greeting cards and gifts arrived. I had not expected that.

Even Bob Curry, who had denied any requests for financial help throughout my life, sent me five dollars and a little suitcase. I was surprised by that, because about two months before graduation he came to see me. Not since I was five years old had he made a trip to see only me. I arranged for him to meet me at a restaurant because, for some reason, I did not want him to know where I lived. We had dinner and a stilted awkward conversation about nothing. I did not realize that he was skirting around a conversation he wanted but feared to have.

After dinner, I had him take me back to the red house, rather than to the apartment on Willard Street, because with Mother just twenty feet away, I felt more secure. We sat in the car in front of the house for several minutes, saying nothing, not knowing how to end this uncomfortable visit. Finally, he got out what it was that he wanted to say. He said he was sorry for all those years that he neglected me, but he was so busy taking care of the other business of his life; he was sorry that he couldn't send me money those two times that I requested it, but he just didn't have it. He said that he wanted a chance to be the father to me that he had not been and that he hoped I would come to Montana and live with him and Margaret.

Only with the brashness of an eighteen year old, and with the confidence I had built up in the last four years could I have answered so coldly and assuredly, "You are way too late and you offer way too little," I told him. I had come this far with the help of Mother and Tom and Aunt Mary and Uncle Marvin and others and I did not need anything from him now. That was my answer to him. He wept, but I was resolute. I went inside the red house and sat at the kitchen table with Mother, Tom and Rosie and felt comfortable and at home. I felt that what had just occurred outside between me and my natural father, was closure. For me it was enough. Forgiveness would come later, with maturity.

Finally graduation night arrived. It was a significant event and came at the best time of the year...lilac time in Sturgis. Many people from my family were in the audience. The most lasting memory is the feeling of completion and joy. I felt more successful and wise than I had ever felt in my life. I did not win high honors but gave them to myself. I had paid my dues and was triumphant.

After the ceremony, I got in the car with my family, and we went to a little restaurant in town. We were joined by Aunt Mary, Uncle Marvin, Jimmy Dale and Sally. We each had a dish of ice cream. I was the guest of honor. There was talk, laughter and reminiscing. It was a shining hour for our family. I felt not only successful and wise but well loved.

There was an important moment at the end of the celebration when the bill was brought to the table. Without hesitation, both Tom and Uncle Marvin reached for it, and they stared at each other. Everyone at the table understood the complexity of that unspoken conversation. In the end Tom won the privilege of paying for my graduation celebration.

CHAPTER 15

Ogden Revisited

High school and graduation were behind me and I was eager to get on with life, which I was sure would begin at Augustana in September. I simply had to fill the time and earn the fare to get there and pay for room and board. Teresa and I dreamed and plotted about this for hours. We came up with a plan. Mother, Tom and Rosie were going to Ogden for the summer and we would go along. We knew we could earn more money in a big city than in Sturgis. I would work at the Air force base outside Ogden, because according to legend, people made a lot of money there. Teresa plans were more modest. She had never lived outside of South Dakota and that was her main impetus for going. She was ready for an adventure somewhere out there in the big world. Perhaps she and I were not quite willing to give up our relationship. We had more to say, more to do together and trusted each other with our feelings more than with anyone else.

I expected to apply and go to work immediately at the base, where I would get a large paycheck every week. I would be ready for Augustana.

Mother was going so she could be with Mary Lou who was expecting her third child in early September. Tom and Rosie were going because they wanted to be wherever Mother was. We all had our dreams for the summer.

How reality worked its way into our dreams is the story of the summer in Ogden. It began before we got to Utah on the first day out of Sturgis.

The first leg of the trip was to Rapid City to spend the night before launching our life in the big world. Mother needed to say goodbye to Grandma and make sure she was settled for the summer. Teresa and I spent the night in the trailer house behind the house on Omaha Street.

The next morning Mother and I went to St. Patrick Street to say good bye to Grandma where she boarded with the Woods family. We found her in poor health. She was having trouble breathing; it was one of her recurring asthma spells. We did not yet use the word "psycho-somatic illness" but Mother knew that every time she planned a trip, Grandma became ill. It was an irritation to her, but she could not leave until her mother was better. So we went back to the little trailer house where Teresa and I slept one more night...and one more, and yet another. Day after day we waited. Our moods alternated between boredom, impatience, anxiety, and giddiness. We were intensely eager to get started on our new life. We didn't go to town or to movies because we were too frugal.

After about a week, we decided to have a party to celebrate our graduation, being eighteen, and the success of our abstinence throughout high school. At this party we would have beer and we would smoke cigarettes. We spent a couple of days making plans but never brought them to fruition because we were too careful about the little money we had to carry us through until we started earning our way in Ogden. Furthermore, that was not who we were. We were in the process of finding out who we were and discovered that we were not party girls.

One night Teresa and I were alone in the trailer house. Mother and Rosie had gone to see Grandma. We had exhausted the reading material available, even the newspaper still lying on the table in front of had been thoroughly perused.

"I'm so bored I could cut out paper dolls," Teresa said. Upon cue, we set out to find scissors and found one pair in a sewing kit and another with a box of first aid supplies. We began cutting out paper dolls...strings and strings of them. We strung them around the walls and windows, and everywhere around the trailer house, festooning every space of the little trailer. It was surprising how one daily newspaper in 1951 could transform a trailer house.

When we heard the car pull up in front of the house, we hid in the closet, knowing that Mother and Rosie would come in to give us a report on Grandma's condition, and to say goodnight. They opened the door and stood a moment, stunned at the sight and then began laughing. We came out and laughed with them until tears ran down our cheeks.

After about a week, which seemed like a month for us, Grandma recovered and we embarked for Ogden. I had been across Wyoming, but experiencing it with Teresa who had never seen it, made the journey more fun than ever before. We were excited as we rode across Wyoming, delighting in the strange names of the little towns along the way...Lusk, Lingle, Torrington, Laramie, and Rock Springs, where we spent the night. Finally, we passed through the last Wyoming town of Evanston. A few more miles down the road, we called out, in unison, "Utah, Here we are!" One more small town, Wahsatch and finally Ogden! At last we arrived at the city where we would start our imagined glorious adulthood.

Our troupe arrived at Grandpa's and spread ourselves around his house and property. I do not remember where we all slept but I know the five of us doubled the population of his family. What I do remember are glorious summer days coupled with a sense of fulfillment and expectation, balanced in exquisite tension.

The first day in Ogden, I found the Civil Service Office. It was a busy place, because of the Air Force Base nearby which was always hiring, but this day was busier than usual, owing to the escalation of the Korean Conflict. I filled out an application and was told that I would be scheduled to take the Civil Service test two weeks later. When I asked about the earliest date that I would actually start work, I was told that it would be "some time" before

I would be called up. "Some time"...what did that mean? A week, a month? My heart sank at that news. It was already June and I was worried about making enough money between now and September to get me to Augustana, pay my room and board, and buy books.

I scoured the newspaper want ads and found a job at a soda fountain at the back of a drug store in the heart of downtown Ogden. It was a pleasant place to work and I made friends with business owners and other downtown workers who came in for lunch every day. One was a hair stylist who offered to cut and style my hair and keep it perfectly groomed as an advertisement for his shop a few doors down the street. That arrangement worked well for him as he gained many customers from patrons at the soda fountain who liked my short pixie haircut.

Another good friend I made was with Thelma, the manager of the soda fountain. She was a woman in her early forties. We became good friends...just as if we were of the same generation. She knew my sister, Mary Lou. I believe Mary Lou knew every waitress in Ogden. Mary Lou had been active in the Union of Restaurant Workers in Ogden.

Teresa despaired that she would ever find a job and expressed her concern to Rosie. Teresa and Rosie became good friends as I was off to work most of the day and they were at Grandpa's house together. Rosie told her, "I can find you a job," and Teresa said, "If you think you can, go ahead!" So Rosie, age twelve, combed the want ads and posing as Teresa on the phone, found a job as a receptionist for a photography studio. Teresa took the job and was working within a few days.

Now that we were both working, and now that the house started feeling too crowded, and still remembering the freedom of living on our own, we rented a small apartment closer to downtown and our work. It was on the second floor of an old Victorian house. It was hot up there on those July days. We spent most of our time at work or in the park nearby.

We visited Mary Lou when she wasn't working. Even in the late stages of her pregnancy, Mary Lou worked. She always worked. I remember her being in perpetual motion, and always productive. Her little girls were well dressed and clean. Mary Lou made most of their clothes, and sometimes I went over and sewed with her. I made a red cotton sundress for myself. Of course, that required a suntan so I had to find time to lie in the sun for a while each day. Ah! The vanity of an eighteen year old! It was the only suntan I had in my entire life.

This summer was memorable. It was fun to be in a big city, big by our standards. Ogden had parks and city buses and things to see and do that were free. There were so many amenities and amusements that Sturgis did not offer. We felt we had graduated into the wide world. We were frugal, living on fruit, peanut butter sandwiches, and milk. Fruit which was abundant and inexpensive there, where, "Lo! The Desert Bloomed Like a Rose," thanks to Brigham Young and the Mormons who had settled there about a hundred years before. Frugality did not quell the anxiety, always there for me...anxiety that I would not have the money to get to Augustana. Teresa's father, in an act of generosity, exonerated me from my debt for my share of the grocery bill we ran up over the school year, and for that I was very grateful. It gave me a glimmer of hope that I might make it, financially, to get to Augustana.

About the middle of July Teresa got a letter from her father saying that he would pay for her to go to Business School in Rapid City, and that school started in August. She could easily see that this was a good opportunity for her. I agreed, but mourned her leaving. I knew it was the end of an era of my life.

On the last day she was there, I stopped by a flower shop near our apartment and bought a little gnome for her. I had been looking at those tiny guys all summer and wanted one, but could not afford it. However it was important that she would have something to remind her of me and of our years together. When I took it to the apartment and gave her the gift, her eyes opened wide, and with tears, she handed hers to me. It was the very same gnome! Yes, we were soul mates.

After she left, I missed her terribly. I do not remember how it came about but a minor social life opened up for me. I dated a young Mormon boy. We had a few dates together, one to a picnic of his Ward of the Mormon Church. He wanted me to meet his parents and I realized he was looking for a wife. I was not ready for that. I had a different plan for my life. That relationship lasted only two weeks.

Teresa's departure caused me to face the fact that I would not have enough money for room and board nor for books at college. I could barely make the rent in Ogden at the end of August. If I could just get to Sioux Falls, I believed that something would open up. I would find a way. Bus fare was all I needed. Surely, I thought, the Civil Service job would open up, and if I got even one paycheck it would take me there.

Mary Lou and I spent more time together after Teresa left. One night I remember, Mother offered to stay with Mary Lou's little girls so she and I could walk downtown. Mary Lou seldom had time or the opportunity to do something just for fun. We dressed up and I wore my new red sundress. We walked downtown and bought a soda at a drug store, and then walked around downtown, looking at store window displays, looking at clothing we could never afford. We walked home through the park by my apartment. We saw young people playing tennis on the courts. Their lives seemed so different from ours. They looked so spiffy and well-heeled in their dazzling whites. They appeared not to have a care in the world, nothing to do but play. They could have been from another planet considering the differences between our lives. I had never known a tennis player. Certainly Sturgis did not have any.

It was the middle of August when the letter from Civil Service finally arrived. I opened it with anticipation and dread. As I read the words, tears welled up in my eyes. I could start work on September fifteenth. My first paycheck would be issued at the end of September...a month after college classes began at Augustana. What a serious dilemma! It seemed like the most important predicament in my life thus far.

So completely had I established my independence that there was no expectation on my part, nor any move on the part of Mother and Tom to get involved in my financial problem—it was mine alone.

I wrote a carefully constructed letter to Augustana College, Dean of Student Affairs, telling them that I did not have the financial resources to start in September but that I would be able to be there by the second semester. The turn-around on that communication was fast. Within a week, I received the terse, harsh, unyielding reply. There was no circumstance whereby they could defer my admittance. They had gone to considerable effort to award me this scholarship and were appalled at my request. I faced the reality that I had reached too high. I remembered one of the sentences Katy Phelps, my sophomore English teacher, had written on the board one day. "One's reach must exceed one's grasp. Else what's a heaven for?" This reach had been in vain but I would keep on reaching. "Augustana was not Heaven," I tried to tell myself.

The Augustana letter came on a Friday morning and I went to work at the soda fountain. It was a hard day to work. It was also my last day there since I had accepted the Civil Service job. Tears were near the surface all day long. My throat was constricted. I could talk to no one and mechanically went about my work.

When my shift ended, I went to the changing room to get out of my uniform into my street clothes and sat on the little cot. The tears I had been holding back all day began to fall. Soon I was sobbing unabashedly. As I sat there, Thelma came to see what was wrong. She knew me well enough to know that I had been having a problem through the day. I told her my story, through my sobs, and she began to cry as well. Soon she was sobbing so hard that I stopped and said, "It's not your problem, Thelma. I will get through this." When she finally got control of her sobbing, she told me she had saved for years to send her son to college. He was to have started this fall also, but just yesterday he had taken all the tuition money she had saved and bought a motorcycle! We held each other and cried until crying had served its purpose. Had I been older and more sophisticated, we would have gone out for a drink. But again, that was not who I was. Thelma and I parted; I never saw her again. I started work at Hill Air Force Base the next Monday.

On Saturday I went to the soda fountain but Thelma was not there. I began to accept what had happened, and worked at convincing myself that there was more to life than college at Augustana. Not one of our family had gone anywhere but Black Hills State in Spearfish, South Dakota. Perhaps I would work at the air force base until the semester break and go back to Sturgis and enroll there.

Perhaps my boyfriend Bob would come back from the Coast Guard and we would get serious. Perhaps we would even get married and have babies. Another thought intruded: I walked by Weber State University every day on my way to work. Maybe I could take some night courses there.

I walked home in the late afternoon in a thoughtful, open mood. What would happen next? I would be open to it. I said some prayers. It was a lovely time of day, just before sun set. That wonderful low afternoon light had illuminated the trees and grass to a dazzling shade of green. Perhaps there was more to life after all!

I had walked slowly by the tennis courts, watching the young people running so nimbly and gracefully over the clay. When a tennis ball came bouncing out of the court, right in front of me, it seemed the most natural thing in the world to pick it up, take it over and hand it to the player who was running out to recover it. That player took the ball from me and said, "A pretty girl like you should not be walking alone in this park. Just wait around and I will walk with you wherever you are going."

Again, it seemed the most natural thing in the world for me to enter the court and sit on a bench in that world where I had never dreamed of entering, and to wait for this young man who I realized was the most handsome young man I had ever seen.

Shortly he won the set he was playing and came over to me. We walked to my apartment, and as we walked, we talked as freely and easily as if we had known each other forever. I discovered that his name was Charles Lichtenwalner; he came from Pennsylvania; he was an airman stationed at the base where I would be starting my second week of work the next Monday. We arrived at my door, he kissed me lightly on the lips and said to meet him the next day at the courts. Thus began the time of my life when he was never out of my mind or my heart or my soul.

CHAPTER 16

More of Ogden

Oh, the glory of young love! No one can express it adequately. Through it, I gained a deeper understanding of the poetry I read with Aunt Mary. In my sparse spare time I reread the poems exchanged between Elizabeth Barrett and Robert Browning. My life was that poetry!

My existence on earth had arrived at its zenith. I believed that with my whole heart. I was loved, really loved; no conditions, no doubts. And I loved Charles with all my being. We spent every available moment together.

He was an airman in the Air Force and that rank afforded very few privileges at the base. Every evening he had to be back at the base by eleven, which meant that he had to leave Ogden by ten. This arrangement probably prevented all kinds of trouble in our young lives. It was much more compelling than parental supervision would have been. I had to get up at 5:30 a.m. to catch a ride to the base with an older woman who was in charge of the unit of Pay and Allotments where I worked. Charles was assigned in the same building in the section where automated devices were tested for use in offices such as mine. We seldom saw each other at work, in spite of our contorted efforts to do so. With every fiber of my being I wanted to see him every moment of the day. I wanted to breathe the air he breathed...walk on the ground he walked upon. I had no doubt that he had the same feelings about me.

We did find enough time to come to know each other well. He would pick me up at the little apartment and we would go to a

Chinese restaurant for dinner. On one of our early dates he asked me if I had a red sundress. I answered, "Yes, why do you ask?"

He said, "I saw you one night at a soda fountain with a woman, probably your sister, and I said to the guy with me, 'That is the woman I am going to marry'." So there it was! In my mind and in his, our life together was pre-ordained, predestined. He never asked me to marry him. It had been arranged in the cosmos. It was as natural and sure as the progression of the seasons.

Before the end of September we were choosing a diamond, wedding ring and the date for the ceremony. We decided on November 10 because we would have an extra day off for Armistice Day and forevermore would have an extra day to celebrate our anniversary

We spent most weekend afternoons driving around in his little black '39 Ford coupe. The real estate market was flourishing in Utah. New homes were being built on the outskirts of town, in the foothills of the Wasatch Mountains. We liked to drive around and look at houses and imagine living in one. We envisioned raising our children there. There were many houses under construction and the roads were not paved nor marked.

One beautiful day as we were driving in the foothills looking at houses, he drove to the top of a steep hill and abruptly stopped the car and asked, "Would you get out and check to see if the hill we will be going down is too steep for this car to get back up the other side?" I stepped out and walked almost to the front of the car. My stomach did flip-flops. I stammered and used my hands to convey to him, "Back-up...back-up! Back up now!" If we had gone one inch further, the car would have plunged over a cliff and landed in a materials dump fifty feet below! He backed up and got out of the car to see what had frightened me. We stood there together, and realized how close we had been to death. After that event we felt we had been saved for a larger purpose in our lives. We believed we had something important to do in our time on this earth and had been saved so that we could move on into that future.

In early October, I knew it was time to take Charles to meet my grandfather. Of my family, only Mary Lou had met my husband-to-be, this dark, handsome tennis player from the East, and she was completely charmed by him. But Grandpa was another hurdle altogether. I knew he would not be charmed. I only hoped they would tolerate each other. I was planning to ask Grandpa to give me away at the wedding. I had butterflies in my stomach before the meeting of these two important men in my life. Charles was so different from anyone in our family. It was not a given that he would be accepted. Nevertheless, I phoned Grandpa and told him that I had met the man I was going to marry and if he would like to meet him, we would be over that evening. He asked how long I had known the young man, and a few other questions about him, and said to bring him on over.

When I introduced them, Grandpa said, "You must be a Jew with a name like that."

My heart caught in my throat. I knew so little about any culture other than the mix of Scandinavian, Scotch-Irish, and Danish of western South Dakota. Furthermore, it would not have mattered one iota to me what religion, culture, race or creed Charles belonged to. He belonged to me and I belonged to him. Charles took a deep breath and with an even tone, tinged with pride, said, "We are German."

Grandpa countered, "German Jews?"

Charles answered him, again with great maturity, "We are Pennsylvania Dutch Germans." That was the end of that conversation.

Although the conversation had ended, I pondered over it for a long time. Grandpa knew and was concerned that I was going to be leading a life in a different culture from our own. I knew he had my interests at heart, but I would have married Charles regardless of what Grandpa thought or said. What I wanted was acceptance. Grandpa and Charles wisely let it go, and by the end of the evening the two appeared to be getting along well enough to talk about the upcoming wedding. Grandpa was pleased when I asked him to give me away.

He even procured a place for us to live after the wedding. When Grandpa had moved to Utah he become a Mormon, nominally, not with strong conviction nor practice of the rituals of the church. However, in Ogden, it was propitious for him to join for many reasons, but primarily because his wife was a practicing Mormon. He had connections with many Mormons in the area, and learned that one friend, Sister Davies, was going to be away for the winter with her daughter, and wanted someone to stay in her little cottage. Grandpa made arrangements for us to stay there. We were delighted to have a place to go to after the wedding.

The wedding was small and dignified in the Good Shepherd Episcopal Church in Ogden performed by Father McGinnis. Mary Lou was my maid of honor. No one else in my family attended. It was too expensive for them to travel and I had too little to afford a reception for them if they did come. The best man was Buzz Burton, a tennis partner of Charles. My supervisor, Miss McClanahan, and a young woman with whom I worked attended the wedding. I provided cake and ice-cream in the hospitality hall of the church. I breathed a sigh of relief when Charles and Grandpa were friendly with each other throughout the day. After the celebration Charles and I drove to Salt Lake City for a two-day honeymoon. I truly felt my life was complete. Here was the man who filled all the empty places that a father or brother might have, someone with whom I could trust my entire being and my entire future. I wanted to have his children.

After that brief honeymoon we went to our borrowed, neat two-bedroom house where the most exciting things for me were electricity, indoor plumbing, a 1940's kitchen and a record player. We played house there, and commuted to the base every day. We discovered Sister Davis had recordings of the *Student Prince*, and in the evenings we listened, danced and sang together. Charles' Aunt Lucy, an opera singer in New York had given him voice lessons all of his life until he joined the service. He had a beautiful voice. Unfortunately our singing and playtime only lasted about a week. I came down with a severe case of the flu and was ill for ten days.

Just as I began to recover, Sister Davies returned. The living arrangement with her daughter had not worked out. She said we could stay for the winter. There was enough room for the three of us, she said. We stayed there together, for about three days and I was sick every morning. Charles and I thought it was a remnant of the flu. Sister Davis stated bluntly one morning, "Just because you are sick every morning doesn't necessarily mean that you are pregnant." My eyes met those big brown eyes of Charles, suddenly alert and surprised. An electric charge went through the room. Of course, I was pregnant! We left the kitchen, went to our bedroom and laughed with joy and ecstasy! We were going to have our baby! We knew that we had to get a place of our own right away. That very afternoon, we went to look for an apartment for no more than sixty dollars a month. We found one and asked the landlord if he would hold it until pay-day, but he let us move in right away. It took my entire paycheck to pay the first month's rent and deposit, but that did not dampen our spirits.

Thanksgiving was the next week. We were so broke we barely had enough to eat on regular days, to say nothing of a holiday! A friend of Charles' went quail hunting a few days before and gave us two tiny birds for our Thanksgiving dinner. It was a meager dinner, especially compared to what we knew our families in Pennsylvania and South Dakota were having that day. We each missed the fun of being with our own family but did not want to admit it to each other and only guardedly to ourselves. We wanted to see ourselves as a grown-up, complete couple.

We knew another young couple, Gill and Joan Hoyt, with whom we had become friends, so we went over to their apartment to commiserate with them. When we got there, we could smell the turkey as we walked in the entryway and were surprised to find them in tears. Their parents had sent them money for a big dinner and they had purchased and prepared the food but were both so homesick for their families they couldn't enjoy it. A lavish dinner sat on their table, untouched. We told our stories of the day to each other and then stepped back a bit and looked at the dinner table.

Charles said, "How about we eat some of this food and see how we feel after that." During the meal, we told jokes, exchanged banter, and were soon laughing uproariously! Here we were, trying to be adults and were caught up like little children, missing our parents, and almost missing the bounty that was set before us. During and after that scrumptious Thanksgiving dinner, we talked long into the night about our common dilemmas and future dreams and thereby we forged a long lasting friendship.

The winter winds of Utah howled cold and dreary outside but we were warm and cozy with each other in the cozy little space we called home. We went to work every day but for me it was routine and took up none of my emotional life. At home I learned to cook for someone whose expectations were very different from Teresa's back in my high school days. Charles' mother, Althea, sent me recipes. The one most often used was for spaghetti, with a decided Pennsylvania Dutch twist...pickled cabbage on the side.

Aunt Chrystal came from Oregon City to visit me and I made my first company dinner for her. It was an opportunity to use the new cranberry glass dishes she had sent us for a wedding present. Dinner was a success and we talked long into the night afterwards. Her decades of nursing experience gave me confidence in her advice about taking care of myself and the baby in my womb. She was still the great story teller she had been when she came to visit our family in Colorado. I remembered her very precious visit in Colorado in 1941. Again I appreciated her visit in the spring of 1952 in Utah.

Charles and I learned how to accommodate each other's personalities and individual quirks knowing they would be there forever. It seemed that neither of us worried about being engulfed or taken over by the other. We were very much in love! One fond memory is of the time after supper when we did the dishes together and sang with unleashed fervor. His beautiful trained voice and mine, honed by all the choruses in high school, allowed us to embellish and harmonize our songs to our great satisfaction and pleasure. We loved singing songs from the *Student Prince,* and other light classics. We also sang old folk songs. I especially remember, *Wait Till The Sun Shines, Nelly.* We were not interested in current popular music.

We had friends from the base, the Hoyts with whom we had forged the bond at Thanksgiving and a few other couples who became only fleeting memories. Charles had friends from his tennis set. Buzz Burton and his mother became our most frequent visitors, and we became theirs. Grandpa came to visit us quite often. We often visited Mary Lou and her three little girls. She was a single mother at this time, and for many years to come. That was our social life in the winter of 1951-52.

Spring, along with the flower gardens of Ogden, brought back the dormant tennis season. On Saturdays I watched the matches most of the day and enjoyed being part of the tennis set...a fringe part, but part of it nevertheless. Sundays I always went to church in the morning and made dinner while Charles played tennis. Often those meals were with Gill and Joan.

My pregnancy was visible by now, and I made my maternity clothes, and a few baby clothes as well. I loved to sew and was a good seamstress. I had made most of my clothes since eighth grade. I had no knowledge of the gender of the child in my womb, so I had to quell the impulse to make pretty little girl clothes, although that was what I wanted to do.

The baby was due in the middle of August and the pregnancy was progressing normally through the early summer. At the beginning of August, Charles was invited to go to a tennis tournament with the team from the base. He was gone for five days. I missed him terribly and felt abandoned. It was the only time we had been apart since our wedding. Grandpa came and took me out to dinner. Just before we left for dinner I fainted, the first time in my life. I gained consciousness quickly and we went out to dinner in spite of the interruption.

The next day I visited the base doctor and he put me on thyroid medication and scheduled a series of x-rays on the fetus. That worried me. I was still working and intended to work up to the week before the due date. However after the first x-ray the doctor told me to stop working and take it easy. The baby was not in a good position for birth. I was directed to go to the base hospital for x-rays three times a week, at which time they would exert pressure and attempt to manipulate the baby into a better position for birth. They would do this under a fluoroscope to determine the progress of their attempts. Nothing was known about the danger of x-ray at that time.

Mother, Tom, and Rosie came from Sturgis to visit us so Mother would be there when the baby was born. It was very comforting to have her nearby. We enjoyed a week of visiting when, in the middle of the night, my water broke. Mother, Charles and I went to the hospital. They stayed with me for a while but as labor progressed I sent them out of the room. I wanted to do this by myself. Soon after they left, I was completely anesthetized and was not awake for the birth. I didn't see my baby until the next afternoon. It had been a difficult birth. I was in the hospital for ten days. Fortunately they kept my baby in the hospital and brought her to me every few hours for nursing.

The baby was a miracle, a wonder, the most beautiful baby in the world. I was head over heels in love with her. The nurses would bring her to me and I would unwrap her and gaze at her little toes, feet, legs, all of her. We named her Marcia Lee. We named her after no one else. I wanted her to have her own name and to be her own person.

My world was perfect and complete except for a few details. Mother, Tom and Rosie had to go back to Sturgis the day before I was discharged, so I came home with a new baby and no one to help me care for her. I was apprehensive and felt totally inadequate for this job. The first night at home, I could not sooth Marcie. Rocking her did not work; nursing her did not calm her. I thought she was too warm and removed clothing; then worried that she was cold and bundled her up tightly. Charles went to the bedroom and shut the door. After an hour he came out, complaining that her crying was keeping him awake, saying there must be something I could do. I had a surge of maternal protectiveness and curtly sent him away. He was cranky because he wasn't getting enough sleep or attention. I nursed her until she vomited. I wept in frustration, fear, and exhaustion.

Morning came and Charles went off to the base. Now I needed to do some laundry. Marcie only had a dozen diapers and we had gone through them. The laundry room was in the basement and I feared leaving her for even a moment but could not carry her and the laundry. Somehow, I did get the laundry done. I don't remember how, and the baby survived. After a few days I began to feel that maybe, just maybe I could handle this...the baby, the laundry, the cooking, and housekeeping.

The biggest challenge came a few days later, when Charles announced at supper, that he would be playing tennis that evening. He walked out to the end of the sidewalk, met the slim, attractive, agile brunette who would be his partner in mixed doubles. I watched them trot down the street gaily. I stood in the doorway holding my baby, watching until they were out of sight and felt a wave of emotion sweep over me. I was an adult now. I had a big responsibility. Charles was going to remain a young fun-loving man for a long time. I was feeling mature...even old. Now there was a gulf between us. As we watched Marcie grow that gulf did not always seem as insurmountable as it seemed that first day, but it was always there.

Marcie was becoming an extraordinarily beautiful little girl. People on the street stopped to exclaim over her golden curls, her big brown eyes and her ready smile. Once a man offered a million dollars for her. We got away from him with haste. She was baptized in the Episcopal Church in Ogden with Mary Lou and Buzz Burton as witnesses. Her Godparents, in absentia, were my high school friend, Teresa, and Beau Blose, a high school friend of Charles. Father McGinnis took a genuine interest in our little family and came to the house to visit several times.

Our parents on both sides wanted to see the baby and sent us some traveling money. Charles was able to get a leave of absence for six weeks. When Marcie was three weeks old we embarked in the '39 Ford coupe, traveling east with our first stop in South Dakota. We had called ahead learning that Grandma was in Rapid City so we arranged to meet Mother, Tom, and Rosie there before we went to Sturgis. We were ecstatic to see one another, and everyone was enchanted with the baby. This was not Grandma's first great grandchild, but it was my first child and therefore very important to her. After that visit we went to Sturgis and drove from there to Whitewood to see Aunt Mary and Uncle Marvin, who were thrilled with the baby, and glad to meet Charles for the first time. He charmed them all. He and Uncle Marvin had a contest that night to see who could eat the most chicken fried steaks. I loved seeing those two interact. They were the two main men in my life.

Almost all of my school friends were away at college or with their husbands in the service. One who was still there was Jocelyn Spencer whom I had met when I was two years old at the sawmill camp in the Black Hills and again in high school. Jocelyn had married a local boy while in high school and moved away for a year.

Within a year she was diagnosed with congenital heart failure and was not expected to live more than a few more months. She and her husband came back to Sturgis to be with her family for the last of her remaining time on earth. She asked me if she could be my baby's mother for a little while since she would never have her own. For a few hours she rocked Marcie and gave her a bottle of water and undressed her and dressed her again. It was an exquisitely sweet, sad afternoon. It seemed a small thing I could do, and yet it meant so much to her. We said a poignant goodbye.

Charles, Marcie and I left South Dakota and embarked on the long ride to Pennsylvania. One night we stopped at a restaurant for supper and an older couple fell in love with our baby. They entertained her and she entertained them while we ate our dinner. The couple left before we did and when we went to pay the bill, the waitress told us they had paid our bill! We were astounded by their generosity. We looked forward to the day when we could do such a thing for someone else.

As we drove through the country further and further east, I recognized the vast difference between the East and the West. We got lost on the Loop in Chicago, but eventually found our route eastward again. When we got to the small towns of Pennsylvania, I was amazed at the population density. So many cars, so many stores, so many streets! As we got close to Easton, I was appalled to find the houses built close together, and each seemed to be a half a house abutting the sidewalk and having no front yards.

I was surprised when I met Charles' parents, Althea and Charlie, and his sister Marlene. They spoke with heavy Pennsylvania Dutch accents and I had a hard time understanding them. Their house was small and crowded, a row house that was built right up against Northampton Street, the main street of Easton. It was meticulous inside due to Althea's housekeeping standards. Everything was in good repair as Charlie never let a flaw go untended. In back of the house was a neat little yard, separated by a picket fence from other back yards, where small gardens and long clotheslines were the backdrop for visiting with neighbors. Pennsylvania Dutch neatness abounded.

The Lichtenwalner family was thrilled to meet me and even more thrilled with Marcie, their first grandchild. They, too, felt she was the most precious baby in the world.

They were kind and loving to me. Marlene took me in as the sister she had always wanted. They all thought I didn't have enough *specht,* the Pennsylvania Dutch word for *fat,* so they decided to fatten me up...just like Uncle John so many years ago. I was introduced to pizza and porter, a thick brown beer that Charlie brought me from the nearby Pub every night. Althea made pot pie, a dish of ham, potatoes and thick homemade noodles and many other foods I had never eaten before. I gained eighteen pounds during the visit. Marcie had more than doubled her birth weight by the age of ten weeks when we left to go back to Utah. I think it was the Porter that contributed to our phenomenal weight gain and our sound sleep at night.

I met fabulous Aunt Lucy and was fascinated by her. She was Charlie's aunt and Charles' great aunt. Lucy grew up in the coal regions of Pennsylvania and was gifted with a beautiful contralto voice. Because of her voice she received a scholarship to Julliard School of Music in NYC. She had earned enough money singing for churches in the coal region to fund her early life in the city. She became a Wagnerian opera singer and taught music for many years after her career in New York City had come to an end. Lucy was a large, imposing woman with a commanding manner and voice. When she arrived in her big black Cadillac and entered the little house on Northampton Street, she seemed to fill the entire space. She came bearing gifts for the baby, an exquisite wardrobe from Lord & Taylor in New York. I knew she would be a force in our lives.

After our month long visit, we drove back west and resumed our life together in Utah. We were now living on Charles' Air Force salary alone and money was scarce. When Marcie was three months old, I went to work as an usher in a movie theater. Charles took care of her for a few hours every night and it was at that time when they came to know each other. Going to work for such a small salary did not make much sense, but the relationship that developed between Charles and his baby daughter was precious.

When Marcie was six months old, I became pregnant again. At the same time, the Korean Conflict was winding down. Airmen were encouraged to take civilian jobs in town. Charles went to the Bank of Utah and was hired immediately. He had worked in banking in Easton before joining the Air Force; he was good at it and had a letter of reference that affirmed his proficiency. With the salary from the bank, his increased service pay from his promotion to Airman First Class, and the added allotment for a child, we could rent a larger apartment and allow ourselves a few luxuries. We were feeling prosperous for the next few months.

One of the first luxuries was a television set. Charles' parents thought we needed it and sent us a partial payment to buy one for his birthday. TV was a new phenomenon in Utah in 1953. When all the other young couples in our apartment complex got their children to bed, they would come to our place which had the only TV. We sat around on the floor and watched whatever was showing on the only channel available. On Wednesdays it was Kraft Theater. Other nights, I Love Lucy, Candid Camera and the Hit Parade were on. There were few choices and we were not addicted to that media in 1953. We enjoyed the camaraderie of a room full of other young couples watching and commenting and laughing about the same things.

In July of 1953, a month before Marcie's first birthday, Charles received his discharge papers from the Air Force. The Korean

Conflict was winding down. We celebrated as if it were over, even though it limped slowly to a finish.

The de-escalation of the war prompted us to make adult decisions about our lives. Charles was working part time at the bank and applied for full time now that he was about to be discharged from the Air Force. The bank executives called him in to a meeting with their board. They complimented him on his aptitude for banking and told him that he had a great future at The Bank of Utah. But there was one condition. He would have to join the Mormon Church. He could go no further than head teller without fulfilling that condition. He balked at that. Added to that factor, Father McGinnis, my pastor at the Episcopal Church had visited us a few days before and talked to us about living in Ogden. He recounted experiences about the difficulty of raising a child of a minority religion in Utah. He said that it was hard for his children to feel a part of and succeed in the school community. He wanted us to stay and would help us over hurdles when he could, but he felt we should know what lay ahead for us if we remained in Utah.

Putting all those factors together, we decided that we should go back to Pennsylvania. Charles could go back to the Bank of Easton. We could live with his parents until we found an available, affordable rental. His discharge would not be final until the middle of November. The Air Force was paying our medical expenses and also paying for the travel back to Charles' home. I was required by their rules to travel before the end of my seventh month of pregnancy, no later than October 24th.

That gave us three months to prepare to leave Utah. My preparation was predominantly in the personal relations area rather than material goods. I spent many hours with Mary Lou and her three little girls, Michele, Mary Lynn and Diane, knowing I might not see them for a long time. Also I had many visits to and from Grandpa. I had the sense I was leaving one large segment of my life and embarking on an entirely different one in a strange, nearly foreign place. I looked forward to it with a mix of anticipation and anxiety...a tension I had experienced before.

CHAPTER 17

Easton

On a cold October night, at ten o'clock I climbed into our little black '39 Ford coupe and Charles put our fourteen-month old daughter, Marcie on my lap. I was seven months into my second pregnancy so there was not very much lap left. I had packed and re-packed the two suitcases in back seat. The Air Force allowed one bag per passenger. It wasn't much. I hoped I had enough for our new life in Pennsylvania. Charles drove Marcie and me to the Chinese restaurant in Ogden where Mary Lou worked.

We drove to the restaurant so my sister and I would have one more chance to say goodbye. Even the late dinner crowd was gone by this time of night so we had time to talk. But time wasn't what I needed. Words were what I needed; words to say, "We have not spent enough time together. I love you and want to be with you, but life is taking us on separate ways now, and I have to follow my own path. With all my heart, I want your life to be easier than it is." There were many other things I wanted to say to Mary Lou in those last moments together.

We hung around the cash register at the end of a counter making small talk about nothing, because saying the things that needed to be said would have made both of us cry, and that would have been embarrassing. I held her hand for a long time, wanting to hold it until my hand had a firm memory of hers. Hers was a tiny hand that had worked so hard...and would go on working. I was already feeling the loss of her in my life, just as I had fifteen years earlier. I knew it would be a long time until we would see each other again.

Finally Charles nodded at the clock, telling me that we had to be on our way to the base and board the plane which would take us two-thirds of the continent away. I wept as we drove away.

Charles got on the plane with us and helped us get settled in our seats and then he and I said goodbye. I would see him in a few weeks so it was not as wrenching as the goodbye to Mary Lou had been. We were flying out on an Air Force transport, a no frills airplane which would take us to the military airbase at Willow Grove, near Philadelphia.

The plane was full as we boarded but many passengers would disembark when we touched down for refueling in Chicago. Whereas I had been excited about flying, I was somewhat disappointed. I had expected something like I had seen in glossy magazine ads...comfortable seats, restrooms, food service and pillows. It was not like that at all. The inside of the plane body was the same as the outside...olive drab metal with scratchy seats in the same dismal color. We were given just one seat, so my restricted lap was Marcie's small domain for the journey, or so it seemed.

In spite of the appearance of the plane, my disappointment surrendered to the excitement of flying. It was my first time in a big one. I had once been up in a Piper Club and was thrilled by the experience of being aloft. This was quite different, but still ethereal. I relished the feeling of being suspended in the air.. Marcie was uncomfortable and cried pathetically. I was not near a window and so missed seeing what was out there. Stars...clouds...I knew they were out there; I wanted to see them. I wanted a look at the great sky and feel myself immersed in it but soon exhaustion took over. It had been a hard day packing all our belongings and deciding what to keep and what to leave. Both Marcie and I were sound asleep in a half hour.

Sometime during the night Marcie slipped off my lap. I woke in a panic and exclaimed loudly, "Where is my baby?" A kindly older woman was holding her and Marcie was sleeping like the baby she was. The woman offered to hold her until she woke up. I allowed that and slept until the plane began its descent. Then Marcie awoke and cried because her ears were hurting.

When the plane came to a stop on the tarmac at a base near Chicago several people got off. Now we had more room; each of us had a seat to ourselves. Now I had a window seat, and was delighted to watch the convoluted ever-moving formations of the clouds. It was an all too short a time until we were again in a painful descent. An announcement was made that we must return to Chicago as the wings were icing up.

By now it was mid-morning and we were hungry. I expected we would be served breakfast on the plane and was very disappointed when an official told me there was no food service on a transport plane such as this one. We were back on the ground in Chicago, so I asked the same guy if I could get off and go inside the airport to find something for my baby to eat. He said we would be on the ground as short a time as possible, but if I did it quickly he would allow it. Uneasily, I let the woman who had held Marcie in the night watch her while I climbed down the steps and ran through the cold blustery Chicago wind across the tarmac and into a rather primitive waiting room. I found a lunch counter where I got a cup of oatmeal, a bottle of milk and scurried back to the plane. Later in the day someone gave me a package of soda crackers. It was meager fare for a pregnant woman and a fourteen-month-old child. After a long day of flying above the clouds, and sitting on the plane for nearly twenty-four hours, the plane descended onto the runway and glided slowly to the parking ramp where we disembarked into a cold rainy night at Willow Grove Pennsylvania. I know I looked like a pitiful refugee, my head covered with a bandana, carrying the toddler on my hip and my coat stretched over my large belly.

Charles' father and mother, Charlie and Althea, and his sister Marlene, were there to meet us. Their concern for me and Marcie was genuine. I was filled with a mixture of excitement and displacement. Snow was falling, covering the ground. This surprised everyone in the car except me. October was early for snow in Pennsylvania. I had lived in South Dakota, Colorado and Utah where it snowed any time after the 1st of September. Charlie said he didn't know if the *machines* were going to get through. I puzzled over that for a while but after riding along on Route 309 north toward Easton, listening to the banter in the front seat, I realized that he was referring to automobiles as *machines*...part of the dialect of the Pennsylvania Dutch. He also said, "And *they* want more of this." I knew he was referring to the snow but I couldn't imagine *who* wanted it. In their dialect they referred to the weather report, as *wanting* rain or snow or whatever was predicted. By the time we reached Easton, about three hours later, I knew I had a lot to learn. And oh! How I missed Charles! I needed him to guide me this new strange land. Yes, I had been there, thirteen months before. That time I was a visitor; this time I was going to stay. That made all the difference in the world.

They were all crazily in love with Marcie. They loved her so much I feared that I was losing my sovereign rights to her. The first day they took her downtown to a very up-scale children's shop and bought her a lovely pale aqua coat and legging set and a couple of dresses. That was sweet, I thought. Next we went to a special shop that sold only children's shoes. I heard Althea say in a hushed voice to the clerk, nodding her head toward me, "She is only nineteen and just doesn't *know*."

I said to myself, "This is going to be very hard!"

After the shopping trip I felt they had little respect for my parenting skills. For example, I had never given Marcie candy or cookies, knowing it was not good for her. Charlie thought that was cruel so he put out a dish of candy for her to help herself at any time she chose. He also loved to hold her on his lap just before bed and give her milk and cookies. I wanted to be strong and assertive. I wanted to be like my sister Kitty, but I could not stand up against all three of them. I felt as if I would crumple like a deflated balloon. I felt that the gems of wisdom I learned from Dr. Spock would fall on closed ears in this house.

On the first Sunday in Easton I went to Trinity Episcopal Church. I knew that there, I would be able to connect with my own strength and would find a supportive family. I was not a stranger when I introduced myself. Father Herschel Halbert said he had been waiting for me, as he had received a letter from my mother, telling him I would be there and that she hoped he would help me get started in my new life. I was both surprised and happy. I would not be alone. The women in the nursery were so warm and eager to make sure Marcie had a good experience, and assured me they would come and get me if she had a moment of distress. This was the beginning of a life-long affiliation with Trinity Episcopal Church. Father Halbert was kind and attentive and understood my situation without me ever telling him. He always had time to talk with me before and after church.

It seemed a long time from October 23 until November 11, when Charles finally arrived by Greyhound from Willow Grove, where his last flight with the Air Force ended. I was so happy to see him, just one day after our second anniversary. Relief and support at last! He arrived in the morning and we talked and played with Marcie all day. Immediately after dinner he said he had to go out. "Out where?" I asked.

He said he had to see his old friends and find out who was still around. I asked who were these friends who could be more important than Marcie and me. John Berger, and Beau Blose were the friends I got to know and there were others whose names I have forgotten or never knew. I got the first intimations that this was not going to be the realization of my imagined storybook romantic life-together-forevermore-till-death-do-us-part. I already knew that tennis was going to come between us and now realized that the gulf widened to accommodate his buddies. I also could see that parenthood was not going to bring us closer...it would increase the chasm.

Two weeks later, I began to have mild labor pains, but did not think it was the real thing. The baby was due in three weeks. The pains lasted through the weekend. Saturday afternoon, Charles and I went to the movie, *Kiss Me Kate*. I wanted to be as feisty as Kate; but that was not my nature. We went for several long walks Saturday evening and Sunday when he picked me up after church. The mild pains continued throughout all the diversions.

On Monday morning I went to the doctor to my scheduled appointment. This was a doctor I had seen but once. When I got to his office he began the examination, stopped after a few minutes and said, "Get to the hospital! You are about to have this baby!" A couple of hours later I gave birth to a baby boy! It was such a surprise to me. I exclaimed over and over again, "A boy! I can't believe it! A boy!" We had so few boy babies in my family. Grandma Michelson had three girls, my mother had five girls. Aunt Mary had two girls and one boy; Aunt Edith had three girls and one boy. My sister, Bobbie had two girls and one boy at this time. This baby boy of mine was the fourth boy child in the three generations.

I knew what I wanted to name him, but had to be somewhat manipulative to do it. We talked about names and Charles thought it certainly should be Charles III. I felt strongly that this child deserved his own name. Finally Charles agreed to that...but what name? After a long discussion, we couldn't agree on any name, so I said, "I will make a list of all the names I would accept and you can pick the one you like best."

Charles agreed to that plan. So I made a list of names: Hector, Reginald, Aloysis, etc, but in the middle of the list was *Daniel.* Charles chose Daniel and I chose his middle name to be Owen after the Pennington County doctor who took care of me as a child.

Danny was a tiny baby weighing only six pounds and looking like a wizened little old man. I wanted to nurse him as it seemed so right, so natural, to me. Nursing was not in vogue then but I was very firm about it in the hospital. Nurses would bring him to me saying, "Mrs. Lichtenwalner, your baby is crying in the nursery and we think he needs more nourishment than you are supplying."

Still, I thought nursing him was best. When I brought him home to Charles' parents' house, they, too, opposed my nursing him. Althea had not nursed her babies and felt it was a primitive thing to do. I was instructed to go upstairs, out of sight to nurse him, as if it were a shameful thing. I was very unhappy and stressed. My milk never came in abundantly. I nursed him for a few more days and by then he had lost a full pound...a lot for a six pound baby. I gave in and put him on formula and fed him from a bottle. I felt inadequate and defeated.

One dark drizzly cold day, when I thought I might never see the sun again, as I was hovering over and fretting about my tiny, frail little boy, a new light came into our lives. Aunt Lucy came to visit him! She brought him trunk full of baby clothes...all in blue and white to go with his eyes, she said. Aunt Lucy, with the flourish of the opera singer she was, dramatically swept up the stairs, her purple velvet cape trailing out behind her, swooped him up from the bed, and held him against her ample breast. She looked deeply into his blue eyes and sang *Danny Boy* as only a Wagnerian opera singer could. It filled the whole house. I was wide-eyed and speechless, transfixed by what was happening. It seemed that she was singing life and strength into his tiny body. She was singing courage into mine.

Little by little life took on a measure of normalcy. Charles went back to the bank where he worked before joining the Air Force and we were happy that he had a job. With the young men all returning from the war it was not easy to find work. We lived with his parents, hoping we would soon have enough money for a deposit and the first month's rent on an apartment. Apartments were expensive because they were in high demand. Many young couples found themselves in the same predicament with this sudden change in their plans, as the war ended and they returned to civilian life.

Charles and I and our two babies slept in one of the two small bedrooms on the second floor of Charlie and Althea's house. The house was comfortably full at that point. However, within a month Charles' sister, Marlene, and her new husband moved in. She was pregnant. She and her husband, who inconveniently was also named Charles, slept in the living room at the bottom of the steps. With only one bathroom, the house was definitely crowded. Tension was high.

To make matters worse, my Charles came home in the middle of a work day with a Mohawk haircut! "What did you do with your hair, and why are you home?" his mother fairly screamed at him!

He said, "I got my hair cut...I can get my hair cut any damn way I want...and I got fired." I thought she would faint. His story got worse. Earlier in the day, he had returned to the bank after lunch, parading in with this wild haircut. He took his place behind the teller's window as if everything was perfectly normal. Soon a bank manager, of much higher rank than Charles, arrived at his elbow and told him he would have to work in the back room until his hair grew out. Charles said to the bank manager, "You can take this job and shove it." He really did say that, long before the Johnny Paychek song was written.

This was the end of Charles' banking career. His mother was devastated. I had mixed emotions about it. I knew he was chafing about living at home, still under the supervision of his parents.

He needed to express his independence. I also knew that part of Charles' charm was his desire to be outrageous. Knowing all of that, I wondered how we would ever get out of our situation, with no paycheck coming in.

The next day, after lunch, while both my babies were napping, I left them in the care of Althea and Marlene and went for a walk by myself. As I walked up Northampton Street, I came to a red brick building with Mack Printing embossed above the entrance.

"Printing, h-m-m-, printing. I know something about printing!"

I walked in to the reception desk and said, "I would like to apply for a job here." The receptionist said I could fill it out the application and give it to her when I was finished. I filled it out, emphasizing my experience at the newspapers in Sturgis. The receptionist told me to wait there. I waited, wondering if I got the job, would Althea take care of the children. Was it worth it to turn them over to her just to obtain our freedom? While I was still pondering those questions, the receptionist came out and led me to another room, where, after a short interview, I was told that I could go to work as a proofreader the next week.

With some trepidation, I went back to the house and told the family I had a job, and asked Althea if she would watch the children. She said, less than enthusiastically, that she would, but would have to charge me for it. I told her I would pay whatever she asked. Charles said nothing at all.

The next week I started the job and loved the work. It was proofreading scientific abstracts for professional journals. There were interesting people around me. I found the abstracts fascinating and I was learning vocabulary and concepts of which I had no previous knowledge. Learning was always exhilarating for me. And reading! I was actually getting paid for reading, which itself, had liberated me years before.

The pay was meager. This was not surprising in 1954. The majority of women did not work outside of the home and those who did were severely underpaid. Nevertheless, I simply had to do it. I had to get out of that house, on a daily basis and also, in the long term; I had to find a way that Charles and I could get out on our own. I was earning thirty-two dollars a week and paying Althea thirty for child care. I prayed that something would change. I knew that eventually I would get a raise.

I was close to despair until Charles got a job as night watchman at the City Water Works. This was very unsatisfactory to Althea. She had raised him to be a white collar worker. She had realized early in his life that tennis would be a way whereby he could meet the right people and acquire a higher station in life than either she or Charlie had attained. She had labored very hard to see that Charles had the best equipment and tennis lessons since he was eight years old. She always dressed him meticulously. But this! This job as a night watchman was not part of her plan. Being a banker fit her plan for him. Being a laborer in the City Water Works did not. I went on working at Mack Printing and he at the City Water Works for a few more months.

In March of '54, Charles got a better job at Dixie Cup Company. He was working in the financial sector of the company learning to use new equipment called "computers." Althea was happier with this line of work for him. Many people, including his father, were skeptical about this new equipment; "artificial intelligence" it was called. "Probably just a flash in the pan," Charlie said. Nevertheless, Charles wore a white shirt and tie to work and could go to Althea's house for lunch.

I found an apartment on Northampton Street, a block from his parents' house. If we didn't spend a dime on anything else, I calculated, we could move into our own apartment the day before Easter. Now we had two incomes, I received a raise in pay and we were more relaxed about money.

Danny was to be baptized on Easter Saturday, the same day we moved into the apartment. His Godmother was Arlene Hahn, a woman with whom I worked. His Godfather, Philip Otis, was appointed by the rector since I knew so few people at church. There was to be a reception for the families of the baptized after church on Sunday. I was both eager and anxious about this upcoming event. By noon on Saturday I was exhausted from packing and moving and getting myself and my children ready for the baptismal ceremony. Carelessly, in the turmoil of all that was going on, I made a caustic remark to Charlie, my father-in-law, during the last moments of the move. He took umbrage, and stormed out refusing to go to the baptism that afternoon. A couple of years later, I realized that he had a strong dislike of church, and was probably quite relieved to have a reason not to go to Danny's baptism. The benefit of not going to that one was that it freed him from going to any of his grandchildren's baptisms ever after. His reasoning, as the years went on and more grandchildren arrived, was that since he hadn't gone to Danny's, he couldn't go to any of the others; "It just wouldn't be fair," he said.

We got through the baptism that Saturday and were into the apartment by dinner time. We were delighted to spend a night in our own apartment and allowed ourselves the luxury of ordering a pizza for dinner. However I was far too tired to go to the church or the reception the next morning.

Later, that Sunday afternoon, while Charles was out with his friends playing tennis, the doorbell rang. It was Philip Otis, Danny's Godfather and his wife. They came to pay their respects to the newly baptized and to bring him a gift. I thanked them and opened the beautifully wrapped gift from a local jewelry store. It was a little silver band about three inches long, an inch wide, with Danny's initials on it. I thanked them and noted how lovely it was to have his initials engraved on it. Soon Charles came home and when he saw the gift, he asked "What is it?"

I answered, "It is a baptismal gift for Danny." I'm not sure if the Otis's realized that neither of us recognized it as a napkin ring.

Napkin rings were not common in our lives...not in the frontier land of South Dakota nor within the Pennsylvania Dutch culture. If the Otises recognized our ignorance they were far too gracious to let us know. Mr. Otis took an interest in Dan's life, always inquiring how he was doing and never missed sending a birthday card with a check in it.

I switched to part time employment at Mack Printing so I could be with the children longer each day. Althea was getting tired of constant child care. She could manage a few hours after dinner, so I worked from eight to midnight. My sister-in-law, Marlene and her husband moved into their own house and had their first child, little boy, Chuckie, who was a few months younger than Danny. I was losing my baby-sitter.

Somehow, even through our busyness Charles and I managed to develop a social life. Most of our friends were having babies and living very much as we were...in apartments, from month to month on small incomes. Several of them remained in my life for the next sixty years.

Betty Berger, my first friend in Pennsylvania, was an American Indian. She and John met in Idaho when he was stationed there. She came to Reading, Pennsylvania on a train from Boise to join her future husband. Charles and I went with John Berger, to meet her train. I was surprised when she disembarked the train and I saw a beautiful young Indian woman. I had never known a Native American who had entered the white world so gracefully and maintained her allegiance to her race at the same time. In the hour it took to get to John's mother's house in Easton, she and I had started a friendship which lasted as long as we were both alive. Charles and I were their attendants when they were married. I was, and still am honored to have such a friend as Betty. We were homesick together; we had our babies together and had more in common than I had with anyone else in Easton. Her two older boys, Paul and Tommy, were nearly the same ages as my children and were playmates as children and friends later on.

Another long-lasting friendship was with the Sampsons, Jim and Jane. They had been classmates of Charles at Easton High School and married as soon as they graduated. Jane called me one Sunday and asked if she could come over to meet me and my children. I admired her reaching out in such an open way. When she arrived at our apartment, Danny, eight months old, was just wakening from his afternoon nap. She exclaimed with great enthusiasm how beautiful he was. I had been so preoccupied with everyday matters, that this was the first time I looked at him objectively and really saw what a handsome little boy he was. The Sampson children, Nancy, Debbie and Jimmy were playmates of my children and their lives were interwoven with ours as the years went on. Jim and Jane had two more children, Michael and Scott.

When Danny was eighteen months old I gave birth to Lorie Ellen. The pregnancy was a surprise, but not a dismay...not to me. Charles' parents were appalled. "How do you think you will manage another one?" It seemed quite natural and normal to me. These were years when, culturally and personally, having babies was the right thing to do. As soon as I knew I was pregnant, I knew that this would be a little girl and I would name her Lorie Ellen. It was as though I had known her before she was even conceived. I wanted her very much. It was an easy pregnancy and birth.

It was fortunate that it was easy because just as I suspected, my in-laws were not going to be helpful with this one. My suspicions were well founded. When I was released from the hospital they picked me up and dropped me and the baby, Lorie, off at the apartment with the two toddlers...Marcie and Danny. Charles could not get away from work that morning. I was overwhelmed with the care of this newborn and the other two for the first two days. On the third day it all fell into place. I relaxed and really looked at my beautiful children and began to feel that I could do this and really enjoy it.

"Marcie, Danny and Lorie," was the lyrical chorus of a song that played on the strings of my heart ever after. If I get an audition with the angels that will be the chorus of my song.

Lorie was an active, good-natured sunny little baby. I was relaxed with her as I had never been with the other two. I had confidence now. I thoroughly enjoyed having that little pod of children so close in age. They liked to do similar things and played together creating their own games and language. And each one was so visually beautiful: Marcie with her golden curls and deep brown eyes; Dan, blond, blue-eyed with intelligence and depth apparent in his expression and demeanor; and Lorie, her sprite-like nature, her sparkling blue eyes, blond hair and her avid interest in everything.

Charles was not an involved father. He played tennis in most of his off-work hours. That was in the daylight hours. He was off with his friends late into the night. His role was similar to that of many of the young fathers in the 50's. I didn't expect anything else from him, but I was sad that he was missing the fun of being with those adorable children. I was sad that the euphoric togetherness I had envisioned before and in the early days of our marriage seemed to have evaporated.

It was not out of boredom or lack of things to do that caused the loneliness to set in. I was busy every waking moment, and even after I finished nursing Lorie and went to sleep, my ears were open for any stirring from any one of them. In the daytime I had the care and feeding of the children, and endless laundry to do. I was still using an old fashioned wringer washing machine, and with two babes in diapers, I was washing, hanging out and folding clothes several hours a day. My groceries were delivered from a small local grocer just a block away, and I was always happy for a little adult conversation with Walt, the older man who delivered them. I talked on the phone with Betty or Jane every morning. Still

I was acutely wanting...no, it went way beyond wanting...I *needed* close adult companionship, someone to share the burden and the joy of being young, healthy and involved in life.

It seemed that just in time to fill that void, Mother and Rosie came to be with me that summer when Lorie was a baby. Mother stayed only a few days as she had to go back for classes at college. Rosie stayed on for a couple of months. It was wonderful to have her with me. That was one summer when I did not have a job. There was no one I could find that I trusted to care for my children. Althea did not offer and I did not ask. She was involved with Marlene, who had given birth to her second one, a little girl, Janet. Charles had a fairly good job by now, and was able to buy an automatic washer and dryer which was deliverance from drudgery for me.

Rosie was deliverance from the loneliness. Now I had someone with whom I could have deep conversations and someone to laugh and play with me and the children. And how we played with them, crawling around the floor, going to the park, and on long walks! Rosie and I were no longer little sister and big sister. Now we were close friends. There was a big void in my soul when she had to return to South Dakota for her senior year.

When Charles had worked at the bank he had been the favorite of an older woman, Jessie Willauer. Jessie had never married, and Charles was just the one she wanted for a son. She took him under her wing at the bank and kept in close touch after he left the bank. Jessie had lived with her father, the only undertaker in a small village, Stockertown Pennsylvania, twelve miles north of Easton. It was not surprising that when her father died and she moved out of the big old Victorian house she offered it to Charles. Not only that, it was at a price we could now afford. That house had served as the only funeral home in that area for more than a half a century. We were going to buy a it! I was going to raise my children in a house, in a neighborhood. I was going to have a house to keep, a nice house, with a lawn; a big house painted grey with dark green shutters. Old, but built to last a few hundred years.

Another era was dawning in my life.

CHAPTER 18

Stockertown —Year One

Old, and built to last a few hundred years, I was told. I had already been talked out of my desire for a new little tract house, an efficient Levittown style house, which several of our friends were buying.

The deal between Jessie Willaur and Charles was completed except for my signature before I even saw the house. The mortgage had been arranged through the bank and with help from a source that was a surprise and a gift of grace to me. Our mortgage would be about the same as our rent. However, we needed a small down payment...not small by our standards, but in the world of finance, next to nothing. We had not a dollar to spare at the end of the month. I wrote to Mother, telling her of our chance to buy this house and our problem with the down payment. Tom, my step-father in South Dakota, stepped right in and lent us part of the money for the down payment...to be paid back without interest, whenever we could afford it. Over the thousands of miles and the span of years, Tom was bridging the gap that had stood between us for so many years. Grace abounds!

Charles had seen the house but I had not until after the financial matters were settled. Our next move was for me to see it. We drove out to Stockertown on a cold day in December. The first thing noticeable was the grayish white cement dust that covered everything...every building, every tree, every blade of grass. Even though the eerie chalky appearance was oppressing, I was being pulled into the unfolding scheme. Jessie assured us that there was a plan underway to put filters on the cement factory nearby, that would cut the cement dust to a fraction of what we were seeing. I remembered that promise and kept it in the forefront of my mind. I wanted to believe it. Otherwise I could not have gone on with the plan to buy the house.

I do not remember my first impression of the interior of the house. How I could forget something that important is a mystery to me. Perhaps I was too busy with the children; perhaps I was numbed by the enormity of what was happening. We were getting into a world of which I knew very little. First there was a mortgage and monthly payments; there would be utility bills and furnishing and heating this immense space. A force much more powerful than my own conscious will was pulling me forward into this adventure.

I had to keep reminding myself...we were going to buy a house! We will raise our children in a house in a neighborhood, on a street named Lincoln Avenue. I will have a house to keep, a substantial house, big and grey with dark green shutters.

We moved into the house on a cold day in January. The first evening we were there, Charles had to work late.

Darkness fell about five o'clock. The house was sparsely furnished. We brought all the furniture we had from the three-room apartment and it barely made a dent in the emptiness of this house of eight immense rooms. In addition to the eight rooms there was a big murky basement, musty attic, front porch, and ante-room in the back of the house. There was an answering echo for every sound we made in that vast space.

The children were happily running from room to room with childlike abandon. All that space in which they were free; free to run and to play hide and seek. I tried to tell myself that this was great. This was wonderful...what I had wished for all my life. However, all my self-persuasion could not dispel the dark pervasive fear that gripped me. That tenacious grip numbed all my sensibilities. I gathered the children around me as I sat in a rocking chair in the family room. I read them all the books we could find...

without venturing into the empty rooms. I read until all three were falling asleep. I put the two older ones, Marcie and Danny on the sofa and held Lorie in my arms until Charles arrived home. I felt foolish that I had been afraid to go upstairs to the bedrooms. He was amused and teased me.

The second day I busily arranged the kitchen cupboards and explored the interior of the house. Even in the daytime I did not enter into the cavernous basement or the ominous attic. It was a very cold day and we did not venture outside. The second evening was a repeat of the first. The fear that gripped me was real and paralyzing. As dusk approached and I began gathering books and pillows in the family room, Danny tugged on my skirt and looked me directly in the eyes and asked earnestly "What are we afraid of, Mom?"

I answered, "We are not afraid; it is just warmer in here." I knew that he knew that was not true; still I could not shake the fear nor could I tell this earnest little boy that I was afraid.

The third day I began to be gripped by the fear even earlier in the day. Also, I began to scan my brain for ideas of how to contend with this dilemma. I *wanted* to be in my own house; I wanted to raise my children here; I wanted to be comfortable and confident. And I was afraid. Somewhere there was an answer to this problem.

As so often happened in my life, the answer was forthcoming, recognized, and very, very welcome. About six o'clock the evening of the third day, Rosie and a friend, Ann, knocked on my door. Never were visitors more welcome! My fear dissolved. I showed them through the house and when we got upstairs, I said, "And this is your bedroom, if you want to stay."

Rosie had left college at the end of the semester and had spent Christmas in Sturgis with Tom and Mother. While there, she reconnected with her high school friend, Ann. Her parents died early in her childhood and she had been raised by an aunt and uncle,

who had been trying, throughout her life, to make her into someone other than her true self. They had enrolled her in a finishing
school from which she had run away just before Christmas. When
she and Rosie met in Sturgis she begged to come back to Easton
with Rosie. Rosie had a job waiting at Mack Printing. Ann was
sure she could find a job nearby. They talked with her caretakers
and Rosie persuaded them that she would be safe in Pennsylvania...
that she had an adult sister who would watch over her.

When I offered them room and board at a price they could
afford, they talked it over for about a minute and decided to take
me up on the offer. At that moment everything about the house
changed for me. My enthusiasm knew no bounds. They stayed that
night until Charles got home from work. We told him the plan and
he agreed to it. He and Rosie had always been good friends. Ann
and Rosie moved in within a week.

Along with Rosie, Ann was my deliverer from fear at that point
of my life. I was her deliverer into the discovery and appreciation
of her true self.

My children and I accepted Ann for exactly the person she
was...a boyish, fun-loving, outspoken young woman. She was a
great addition to our family. With both Rosie and Ann there,
the flavor of our life was immensely improved. Ann worked at
Ingersoll Rand in Phillipsburg New Jersey across the Delaware
River from Easton. They came home almost every evening. Our
dinners became a source of nourishment for our bodies and souls.
After the evening meal we would sit at the table for a long time,
playing games, telling stories. The children loved that after-dinner
time. After a time Rosie and Ann brought their current boyfriends
to the table, which provided even more amusement to our lives.
One boyfriend of Ann's was Larry, a sweet, usually quiet young
man, who was welcome at our table. One night when we were telling stories I told about Grandma Michelson bringing watermelon
pickles for a condiment to a family dinner at Mother's in Sturgis

while I we were visiting. Charles praised her offering effusively, and she was thrilled. Thereinafter, she sent him jar of watermelon pickles every chance she had. The truth was that Charles did not like them at all...he had just been charming her as he was prone to do. As we were laughing at the story, Larry was noticeable quiet. Conversation around the table resumed. When there was a break in the conversation, Larry spoke with a puzzled voice, "Where do they get jars big enough?" We laughed uproariously and that became one of our family stories.

I was making friendships with the neighbors in Stockertown but our friendships seemed to have unspoken limits. It would take years before we were not "the family that lives in the Willaur house."

One cause of the distance between me and the other women on Lincoln Avenue, was that every Sunday I went into Easton to Trinity Episcopal Church. Trinity was so good for my personal and spiritual life, but at the same time created a social barrier for me in Stockertown. Most of the people in that little town went to church every Sunday. They were either Roman Catholic or Lutheran. We were the only Episcopalians. I simply could not give that up. It was very important to me that my children have the experience of going there. I wanted them to have a body of people who cared for them in a spiritual way. I wanted them to be comfortable with people of varied backgrounds. I wanted them to have a larger life than one confined to a town of eight-hundred people, most of whom were supported by the cement mill, nearby.

Some Sundays, it was difficult just to get to church...getting the children ready, making the car accommodations with Charles and other minutiae of having three small children, a large house and a non-involved partner. Charles was tolerant but not helpful or supportive of this part of my life. We could not even discuss religion. That subject that was off the table in our life together, except for giving thanks at the evening meal.

One particular Sunday morning, as I sat in the pew alone, the children in Sunday school, I was graced by a powerful revelation. I suddenly realized I was too young and too naive to be responsible for these three precious little ones who were my responsibility. I was nearly overwhelmed by the immensity of the task before me. In the flash of a moment, that morning, I turned them over to God, to whom I knew with certainty, they really belonged. I promised to provide unconditional love, nurturing and positive acceptance for each one of them, just as they were. I promised to provide the place where they could learn, grow and evolve. I would sit back and watch each unfold as one watches a living plant grow, thrive and develop. I expected that each one would be a unique person, different from each other, and vastly different from me. I realized that if I held them too tightly, I would thwart their growth, just as grasping a rosebud too tightly would cause it to wilt. I trusted the process that was persistently revealing itself to me. What followed after that great Sunday was confidence, wonderment, joy and trust through the years that followed. I was privileged to witness Marcie, Danny and Lorie each become the person they were meant to be.

Every weekday afternoon during that first winter in the house, the children and I would go up to the master bedroom and lie down on my bed for their naps. I would sing to them. Each one had their own song. For Marcie it was an adaptation of Margie. I would sing, "Marcie, I'm always thinking of you, Marcie..." For Danny predictably, it was "Danny Boy," And for Lorie it was my own interpretation of "Annie Laurie." I sang and appreciated each one of my children separately and would thank God with a full heart. I would sleep with them for a few minutes and then go out of the house, and walk to the post office, get the mail and hurry home as I was uneasy leaving the children alone.

One early spring day as I came up through the yard, under the huge evergreen tree at the east end of our property, I looked down and saw a little wild violet in bloom in the tender green grass. I knelt down to get a better look and a sense of awe came over me. For the first time I saw the yard of which we were caretakers. It was a beautiful yard, with a lawn, just beginning to turn green. There was a rock garden, starting to show its shape and form. A hedge of what I came to learn was japonicas, boxwood, and forsythia which formed a soft boundary around the property. A rose garden was just beginning to show signs of life. And the cement dust was not the first thing I saw. It was barely visible now. The filters had been installed just as Jessie said they would.

As winter was easing up, Saturday nights were usually spent with the Bergers, John and Betty. The men would go "up the line" which meant driving up the road between Stockertown and Belfast, stopping at the many small "Hotels," as the bars were called in Pennsylvania. Betty and I would stay home and play with the children, until they were bedded down. Then we would go to the piano, we would sing every song we knew, until our drunken husbands came home, ending the evening.

Charles' parents, Charlie and Althea, came every Sunday afternoon and stayed through the evening for dinner. After dinner Althea and I played cards or games with the children. Charles and his dad went to the Club, an offshoot of the Stockertown Fire Company. There they drank and were in the company of men.

Increasingly, I experienced joy in the house and its surroundings. Charles hired a neighborhood boy to keep the yard well groomed. When spring came the place was vibrant with color...purple hyacinths, yellow, red, pink and white tulips, a cherry tree that bloomed gloriously. The wisteria which climbed thirty feet upon an old tree skeleton, was intoxicating with its pungent clove-like aroma. A birdhouse for the Purple Martins was on a high pole and the Martins were a bird we came to know well as we watched their antics. Daily I was dazzled by the beauty of the life that was taking us in. I baked about a dozen cherry pies and took them to the neighbors.

Later in the spring, children of the neighborhood took to the streets. There was more rolling stock on Lincoln Avenue than on the Reading Railroad, so our neighbor, Jake Metzgar, used to say as he sat on his porch and took it in. There were tricycles, bicycles, scooters, wagons, roller skates and toy cars. Lincoln Avenue ended with a cul-de-sac so there was no through traffic. Every house had more than one child in it. And every child had at least one wheeled vehicle.

We, as most, had a dog that frolicked and played there too. First we had Dutchess, who was well named; she had dignity. Later we had Boots, an Irish setter who was the bad boy of the street. Eventually, we had to find other quarters for him because he became too protective of our children, and we feared he would injure some other child in the midst of a children's skirmish. While we were pondering this, one Sunday he came running through the dining room just as I was about to serve the roast for dinner. He grabbed it off the serving tray and ran off with it. Monday was his last day in the neighborhood.

Along with our neighbor Jake, most of the neighbors sat on their front porches in the evening. We often sat there and watched the Martins return to the house and the lark who had built a nest in the upper corner of the porch. The ice cream truck from Hartman's Meat and Dairy Company came through two times a week just before bedtime. When the truck stopped in front of our house and the bell rang, I delighted in seeing my little pod of children arrive and choose their treat. It was a charming scene, a beautiful life.

Through the children, I became acquainted with almost everyone on our street. There was still a barrier, a distance than I could not breach. Was it my Episcopalianism, or my Western heritage? They both were at the core of myself.

Charles did not sit on the front porch. Most often he worked late and as the days grew longer he played tennis until dark. I had acquaintances, but no deep friendships. I was mostly satisfied with my life but also missing a close friend. Rosie and Ann were what saved me from despair about this. They were there many evenings, but being young adults, they had social lives that were not centered in Stockertown.

Another dissatisfaction was a perceived lack of money...of course I could fix that. Charles made a fairly good salary for those times, but he had expensive taste. His tennis equipment cost a lot. His going out with the boys took its toll on our resources. He liked to buy cars and guns and collect stamps. He was not generous to me or the children. I had been independent for quite a few years before I was married, and it went against my grain to ask for money.

I was as frugal a housekeeper as I thought possible. Nevertheless, there were things I thought were important, for which there were no resources for me to use. When each of my children was down to one pair of socks, and I had to choose between adequate food or acceptable clothing I decided I *must* get a job. Then began the babysitter rigmarole. It was summer so teenagers were out of school. Through the next few years we had a series of them. Their lives were always changing and were pulled away by the slightest tug. However due to this problem I came to know many young people in Stockertown.

My first job after we moved to Stockertown was selling cosmetics in a downtown drugstore in Easton. Now I was far too busy to be lonely. I made new friends in Easton at my work, and I was able to see Betty Berger and Jane Sampson who lived in town. I could buy the things that I felt the children needed and sometimes things they simply wanted.

Once I brought home a little white kitten I bought for a quarter from some children on the street. She was Lorie's fifth birthday present and was named Sugar. After Sugar we had a series of cats over the years...Momma Cat, Big Cat, Little Cat, Oogle, Philip and Gracie. This was the start of a dynasty that lived on in our home and the homes of friends over the years.

When September came that year, changes occurred in our household. Rosie went back to college, and Ann got married. The teenage baby sitters went back to school and I needed a dependable helper to care for the children. I placed an ad in the local paper and found an older woman, Mrs. Gold, who was willing to care for my children for a salary I could afford. She was a former nurse, so I trusted her to take care of my little pod. She took an active part in the housekeeping and it was a sweet time for me... for a while.

Marcie started school, in a small red brick schoolhouse at the end of our street. She was a good student and extremely earnest and hardworking. Lorie and Danny were at home with Mrs. Gold who was satisfactory, or so I believed.

However, I was told by one of the neighbors that Danny was running across town, crossing a busy street and going to the Rod and Gun club pond. He was four years old. We had taken him to the Rod and Gun Club's fishing contest in late summer. The first fish he hooked really hooked him. It was a passion that lasted throughout his life, but at four, it was not safe for him to go alone. I spoke with Mrs. Gold and she told me "He will not obey me!" I had to let her go. I left my job and stayed home for a few months.

Just about that time, Jim and Jane Sampson were having difficult times. Jim was recuperating from a serious illness and could not work. They had three children and Jane was a few months pregnant. I thought we should share our house with them. Charles, not very enthusiastically, agreed to my idea.

It was a good time for me. Jim, Jane and I were good company for each other in the evenings. Jane and I got along well sharing the kitchen, taking turns cooking, and managing other house-hold tasks. Our children had fun together. Our two-family house seemed to be working well. Through the rest of my life, when I think of good husbands and good fathers, Jim Sampson is at the top of the list every time. And when I think of everlasting friend-ships, Jane's face comes to me.

It worked out well until the sicknesses began. First all the children got chicken-pox which lasted quite a while. Then, be-cause their immune systems were already compromised, they all got Asian flu which was rampant that year. All six children came down with it and in a few days Jane joined them in the upstairs of the house. For her it was more serious because she was pregnant. We called Dr. Snyder, our family physician, but he was making house calls His receptionist, who was also his wife, said he was not expected home until midnight. We called the other doctor in Nazareth whose nurse said he would be there when he could. He arrived about ten pm and lined the six children up in the cribs, examined each of them and administered a medication. He talked to Jim and I about how to treat them, and left us with bottles of medications and told us how to use them. He did it by numbering the children, "2 tsp. for child #1 every two hours, 3 tsp. for child # 2, and so on."

When we escorted him out, both Jim and I thought he seemed quite tipsy. But his prescriptions worked to lessen the coughing while the flu ran its course. Charles was incapacitated with a bad back. For a week Jim and I were the only ones in a household of ten inhabitants who were well. We were busy taking care of the other eight. They all recovered from the flu, but the siege was not over.

The next week Jim Sampson found a job and they moved back to Easton, which was hometown for them. The day they moved three of their children came down with mumps. Mine came down with it a few days later. Then I got a bad case of bronchitis, which lasted most of the winter.

Spring was so welcome that year!

CHAPTER 19

Stockertown, Extended

Many days during the winter of '58 I was too ill to go for the mail; barely got meals on the table, and zombie-like went through the motions of motherhood and house-keeping. The incessant coughing made me think I had tuberculosis, and I remembered the cure for that was to lie in the sun on cold winter days. So each afternoon when the two younger children took naps, and Marcie was at school I would open the window in our bedroom, facing south and lie in the afternoon sun. Day by day I felt health creeping slowly back into my body. One day while the two younger ones were napping I got up, took a bath, looked in the mirror and was shocked at what I saw. I determined to do something about it. I put on lipstick, combed and curled my hair and went down to meet Marcie. Before she got there, Danny awoke from his nap and came down to wait with me. He looked at me with his wide blue eyes, astonished, and said, "You are the most beautiful Mommy in the world!" I realized then, how sick I had been and how neglectful of things that mattered to the children. The next day I enlisted the neighbor girl to stay with the children, called John Berger who was laid off from Ingersoll that winter and asked him to take me grocery shopping. I nearly fainted at the end of the shopping but it was the beginning of becoming strong and healthy again. I was never that sick again for thirty years.

In April I planted a garden, and found wild berries in the hedgerows that grew wild at the edge of town, two houses away. A cherry tree grew in our yard, at the end of the walk out to the huge barn. That year there was such an abundance of cherries I spent two weeks making cherry pies, taking them to the neighbors, and also making cherry jam, enough to last until the next year. Sadly, that was the final year for that cherry tree. It gave us its swan song, and then it died. We never forgot it.

There are a multitude of stories I want to tell but there are limitations I must reluctantly acknowledge...constraint of time space, and mortality. I will go on to tell you my story by unveiling crossroads that led me forward and others that caused me to change course...the nodal points of my life, I call them. I use that word in the botanical sense; *i.e.* a place on a twig, branch or stem of a plant where new leaves emerge and go off in a different direction thus giving the plant its shape and size.

Marcie, Danny and Lorie; the chorus of my life song, continued to grow and thrive, each one becoming a greater wonder and delight to me as their personalities unfolded. When Danny started school in the fall the next year, Lorie was at home alone. One of the first days of school, while she was playing outside chattering with the dog, Dutchess, I was working in the house. Suddenly I realized I could not hear them. I went out to the end of the yard and found Lorie and the dog, trudging sadly toward home, Lorie singing to the tune of *The Arkansas Traveler*, "*The teacher send me home, home, home, home, home.*" Lorie and Dutchess had tried to enter first grade but were soundly rebuffed and took it sadly, but with resignation.

Charles became involved in the government of Stockertown. He was chosen to be the Civil Defense Com-missioner. The nation was in The Cold War, so each government entity, no matter how small, had some level of defense against the presumed threat of a Russian invasion. This meant that Charles attended the City Council meetings and therefore became a true citizen of Stockertown. He was still out every night but sometimes in an ostensibly civic endeavor.

I was elected president of the PTA, a position I held for one year only. At the end of the year, the organization had some excess money from an event that was more successful than we expected. It was enough money that we had to decide on a use for it. Two projects were considered. One was to sponsor a Easter-Egg hunt and the other was to provide a scholarship for a Stockertown graduate from Nazareth High School. I lobbied strongly for the scholarship and it was the chosen project, but not without incurring some rancor from those on the other side. I did not run for a second term. Politics, with its accompanying polarization, was never going to be my strong suit.

I remained active in the church, at that time teaching Sunday School. I did not recognize this as one of the crossroads in my life. So small a thing. At a meeting of the teaching staff of the church, someone said to me, "You have the gift to be a teacher. Did you ever consider that?" It was a small seed planted. Did I ever consider that it would germinate? Certainly then there were no prospects of pursuing that in my life. We were barely keeping our heads above water, and paying our bills at the end of the month.

By fall that year I was out looking for a job again. I worked as an accountant at Schaibles Bakery. Accounting was not my forte, but I could do it, and did for about a year. During those next few years I worked at several places, sometimes leaving the job because of illness of one of the children, or of myself or having baby sitter or car problems; most of the time for reasons I do not even remember.

Our house was seldom a single family dwelling. Always, there was someone needing shelter for one reason or another. Sometimes they paid for room and board and sometimes they did not. It depended on the circumstances.

One year our boarder was a young girl, Ellie, with whom I had worked at the bakery. She found it impossible to live with her parents, immigrants from Poland. The American ways were unacceptable to them. For example, the reason for her leaving them was that Ellie was expected to give all of her earnings to her father to administer to the family as he saw fit. Ellie had become a thoroughly American girl and she had met the man she wanted to marry. She was not willing to be dominated by her father, and asked if she could come and live with me and my family. I, of course, said yes. It was an endearing relationship. We, my children and I, helped her prepare for her wedding. We helped her with invitations, reception favors, spending many evenings around the dining room table making things. The children and I attended the wedding, the only wedding I ever attended where the bride wept, with deep loud sobs, throughout the service, because her father was not in attendance. After the marriage and her first child, her father accepted the Americanization of his daughter. Ellie now lived a typical American life. Assimilation happens, but not with-out pain and drama.

For two years after that, the Donneley family came to live with us. They had been the storekeepers at an independent grocery store in Stockertown and had suffered bankruptcy during an economic slump in 1959. The family consisted of Dot and Frank, and their two sons, Michael and Buddy. Frank worked at the Club in Stockertown. Dot, a gracious woman, took care of the children and was a wonderful nanny for them. This was a pleasant arrangement for me. Dot had a certain elegance, something of a New England grace, which I admired. She was kind to the children and she cared for them lovingly and competently. After a couple of years the Donnelleys rented a house in Stockertown and we continued our friendship for many years.

After that we were living alone as a single family in our house. It was in the early sixties...the economy had improved for us and other young couples. It gave us opportunities to become more social with neighbors and friends.

It was then that the party circuit started and life took on a different tone. There were several couples involved. It started modestly, each successive party became more expansive, expensive and wild. There was an excess of drinking and flirting and really an excess of everything except restraint. I remember entering my living room one night, where two women friends of mine, were slightly tipsy and were discussing my husband. One was saying to the other, "Oh, sure! I am a little in love with Charlie...You, too?" I backed out of the room silently and sold myself the fiction that sustained me for the next few years, "They may all love him, but he always comes back to me."

Nevertheless, one more seed was planted down in my deep secret well, waiting for germination or extermination. After that event I told Charles that I did not want to be in that party circuit any longer. He must have agreed, because I do not remember any more of those parties.

Something happened that year, that I would rather not write about. However, it was such a turning point in my life that to leave it out would be somehow, dishonest, or at least an omission of an event that explains so much of what followed for the next few years.

One night Charles did not come home. I slept downstairs on the sofa, as I often did when he was out late and then went up to the bedroom with him when he came home. Throughout that long night I wavered between anger and worry. Charles came in about five in the morning and caught me when I was on a high wave of anger. I ranted, quietly, as I did not want the children to wake up and hear this. Charles was not generally a violent man but on this occasion he lost control and hit me hard on the side of my face. I became coldly calm and walked away. I did not cry or answer him with any words. I simply walked away. It was not as though I did it myself; it was as though some force within turned me in a different direction, physically, emotionally and practically.

The next day, covering my bruised face with makeup, I went to the Employment Office in Easton and looked for a better job. I knew I needed more money. I knew I had to find a way out...not immediately, but sometime I would be out of this. I wanted to exit with dignity.

At the employment office I found a good job as a Lab Technician at Davidson and Hemmindinger. They were physicists who owned and operated a company specializing in color technology. Theirs was the company that standardized colors for many industries throughout the world...colors for Bell Telephone, Ford Motors and others. In the lab, colors were mixed by the technicians and measured by a spectrophotometer. My first job was mixing the colors, and in a few months I advanced to using the spectrophotometer.

What an exciting job this was! I was learning something every moment. I was working with intelligent and educated people. Deep friendships were forming. I was learning and earning more than I ever had. Soon Betty Berger came to work there as a secretary. A reconnection with such a good friend of so many years was particularly satisfying for me.

It was not the product of a single seed planted in my psyche, but a whole crop blossoming at once. I could not quell the growth of the idea that I wanted more...more than even this exciting job was offering. When I allowed that idea to come to the surface, it could not be stowed away again in the recesses of my soul. What I wanted was more education. I wanted to go to college.

The first thing I did was to talk to a family counselor in Easton. I talked with her for an hour and told her about my family and how my mother had gone to school late in life and succeeded against all odds. I told the counselor that somehow, I thought I might be able to do it. I wanted to become a social worker. She said that one needed a Master's Degree in social work to become employed in that profession but she thought I would be a good teacher, and there was a lot of social work in the teaching profession. She also said there was a shortage of teachers in Pennsylvania and New

Jersey so one could teach on an emergency certificate after accumulating slightly more than half the credits needed for a Bachelor's Degree.

I thought about that and how it would be good to have vacations at the same time the children had theirs. There were so many teachers in my family. By this time Rosie was teaching. Mother, and of course, my main mentor, Aunt Mary were teachers. I thought about that meeting of Sunday School teachers and someone telling me that I would be a good teacher.

I decided that was what I would do. The counselor directed me to take the SAT exam soon, which I did. At this point I had told no one of my plans. I sent for material from East Stroudsburg State College, the nearest state school and when it arrived by mail, I kept it hidden. This whole endeavor was taking on sub-stance and speed like tumbleweeds blowing across the prairie, getting larger with each turnover. I got my SAT's back and they were good enough. Not great in math but high enough in the verbal section to give me a respectable score that would be accepted in most colleges.

Finally, I had to talk to Charles about it. He was surprisingly agreeable to the idea. He said he had always felt some guilt and sadness that I had not been able to claim my Augustana scholarship. He said that the money spent on my courses and books would pay off and would be like insurance in case anything happened to him. After that, I was bold enough to bring it up in a conversation with a friend of ours who said with incredulity. "But, Dolores you will be thirty-four years old when you get finished!"

I answered, "I will be thirty-four years old even if I don't go to college."

It was about a year and a half from the time I visited the family counselor until I was able to enroll in a summer session of East Stroudsburg Teacher's College. Before I could go, I had to earn enough for a semester's tuition.

The first thing I did was to stop smoking. I had been introduced to cigarettes while in the hospital after Lorie was born. The volunteer women came around to the rooms with gifts for the new mothers. A pack of cigarettes was one of the gifts. This was in 1955, long before the dangers connected with smoking were generally realized. I asked my doctor if he thought this was good for the baby. He said, "Dolores, you have three children under three years old! You need some time to relax and be calm. Take some time out with a cigarette a few times a day. It will do you good."

Thus by 1962 I had an addiction to nicotine. By a firm and strong resolve I managed to overcome it. Every week I put aside the money I would have used for cigarettes into a special account for tuition. I was still working at Davidson and Hemmindinger but I also found many additional ways to make money that year. I did ironing for a family in Nazareth. I took the census in Stockertown. I sold cosmetics door to door. In every way I could think of I earned money and put it aside to get to college by the next summer.

It was a good year, that time of working at Davidson & Hemmindinger, and working toward the dream that seemed to be going in the right direction. The best thing that happened was that the Bartletts came into my life.

I was attending a baby shower one Saturday afternoon in Stockertown. A new woman in town was there with her six months old baby girl. The new woman was Marianne Bartlett. Her darling baby was MaryBeth. After exchanging a few words, it became obvious to us that we were kindred spirits. We were eager to get out of the baby shower so we could talk with each other away from the chatter inside. We walked to her home on the other side of town, in one of the other big old Victorian houses in Stockertown. She was the wife of a young engineer, Bill Bartlett, who had recently been hired by Davidson and Hemmindinger. I knew that a few new engineers had been hired, all from upstate New York, graduates of Union College. And one in particular was the husband of the woman who was to become my best friend. On that walk home I learned that they were Catholics...Irish Catholics in this little town of Pennsylvania Dutch Lutherans and Italian Catholics. They, too, were finding it difficult to find their place in Stockertown. They were practicing Catholics which meant that their family was growing at a rapid rate. She was wheeling MaryBeth in a carriage and was expecting another in six months. We talked about our backgrounds, about music, babies, religion and by the time we arrived at her house we had started a conversation that was to go on for nearly fifty years.

The PTA was looking for a project that spring, the year before I went to college. I was on the committee and remembering my early days on the prairie and how much fun the Farmer's Union dances and socials were, I presented a plan to have an auction and dance. We would solicit merchandise and services from local businesses which would serve three purposes. It would get the business people involved in the school, would advertise their businesses and would make money for the PTA. After the auction we would have a dance.

The event was a huge success, held in a public building in Tatamy, a little town near Stockertown. The event was so successful that we had to turn people away as the number of people in the building was exceeding what the fire company considered safe. The event went on and after the very lively bidding and buying of the goods and services, the band began to play for the dance. It was an astounding success! About a half-hour after the dancing had started, the electricity went out. Several flashlights were found and the dance went on. Someone found me in the darkened room and said, "I can fix that electric problem, if you want!" Of course, I accepted the offer and in a short while the lights were back on. I looked for the electrical genius who had solved the problem so efficiently and graciously and was introduced to Bill Bartlett...the husband of my new best friend, and the new engineer at Davidson and Hemmindinger.

The next day, a Sunday afternoon, I answered a knock on the door, and there was the same Bill Bartlett, with an armful of 33rpm records, asking, "Can Charlie play this afternoon?" I laughed and told him he would have to ask Charlie.

Bill came into our living room and into our lives that day, saying he had heard that we liked music and he had some to share. Charles came down from upstairs and we sat and listened to folk music for a couple of hours that afternoon. Bill liked folk but Marianne was a classical vocalist and was being auditioned for the Bach Choir in nearby Bethlehem, PA. He was looking for someone with whom to share his music. Among our favorites were the Brother's Four, The Weavers, The Kingston Trio, and Burl Ives. His taste was similar. When he and I talked about our mutual employer, we agreed to car pool and share the expense of commuting to Easton. That Sunday certainly was one of the nodal points in my life.

On Memorial Day that year, I was having a family picnic in the yard.. Charles' parents and the Bergers were invited and we would eat at three. About noon, the phone rang and Bill was on the other end. He said, "Heard you are having a picnic...could I bring my family?" I was disconcerted, as I quickly calculated that their family would add six more attendees.

I answered, "Of course! What would you bring, besides your family...such as food?"

He said Marianne had just taken six loaves of homemade bread out of the oven and would bring that. What a wonderful day it turned out to be. We ate, and sang and played with the children, and laughed and reveled in our good fortune. It was a picnic the likes of which we had never had before.

After everyone else had gone, the Bartletts lingered on. We walked around our property and found that grape vines which had not been tended for years had wound their way up the tall ever-greens bordering our yard. They were dripping with bunches of luscious grapes. Bill and Charles got ladders and buckets and by evening we had bushels of grapes waiting to be used. Marianne and I set to making jam while the men played and sang. It just felt so good, so right! I watched Bill with his children, hanging off him like appendages, as he tumbled and played with them. I hoped some of that behavior would be seen by Charles and that he might be inspired to play with his own children that way.

The Bartlett children and ours got along well. They were not best friends until high school as they were never in the same grade in the lower schools. But the Bartlett children, were closer to me than many of my nieces and nephews, way out West, and mine were the same to the Bartletts. We did child care exchanges and our children were entirely comfortable in each other's home.

After that Memorial Day, there was not a weekend for years that we did not spend most of it with the Bartletts. Every Sunday morning I would stop there on my way home from church and after years in a dry desert, as far as theological discussions were concerned, I had come to an oasis. We had deep and intelligent conversations about church, religion and ecumenism, spirituality... and the differences between those four subjects.

We saw the Bartletts throughout the week too, as I went to their house in the morning so I could visit with Marianne before Bill and I went to work. Bill and I were forming a friendship of which I was both cautious and enriched. I had no brothers, and there were so few men in my life, I really didn't know how to shake my self-consciousness with men. This was different. He respected me; he listened to ideas and even elicited my opinions on deep and complex issues. I worried that Marianne would be jealous of the time we had together on the drive to and from work, but we talked about it openly and honestly. Somehow, it worked. It worked be-cause Marianne and I were so blatantly honest with each other.

At Davidson and Hemmindinger I was promoted to the engineering department where computers were being developed to measure the various properties and uses of color. Soon I, myself, was building computers. My speciality was a tri-stimulus differentiator.

Bill and Charles formed a Boy Scout troop which was the best thing that ever happened to Danny, and served him the rest of his life. Charles had tried to get Danny involved in Little League Baseball but Danny had not a competitive bone in his body. He wanted to be in the woods, and to fish and hike...never out in a baseball field, trying to beat his friends. Our Stockertown troop did not aspire to medals and rank. They focused on cooperative ventures. They were always busy building a shelter in the woods, planning a fishing trip...things of that nature. Their leader, a young man, Sherman Metztgar was a major force in the development of Danny and many other young men of Stockertown.

From the beginning of our friendship with the Bartletts, Bill and Charles got deeper and deeper into folk music. Soon they each played a guitar, and Charles devised a washtub bass. They began to sing and harmonize together. Both had rich, strong melodic voices. They sang for hours on Sunday afternoons.

After a couple of months of this, I saw that a folk concert featuring Odetta, was being offered at Lafayette College in Easton. I pleaded with Marianne to go with me, although she had little regard for folk music. We went together and were both enchanted by Odetta and her rich voice and powerful presentation. From that day on we were all were caught up in the legendary "Folk Craze" of the Sixties. From that day on, we sang, collected, uncovered new talent, learned new songs, followed the Weavers, Dave Von Ronk, Tom Paxton, Judy Collins, Joan Baez and others. In other words we were saturated with folk music. More than listening we all sang and harmonized. Marianne's beautiful soprano voice made every song magic.

Our Sunday gatherings grew in size and importance. Many people, including The Bergers, the Sampsons, the McLaughlins, the

Wichies, all brought their families and contributed to the food and talent. Sometimes the gatherings were at our house and sometimes at the Bartletts. There was an abundance of children running in and around the house entertaining each other without adult interference.

I started college during the summer session of 1963 at East Stroudsburg State College, fifty-one miles from Stockertown. The first summer I found the Letson family with their three older girls who provided child care for my children. The Letsons became good friends and joined our circle of friends. Linda, one of the daughters from that family became a lifelong friend of mine.

When I registered for the first session of college I chose the subject of Physics. I reasoned that if I was going to fail, that subject that would be the cause of my failure. It was a requirement for the degree I was pursuing. If I was not going to be able to do it I wanted to know early, rather than expend the time and money and then find I could not attain my goal. I wanted to get over it at once. As I expected it was very difficult for me. The first day of classes, on my way home from college I stopped at the Bartletts with my text book and told them I might not get any further than this one semester. The textbook, itself was daunting. Bill offered to help me and with his engineering skills and his patience, honed to perfection through child raising, he did get me through it. Also my professor was an older man who was impressed by the fact that I had entered college at the age of thirty, and he made it impossible for me to fail. There were five students around my age attending the summer session of 1963. We were considered a special group. It was not usual for anyone, especially women, of that age, to be attending college. They provided special physical education classes for the five of us. Ours was golf...just driving balls, nothing serious, such as learning the game. The second session of the summer we were given Folk Dancing.

The second session I took Psychology and felt, when I had my first class, that I had stepped into a warm bath. I had found my life path...or it had found me. The third session was Philosophy, a revolutionary way to think...for me. I ended the summer with a respectable grade-point average.

By the end of the summer, I had used up all of the money I had saved for college, and did not have enough credits to apply for the Government Education Loan.

Remembering Augustana, I resolved to do something about this. My college education would not slip away again. On one of the last days of the session, I waited in sight of the college President's office until all the secretaries had gone out to lunch. I approached his office with determination and trepidation. I knocked on the door and the President answered with a questioning "Yes?"

Opening the door and summoning all my courage, I told him my story....my background, my goals, my dreams. The problem was that I had no money to continue.

What questions he asked, or anything else that was said, except his welcome words, "We can find a way around that are lost in memory. "I will put in a waiver for the credit requirement and you can go to the bursar's office and pick up a voucher and register for the fall semester."

I was dizzy with wonderment and joy at what had just transpired. I walked across the campus saying to myself, "You are a college student; you, Dolores, are about to register as a full-time student for a semester! You are going to do it!"

Looking back at all the years of my life which led up to this moment I am exhilarated. It was as though I stepped out of my skin and watched myself walking through the years and onto this campus. I said to myself, "You *can't* get here from there," and answered myself, "But I did!"

CHAPTER 20

Stockertown Part Three

Most of the Saturdays mornings I remember from the days when I was going to college were lighthearted and fun...except for one which will remain etched clearly in my memory. Usually it was get the chores over with and then on to Easton for choir practice and whatever adventures were in store for us on the way home.

This particularly memorable cold Saturday morning, like the others, started with the ever present laundry. That had been a bigger chore for the past six weeks when the dryer went out. I was hanging the wet clothes in the attic as January and February had been too cold and dreary to hang them out. What was alarming this Saturday was that the washer quit just after filling with water on the first load of the day. Nothing I could do would make it budge. I hated to bother Bill Bartlett, but he liked to fix things and usually could. He had a lot of experience with washing machines gleaned from the experience of having eight children and monumental amounts of laundry. Today his experience told him and he told me that this was the exception to the rule; he could not fix it. The washer was ten years old and burned out.

The children and I left for Easton where they had choir practice. Try as I might, I could not chase the gloom that was settling over me. What was I going to do? Usually I could think of something, but this time I was overwhelmed. I could not get the laundry done by hand, over a weekend. The fact was that I had to get a new washer and dryer, and I knew that our budget simply did not support that fact.

I pondered the problem on the way to town and when I arrived at the church to drop the children off for choir practice, I had decided that I must leave college and get a job. It was a wrenching decision and not made easily. I had been awake many nights even before this pondering how I was going to afford the next semester. Even though I had the government loan for tuition, we were having trouble making ends meet. And now this! I would have to start paying back the government loan right away and would not be able to get another. Not again! Oh, God! Not again!

When the children were safely ensconced in the choir loft, I went into the small chapel to pray about it, to think about it, and to absorb the enormity of what I had to do. When I got inside the chapel, I could neither pray nor think. I knelt in a pew and cried my heart out. I let it come out, and sobbed with abandon.

When I was exhausted and had no more sobs in me I went out into the cold rainy morning, walked to Sears and selected an economy model washer and dryer. I put it on credit and contracted to pay in monthly installments. There was no joy or sense of satisfaction about the purchase. It simply had to be done. I walked back to the car dejectedly and climbed inside to wait for the children.

There was a knock on the car window and I looked up to see the sexton motioning for me to roll down the window. He told me that Father Harvey wanted to speak to me in his office. "Oh, God," I thought. "Has it something to do with one of the children? If they have broken something, I cannot afford to pay for it."

Father Harvey, a man of my age, said, "Dolores, I don't want to pry into your affairs but the sexton said he saw you in the chapel this morning. If there is anything you want to talk about, I am here to listen." I poured out the whole story, sometimes breaking down and crying. I told him about the scholarship to Augustana and how I could not redeem it because of money. Again, because of money I would not be able to carry out this dream of attaining a college education.

While I was talking he seemed to be suppressing a smile, and there was a twinkle in his eye, and I thought he did not show any empathy at all. Before I got to the end of the story, he broke in, "Dolores, Dolores, you will never believe what I am going to tell you, but I can show you proof that it is true. In the morning mail today, I received an envelope addressed to me personally. It contained a check for $500 dollars, with instructions to use it for whatever I felt most appropriate. I have been sitting here for an hour trying to determine what was needed or wanted here at Trinity and up until this moment, I had thought of nothing appropriate. Our budget is good now; I thought of paneling the walls in this office but that didn't feel right. This money is for you, Dolores. Clearly, it is for you!"

I was stunned for a long moment and then flooded with gratitude, happiness, purpose, and of course, with unfaltering Belief. From then on I believed my college and my career were pre-ordained; that I had God on my side. Nothing could stop me now! Father Harvey also said, "Dolores, you never have to go through have this again. You can call upon me whenever you get to a point where you need it and this benefactor will supply whatever you need."

I never asked for it, but a few times every year, always at a crucial time, I received an envelope with a money order for two, three or four hundred dollars in it. I never knew who my benefactor was, but suspected it was Fred Conine, an older man who was an executive at the Crayola factory in Easton. Fred and his wife had lost a son who was about the age of Danny. He was always kind and interested in my children and my progress in college. I will be thanking him from my heart the rest of my days. And just in case it wasn't Fred, I am thanking an unknown benefactor.

Trinity Church was a big portion of my life, before that incident, and even more so afterward. The children were involved in all the activities in which they showed an interest. Summer camps were wonderful events that developed skills, companions and adventures so important in their lives and development. Danny decided, when he was about ten years old, that he wanted to be a priest when he grew up. The Harvey family and I were becoming good friends. Father Harvey and Grace had children near the age of mine, and our children formed important friendships.

Along with the church, the Bartletts and the music formed another major part of my life. Charles and I now had something we shared and I felt that perhaps this marriage could survive. I wanted that with all my heart. As a child, when living with various families, I would observe the relationships and decide that this or that was the way I would live my life...and I would never, never get a divorce. For a little while, during this middle period of our marriage, I thought it was going to happen just the way I planned.

By necessity, college and the accompanying study and school events of my children, along with church, took most of the time, for that period in my life. Many mornings I awoke with my head on the dining room table, as I had been working on a project or reading a textbook until I was too tired to go to bed.

I felt that I was doing the necessary things...always making sure the children had a good breakfast and dinner for the family, always being sure my children were well dressed and cared for, always attending every scouting and school event in which they were involved. I also made sure every Monday, that Charles had five white shirts perfectly ironed, and I certainly tried with all my heart to satisfy his needs and desires. However, if there was one area of my life that got neglected, it was probably my marriage. We were both responsible for letting important linchpins in our relationship come loose.

In early spring, before the summer of 1964, word spread throughout my South Dakota family, that we would have a family reunion in Sturgis. Mother was insistent that all her daughters be there at the same time. I promised that I would be there but had no idea of how to pay for it. Bus fare for three children and one adult was more than I ever had on hand.

The first hope that I might make it to the reunion was that Davidson and Hemmindinger had called me and asked if I could come back and work for the summer and build seven tri-stimulus differentiators. This was a computer that I had built many times in my years there. It was my specialty. So I was relieved that I would have some income for summer expenses, and baby sitters. I worked throughout that summer and finished the computers by August. Still, it was almost time for the reunion and I did not have bus fare.

On the last day of work, I was handed a note from Dr. Hemmindinger. This was highly unusual. He was a shy, reserved man and seldom interacted with the technicians. We were in awe of him. I opened the note and was even more surprised. It was an invitation for lunch! I was filled with anticipation and trepidation through the morning, and when lunch time came, I met him in his outer office. He drove me in his Cadillac to The Old Stone Inn for an elegant lunch. Conversation was cautious and stilted. He asked me about my courses, and about my children. I asked him about his college aged children.

When we were finished, he cleared his throat, and said, "Dolores, we sold those computers you have been building for a lot more than we expected, and considerably more than what we paid you to build them. This has been an embarrassment to Mr. Davidson and me, and we want you to have this." He handed me an envelope with a check inside which was more than adequate for our trip to South Dakota. I thanked him profusely. With the check in hand, I was once more reminded that I could trust the process... the process of life itself.

My children and I went to Sturgis by Greyhound bus. They were ten, eleven and twelve years old. We were on the bus three or four days and nights. It was quite an arduous trip but all the way I felt like singing. It would be the first time in twelve years since I had seen Mary Lou, Kitty and Bobbie. There were several nieces and nephews I had not seen at all.

From the West coast, Rosie, with her two-year old Karen, Kitty and her three-year old Tracy, Mary Lou and her thirteen year old Diane, all came in a little Volkswagen Bug, from Bothell Washington. Their odyssey was remarkable...almost legendary. To add to the sheer number of bodies in the car, Rosie's leg was in a cast due to a motorcycle accident she had been in a few weeks before the reunion. Kitty and Mary Lou took turned driving. Mary Lou had never learned to drive a stick shift so when she drove, Rosie sat beside her and shifted the gears.

Bobbie and her husband Jack now lived in Rapid City having spent several years in Guam, and Louisiana as he was a career man in the Air Force. In 1964 at the time of the reunion they had six children; Jackie, Cleanne, Jenice, Jon, Kayla and the baby Steve. How wonderful it was to get to know that family again.

Rosie and I had forged such a tight bond in Pennsylvania that we were inseparable at this reunion. The first night of the reunion, after we had bedded all the children down on the kitchen floor of Mother and Tom's house, she and I slipped away and went to the diner at the end of town, where we had coffee and talked all night. Memory does not serve me well enough to know what we talked of, the tenor and tone of our conversation will stay with me forever. We slipped in just before the sun came up, and were careful not to step on the five children sleeping on quilts on the floor of the kitchen in that little house.

Along with my children, there were nine of my nieces and nephews, plus Dorothy's four oldest children. Those thirteen children had a wonderful time together. I would love to hear their memories of that time. Also the toddlers provided us with entertainment and stories that have lasted for years.

One of the memorable things about the reunion was that each of us five sisters, chose one night to cook a meal for the entire group. It was to be a favorite of our family...not our family of origin but our family of now. The dinners were good, with- out exception, food was ample and we laughed and told stories as we sat around the table. Even the children ate with appreciation and enthusiasm. It seemed they wanted to share that part of their lives with their cousins. My offering was Italian spaghetti and Pennsylvania Dutch pickled cabbage, the meal my children always requested for their birthday dinners.

In Sturgis, there were no ingredients for spaghetti. For that dish, which seemed so ordinary and simple to us Easterners, I had to go to Rapid City to find oregano, Italian cheese, bread, and the pasta itself.   Sturgis had only macaroni; nothing foreign on their shelves! That, above all other aspects of the visit, defined so clearly, how far I had moved from my family of origin.

We never know the seriousness of certain aspects of an event until much later. At this event, Tom was quiet and seemed to want to be alone much of the time. He acknowledged my presence but did not converse with anybody. The rest of us were so busy with the children, laundry, and the camaraderie, that his condition went by without remark or action.

At the end of the reunion Kitty and I listened as Mother talked about his condition and how she did not want to leave him alone while she went to teach in Wyoming. We let her lead the way in determining her action. Then we helped her do it. He would be staying in a private home in Whitewood, with a woman who cared for elderly people such as Tom. He died that winter.

After the reunion the children and I went back to Pennsylvania. I continued through the college curriculum, working toward a BS in Education. In the summer of '65, I went to college in the morning and worked at Davidson and Hemmindinger in the af- ternoons. Cleanne, my sister Bobbie's oldest daughter, came from South Dakota with Rosie and Mother to be my baby sitter for the summer. Cleanne stayed for the rest of the year, working in Easton. She was a welcome family member.

While Mother and Rosie were there, we took my children to the World's Fair in New Jersey. That was a great day in the life of my children. Most of their friends had been to the fair, and it didn't look like a possibility for us with our limited budget. However, Rosie came with her Volkswagen camper, I took a day off work, we packed lunches and went off to the fair. The children referred to it as "The Best Day of Our Childhood."

By the fall of 1966 I had enough credits and had finished my student teaching so I could obtain an emergency certificate in New Jersey and begin teaching first grade in Stewartsville in September. I was extremely happy and proud when I signed the contract. When I got home that evening with the contract in hand, Charles was there with Bill. I burst in with great excitement, "I got it, I got it! My first contract!" Charles looked at it and expressed his disdain. "Eight thousand a year! You signed a contract for eight thousand! Why, I make more than that without a degree!"

I was abashed, deflated. I rallied and pointed out to him that I did not yet have a degree, and that someday soon, I would. Then I would make more money. I voiced the fact that this contract was for more than I had ever made, and it was a contract...I was guaranteed to make that much. Charles gave me a deprecating look, almost a sneer. As the two men walked toward the door to go out, Bill turned, winked at me and mouthed, "Good for you!"

I should have realized then that Charles was self-conscious about not having a college degree. How this manifested was that he felt disdain for the degrees held by people with whom he worked and with whom he played tennis. His life constantly put him in close relationships with college-educated people...he even chose them, such as Bill Bartlett. Sensing that, I had a slight discomfort about attaining a degree but failed to see the effect it would have in our relationship.

We had discussed it before I started college. It was like an insurance policy, he had told me.

Setting up my school room in early September was exciting for me. I remembered helping Mother set up hers. My co-teacher, Helen Deiterley had one year of experience. We would be teaching the two first-grade classes in a little New Jersey town, whose child population had grown to the extent that it had exceeded what the school building would hold. The school board in Stewartsville had arranged with a church about two blocks away to use two rooms in the basement for the two first grade classes.

Helen was an intelligent, progressive thinker and an excellent, creative teacher. This was early in her teaching career and I learned more from her than I had in all of my classes at East Stroudsburg. One of the things we strongly agreed upon was that first-graders should love school. This would be the year in their lives where they would establish their attitude toward school and learning. Helen and I would work on projects together and always evaluate them on how they would impact the children's concept of school, and their self-esteem. We believed that the first event in the morning should be something that they eagerly looked forward to, and the last thing of the day should be something that left them feeling good about the day and about themselves. We wanted to see excited faces in the morning and self-satisfied smiles as they boarded the bus to go home. I felt we succeeded in that and we had a good time ourselves.

I enjoyed teaching and being part of a school system; I was on the way to becoming a professional. Also I was learning that it was the child who had the most trouble learning that interested me most. The average and above student absorbed learning like a sponge absorbs water. You could see the slow-learners striving for understanding, and you could literally see the process of learning. I found that fascinating and absorbing.

For example: The youngest child in my class, also the smallest, simply did not get it for the first three months of school. He was compliant and pleasant but with an aura of sadness about him. He knew he didn't get it, and he knew the other children did. Suddenly one day, while I had the privilege of witnessing, the light came on! He looked down at his name, printed in large letters on the upper left hand corner of his desk, and he looked up at the letters above the blackboard, displayed in every first grade classroom. He stood up and said with wonder and amazement, "Every letter of my name is up there!" He had made a connection that was truly like unlocking the door to a treasure trove that previously belonged to everybody else, but not to him. He was now in on the secret, unlocking the door to the mysterious treasure. It brought tears to my eyes then and even when I think of it fifty years later.

That was the beginning of my interest in teaching and working with developmentally disabled children and adults. I was taking courses two nights a week at an extension of Penn State University, to complete my degree. Whenever I had an elective, which was becoming more often as I neared completion of my course, I steered it toward Special Education and Psychology.

Mother was pleased that I had become a teacher. Tom died in 1965 in the nursing home in Whitewood South Dakota. Mother had been living in Wyoming where she taught. Mother was twenty-five years younger that Tom. At age fifty-five she was not yet ready to give up on life. She continued teaching and it gave her purpose and determination and raised her self-esteem.

Also it was more money than she had ever had earned before. Teachers were always considered to be a good catch for the Western men. It wasn't long before she was being courted by Spike Olson, the former sheriff of Sundance County. She and I spent more time on the phone than we had for many years. She had much to discuss about Spike and their relationship. We now had two elements which bonded us in a different way than ever before...teaching and problematic men. It seemed as if the difference in our age was diminishing. We were closer than we ever had been.

At Christmas time, in our school, as in every public school in America, there was a school program where each grade prepared a presentation to perform for their parents and the town. Helen and I worked diligently to make sure ours were outstanding, and with first graders, it was not difficult to do; they are so endearing. They simply need to show up on the stage and the heart of everyone in the audience melts. We enjoyed the preparation and the program. Helen and I were drawn into a closer friendship.

After the program, she and I had arranged to meet with our husbands at a restaurant and have dinner together. It was the first time Charles had met any of the people I worked with at the school. From tennis connections, he knew the principal, but no one else. I had a foreboding about the evening and was nervous when he arrived at the restaurant. The evening did not go well. Charles' reaction to people who, in his estimation, had too much education, was to be outrageous...to say crude and rude things, and to make off-color jokes. It was that kind of night. Before we finished dinner, without provocation, he said, "Well, I've had enough of this!" and left.

Charles' behavior was embarrassing for me. Even the very good friendship that Helen and I had forged, did not redeem the evening. I departed shortly thereafter. Charles was not at home when I got there but that was not unusual. He was seldom home before midnight or one o'clock.

The next morning, Saturday, I was up early to start the things we did on Saturdays. This season the children were in adult choir which met on Wednesday night so we had different activities on Saturday. Dan had to be a church for his confirmation classes, Marcie to Wind Gap for her gifted art class, and Lorie somewhere else for the gifted music class. I was picking up things in the family room waiting for them to be ready to leave the house with me.

Charles' sheepskin jacket was thrown over the back of the rocking chair and I picked it up to hang in the coat closet. For some reason I reached into one of the pockets and pulled out a receipt for a motel room, in East Stroudsburg, dated the night before. For the second time in my life, my knees turned to jelly; I had to sit down. I felt everything, *everything* drain from my being. This was now something I had to face...to deal with. It was the thing I had ignored, rationalized, deluded myself about, but now that was no longer possible. I had to deal with it. But how? How do you end the life you always wanted?

Mechanically, I took the children to the various places they had to be, and then drove to a secluded place by the Bushkill Creek to think. What to do, what to do? I decided then that I didn't want the confrontation with Charles until after Danny's confirmation at Trinity in January, a month away. Once that was decided, I felt I could do this, one step at a time. That would be the first step. Immediately after confirmation I would tell him what I had found and then decide the next step. Confirmation was going to be on the 19th of January. That was a month away. I was able to put the problem on hold in my mind and actions.

Naturally Sunday afternoons were still singing events with the Bartletts but Charles was often absent. This was the year my children started the Christmas Eve caroling through Stockertown. I wanted this last year in their home to be special and memorable. The trio left our house and picked up several more children on Lincoln Avenue. They continued to Main Street and picked up children in almost every house where they stopped to sing. They went through the town, gathering carolers and ended up at our house where we had hot chocolate and toast. After that we piled in the car and drove to Trinity Church for the midnight mass. A few of the Stockertown children came with us to Trinity and were awed at the beauty of the midnight mass there.

Christmas came and went; a new semester began, both at my school and the school of my children and my night college classes. Finally it was January 19th, the day of confirmation. It began to snow early in the morning but we managed to get to the service. I was moved to tears as Danny was confirmed. He was committed to and believed in what he was doing. I knew his life was about to change in a major way. I knew I would have to tell him about that change soon. It was heartrending.

The snow accumulated and by the end of the day was piled high and the wind was blowing it around like a blizzard out on the prairie. As I had made a promise to myself I had to confront Charles with the evidence I found in his pocket over a month before; I must do it. Procrastination was no longer an option.

"I want to go for a walk," I said, after cleaning up after dinner. He said, "Are you crazy, woman? There's a helluva blizzard out there! You want to go for walk?"

Something in my face or my resolute stance, caused him to follow me and get his coat and we started down Lincoln Avenue in silence. Finally I told him what I had found and when I had found it. He answered, "She is a wonderful woman and I am not going to give her up!"

I was silent, digesting the fact that I was reliving my mother's life. My father probably said the same words to her, and she probably felt as empty and frightened as did I at that moment. What I said next was reflexive, rather than rational and well thought out. "I want to stay here until school is out and then will take the children with me and go back Home."

He echoed my last word "Home? Where is Home?"

I answered, "South Dakota, of course. I'll have family support there and I know I can get a job teaching in Wyoming next year." As was characteristic of Charles, he had to rush home to the bathroom, right then. I walked alone in the blizzard for a long time that night. The weather seemed to be in synch with my life that night...cold, bitter and dangerous.

It was a long spring that year. There were so many important things that had to be done before my life fell totally apart. Each day was one more small chunk of it falling away and my very being transported into an unknown new life.

If I passed the three night courses I was taking I would have enough credits by May, to attain my B.S. in Ed. with a minor in Psychology. Two nights a week I drove to Allentown to the extension courses offered by Penn State University. It was a trial to keep up with my pre-teen and two teenagers, getting them to their various activities. I had to inform the school administration that I would not be returning to teach next year. I had to decide what to keep and what to leave of my life in Stockertown.

At home in waking hours with my family I chose to act as if life were normal and would go on like this for ever. I simply could not tell my children what was happening. I could not bear to answer the questions I knew they would ask, nor could I face the pain and anxiety they would experience upon leaving their friends, their wonderful yard, their bedrooms and every part of Stockertown that they took for granted now, but would come to miss with acute pain.

When I told the Bartletts, they were nearly as devastated as I was. Bill, of course, thought it could be fixed. If anything was broken, he thought it could be fixed. Marianne understood what I was going through and she and I spent many hours sitting with the pain. The friendship between Bill and Charles came to a standstill. Bill missed it more than Charles did because Charles had other things to occupy his mind and his time.

As the end of school neared the children asked about summer camp. I told them that we were going to forego summer camp for a long visit with Grandma in South Dakota. We were going to stay the entire summer. They had pleasant memories of time there so did not balk at the idea of being in the West all summer.

College graduation day was nearing, the day that I had always felt would be triumphant and joyful. Charles and I still were living in the house together but conversation was sparse and interaction stilted and awkward. The day before graduation, he said, "I hope you don't expect me to come to graduation."

I didn't reply, because the lump in my throat precluded any words I might have uttered. I was sad that my children would not get to see it. I had to be there at seven in the morning and it was not allowed to have them on the campus unsupervised for four hours. Always my champion, Marianne showed up with my three children just as we were lining up for the procession to the event. Tears ran down my face throughout the bittersweet ceremony. My children were appreciative of my accomplishment. Marianne knew the importance of their attendance that day.

Finally, the day came when the four of us would fly to the Rapid City Airport; my mother would pick us up and take us to Sundance Wyoming, where she was teaching. She had married Spike Olson and moved there a few months before we arrived. Her mother, my grandmother, Hattie, had moved into the Sturgis house.

We arrived in Sundance shortly before the 4th of July. Dan enjoyed our time there. He liked hiking around Sundance Mountain and exploring the terrain. Marcie and Lorie were appalled. They believed I had taken them to the end of the earth...to the dark side of the moon. There were not even sidewalks, they pointed out to me.

A few days after our arrival in Sundance, I mustered the courage to talk to Marcie...to tell her what was going on. She was relieved rather than dismayed. She had seen Charles with the other woman, and had wondered how she would ever tell me. However, she told me, with no uncertainty, she did not want to stay in Sundance, where there was not even a movie theater.

I was having doubts about the wisdom of that myself. In the middle of my quandary, Bill Bartlett who was on a business trip in the West, called and asked if I could meet him in Rapid City. I borrowed Mother's car and met him at the airport. True to character he wanted to fix the problem and we discussed it from every angle. He stayed for a couple of hours, we had lunch, talked and cried together and he flew back to wherever he was working.

At the end of that discussion, my solution was to turn to Rosie. She also was now a single parent. In answer to my problem, she said that my coming to live with her would be the best thing she could imagine. She would love to have me and my children come to live with her. That became our plan; that we would go to California right after the July 4th celebration in South Dakota.

Mother, Spike, the children and I drove to Belle Fouche where Dorothy lived, for the parade and carnival. I suspected that Dan and his second cousin Tucky had a wild time that but could not confirm just how wild it was. In the evening we drove forty miles back went back to Sundance for fireworks. Dorothy, Carl and some of their children came back with us. The boys got in a little trouble shooting off firecrackers in an undesignated place, and the police came to tell us to keep them in check. We remembered that day the rest of our lives. It was a difficult day for me. I did not want to talk of what was going on in my life, my marriage. I also wondered if I could raise a son alone.

The day after that Mother, Spike, my children and I piled into Mother's station wagon and drove west to California. What a trip that was! Dan was surly and not feeling well, which I discovered was because he and Tucky had shared a pint of whisky to celebrate the 4th of July. He had a hangover! I was appalled! My Boy Scout son! I felt very guilty that I had been so self-involved that I did not know what they were doing the day before. I also showed no sympathy for Dan and his condition. While he was still suffering, we went through Yellowstone Park.

We captured one great memory on film of our stolen picnic lunch. A mother bear with her three little ones took over our picnic table and ate our lunch while we watched helplessly from the station wagon. None of us never forgot that!

After lunch we went to see Old Faithful perform and were appropriately stunned by the wonder and beauty of it. However, as we walked through the geyser fields, where there were ample signs, warning us to stay on the walkways, Dan stepped into a geyser pool, just to test the authenticity of the warnings. He got a painful burn on his foot, which we treated as best we could with the limited resources at hand. It did not improve his disposition and added another layer of stress to the trip.

It was a long, hot trip in a 1965 station wagon, without air conditioning. The six of us...my mother and her new husband, Spike Olson, three contentious teen-agers and me, the anxious mother, finally arrived in Sunnyvale California. Rosie had rented a two bedroom apartment in which we would live for the time being. Mother and Spike dropped us off, stayed one night and drove off in the morning. I didn't blame them one iota.

CHAPTER 21

California

As Spike and Mother drove away, Rosie already had a plan for the day. She said, "Let's all go to the beach!"

My children enthusiastically endorsed the plan but I said, "I'm never getting in a vehicle with those children again." Of course, that was hyperbole...I would get in a vehicle with them a thousand times and more, but not that day! Rosie had no idea how tired I was of being in the car with them.

They took off for the beach and I went to the Yellow Pages, and found the phone numbers of several computer companies or enterprises that had to do with electronics; places where I could get a job. I called three of those companies, inquiring about employment and was able to get an interview that afternoon with one of them and the other two early the next week. I also found the number for public transportation and ascertained that I could take a city bus to the place where I had an appointment that afternoon. That was all I needed.

The electronic business was flourishing in the Silicon Valley in the summer of 1967. They were eager to hire anyone who had any experience. I was hired that afternoon at my first interview and would start work the next day at three in the afternoon. I would be working until midnight five nights a week. The salary was good.

By the time Rosie and the children got home I was confident that we had a future in California. They arrived at the apartment in high spirits. Of the children, only Marcie knew that the plan was for us to stay there in California indefinitely. I knew I had to tell Danny and Lorie very soon.

We were renting a two bedroom unfurnished apartment on Garland Street in Sunnyvale. Rosie had put out a notice through her network of school friends that we needed some basic furniture. From that one little notice, every time we came home from anywhere, there was at least one piece of furniture on our door step. One afternoon as we arrived home and saw yet one more dresser on the porch, Marcie turned around with her hands on her hips, looked at us and said, "Whoever is praying for furniture had better stop!"

We were lightening up. I felt as though a heavy shroud that had been wrapped around the spirits of my children and me was slowly being unwound. Later in the week, I opened the refrigerator to retrieve something, and the old uneven shelf holding four baked potatoes, came loose from its moorings, causing the potatoes to fall out on the floor, one by one. The children froze. Such an incident in our old life would have started a stream of invectives from Charles, "Who the hell....."

I saw the distressed faces of my children as the potatoes fell to the floor, and I chanted, "One potato, two potato, three potato, four!" It released a long pent up dam. We laughed until tears ran down our faces.

Meals had always been a tense situation in Stockertown with one of the children often leaving the table in tears for a harsh reprimand from their father for some minor transgression. Now, in a moment, we all realized that we were going to have fun! Even at meals, we were going to have fun! We were free to have fun with whatever happened. And that we did, in California.

Shortly thereafter, the children made up new words to a popular song, in reference to the garbage disposal which we had never had before. "*Puff, the magic dragon, Lives in the sink. He eats the food that we don't eat, and drinks that we don't drink.*" Their playful, creative, witty selves began to emerge. Dan had brought a small four string guitar with him and the three of them had learned a few songs. I'm sure when they sang for a family party in South Dakota, *The Times They Are 'a Changing,* they had no idea how prophetic Bob Dylan's song was in the summer of 1967.

Rosie was planning to take a couple of morning classes at San Jose State, working toward her Masters of Education degree. We felt that the children would be all right. They were not exactly children anymore. They were twelve, thirteen and fourteen, certainly old enough to take care of themselves and baby-sit for Karen, age five, a few hours a day! Rosie was looking forward to spending the afternoons with them. However, after a short time she gave up her classes as it was not practical to continue, either in time and energy. She chose the children.

I harbored some guilt about that for several years; guilt that my problems had prevented her from completing her Master's Degree. After a while, it became apparent that she did not need a Master's to succeed in teaching. She was highly acclaimed as a Master teacher in the Santa Clara School district for many years. One year she won the high honor of being designated Teacher of the Year in that large district. She confessed to me that she had more fulfillment with the children that summer than any advanced degree would have provided. I gave up my guilt.

One morning, before I went to work at the electronics lab, I applied for a teaching job in the Santa Clara Unified District and was granted an interview. It was a successful interview and I was elated to be hired and eager to begin teaching in September. Now I had to start finding schools for my children. That was a bit more troublesome.

I was apprehensive about having them in a big California school. Marcie had made friends with a girl and they went into San Francisco to a book store. That sounded quite innocent to me but the next morning she confided to me, in awe, that she had been invited to smoke marijuana. Marcie, being Marcie, declined, but just knowing that there was an opportunity for her and for the others to get involved in drugs so easily set a cold fear in my heart.

Nevertheless, I felt the die was cast and we would stay in California. I would find a church where they could get involved in wholesome activities and hang out with other teenagers who were well cared for. I carefully set the stage to talk to Lorie about our real plan...to stay. I seriously conveyed the news to her, that we would not be going back to Pennsylvania. She was rather matter-of-fact about it. "So that's it...that's what you wanted to talk about?" She was looking forward to adventures in California.

Later that morning, I told Danny. His reaction was exactly the opposite. He said, "Well, you can do whatever you want, but I am going home! I'll join Hell's Angels if I have to!" His face was a blend of anger, pain and sadness. He took off running across the parking lot, jumped over a fence and ran...and ran and ran, out of sight in less than a minute.

What a difficult afternoon that was as we searched the neighborhood for him! I pondered the cost of the debacle Charles and I had made of our marriage. What had we done to the children? Maybe there was another way. I simply could not sacrifice one of them for...for what, I asked myself. For my disappointment, my failure? No, there had to be a solution that we simply had not yet discovered.

We looked for Danny all morning and into the afternoon. While I was deciding whether to call the police or to go to work, he reappeared, still angry but with more sadness and pain than anger now etched on his beautiful tear-stained face. Before I went to work I let him know that I was looking for another way. I assured him that we would all stay together and we would talk about it in the morning.

I worked through the night, mindlessly following diagrams, soldering connections, all the while letting my mind sort out the problem before me. By morning I knew that we must go back to

Pennsylvania. I would have to face all the things and people I did not want to face. I realized it was mainly pride that was standing in my way. All I had to do was set it aside, strip it of the power it had over me and get on with my life. It would be difficult to get my life together in Pennsylvania without the help of Rosie and my family in the West; but for the children, I had to do it. One step at a time, we would do it.

The next morning we sat down at the kitchen table to talk about it. I told them that if we all worked and saved as much as we could, we could afford our tickets back to Pennsylvania. We were going to need more money than I could earn in that time. The children agreed to help solve the problem.

It was as though I had set in motion an engine that ran on its own power and never stopped. Those teenagers found jobs where none were to be found. They painted fences, walked dogs, watered gardens, baby sat, fixed bicycles, delivered newspapers...whatever came within their radar they seized upon and made money. Every cent of it went into a teapot on top of the refrigerator.

I continued to work nights and occasionally was given overtime. By the appointed date, the deadline, we had saved just enough to order the tickets. We would be home before school started.

We did have time and a small amount of money to enjoy California for the rest of the summer. We went to the beach at Carmel where the children had as much fun as they had ever had. Dan lamented when we left, "We will never again find a beach as good as this." Now, that he knew we were going home, he could enjoy California and the time we had left there.

Rosie and the children, my three and her one, had many adventures while I was at work. The people for whom the children worked were captivated and enchanted by them. They were friends of Rosie. Those friends included us in many festive occasions.

There was one last celebration, the day before Marcie's 15th birthday, in a beautiful Los Gatos park. Many of the friends they had made over the summer attended. One of my all-time favorite snapshots was taken that day. It was of a huge California oak festooned with children and young adults in its low hanging boughs.

The next day, Marcie's birthday we boarded the plane in San Francisco which would take us to Allentown Pennsylvania. We were excited about the flight and about going home.

I was pondering questions during that long flight. Where we were going to live? Where would I get a job? How we would deal with Charles? I had relinquished the house to him when I went West. In spite of the counsel of my friend and attorney, Chauncy Howell, I was determined I would not sue Charles for child support.

I knew how Charles was about money and that such a suit would result in acrimony and bitterness and probably not enough money to warrant the fight. I did not want to depend on his generosity or his enforced duty. I did not want to be involved in arguments over money. No one would benefit by it. Also there was a selfish whim of mine. These were now my children. I wanted to raise them by myself. I wanted them to be independent and self-sufficient. The question hung around, "Could I?" and I confirmed it with a resounding, "With God's help, I Will!"

The plane landed at the ABE Airport at about 9 p.m. I went down the steps first and was surprised to see Charles and his mother, Althea, waiting at the edge of the tarmac. Then I saw Charles' face as he saw the children coming down the steps of the plane. It was as though he saw them, really *saw* them, for the first time in his life. They were extraordinarily beautiful as the lights shone on them when they descended from the plane to the tarmac. They glowed with their California tans and sun-bleached hair. It was a tumultuous greeting; hugs and kisses and tears as we all met each other...well not all of us. Charles and I were careful not to touch each other and barely made eye contact.

As we drove away from the airport, I asked, "Where are you taking us?" thinking that perhaps we were going to his parents' house.

He said, "You can stay in Stockertown tonight." We were dropped off at the curb of our house on Lincoln Avenue. As I walked up the sidewalk, I touched the balustrade on the steps and felt a love for that house that was visceral and complete. I had made a home for my children, and they would remember it even if we only stayed for one more night.

We were all tired and our beds were still there, made up just as we had left them. The girls climbed into theirs and were asleep in minutes. Dan could not sleep and neither could I. With the quilt my grandmother had made for me, I covered him and sat by his bed. We talked long into the night. He, nearly fourteen, was trying to understand the inscrutable ways of adults in their relationships. He was also concerned about what we would do next. We could see that the house and yard had not been tended all summer and we vowed to each other, no matter what, we would put the yard in order in the morning. About daybreak, we both went to sleep for a few hours.

No morning could have been more beautiful than that one, our first day back. The sun was shining, and it was not too hot, as an August day in Pennsylvania can be. We got up, ate cold cereal and milk which Charles' mother had thoughtfully left in the kitchen. Then we tackled the yard. A summer's growth in Pennsylvania is considerable.

I called the Bartletts, of course, right away. Bill was at work; Marianne and a few of their children came over with tools and helped us for as long as they could. About 11 in the morning, we were taking a break when to our surprise, Charles drove up in front of the house. He was somewhat awkward and stuttered a bit when he told me that he had decided to give the house to me and the children. I was shocked and overwhelmed! He wished us well and drove away.

I immediately went in the house and phoned my lawyer, Chauncy Howell, who was elated at the news, and promptly drove out to the cement plant where Charles was comptroller. He had the papers ready for signature and they completed the transaction over Charles' lunch break.

I got the call from Chauncy that the deal was complete. I was the sole owner of the house. I felt a surge of power and confidence. I phoned the school district where I had done student teaching. Because it was summer time the secretarial staff was not there. The principal answered my call. I said, "This is Dolores Lichtenwalner."

Before I could say anymore, he remembered that I had been a student teacher there, and offered me a job teaching first grade, starting in two weeks.

What an amazing morning! The day before I had been an unemployed, single parent without a home. Before one in the afternoon I became a homeowner, an employed teacher and a confidant mother of three. Life was good...it was better than good.

CHAPTER 22

Life Goes On

Ah, yes, a new life...a divorced woman, mother of three, a home-owner and a teacher. I tried to be confidant and assured about my situation but did not succeed. I would not walk to the Post Office or to the little store in Stockertown. I did not want to see anyone to whom I would have to explain or make excuses. I did not want to see pity in their eyes, nor accusations, nor questions. Every weekday morning I would go to my car parked in big barn behind the house, drive to the school in Nazareth where I was teaching first grade, shop after school in Nazareth where not everyone knew me. I would return the car to the barn and stay in the house until the next day. Saturdays I took the teenagers to where they needed to be, to shop in Easton, and return home, staying in until Sunday morning, when the children and I went to church. I did not feel that uneasiness at Trinity. They were a forgiving and loving gathering of kindred souls.

I saw the Bartletts several times a week. I drove to their house at night or on a Saturday or Sunday afternoon, although it was only a block and a half away. I could have easily walked, but by driving I did not take the chance of seeing a neighbor or someone with whom I might have to make eye contact. My visits with Bill and Marianne saved my dignity, self-esteem, sanity and my soul.

About the middle of October, Charles came over and said he thought we should try again, try to save our marriage. I don't recall that he ever said why he thought that or why he wanted to try again. I was willing to give it another chance and felt that I could put my whole heart and soul into it. However, it was flat from the first day and never took on any substance, joy or authenticity. It was a charade; I felt he was pining for *the good woman*, the one he said on that cold December night nearly a year before, that he wasn't going to give up. We didn't last through the Christmas Season.

One night a couple of weeks into December there was the Festival of Lights and Carols at the church. The service touched the children and me deeply. We tried to keep our candles burning as long as possible. One of the children managed to keep their candle burning until we got home and sat it down on the dining room table. While we were taking off our winter clothes it burned down making a charred mark on the table. In the past this would have enraged Charles and he would have upbraided the culprit and sent them to bed.

This time there was a different feeling about it from every angle...we were free from the fear of temper tantrums and put-downs. Also, Charles was free from any commitment to this house, its furnishings or inhabitants. He had an agenda quite different from preserving any aspect of his life with us. He flatly said, "I won't be staying here anymore," and left the house. It was as though a pall had been lifted and oppression was over. That life was gone, dead; we were willing to allow it to leave our presence. Thereafter we always looked at the burned mark on the table as a symbol of our deliverance. It was unspoken, but we all knew.

The stigma of being a divorced woman disappeared not long after that. It was a Saturday night and the Bartletts were having a party. Of course Marianne entreated me to attend but I declined. It was so difficult to be there. I felt the men were sorry for me; that is, those who weren't predatory, and the women saw me as a threat. I told Marianne that I had a good book and wanted to stay home and read it. That was true. I was reading *The Secret of Santa Vittoria* by Robert Crichton.

As the evening went on, I forced myself to persist in reading although the feeling of being left out of the party sneakily crept in. Soon I was feeling quite sorry for myself; that feeling fueled by the pervasive disappointment in how my life was turning out. Throughout my childhood, when I had lived with so many other families and looked for what was good and what was not good in their family life and relationships, I devised a plan for my life. I would find a husband, have children and make a home for them that would last all of their lives and after they were grown my husband and I would grow old together "till death do us part." I was going to be one of the few in my family not to have a divorce, no way, not ever! It was a personal oath. Now I had failed my oath to myself.

However, in spite of my self-pity and disgust, I began to get into the book; it was very well written and absorbing. The theme of the book was saving the precious wine from the German forces of WWII who were about to take over a small village in the mountain wine region of Italy. The wine was the sub-hero of the book. Suddenly, it occurred to me that there was some wine left on the shelves of the entry way into the cellar. It was wine left over from the party times a few years before. To my pleasure and surprise I found a bottle of Italian wine, uncorked it, poured myself a hearty glass. I read on and each time I took a break I had another glass of wine.

At some point there was a shift in my perception. I started thinking about divorce itself and the many divorces in my family. I began to think about divorce objectively rather than subjectively. I began to think of all the marriages in my family that had ended in divorce...some before I was born. For example, my great grandparents must have obtained one of the first divorces permitted in the Territories. After that my maternal grandparents, my parents, my sisters, even my highly esteemed cousin Dorothy had been divorced. Then I thought of the condition of the marriages before the divorce and of how the women had succeeded afterwards. How beaten-down they would have been if divorce were not possible. Each of those women had made their way in the world...had made great contributions to the world, had maintained their dignity. I was proud of them, each and every one! They had been set free! Most of them had been given second chances at marriage which turned out to be loving life-time partnerships. .

By the time I finished the book and most of the bottle of wine, I was ready to start a movement, lead a parade, carry a banner and wear a badge, extolling the Institution of Divorce. I was feeling exultant, not beaten down. I was free!

That feeling sustained me and carried me through that sad time of my life. Later my thoughts about divorce extended with less strident gender specification. I met and knew many men who also had been set free and lived more authentic lives after a divorce than they were living in a disappointing, hostile marriage. I could applaud them for their courage in going on with their lives. I also knew and had great relationships with many couples who honored the institution of marriage through better and worse. Nevertheless, I needed that night to release me from the shame and disappointment of the failed marriage of which I was a participant.

My new feeling of freedom, however, did not help in covering living expenses. I was foundering, financially on a first-year teacher salary. There were dental bills, school lunches and other school fees, groceries, utilities, insurances, property taxes; all the usual expenses of running a family and home ownership.

The biggest blow came with the cost of heating the big old Victorian house. Charles left without paying the coal company. They would not deliver another load until the balance was paid. It was nearly the end of the month and I would pay it when I received my check, but the bitter cold came sooner than the check. With a week to go before pay day, the temperature was going down through the day and by nighttime had dipped below zero, and we had no coal. As evening came we huddled in our coats in the innermost room of the house, and we shivered. I called the Bartletts and they said to come on over. What were four more bodies in their family, now a family of ten?

Before we left for their house I could see that Danny was struggling mightily with a great problem. He haltingly told me he had a semi-solution to our problem. He was active in the Scouts and they were always selling something for the benefit of the local troop or the larger organization. Danny said, "I have thirty dollars hidden in that guitar hanging on the wall. It's Scout money but if you are absolutely sure you can replace it by next week I can buy a load of coal tomorrow."

I could see how he was struggling with the integrity of what he was doing. Weighing the gravity of breaking his oath as treasurer of the troop, against the duty of keeping his family warm and together in their own house. We stayed that night with the Bartletts and the next day used his money to buy a month's supply of coal. I paid him back immediately upon receiving my check. It was a sobering event for me and I know it was character-forming for Dan. He was always called Dan after that event. "Danny" was the child of the past. Dan, the man, had emerged. He asked me to show him on paper just where our money went. He was surprised that so much of it went for things, he said, "Things that you can't even see!" Things such as insurance and taxes, were astonishing to him and he had never realized that we paid for water and electricity and phone service.

Marcie, now sixteen had found a job cleaning a house for a family in Nazareth. That job provided her spending money and she spent it wisely. She was always well dressed and groomed and she asked me for very little in the way of cosmetics or entertainment. Dan, at fourteen, did odd jobs in Stockertown as well as his trapping business. He and his friend Bobby Reuss had learned to trap as an extension of Scouting. How they learned the marketing of the furs was something of which I knew nothing. Dan was active in the Rod & Gun Club of Stockertown, where one of the older members, Mr. Messinger, took Dan under his wing and taught him many of the intricacies of fishing, hunting, trapping, forestry, and wildlife management. Mr. Messinger had three beautiful daughters and had always yearned for a son. Dan was just the kind of son he wanted. Mr. Messinger was one of the great surrogate fathers to my son.

In spite of my endeavors and those of my children, I needed additional income to meet expenses. As so often happened, the Bartletts had a solution for me...or so we thought. Marianne's sister, Jane, was recently divorced and was moving from upstate New York to Stockertown for financial and emotional support from Bill and Marianne. Jane had five children, the oldest of whom was about the same age as Dan, and the youngest five months old. They moved in with Bill and Marianne and within days it became apparent that fifteen children and three parents in one house were stretching the limits, both of the capacity of their big old Victorian house and the patience of the adults; even saints like the Bartletts had human limits to their largesse.

It seemed that moving in with me was a solution for Jane and her children. We figured that with my salary and her child support we could make it financially. I was happy to have another adult in a similar situation with whom I could talk and share some of my anxieties and ideas. Jane was intelligent, educated and well informed. She brought books and music in the house that stretched my repertoire. Our house now was often filled with the music of Beethoven's 9th Symphony or something comparable. Together Jane and I read and discussed the *Myth of Sisyphus*. I really liked Jane and we started out with excellent compatibility.

However, after a few months, Jane began to feel stifled being at home all day, while I was out in the world, having the exciting adventures of teaching first grade. I did enjoy the teaching experience even though I knew I was not going to be a life-long teacher like my mother, Aunt Mary and Rosie. This was a pathway to something else. One particular day of teaching was more exciting than I ever thought it would be and perhaps that was when Jane decided she should be having more life to her days.

I came home that evening really enthusiastic over what had happened.

It had been a field trip for the first graders to the Trexler Park Game Preserve in Schnecksville about fifteen miles west of our school in Nazareth. The teacher of the other first grade class of thirty students, same size as mine, called in ill and I was responsible for all sixty children that day. I felt some anxiety but had no choice in the matter. The bus was there; the children were excited, so off we went early in the morning. We arrived at the Preserve and the children, who had been primed for seeing the buffalo, all queried, "Where are the buffalo...we want to see the buffalo! The attendant in charge told us they were down in the gully just beyond that little rise of land pointing to the south of us. She said they were down there because they had not been fed yet and we could go look at them if we wanted. Off we went to the little rise of land, the children about two feet ahead of me. When we got to the edge of the rise, the buffalo in unison, about fifteen of them, raised their heads and started walking toward us, probably believing we were there to feed them. Very shortly they were trotting and the distance between my children and the buffalo was diminishing much too quickly for comfort. I could see that we could not get to the shelter before those huge creatures were upon us. Strictly by instinct, I faced the children and in a very loud commanding voice bellowed out, "Stop! Stop right where you are!" The children came to a slow stop and with their stopping, so did the buffalo. I was shaken but also exhilarated. In all my years of living in the West I had never encountered and triumphed over a herd of buffalo. In the gift shop I purchased a stencil set of several buffalo and when we go back to the school that afternoon, we wrote "experience stories," my favorite teaching tool, using the stencils to illustrate them. The stories were wonderful and I was quite excited when I got home that night.

Jane had apparently had a hard day at home with the children. She was not amused by my story. The very next day she got a job at Gracedale, the county home for the aged, where she was a night nurse. She thought she could get enough rest at home in the daytime while the younger children took their naps and the older ones were at school. After about two months of this regime she was taking pills to help her stay awake, and pills to help her go to sleep. It was a dangerous situation. When I tried to talk to her, her judgment was clouded by the chemicals in her body, and she became quite angry with me. She wanted to move but had nowhere to go.

In stepped my rescuer, Chauncy Howell. He owned a house in Martin's Creek, that he had been trying to rent. He rented it to Jane for a very small amount, as a favor to me, and we got her moved in the spring. At first she had a hard time getting her life back in order and held me responsible for her difficulty. Later that summer we reconciled and she was satisfied to be living in Martin's Creek. It was near Stockertown, so she could maintain her relationship with Marianne. Bill could help her with household maintenance problems. Her children were thriving in that little town. Her boys were involved in baseball, were very good at it and were becoming small town heroes. It was a good place for her and her children to live.

When spring arrived the heating expenses diminished and I could make it on my teacher's salary until the end of the school year. However, summer was coming and there was no teacher salary in the summer. I found work at the Allentown State Hospital (ASH). It was fascinating work and more in line with my motivated skills. It was an extension of my education, being with, and understanding people afflicted with mental disorders and deficiencies.

The first few days at ASH were spent in orientation, where I learned one important lesson...that the "mentally ill are not ill all the time." There are times when they seem completely normal. I found they have insight into their own disorder. However, when their illness manifests itself one must be prepared to handle it, to avoid mental or physical damage to oneself or the patient.

Another phenomenon I witnessed that summer was the impact of the new tranquilizer drugs that had recently come into use. My first month there was before tranquilizers were used. At the onset of the full moon there was constant moaning, screaming and general unrest among the patients which continued for about three days. The drug, Mellaril, was instituted the second month I was there and the entire grounds of the hospital seemed eerily silent as I walked up the path to the entrance on the morning after the full moon. Eerie, because the clamor was expected, but also satisfying with the realization that the patients were no longer anguished by their demons being set in motion by the lunar force.

As that summer went on my daughters were spending a few days a week at Saylor Lake with their grandparents. Actually, their grandparents were in their cottage at Saylor Lake and Marcie and Lorie were spending their days at the lakefront with an abundance of other young people.

They were becoming beautiful young women and I was concerned about them and my ability to keep them safe from the young men who were naturally drawn to them. Marcie was quite circumspect, and I did not worry about her very much. Lorie, on the other hand was more adventuresome. My fear for her was great. It took a serious measure of fear to prompt me to call Charles and ask if he might take her for the school year. He said he would have to talk with his wife. That was the first time I had talked with him for a year and to hear him say, "his wife" was a jolt for me.

Charles called me back the next day and said that they would take her but I would have to make sure she had a proper wardrobe, that her teeth were taken care of and I would have to pay them room and board. His conditional acceptance took my breath away! The audacity of it! I said vehemently, "She is not a commodity, she is my daughter. Forget I ever asked you!"

We got through the summer safely. Shortly before school started, Dan got a letter from the Athletic Department of the high school, asking him to try out for the football team. He thought he should try it; so on a hot August morning he caught a ride to Nazareth for the first practice. I was working in the garden when, a few hours later, I saw him come limping into the yard, tired, hot and puzzled. He said, with great earnestness, "Why would anyone want to spend a beautiful summer day knocking down their friends when they could be out fishing in the woods!" I was pleased and amused at his assessment. He never went out for another sport, and became the best fisherman on the Bushkill Creek.

A couple of weeks into her sophomore year it became clear that Lorie needed an educational setting other than a public high school. Perhaps she needed to be a person of her own, not the younger sister of two older siblings who were well known and well liked. She refused to ride the school bus so I drove her to school. However, I would drop her off at the front of the school and she would go out the back and I would get a call from the office.

I called Notre Dame, the Catholic High school in the area, and arranged for her to attend there. The school was about twelve miles away and in the direction of the school where I was now teaching a special education class in Easton.

The first week was difficult for Lorie at Notre Dame but she was taken under the wing of one nun who really liked her and taught her to love learning. After that she seemed to like going to Notre Dame. The commute was healing for both of us. We had adventures, on the way...adventures connected with driving in the winter on small country roads; such as livestock on the highway, and car problems. We talked on the way to and from school. We sang songs. We became good friends. She did well at Notre Dame and returned to Nazareth for her junior and senior year of High School. She did well there as well, excelling in music and art.

Marcie was a stellar student, a good worker outside of school, and active in the church. She always entered her work in the art shows and always won ribbons. She was Homecoming Queen in her senior year. Some parts of her competence were a burden to her. Later she said that she felt like the oldest child in the universe… always asked to baby sit…always expected to lead the others out of trouble and always to set an example for the younger children, both in our family and among our friends. She provided emotional support for me and I will be grateful to her for that forever.

During that time we began to have Sunday dinners, early in the afternoon, before the sings at the Bartletts, where I always went after dinner. The dinners were attended by my children and several of their friends and friends of their friends. Usually there were about a dozen at the table. We always had spaghetti, Italian bread and salad…sometimes dessert. After dinner we would sit around the table and talk for a long time about many things…current trends in music and clothing and often just the way of the world. I loved those dinners and so did my children and their friends. I was given the nickname *SKAM*. They said it meant *Sweet Kind And Motherly*.

This was a time when many teenagers were estranged from their parents. It was the Age of Aquarius, long hair on the boys, short skirts on the girls, the Beatles, and the beginning of Rock 'n Roll and drugs….the late sixties and early seventies. I embraced that culture, from the fringes. I did not fully enter into, but tried to understand it. I did not want to become estranged from my teenagers and I saw value in the ways they were becoming disaffected with the mainstream culture of the 60's and early 70's. I, too, protested the war in Viet Nam. The conventional culture didn't work for me, either.

Folk music was one of the ways that I entered into the new age. I took my teenagers and several others to folk festivals whenever I could. The first time I took them, was after Bill and Marianne had attended the Old Songs Festival in upstate NY. It sounded so wonderful! I looked for one I could afford that was within driving distance and it was the Philly Folk Festival just north of Philadelphia. I had to talk my children into it, as they thought it was "Square"... something only old people did. However, we reached the stage area, just as Joanie Mitchell was singing *Clouds,* the first time most people had heard it. She was followed by Janis Ian who had just enough punk and sass to let my children know it was not so square after all. Also at that festival were the Fairfax Convention. My children and their friends were hooked. We attended the Philly Folk Festival several times, the Union Grove Fiddlers Festival in South Carolina, and small festivals in Virginia and West Virginia. We met musicians from all over the country. Many slept in our house, played in our barn. Music was always there.

We were so busy and active that the chronology of events is blurred in my memory, but somewhere in there, on a Saturday afternoon, I got a phone call that surprised me. Before I go on, I must go back and fill in the prelude to this phone call.

About a year before the divorce, on a Sunday morning in October, I arrived at church an hour early as daylight savings time had ended and I forgot to adjust my clock. It was fortuitous because that morning I met Mary Wichie, a woman who was to become very important in my life. She also had forgotten to turn her clock back and I found her in a Sunday School room washing the windows. She said, "I might as well be doing something, rather than wasting my time. Not many can do this without standing on a stool." Then I noticed that she stood about a foot taller than I. She was a beautiful, stately and well-spoken woman, who I immediately knew, would become one of my best friends. By the time church started that morning, we were well connected. The next week I visited her in her home where she was mother to four little children and was into the pregnancy of her fifth. She was married to Tom, an engineer and a Catholic, to whom she was not only married, but with whom she was passionately in love. They were full participants in many of the Sunday sings at either our house or Bartletts. I came to know Mary's whole family including her brother, Jim Mehring, who was the best guitarist of all in the group, and had a wonderful singing voice.

Back to my story of the phone call on the aforementioned Saturday afternoon, a few years after meeting Tom and Mary and her brother Jim. On the phone was Mary's brother, Jim, asking me if he could take me to dinner at the Candlelight Inn. I stuttered and stammered; I was nonplussed. Gathering my wits, I told him I would like that very much but had to arrange for my children to get to the football game and home again. One of the girls was standing at the landing of the steps and had heard my end of the conversation. She said, "We can get there and back by ourselves. Mom, say Yes!" I accepted the invitation.

When I hung up the phone I realized Charles was sitting in the next room. He, too, had heard the conversation. This was unusual because it was the only time since he had left the house nearly a year before, that he had ever come back into it when I was there. He made a sarcastic remark about my new boyfriend, and somehow, I felt a little embarrassed, but I said nothing, nothing at all. Charles left the house with an attitude of disdain. I let go of my feeling of embarrassment and realized that I was free from a reaction to his judgement about me. I really could let it go and start preparing for the evening. My children were excited and happy that I was going out on a date! The girls found something for me to wear...one of Marcie's pink party dresses. Dan said, "Now, Mom, when a man takes you to a place like that, do not order a hamburger!"

It felt strange, not awkward or uncomfortable; just strange to be going on a date at this stage of my life. I had not thought about dating or even interacting with a man. I had been so busy just getting by that there was no time or energy to devote to that kind of thinking. Driving to the restaurant, I realized I did not even know how to spell Jim's last name, and yet, here we were, conversing easily as if we had known each other for years. Jim had recently been delivered divorce papers by his wife and he wanted to get on with life. Jim was an elegant man, with perfect manners and an intelligent conversationalist. He had been an Episcopal priest and he took it for granted that a college education was normal. He had graduated from Harvard Divinity School. I smiled to myself when he told me that, because when Charles and I were having one of our last conversations he said, "You probably will want a man from Harvard or Yale for your next husband." A strangely predictive remark.

Soon Jim became a regular visitor to our house, and took me to places I never dreamed I would be going. He bought me gifts of pearls, perfume, flowers, music albums. He got along well with the children, and they liked him. Of course, he fit right in with the music Sundays. He was a great addition to the group. He took me to Maryland to meet his parents, who lived in a mansion on Old Lawyers Hill, Ellicott City Maryland. Furthermore, he went to church with me every Sunday! I must admit, I was bowled over by his attention and regard. He seemed to be a perfect man and he seemed to love me!

I met his stepdaughter, Julie, who was in the age group of my children. She visited us for a week at our house. She was a sensitive, nervous young person and was not compatible with my children, but it did not seem like a huge barrier to the relationship between Jim and me. I got along well with Julie but was not going to invite her to live with us...not that she ever asked.

Soon it was apparent that Jim and I would get married. We talked about it very seriously. The first important thing we talked about and agreed upon was that we did not want more children.

Raising three teenagers, and paying support for Julie, would be quite enough. Next we decided that we wanted to have a long healthy life together so we decided to stop smoking. I had started smoking again when he and I started dating. It seemed so companionable. Jim had diabetes and smoking was one of the worst things he could do, if he wanted to live a long and healthy life. Part of our courtship was going to SmokeEnders. When we finished the program, we vowed to each other that we would never smoke again. We used the money we saved by not buying cigarettes to pay for our honeymoon in San Francisco.

Jim courted me for about two years before we were married by Judge Palmer in the Chapel of Trinity Episcopal Church. The Episcopal Church did not allow divorced people to be married in the church but our interim rector, procured a dispensation from the Bishop and we were allowed to use the chapel. I remember nothing of the service. It was a blur to me. Alice Bower, a teacher with whom I worked, hosted a tasteful reception in the hospitality hall of the church. My children and several of their friends attended. Alice had involved them in the preparation of the reception. She knew how important it was that they felt part of my ongoing life.

When Jim and I left the church and went to our car we found it festooned with crepe paper and a sign that said, "Just Married." There were tin cans tied to the bumpers for a noisy celebration when we were to drive away from the church. As we approached the car Jim was appalled. I was disturbed that he was appalled. I knew this was the teenagers' way of celebrating our marriage. Nevertheless, at Jim's insistence, they cleaned the car before Jim and I drove off to the airport, bound for San Francisco. We had ample champagne on the flight causing me to forget all about the disturbance of the decorated car.

It was a great honeymoon. We did all the touristy things one can do in beautiful San Francisco for the next few days. We stayed with Rosie and Allen in Santa Clara and had a good time with them. Then the honeymoon was over and we boarded the flight from San Francisco back to the ABE Airport. Bill and Marianne picked us up at the airport and took us home.

Home, of course, was my house in Stockertown. The dissonance began right away. As we were on our way home from the airport, Jim asked Bill to stop so he could pick up a six pack of beer. At home he sat in front of the TV, which had seldom been turned on, and he turned it up loudly and watched until the six pack was gone. OK, I can get over that, I told myself. The truth is that I never quite got over my distaste of having him come to bed drunkenly night after night, year after year. I detest the smell of stale beer breath.

Less than a month went by before the evening he came home and I could smell cigarette smoke on his breath and his clothing. At first he denied it, but finally, sheepishly admitted that he could not resist. Everyone at work smoked and the temptation was too great. I felt disappointment and betrayal. OK. I can get over it, I told myself. There are worse things. I certainly tried to let them go.

We, at my persuasion, went to marriage counseling within six weeks of the wedding ceremony. There were four other couples in the group to which we were assigned. Jim sat in a corner and seldom said a word. I gave it up after about six sessions, and thought I would work it out some other way. He was a gentle, kind man and my children got along well with him. I loved his sisters, Mary Wichie and Sally Burgoyne, and his sister-in-law, Kim Mehring. There were so many reasons to stay with it and try to make it work.

Both he and I were satisfied and content that our financial situation would be greatly improved with our combined incomes. However, that satisfaction was short-lived. Within two months a blow shattered our financial contentment. He was notified that his ex-wife, the mother of Julie, was suing him for additional child support.

With great diligence he prepared a detailed account of his financial situation to present at the appeal hearing, which was to be in two weeks.

The day we arrived in court with his very expensive Princeton lawyer, we found the courtroom packed with people presenting similar cases. We were about thirtieth on the list of hearings. There was a new judge hearing the cases and the outlook was not looking good for any of the fathers in court that day. We sat through seemingly endless stories of the dissolution of marriages and the financial and emotional turmoil that ensues. At five o'clock the judge said he could hear more cases but there would be no court reporter so they would be "off the books"...whatever that meant. Jim was paying the lawyer by the hour and had spent so much that he was willing to go on with the hearing, even if it was "off the books." His hearing did not go well. The judge would not even look at the detailed account Jim had presented. The judge asked to see the "new woman" in Jim's life, which I felt to be very inappropriate. He called me to appear at the judge's desk. He looked at me salaciously and said, "Not bad!"

It was embarrassing and demeaning. The judge gave Jim's ex-wife everything she asked for. The new child support payment would consume his entire take-home pay and it was to continue as long as Julie was in school; that included college and any post graduate studies! We left the court in stunned disbelief. On the way home we stopped at a drive-in movie where "The Godfather" was playing. As we watched the movie, we both felt that justice was served better by the Mafia than in court that day. I was very sad as now I would be supporting one more person, Jim. I asked myself why I never seemed to get out of financial worry. By now, with my life experience, I knew I could deal with it, but I did not like it... not one bit!

Again, unsuspected deliverance was just around the corner; we spent only one month living with the angst of the child support decree. Then Jim got a sad call from his ex-wife. Julie had dropped out of school and ran away with a young man that she intended to marry. I felt sad for Julie, starting out her adult life on such an unpropitious track but I have to admit that it was a relief for me... ah! Yes, The Process again.

One glorious Sunday morning, we were meeting the new Rector, Jim Gill, at Trinity church. He gave a marvelous sermon and we were certain the committee looking for a priest for Trinity had made a good choice. After church we attended the reception of the new Rector, when I caught sight of a woman I knew I wanted to meet. I introduced myself and was a bit surprised that she was married to the new Rector. She was nothing like what most spouses of Rectors, Ministers, Pastors or Reverends were at that time in the culture of the church.

This woman, Kay Gill, was distinctly her own person. She wore sneakers, blue jeans and a plaid shirt. She had lively blue eyes, short hair and her demeanor was of depth, intelligence, integrity and humor. When we had exchanged but three sentences we both sensed that we had met a soul mate. Her children were flitting about the room and she gathered the younger two up and told me their names; Jamie and Christie.

My daughter, Lorie was nearby and she was enchanted with them and asked if she could take them home with her. Kay said, "Sure, if you want to. But, be prepared, they might be a handful!" We took them home and Lorie played with them at the school playground down the street from our house. Kay, following our directions, came to get them later in the afternoon, bringing her daughter Laura, to meet us. That too, was love right from the beginning.

As the children returned from the playground, we sat down at the dining room table, each had a beer and we began to talk. How we found things to talk about, real things, not small talk, for the next two hours is a wonderment to me. We never, as long as we were both alive, ever ran out of things to talk about. My life and that of my children were enriched in ways that words could never convey by my friendship with Kay, Jim Gill and their three children. My life became larger and richer with love, understanding, companionship, spirituality and community.

CHAPTER 23

The Golden Years

That day in early June of 1968 was positively intoxicating with its vibrancy and sense that all was right in the world! The trees were at their finest in their early spring greenery. My eyes were bathed with beauty at the abundance of flowers in bloom. My children were all set for the summer; Lorie working at the Jaycees Camp for Handicapped Children; Dan at a gas station in Allentown and Marcie was going to summer classes at Kutztown State College. The newly formed friendship with Kay Gill had lent a zest to my life; with her I had conversations of deep meaning interspersed with unabashed laughter. A week before this pivotal day, I had come to the end of a difficult school year, dealing with pre-adolescent emotionally disturbed boys. I was vaguely looking for work through the summer, because even though money was not quite such an intense problem now, I wanted to have my own earnings. I never felt comfortable asking Jim for money.

This particular morning I had a meeting with Jim Gill in his capacity as priest of Trinity church. He made it a point to meet every person in the church on a one to one basis, and it was my time to visit with him. We already had made a good connection through the friendship flourishing between Kay and me but Jim and I not as yet had a private pastoral visit. We met at a small quiet restaurant on a side street in downtown Easton. As we talked we got into discussing our worries about the drug problem that was developing in Easton. As the conversation developed, we wondered what could be done about it and could we, as individuals do something constructive. The ideas seemed to take on a life of their own and soon we were verbally implementing a drop-in center where teens and young adults could come in for conversation and guidance, especially about drug and alcohol use.

Marijuana had been on the streets of Easton less than a year. Heroin and other drugs were coming in with the returning veterans from Viet Nam. Many of the servicemen became addicted during their time in the war. Some of the children of professional people in Easton were on the fringes of the drug culture.

Jim Gill and I quickly established a Board of Directors: two attorneys, two college psychology professors, two physicians, a journalist and three parents. We rented an abandoned store on one of the busy downtown streets of Easton and in a very short time had established The Drop-In Center. I was the director!

There were no certified drug counselors then. The problem was too new. I attended a gathering in Philadelphia of people like myself, interested professionals learning how to solve the disasters developing around this exploding problem. People I met at that gathering formed a loosely connected support group, sharing any new techniques or ideas we gleaned from our experiences with this new drug culture.

The Drop-in Center was an instant success. Young people did come in. Middle-aged people came in. Even old people came in for help. One of the first clients, which established the credibility of the Center to the young people, was brought in by Jeff Vitelli. Jeff was the son of Tinker and Jim Vitelli, a highly respected college professor in Easton. The young waif Jeff brought in was a runaway girl from the Easton Children's Home. What I did was decidedly unprofessional for a social worker, but it established me as a person who was on the side of the youth. After talking with the head of the Children's Home, I gained permission to take the girl home with me.

That action constituted a very important part in my learning the intricacies of becoming a social worker. I learned that never, never, under any circumstances should a social worker get personally involved with a client. The young girl I brought home instantly fell in love with Dan and we spent much of the summer getting dis-involved with her.

The Drop-In Center was developing a good referral bank and through it we found a good foster home for the orphan girl. Gradually my family and I were freed from the entanglements that ensued from my misjudgment. After that, I became more objective in handling cases.

Word spread quickly among the youth of Easton that the Drop-In Center was a place where they would be listened to and heard. The volume of cases would have been overwhelming if not for the competent and helpful volunteers. There were several college students and professors. Sidney Watt, wife of Dr. Watt, head of the English Department at Lafayette became my co-counselor. Her presence was helpful in establishing the credibility of the center to the establishment community of Easton. That was important in that it made it easier to raise funds for running the center. Sidney also became one of the wise and loyal friends who has shown up in my life when I needed her most. After the Drop-in days she and I would meet for coffee and talk for hours. This went on for a few years until she succumbed to cancer.

I had read, digested and incorporated the teachings of Carl Rogers, from his books, especially *On Becoming a Person* and *Client Centered Counseling*. His philosophy was at the core of our trainings and staff meetings. Many of the young people who came in and received this sort of training became staff members. We had staff meetings and trainings that were so much fun that people were knocking on the door to get in, and I had to hold a few back. We were all learning as we went along. We dealt with bad trips on hallucinogens, runaways, severe alcoholism, heroin addictions, and returning veterans with Post Traumatic Stress Disorders, before it had an official name. We made presentations at assemblies in high schools, taking with us recovering addicts and alcoholics. We obtained excellent publicity as DeWitt Scott, the editor of the Easton Express took an interest in our work.

The Drop-In Center was the most satisfying work I had ever done. It went on for two years until it was taken over by Mental Health and Mental Retardation, (MHMR), a County Bureau. They said they had no place for me at MHMR because I did not have a degree in social work.

Very disappointed at losing my part in the Drop-In Center, I went back to teaching Special Education in Easton. The year looked as though it would be just as hard or worse than the year before. About a month after school opened, on a day when I wondered if I could get through the year, I got a phone call from Nancy Haley at the County Children's Bureau, asking me to be their social worker in the Children's Placement Unit. There was an increasing volume in their cases involving drugs and addictions, and no one in the agency had experience in this field. She had been following the stories about the Drop-in-Center in the newspaper. I told Nancy that I was honored to be asked, but I was under contract with the School board to teach that year and furthermore, I did not have a degree in social work. She told me that if I wanted the job, I could resign from the school contract with a sixty day notice and not to worry about the social work part of it. I could take the Civil Service Social Work exam. If I passed, I was a social worker. She said I should take the test which was being offered very soon. I took the test and passed with a high score, and Behold! I was a Social Worker within two weeks! I was elated! Exactly what I wanted to be before I started college seven years earlier.

I gave my resignation to the school district and expected to wait sixty days to fulfill the terms of my contract. I accepted the fact that I would work there two more months when another deliverance occurred. At school we were at an in-service program whereby a young presenter was doing a program on handling difficult adolescents in a class room. At the end of the day this young man asked our supervisor if he could apply for a job in our district. He was hired immediately for my teaching job. I was released from my contract and went to work for the Northampton County Children's Bureau as a social worker. I worked there for two years. Incidentally, the young man who took over my job lasted a day and a half, before walking out abruptly. I do not know how the school district solved it but by then I was immersed in solving other problems, at which I could succeed.

It was during that time that I was invited to join the book group. It was made up of women from the country around Stockertown and Easton, who had been meeting and reading books for several years. I had wanted to join but had been turned down twice before the final acceptance. The first rejection was because I was a working woman and the others were housewives and mothers. They were rural women who baked their own bread, and were dedicated to living simply. The second time I was rejected was because I was divorced. Marianne had been reading with them for several years and never ceased to lobby for my inclusion in the group. Each time someone in the group moved or dropped out for any reason, Marianne would try to have them consider me for membership.

Finally, when the person most resistant to my inclusion moved away, Marianne simply took me to the group with her. I was enthusiastically received and stayed connected to the group no matter where I moved or what I did. Those members became a close sisterhood for me. They accepted me wholeheartedly despite all of my nonconformity. Friends for life from that group were Doodie Genthner, Faith Shireman, Jo Lysholdt, Carmen McCray, Kay Gill, Mary Wichie, Loy Tolson-Jones and Anne Hogenboom.

Book group prompted us to think and consider deep philosophical issue. When I started with the group we were reading Martin Buber's, *I and Thou*. Through the years we read complex books that opened me up to a part of myself that had been dormant since my awakening on the prairie thirty years before. I have learned as much, probably more, from book group than I learned from any college course.

During these years Marcie, Dan and Lorie, the chorus of my life's song, finished high school and commenced with their young adult lives.

Marcie went to Kutztown State College, where art was the specialty and was her forte. She worked hard, both academically and in the cafeteria to augment her tuition. She managed the Folk Music Center where music was performed every weekend. Everybody loved her, which included the people who rented her a room in their home, the staff of the cafeteria, and her college-mates and Dave Van Ronk who came to perform at the coffee house. She was adorable and she was on fire, on fire for everything!

However, she entered Kutztown when big, graphic art was the rage. Her artwork was fine and detailed and not appreciated there. That was a major disappointment for her. After two years of burning like a glorious candle, she burned out and tearfully phoned me to come and get her. Very sadly she returned home. It was not long before she regained her momentum and went to work as a tour guide at Martin Guitar Factory in Nazareth. She was an excellent tour guide and it fit well with her experience in folk music.

Marcie organized the first big folk music party at our home and in our barn in Stockertown. It happened between Christmas and New Year's. A few days before Christmas she asked if she could have a party two days after the big day. I said, "Yes, of course. I'd like to meet your friends." It was a busy time of the year and I was getting ready for the holiday. Not until the night after Christmas did I put together bits of conversations I had heard between my teenagers. "Let's be sure to ask Pete and his group, and Twig will bring Steve, for sure."

I asked, "How many do you think might be here at the party tomorrow night?" Marcie answered, "Oh, probably no more than a hundred."

I got little sleep that night. How would I handle a hundred teenagers and college students. I woke up in the night and wanted to go out and turn the road signs pointing to Stockertown in the opposite direction. I didn't do that but I did worry quite a bit the next day. It appeared that they had preparations well underway. Marcie had been managing the folk music center at the college and was undaunted by the numbers. So the party happened. I was nervously walking from room to room and discovered a group of young people playing all manner of acoustic instruments, and singing and doing absolutely nothing else that would or should worry me. I called Bill and Marianne to come over and join the party. It was a gloriously wonderful party and ushered in many more over the years of their teenage into adulthood.

After that first one, there were several more, through the years. Up to a hundred people would come and play music throughout a weekend. We heard wonderful music for the price of a big pot of barbecue. Years later I met a musician at the Newport Folk Festival and thought I recognized him. I asked him if he played music in my barn in Stockertown. He said, "SKAM, everybody played music in your barn!"

While working at Martin Guitar, Marcie met and fell in love with Charlie Reusch. One more Charles in our life! He was a twenty-one year old Viet Nam veteran. He had not been back from Nam very long and was eager to get on with his life. He believed there were better opportunities in Long Beach California to pursue a career than in the Lehigh Valley of Pennsylvania. He went there to try it out. It was not long before Marcie was on her way to California to marry him.

Her leaving was wrenching for me...the first of my children to leave home. The night of her departure she and I went out for dinner at The White House, a Chinese restaurant in downtown Easton. It was an enterprise in an old Victorian building, owned and operated by an Irish woman and her Chinese husband. After bringing your food, which was of high quality, the waitress, who was also the owner, would abandon you for the rest of the evening. You got up to get more tea, or whatever you needed. Sometimes finding someone to whom you would pay for your meal and service was difficult. It was a good place for us that night. Marcie and I sat there and drank tea until midnight, neither of us wanting to say good-bye. It was very difficult for me to have one of my children going so far away. When she was gone it was like a hole in my heart, and a voice missing in the chorus of my life's song. I would not miss the wedding. Nothing could keep me away.

A month before the event I asked Marcie what I could do for the wedding. The only thing she asked was for me to make for her a floor-length dark green velvet cape with floral lining. Not very much to ask. I was excited to do it.

First I had to scour the Lehigh Valley to find a length of green velvet long enough that it would not need pieces sewn together halfway down the garment. I completed that first task barely two weeks before the wedding. After finding the material, I worked on it every moment I was home and had it nearly finished when I became ill with strep throat. Ann Scott stepped in to finish it, all except the final hemming which had to wait for Marcie to try it on and determine how long it should be.

Kay and Ann took me and the green velvet cape which we had named "The Cape of No Hope," to the Kennedy Airport. We had a hilarious time on the trip to the airport, stopping at Coney Island on a cold day in January. We had the privilege of seeing a female whale in the aquarium, in labor preceding the birth of her baby.

We couldn't stay long enough for the culminating event. Somehow, we found everything about that day hilarious.

On the day of the wedding I met Jim in Los Angeles where he had been on a business trip. When we arrived at the very small house Marcie and Charlie had rented, Mother, Rosie and Allen and Karen were there, having driven from their home in Santa Clara. Mother and I took up most of the room in that little house, sitting on a sofa and hemming The Cape of No Hope; she starting at one end, and I at the other.

When it was finished we went to the little Episcopal Church where the wedding would take place. Charlie's best friend, who was to be the best man, was not there yet. We went ahead and prepared for the ceremony and were about to assign his duties to someone else when he showed up, hot, sweaty and road-worn. He had just hitch-hiked in from Fresno.

Marcie came down the aisle as the most beautiful bride who had ever been seen, I believed. She wore a long cotton lace adorned gown, under The Cape. At the altar were Charlie, in dubious formal dress, and his best man in the shirt Charlie had recently taken off to don his wedding garb. Rosie was her bridesmaid. It was an event overflowing with love.

My sister, Kitty, and her husband, Jim, drove down from Oregon. At some point in the preparation, Mother broke a toe and needed medical attention. Rosie and Allen's twelve year old daughter, Karen, had come down with measles. As soon as possible after the ceremony the four of them flew back to Santa Clara. My Jim and I drove Rosie and Allen's car back to Santa Clara, in tandem with Kitty and her Jim. We drove north on Route 101 along the California Coast. It was the first time for all of us to see that spectacularly beautiful seashore. We stopped many times just to breathe the sea air and enjoy life itself. For Jim and I, it was one of the best times in our marriage. It was the most time Kitty and I had spent together since we were teenagers and we did a lot of laughing and playing on that trip.

As the plane took us back East, I had as strange mixture of feelings; satisfaction and completion at having launched one of my daughters into her own life, and the sadness of losing my first-born to someone else. Now I had only two children at home...and I ached for the other one.

Throughout his school years Dan had been a good student in every subject but math. He wanted to go into forestry after high school but his grades were not high enough. This he discovered as a junior in high school and was disappointed that he could not spend the rest of his life in the woods.

The summer after his disappointment, Rosie, Allen, and Karen came for a visit. Allen, a teacher with a gift for teaching math, gave Dan a few hours of his time and taught him something that turned Dan's math ineptitude around. When Dan went back for his senior year, he was on the honor roll every marking period. His math block was gone. We were immensely appreciative of Uncle Allen's help. However, Dan's grade average was still not good enough for Forestry School.

After high school, he went to Williamsport Community College and studied horticulture for two years, graduating with a 3.9 grade point average, second in his class. After that he went to work for a landscaping company in Easton to prepare himself for his own landscaping business which he would open as soon he could make enough money to get it started.

Lorie continued to be the delightful person she always was. She was dating a young man I liked very much. Everybody loved Charlie Barnett. We called him Charlie B to distinguish him from the many other Charles' in our life. He was a budding musician and had an effervescent personality.

He and Lorie lit up every room they entered. Charlie B's parents, Martha and Charles, and his sisters all became good friends of ours. Charlie B was a good music teacher for Lorie and she was becoming a fine musician herself. They were a delight playing music together, and were often at the Sunday gatherings.

School was not Lorie's forte. It was something she had to get through; music was her driving force. She learned to play the guitar and was always popular at the festivals we attended. At one festival in South Carolina she met a man whose name was Carrolton, playing a hammer dulcimer. Lorie had to have one. So she discovered from the player that Sam Rizetta was the person she needed to contact.

Sam was the archivist at the Folk Music Department of the Smithsonian Institute. Lorie contacted Sam and he agreed to build her a hammer dulcimer. He would build it for her, only if she earned the money herself, to pay for it. He explained to me that he would not build an instrument for a youngster whose parents bought it and his handiwork would likely end up under their bed. He wanted only serious musicians to play his instruments. Lorie was serious, so she would send him ten dollars out of her salary from her job at a local snack bar and he would send her a progress report on how the building of the instrument was coming along.

Hammer dulcimers had recently reentered the world of American folk music, thanks to Sam Rizetta. When her instrument was finished, Sam brought it to Pennsylvania and stayed with us for a few days while he taught her to play it. We enjoyed her music through high school. The music scene surrounding her buoyed her up sufficiently to get through high school.

After graduating from high school with no desire to go on to college, she found several little jobs, none of which were fulfilling for her. But she was always looking for a way to make music the center of her life.

One day I was getting ready to leave for a church retreat up in the Pocono Mountains and Lorie asked me, "Why are you doing this, Mom?"

I said, "I suppose, to find out what to do with the rest of my life."

She said, "Well, if you find out something for me to do with the rest of mine, let me know."

Through the weekend I was thoroughly occupied with the retreat, and forgot her request. However, on the way home, as we were waiting at a church for a bus and I turned and looked at a poster on the wall behind me. It said, "Don't know what to do with your life? Try the Church Army."

Then I remembered Lorie's request and was eager to get home and tell her about it. She asked, "What is the Church Army?" with much skepticism in her voice. This was near the end of the Viet Nam War and "Army" was not a popular word or idea in our circle of friends. Nevertheless, she followed my lead when I told her to ask Father Gill. He would know. She promptly did that.

She found that it was an arm of the Episcopal Church similar to the Vista Program. They sent people around the world doing volunteer work where the needs were the greatest. Lorie was more than interested. Immediately, she was involved and enthusiastic! She filled out all the papers, and eagerly waited for a letter of acceptance. When that letter came, she was told she could volunteer at a day care center for children of migrant workers in Florida.

Around this time, Dan moved into a house with four or five other young men who were asserting their independence. He could see that his childhood had come to an end. One sister was gone and the other, younger than he, was preparing to depart. His leaving was very simple, accompanied by no drama, whatsoever. He came to me one day and said, "Mom, I will be living in Easton from now on. I'll come home often to visit but it is time I got out on my own." Dan did come home often, sometimes for several days, but essentially he did not live at home again.

I remember clearly the day of Lorie's leaving. She was packed and ready to go. A friend was picking her up at the house and driving her to Florida. The house already seemed eerily empty when she came downstairs with the few things she would take with her. We played scrabble at the counter that divided the kitchen from the dining room while we waited for her ride. When the ride came I walked out to the car with her and with tears in my eyes, said goodbye. She was not tearful. Her eyes were sparkling with excitement. She was starting out on an adventure of her own.

As she drove away I went back into my empty house, sat down on the floor of the living room and sobbed great wrenching sobs. My last child had left. I was only forty-three years old and my life was over. What would I do for the next forty years?

Jim came down the steps and asked me why I was crying. I had a hard time explaining it to him. I could see that for him it was a time of opening, not a time of closure.

He had been patient, and a good stepfather to my children, but he was ready to move on. He said, "Let's go for a ride." I was too depleted to resist, so I went along. He drove down to New Hope Pennsylvania, and went to a place that was selling condos, a new idea in housing. The salesperson, very friendly and cheerful, asked me earnestly what I really wanted in a house. I could not answer and started crying again. All I wanted in a house was my children.

Somehow we got through that day and went on. It was quite clear that Jim wanted was restless. He had complied with my desire to get my children raised in the house in which they had their childhood, but he was now eager to move on. Thinking it might add some life to our flat marriage, which I still wanted to preserve, I joined him in looking at houses for the next six months.

Interwoven in the web of our lives were my children and their emerging adulthood, our careers, our friends, and the church. Looking back I cannot conceive how we did so many things in a time that in retrospect seems like a wink of an eye. It was a rich time in our lives and I look back on it as The Golden Years.

We became friends with DeWitt (Scotty) and Ann Scott. He was editor of the *Easton Express*, the leading local newspaper. Jim and I met the Scotts at a church picnic. As several of us Trinitarians were sitting at a picnic table, Scotty asked me where I grew up, recognizing my midwestern accent. When I told him I grew up in South Dakota, he told me that there had just been a flood there which he had seen on the wire before he left the newsroom that morning.

The flood was in Rapid City where my sister Bobbie and her family lived. I was acutely alert. He said, "We can go to the newsroom and look at the list of victims if you want," Of course, I wanted, so we, Jim and I, Ann, Scotty and their two toddlers, Amy and Sarah, left the picnic, went to the newsroom and read the names on the wire. We found no names of my family on the list, for which I was grateful.

There was still much time left to the day, so we went to my house in Stockertown. By the time the Scotts left that evening we were firm and eternal friends. Ann was a fine guitarist with a pure and vibrant voice for folk music. One more participant at our Sunday sings. They were also Episcopalians. They fit in very well with us, the Gills and the Bartletts.

It was during that era that Trinity Church was introduced to a Cursillo. A Cursillo, which translates into *Little Course,* is a weekend retreat, started in Spain by the Catholic Church. It is an intense course in basic Christianity. The Catholic Church was reaching out to the Protestants to share this experience. It was in the era of Ecumenism. Trinity Church was the first in our area to be invited. Jim and I, Kay and Jim Gill, Scotty and Ann all participated in these weekend retreats. They were powerfully invigorating. We all came out with a new enthusiasm for living and spreading the basic tenets of the teachings of Jesus Christ. All of us had belonged to the church for years and years, but this was something else. Personally, it changed the way I would look at my life's work...how

I would spend the rest of my days...to what I would dedicate my intents and purposes.

Not long after that I volunteered my own spouse, Jim, and Bill Bartlett to provide music for an informal gathering at the church with the Bishop on the eve of his annual visit, a celebrated event in every Episcopal Church.

It happened that the week before the event, both Jim and Bill were called out of town by their work, and could not do the music. I was mortified. I had promised to take care of the music for that important event.

Then I realized that the four of us...Marianne and her autoharp, Ann and her guitar, Kay and her violin and I with my penny-whistle, could provide the entertainment. All we had to do was sing a few very simple folksy gospel songs. That would be enough! We met a couple of times in Ann's living room, with her toddlers, Amy and Sarah and their obstreperous dog, Bonzo, a Weimaraner, wandering through our practice sessions. There was as much laughing as practicing, but we managed to polish our version of *Swing Low, Sweet Chariot, Rock-a My Soul* and *When the Saints Go Marching In*. The evening of the Bishop's visit was a smashing success! The Bishop loved it and taking his lead, so did the congregation. We were asked to perform for the next event of the church...and the next and so on.

The four of us, Marianne, Kay, Ann and I got together again after that, every time we possibly could. Soon we were joined by Mary Wichie, who added her own inimical style to the group. We discovered that we would *druther* play than anything else. That was the beginning of "The Druthers," a group of women who played for Head Start Centers, nursing homes, prisons and, as we said, "for any captive audience," we could find. Later we were joined by Betty Berger, my first friend in Pennsylvania, also an accomplished musician. It was a glorious season of our life. After I left the Easton area The Druthers persisted for a little while.

Ever since that day when we looked at condos in New Hope I knew we were going to look for another place to live. Leaving the area was not easy for me. I had gained my self-respect back after my divorce, and felt that Stockertown was my town. Even Easton had become my town, with my many years of employment there, my connection with the church, along with a large circle of Easton friends.

However, leaving the house in Stockertown was the most difficult of all...the house I had almost lost several years before, regained by a miracle, and finished the dream of raising my children in *one* house...all of those things troubled me about leaving it. Jim did not love the house. I suspected that living in a house another man had chosen and owned was part of his discontent. Also, he was driving a hundred miles a day to and from work, at Western Electric in Princeton. So we looked and looked at houses in that area. There were some that I liked and he did not, and some he liked and I did not. It was a long process.

Then I found a house in Trenton New Jersey, almost on the Delaware River. It was a very well built rambling ranch house and beautifully landscaped. You could see the river from the front yard and there was only one house on the street between that house and the river. I had come to love the Delaware River and as it flowed through Easton and on southward to Trenton, I felt that a bit of Easton was coming with me...that I was still connected with Kay and Jim, Marianne and Bill, Ann and Scotty, the Bergers the Sampsons, book group, The Druthers, and all my friends at Trinity Church.

After finding the house there were many things that had to be done before moving. First, we had to get the Stockertown house in condition to sell. Sadly, all the things I had always wanted to be done, were now important enough to do. Also we had to clean out an extensively cluttered attic, basement, chicken coop that the children had used for playhouse, club-house, coffee house, through their growing up. Of course, there was the selling of the house. We put it on the market and went through the preliminaries of selling it.

During that time Dan had been at home for several days. He was good company and his help was greatly appreciated. One night after Jim and I had been out quite late, I noticed that Dan had not come home. At first I assumed that he was simply out late, or perhaps had gone back to his place in Easton but he always let me know where he was. I worried about it most of the night and went into his room about 4am. I noticed that the quilt was gone from his bed, which told me that he had been home and taken the quilt. Through the night I alternated between imagining various disastrous scenarios,

In the morning I received a collect long distance phone call from Lorie. I answered with trepidation. She was supposed to be caring for children in a day care camp in Florida. This call came from South Carolina. She told me a strange story of how she and another teenage girl, Allie, also with the Church Army, had discovered the couple who were managing the center were not spending their allocated funds on the center which was in an abominable condition, while the managers were living in grand opulence. While the girls were contemplating what to do with this knowledge the manager overheard their discussion. Fearing for their safety, feeling that they were in danger because of this knowledge, they fled when darkness fell. They quietly and carefully got out of the church compound, arrived at a highway, hitchhiked to a town in South Carolina, where they called our house and Dan answered the phone.

He immediately grabbed a quilt, jumped in his car and was on the way to rescue them. Lorie said they would call me later when Dan arrived. I received that welcome call after about two hours of waiting and worrying. Dan, Lorie and Allie got to our house that night, much to my relief! Lorie and her co-worker firmly believed that they must report this to the Church Headquarters in New York City immediately.

The next day they went to the Church to talk with Father Gill and he directed them to the people at Church Headquarters in New York City who would handle a case such as this. When they made their report, people at church headquarters were very impressed that these two young girls had acted with such integrity and courage. They were held in high esteem by the officials at the Episcopal Church Headquarters in NYC. The two girls were told that they could choose any site on the list of volunteer placements.

Lorie chose Innisfree Village, a community in Virginia that was founded as a place where handicapped adults would have a permanent home, that was their own, where they could engage in productive work and live in a healthy, positive environment. She was attracted to the concept and philosophy of the village. She also chose it because it was in the heart of the Blue Ridge and Shenandoah Mountains, where the mountain music she loved was alive and flourishing.

I put my moving project on hold for a while to take her down to Virginia to look at Innisfree Village. We both were enamored by it, and she eagerly put in her application and waited for acceptance. She was accepted, moved into Innisfree Village just about the time our house was sold. I resumed the work of leaving Stockertown.

My children wrote the ad for the paper, an ad which I carried with me the rest of my days. It said: *Looking for a perfect childhood? Apple trees to climb, outbuildings to play in, four bedrooms, cozy family room, living room, dining room, and a huge barn for cars and hobbies, cats, dogs, other pets, and gatherings.*

The ad went in the paper on a Sunday morning. When we got home from church a family was waiting in front of the house. They enthusiastically signed the agreement to buy the house. The sale would be complete in sixty days.

There were several more details to be done. One was leaving my job at Northampton County Children's Bureau so that I would have time to get ready for the move. After resignation and finishing up work details, I was systematic about the process of moving. Each day I worked eight hours, taking time off for lunch. Often at the lunch hour Kay, Marianne, Ann, Charlie B and other musicians would come in and we would all play music for that hour. Then I would get back to the packing and sorting.

Near the end of the two months, I had a garage sale which was big, and somehow both festive and poignant. There were several going-away parties...one at the church...one from the book group and one last party in the barn. That was on the eve of the Bartletts departure from Stockertown. They left Stockertown to move to a farm in Ohio shortly before we left to move to Trenton. Again... the end of an era... Charlie B told me years later that for the first week we were gone, on his lunch hour he would go to our house on Lincoln Avenue, sit under the big tree in front of the house and play his guitar, unwilling to believe we had gone and unwilling let go of his part in The Golden Years.

CHAPTER 24

Trenton and Beyond

Moving from the Easton area of Pennsylvnia to the Trenton area of New Jersey felt as though half of me was moving on and the other half was staying. I had the sensation of being torn apart. Stockertown had been my home longer than any other place in my entire life. It was there, in that geographical divide, where the Delaware River separates Pennsylvania from New Jersey, that I transitioned from a nineteen-year-old bewildered, displaced young girl to a mature woman of forty-two. I had lost and regained my self respect and now felt I had become an accepted member of the community.

I had a hard time selling myself the idea that this move was a good idea. The selling points I told myself were that, perhaps it would save a faltering marriage; perhaps this would make our life together more interesting and endurable. Jim, I reasoned, had helped me with my children, bringing them from teenage to young adulthood, and he had done it with a large measure of respect and love for them and gained the same from them. I certainly owed it to him to find a place he wanted to live where he would not have to spend three hours a day commuting. Also I thought, buying and furnishing a house together would give us a common purpose and interest. We would make a home together.

Leaving Kay, Ann, Betty Berger, Jane Sampson, the Barnetts and others, including all of Trinity Church made the move painful. At the same time they were the elements that made it bearable.

Kay and Ann drove down the river from Easton many, many times carrying my house plants, bringing their children to swim in our very large and beautiful swimming pool, some-times coming just to play music. Those visits made it seem that all connections were not cut. It was just a little over an hour's drive. I still had access to much of what was valuable to me in the Easton area. Jane Sampson drove halfway down the River Road one day and I met her; we browsed in an antique shop and had lunch along the river. Once Marianne came through Trenton from Ohio on her way to visit her elderly father in upstate New York. I was having a gathering for many of my Easton friends that Saturday so she stayed quite a while before moving on to drive northward. She left the three youngest children at my house for the weekend. I still felt connected to her and to Easton.

We had a few music parties in our new home. Our music experience was enriched when Lorie brought her friends from Virginia to our house and christened it with a new flavor. Those Applachian fiddles were lively and refreshing. Kay brought a new friend, Loy Zaremba, to one of the parties. Little did we know at the beginning the convoluted paths our lives would take and still keep our friendship. She had joined the book group and the Druthers within a week after I moved away. In Easton she was meeting many of the people I had known. Often people would ask her if she and I were related. In some ways it felt that she had slipped into the place I had vacated.

When all the transactions connected with selling my house in Stockertown were complete I had in my possession the largest amount of money I had ever had. My decision was to divide the proceeds into four equal parts, one part for each of the children and one part for myself. It was not a huge sum for any one of us and it was interesting what we did with the money. Mine was largely spent on furnishing the new house, a trip to California, and living a full year, willingly unemployed.

Marcie and Charlie used their share to buy a Volkswagen and made a trip across the country, moving back into the area Marcie had known as a child. They wanted to start a family and be nearer grandparents when their children were growing up. They rented an apartment in Northampton.

Lorie bought a truck and traveled throughout the South exploring the music she loved. She told me that there was no place too far, nor was it ever too late, too cold or too hot to go play music. After she left Innisfree she went to the UVA School of Nursing and remained in Virginia where she became an accomplished and well known musician who always had a band playing somewhere. She also became a competent nurse who was in demand for her skills and her vibrant personality.

Dan used his share of the house money to start his landscaping business. He bought a truck, and employed a business manager. Very soon he had his first contracted job. Daniel's Landscaping got its start. This first job was for a man from Trinity Church who was building a house in a new development in Easton, Old Orchard. He told Dan that he wanted unusual and interesting plantings and money was not a factor. Dan could spend as much as he needed to obtain the plantings to make the grounds unique. Dan hired some of his friends and they did a spectacular landscaping job. The property was at the entrance to Old Orchard so it was seen by everyone entering the community. Dan and his crew were given most of the contracts for landscaping for Old Orchard. His was one of the first landscaping businesses in Easton and was a huge success right from the start.

What a year for me it was! This was the first time since I was thirteen years old that I was not employed full time. Now opportunities exploded for things to do that I had only dreamed of before. First, I cultivated a wonderful garden, gleaning all my gardening wisdom from Rodale Press's Organic Gardening magazine. It was a compact garden which produced the best corn we had ever eaten, and tomatoes which could have won prizes. I found a friend who quilted and we made a quilt together. We got hers finished but mine didn't quite make it before another life opened up for me.

I made friends in the neighborhood, and opened our pool to all the children living on the spit of land by the Delaware River. This caused some consternation in the neighborhood because I invited Afro-American children into my pool along with the other neighborhood children. Integration was slow in coming to Trenton. We had some visits from neighbors warning us dire things that would happen if we allowed this kind of mixing races. They told us that we were going to affect the property value of the neighborhood if we kept this up. It only made me more determined to welcome them. The children quickly and effortlessly found their commonality and accepted their differences. I saw the fear disappear from the children on both sides of the color barrier with the first splash. In fact I saw the barrier melt away. It was an object lesson in integration. And the neighborhood remained intact.

When summer ended I decided it was time to answer my yearning to hear hammer dulcimer music. I missed hearing Lorie play hers, and thought that this might be a time when I could learn to play the instrument. I wrote to Sam Rizetta and asked if he would make a hammer dulcimer for me. He agreed to make it and I went to Virginia to pick it up early in the fall. It was custom made to fit me...not so big that it would drag on the ground when I carried it. I spent many hours of that fall and winter learning to play it, and several times drove to Easton to play music with The Druthers.

Only one time did I get to play with both Kay and Ann because in the fall of that year Ann and Scotty moved to Walnut Creek California. Scotty was a newspaper editor with a deep sense of ethics. Because of that, he often ran into opposition from some sector of the newspaper business. The lives of Scotty and Ann had been a series of living two or three years at a location and then moving on. This time, after a disagreement at the *Easton Express,* Scotty resigned and was hired as night editor of the *San Francisco Examiner.*

I went to Easton to help with the move, which was dramatic and chaotic. Scotty had moved to the San Francisco area to start his work shortly after he was hired. He went ahead of Ann and the children to find a home for their family and Bonzo, the dog. Ann stayed in Easton to sell their house and organize the move of their furniture and household goods. When those transactions were done, she packed up the contents of their big house and took a houseful of boxes to Kay and Jim's house to be picked up by a moving truck.

The night I arrived to help with the final move could have been sad and gloomy but there was just too much going on to find time for grieving. Instead we found everything uproariously hilarious! Kay and Jim's house was filled to the ceilings with boxes. We had a going away dinner during which we laughed hysterically. That night the three Scotts, Bonzo and I found places to sleep in the Gill's house which was already filled. We slept on cots, couches and the floor.

The next morning Kay and I took Ann, Amy, and Sarah and Bonzo to the Newark Airport to help them get launched on the plane to San Francisco. Bonzo required a tranquilizer to be accepted on the plane. Ann had to climb into the container to lure him in as the airport attendants were not having any success with him. We laughed through this maneuver. Someone had given the little girls a box of donuts and predictably they had opened the box, managed to spread sticky sugar over themselves as well as on everything and everybody they touched. They were on a sugar high which added to the drama of the day. As they were walking up the ramp to get on the plane, little Sarah, then about two and a half, turned and came running back down the ramp, shouting, "Oh, Dolores! You are going to miss me so much!" She was so right!

Their leaving was a never-to-be-forgotten epic event. After their plane was out of sight, Kay and I turned to each other and wept. We drove back to Easton in a sad, yet companionable silence, too deep for words. The absence of the Scott family was painful. It was one more diminishment of our Golden Age together.

The Scotts arrived in Walnut Creek in early winter. I was concerned about them being in a new community, without friends or family for Christmas, so I arranged for them to go to Rosie and Allen's for the holiday. When they arrived on Christmas Day at Rosie and Allen's house, they presented themselves as a Christmas present from Dolores. When Rosie hugged Amy, about four and a half, Amy said, "Oh, good! You smell like Dolores." My sister and one of my best friends and her family bonded immediately and have been close friends ever since.

Trying to fill the gaps in our lives, the holes that were the result of all the changes, Jim and I tried very hard to get involved in a church near our new home in Trenton. We found a small Episcopal church across the Delaware River in Morrisville Pennsylvania. We immersed ourselves in all they had to offer. We took in the children of a couple who were going through a messy divorce. We visited at the homes of other parishioners and became friends with the rector. We invited couples to our home for dinner. Nevertheless there was a social vacuum in our life, accompanying and magnifying the emptiness in our marriage and the spiritual hunger in my soul. The Cursillo had left me with a yearning. Something like a quest was always roiling restlessly deep inside me. It took a long time to understand what would feed that hunger. That church we attended was all right, but it wasn't Trinity Easton, nor was it Cursillo, nor was it the answer to my quest.

We had several supposed-to-be exciting weekends with a group from Jim's workplace. We went on a whaling ship out of Rhode Island. We went on a whitewater rafting trip on the Youghaghenny River, along the Pennsylvania-Ohio border. The people with whom Jim worked were intelligent, fun loving people but they did not become lifelong friends and the adventures did not fulfill the restlessness and hunger that was in me. They consisted of superficial fun...I wanted something more earnest than that.

By spring I decided that I should go back to work. It was surprisingly easy to get a position with the Division of Youth and Family Service (DYFS) in the state of New Jersey. My work with the Children's Bureau provided good background and good references for the job. The work was similar to what I had done in Easton. It felt good to be back working, and that sated some of the hunger in me. My work felt like a calling. I made very good friends at DYFS, who were to remain and return to my life years later. I had taken a course in Parent Effectiveness Training (PET), when I worked for the Northampton Children's Bureau, in Easton, and conducted PET sessions for foster families in New Jersey...very satisfying work. It kept me occupied and satisfied for a year and a half.

Because of the time Lorie had spent in the Church Army, we continued to get newsletters about that organization. A newsletter arrived announcing that the name of Church Army had been changed to the National Institute for Lay Training (NILT) This was new not only in name but in mission. The mission of NILT was to train lay people in the church to become ministers in the world, ministers in whatever position they were in. It was not to encourage people to go into the church ministry, that is, to become priests or deacons, nor was it to prepare them for work within the church. It was to teach them to inject the social justice issues that Jesus taught into their secular work. When I read that issue of the newsletter, something in me stirred. This sounded like a possible answer to the quest, the restlessness, the hunger in me. The more I studied it, the more interested I became.

The training site of NILT was at General Theological Seminary in NYC, one of the major Episcopalian seminaries in the country. One had to apply, take a battery of tests, meet with the Bishop of the Diocese in which you lived, and be able and willing to live a full school year on the campus of the seminary. Many classes were taken with the seminarians, and many were specifically aimed at Lay Ministry. As I read into it more deeply I wondered if I wanted to pursue the priesthood. Women in the Episcopal Church at this time were fighting for their right to become priests. Although there was initially much opposition, the women were winning the battle. This NILT program might be the place where I could sort that out for myself.

I filled out all the papers, took the tests in NYC, had my interview with the Bishop in Philadelphia, and was accepted into the program.

Jim had been noncommittal as I went through the preliminaries. He had said very little about it, until it was time for me to go to NYC to live for a school year. Then he expressed his feelings and opinions. If I was determined to do it, he said would not stop me. But he let me know that he did not like it, not one iota. However, I was already on the train and it was moving!

Before I started seminary a very powerful event in my life and the life of my family occurred. Marcie and Charlie became parents of Joya, making me grandmother. I was deliriously happy. It felt like a precious pearl had been added to the string of strong women in our family.

What a celebrated event it was! Marcie and Charlie had been to a Cursillo event and the entire diocese of Bethlehem became involved with their life, rejoicing at the birth of Joya. On the day of her birth, Joya was visited by five ministers from the Lehigh Valley, two of whom shared her birthdate. Later on, she would tell her brothers, "Don't you forget it! My father was a carpenter, I was born in Bethlehem, and five wise men came to visit me a few days after my birth."

She was a delightful baby, smiled and interacted with others immediately. She began talking at eight months. Her arrival made it more difficult for me to go through with my plans to live in NYC for a year, but I was on a mission! Also I told myself that she was not my baby. She belonged to Marcie and Charlie, and I would be doing them a favor by getting out of the way. I trusted they would be excellent parents. Jim's involvement and love of this precious baby was remarkable. I believe the strength of his love for Joya surprised him and eased the discomfort of my departure.

Arriving at the Seminary, I felt as though I had entered another universe. General Seminary is in the heart of NYC, in the section of the city known as Chelsea. The seminary grounds are called "The Close" because the area is a city block closed off from the city by brick walls and the backs of buildings. The Close is entered by a gate, and all the buildings face away from the street, onto a lawn partitioned by majestic old trees and brick sidewalks. All the buildings except the new Library and Administration office, are over a hundred years old. The room which was to be mine for the next school year was on the third floor of an old turreted building, where the floors were of marble tiles, the woodwork old mahogany, and the showers three floors below. My bedroom opened out onto a large living room with a fireplace. The three large bay windows looked out on The Close. One other NILT student, Christie Balsam, had in a bedroom next to mine and we shared the living space. We had our meals in "The Refectory." New words, new ideas and concepts...an entirely new life!

There were six other students from all over the United States, enrolled in NILT that year. They brought together vastly varying backgrounds and cultures ranging in age from twenty to fifty. Five were female and two were male. Our leaders and mentors were Pat Page, a former missionary to Kenya, and Tom Tull, a seminary graduate who had been with the Church Army for several years.

That year was rich and full of experiences and people I was astonished to meet and with whom I could hold my own in discussions and learn the theological language I had heard so many years before in El Paso when I was sixteen. There was chapel every morning and evening. The NILT students were assigned liturgical duties just as the seminarians were. We had classes with the seminarians led by notable clergy and professors. We also had insightful assignments outside of the classrooms.

For example, one early assignment was for us to go out in pairs and interview the leader of every church in a ten block area of NYC. We were to interview them, regardless of denomination, and ask what was their view of the laity. What did they expect their parishioners to do for the church and in the world? Where and how did they incorporate the social justice issues that Jesus talked about during his brief stay on earth? Their answers provided us rich material for studying and defining the ministry of the laity.

Early in the year we studied Kohlberg's Theory of Moral Development, and were assigned to choose a notable person and write his or her story from the perspective of moral development. I chose Mahatma Ghandi. Reading his autobiography and several books about him I became increasingly drawn to Eastern Spirituality. I was questioning my religious beliefs and my commitment to the Episcopal Church.

One day, in the midst of this turmoil, I fell asleep as I was studying. I had a vivid dream of being in the presence of a white-robed man of Eastern origin who held his hand out to me palm up, at first beckoning me to come closer and then as I got very close, held me back, saying something in a language I did not understand. He spoke kindly but firmly. I woke suddenly with the words he was saying clearly embedded in my memory. On campus there was a seminary student from India. I found him and asked him what those words meant. He told me they translated into, "No farther, no closer!" I took that to mean that I was not go any further down the path of the religion of Ghandi. I was puzzled by it because it really made so much sense to me and I did not want to give it up entirely. I did keep many of the precepts of Eastern religion as I continued my studies in the Episcopalian Seminary. I wish I could remember specific courses and concepts but the memory is something like a Gestalt experience; that is, a whole concept and acceptance, rather than any courses or parts I could separate from the rest. A bit like a quilt you put together piece by piece and when you are finished, you have a complete, warm, comfortable entity, with which you cover yourself.

A few days later Dean James Morton came to speak to our class. It was more his style to speak *with* a class than *to* a class. He sat down at one of the desks in the middle of the classroom. Being a huge man he barely fit there and did truly seem larger than life. He was the Dean of the Cathedral of St. John the Divine, in NYC. He had recently been castigated by many of the more conservative members of the Episcopal Church because he had allowed diverse religions to set up altars along the sides of the Cathedral.

As he talked with us, explaining his reasons for the many altars in the Cathedral, he said, as he flung his big arms out as if embracing all that *is*, "I believe in everything!" It was as if fireworks went off! I remember that moment as if it were burned into my soul, and I said, "You Can DO that? You can really DO that?" It seemed so right to me.

If I am to believe in the Creator of everything, the ultimate intelligence, the overarching authority, I had to believe in *everything*. I had been looking for a religion that had no boundaries, as I believe our Creator has no boundaries. I do not believe our Creator has only one name or that we can ever totally understand the entirety of what it entails. I gravitated to the Episcopal Church because it allowed more latitude, more questioning and less certainty than any other church to which I had been exposed.

It was here, at the seminary where I came to know the difference between Spirituality and Religion. The very word, Religion, has its origins in the Latin word *religare* which means "to bind, to tie up." The word Spirit, derived from Latin *spritus,* means breath, vigor, courage. That, to me, means spirituality is very different from religion. I was challenged by many other students and even our mentors, by this stance I had taken and expressed. "Does this mean you believe in 'Evil'?" I was asked. I had to answer that I do believe that Evil exists...not that I think it is good, but it does exist. I believe that you have to allow the darkness to be part of your experience if you want to fully experience the light. The good part is only half of it.

When I went home that weekend and discussed this with Jim, he said, "If you believe in Everything, you believe in Nothing." I pondered that deeply for a long time and came to understand that I do not believe in a bounded religion; I do believe in limitless spirit.

My philosophy of life was unfolding as I absorbed what I was learning at NILT. I knew with certainty that I believed in whatever breaks down the boundaries between people and enables them to love and embrace every living thing, and the planet they live upon. I also came to believe that it is a process. We will continue to learn and grow as long as we are open to that process. Once we believe we have all the answers, we stagnate. The ultimate knowledge is unknowable.

One NILT assignment was to go to the Catholic Worker Soup Kitchen on Saturdays and help serve the poor at that location. The Catholic Worker, started by Dorothy Day in the 1930s' during the Great Depression remains in action around the Catholic Worker Mary House in NYC. There are many other communities of Catholic Worker centers around the world, and the headquarters are in Lower Manhattan, where we were assigned to go. I could not do this assignment with the class because I went home every weekend.

Because I could not go to the Catholic Worker on the weekend I was released from class to go one day during the week. I was still quite intimidated by NYC itself. Never before had I felt so alienated from my surroundings. Such a big city for someone who still considered herself a South Dakotan. I felt so alienated by my surroundings that I went to several counseling sessions early in my time in the city.

On the day I was to go to the Catholic Worker, I started walking south toward Greenwich Village. I got as far as The Bowery before my courage gave out. I accidentally walked into Skid Row and fear took over. I walked briskly, my knees trembling. I tried not to make eye contact with anyone. Men who had lost themselves in their addictions and afflictions lined the street, leaning against the buildings; holding tightly to the paper bag which contained the bottles that provided their comfort.

As I approached, a few rose up and confronted me, face to face, eye to eye; smelling of sour wine and worse. They blocked my path and cried out with various pleas, such as, "Just a quarter, ma'am, please, just a quarter."

One man said, "Lady, you've got on a cross...help me!" That did me in! I fled from them and caught the very next city bus in sight, willing to go wherever it would take me....anywhere away from there. When safely on the bus, a few blocks away, the fear subsided. Now I was angry at my lack of courage and conviction. I felt the man in my face was right...how could I wear a cross and be too afraid to help...too frightened to even look him in the eye. I was embarrassed, angry and ashamed.

Somehow, with a few bus transfers, I got back to The Close. If not for the care and consideration of my classmates, I would have dropped out of the program right then. My classmates persuaded me to stay at Seminary by reminding me that Peter, the Rock on which the church was developed, had denied Christ three times, and had managed to go on spreading His Spirit and Word. They reminded me that Paul who had persecuted and killed Christians, was redeemed and wrote the first accounts of the emerging church. I conceded that I could understand redemption and believe that it was available, even to me. I decided to stay with NILT. I never again felt comfortable wearing a cross.

Three years later when I went back to NYC by myself on a bus from Easton, I took a city bus to The Catholic Worker, walked into the soup kitchen and served those who came for food and spiritual sustenance. I was assigned the task of serving the water. A grisly, tough looking man said harshly, "Lady, for Christ's sake, give me a drink."

I looked him in the eye, and said with conviction and compassion, "Sir, for Christ's sake, a drink of water for you."

Something happened to me at that exchange. It was a powerful spiritual experience. We met each other's eyes, held the gaze for a long moment and a spark passed between us. After that event I was never afraid to serve, or touch or care for, or meet the eyes of anyone in need. No one was beyond Christ's care, and I now knew that basic solid truth with my whole heart and soul.

Back to my year at Seminary; going home on the weekends proved to be an elixir to our marriage. Jim would meet me at the train station at Princeton Junction and we would go to dinner, talk about our week and our plans for the weekend. We even talked about ideas, concepts, religion, politics, and occasionally skirted around conversations about our relationship and marriage. It was the most conversant we had been with each other since our courtship. I had things to talk about that interested him and he had things to tell me. On Monday morning he would take me to the train at Princeton Junction and I would return to the city, always a foreign and exotic place for me.

It is amazing to me how NILT could pack so much into nine months. Study and discussions were never dull or meaningless. They were filled with information, ideas, and new ways of looking at things normally taken for granted. We saw movies, had a segment of sex education that went way beyond any high school, college or social work sessions ever did. We went to plays on Broadway such as *Equus, Chorus Line* and *Why Colored Girls Cry When The Rainbow Is Not Enough*. Discussions of the movies, readings, and plays always revolved around finding the sanctity, the soul, the spirit of them.

One Friday evening when Jim met me at Princeton Junction he was as animated and excited as I had seen him in a long time. He said he had something big to talk about but wanted to wait till we were sitting down in a restaurant face to face. I could hardly wait, but managed to do so until we were sitting down in the dining room of The Milford Inn, my favorite place to eat dinner on the Delaware River.

He had been up to Northampton to visit Marcie and Charlie and of course, the baby, Joya. The three of them decided that there were far too many miles between us to develop a relationship and be involved with Joya, our first grandchild. Also Marcie and Charlie were struggling to get by on Charlie's carpenter earnings. So the three of them had devised the plan that we would find a big place in Bucks County. Jim and I would sell our house in Trenton, and we would all move in together. I agreed to the plan.

Within a week Jim had taken a day off work and found a beautiful place with ample room, along a little creek in Northern Bucks County, not too far from Easton; farther from his work than Trenton but not a distance he was unwilling to travel. I had not seen Jim as enthusiastic about anything since our marriage. It didn't take long to realize that this was really happening, and would be completed very soon.

By the end of October the five of us, Marcie, Charlie, Joya, Jim and I, moved into the Carriage House, looking out onto the stream which was spanned by a historic covered bridge. The first night after we moved in I watched Jim, lying on the sofa, with Joya on his chest; both in total contentment, and I knew why this had happened. The wondrous power of unconditional love!

I continued at General Seminary and by November had firmly decided that I did not want to be a priest. I felt I could carry out the ministry of the laity more effectively as a social worker. This realization came about as the result of a weeklong workshop with The Haldane Association.

That association usually worked with corporations and large companies to help their administrators learn the skills of their workers, to enable them to be placed in the most effective slots in the workplace. Also individuals who were trying to find what profession or career path to pursue used the Haldane Association to find their motivated skills. The Haldane Association was brought to us at NILT to enable us to discover how we could best use our skills in total ministry. They spent a week with us at the seminary, administering tests, discussing our motivations and helping each of us to better understand ourselves. The results of my week indicated that my motivated skills had to do with social work in a community.

While in our year at NILT we were to develop a project, a working thesis, and were to have it completed by spring. I started out being very interested in developing a small working community made up from families I handled at DYFS. I had found generous support for this idea from many people who could help me get it established.

For my field study I went to Virginia and stayed at three different communities, one of which was Innisfree, studying what worked effectively for the community and what did not. I also studied what would be applicable to the community I was formulating. I wrote a paper on it and it was approved by NILT. However, the stumbling block in my plan was Jim. The Charles Manson debacle had been in the news that winter, and all Jim could imagine about a community revolved around that tragic scenario. I pursued my idea for a month or so, but came to realize that it certainly would be the death knell to the marriage. I gave it up.

I turned my thoughts to developing a workshop somewhat like that of The Haldane Association, which became an entity titled

"Discovering Your Gifts for Ministry." This became my NILT Project, and was well received by the faculty and NILT students and by my spouse. I presented this workshop across the country for various churches and groups, long after the NILT experience was over.

It was invigorating for me and gave many participants a sense of the sanctity of their daily work. Store clerks, teachers, farmers, stay at home mothers, waitresses, executives and others working at various jobs and professions felt they had discovered their ministry. Presenting these workshops was satisfying and fulfilling. I felt I was doing what I should be doing.

After completing the NILT program and doing several of the "Gifts" workshops I received a very surprising gift...a complete tuition scholarship from the Episcopal Church Women (ECW) to attend the college of my choice for a Master's Degree. What a surprise that was! I subscribed to the *Social Work Journal* to help me decide on which school I might choose.

I had decided on Marywood College in Scranton Pennsylvania as it seemed to have the most respected curriculum to obtain an MSW and it was within a reasonable distance from home. Jim did not approve of it at all. It wasn't the degree he objected to, or the school...but the distance I would be traveling from where we lived. My year away at Seminary and the several weekends away with the Gifts workshops had taxed his patience. I pondered this, and reckoned the cost to the marriage, against the gains of studying at Marywood and obtaining a MSW. I started looking closer to home and found that Lehigh University in Bethlehem had a M.Ed program with a concentration in Community Counseling. That seemed to be right in line with my motivated skills and experience, so I set about getting accepted for that program.

I started classes at Lehigh that fall, just after Marcie became pregnant for the second time. It was a rich time for me; classes were interesting and not very difficult.

I relished being at home with our extended family, especially Marcie and Joya. Being in Bucks County, driving around the beautiful countryside, picking wild strawberries, simply living in the country is a rich experience. We were all involved in Trinity Church in Easton, so our friends and interests converged in satisfying ways. In spite of all that satisfaction I still felt the need for my own income. I felt I could also fit in a part time job and could thereby exercise my own ministry as a social worker.

During the semester break I went to a Scottish Dance group and there met a woman who introduced me to school social work. She was a Learning Disability Specialist and at our first meeting, told me her school was looking for a School Social Worker. With a degree in Education, a Civil Service designation as Social Worker, and the fact that I was pursuing a Master's Degree in Education, she was quite sure I would be hired. I drove across the Delaware into New Jersey and found my next career, as a school social worker.

My nights for the next two years were filled with classes, and my days at three different rural schools in NJ. Child Study Teams had been mandated by the State and I became the social worker on three different teams. It was satisfying work for me. At Lehigh I steered myself into all the counseling classes I could and became certified as a Mental Health Counselor. I spent most of the next summer in Glassboro NJ, obtaining the official Certification as a School Social Worker.

Even though I was working full time I spent as much time as I could with Marcie and Joya. I was there for the birth of Marcie's second child, my first grandson, Eli. Marcie had decided to have a home birth, assisted by a midwife. I was a bit worried by this, knowing all the things that can go wrong with a birth, but honored her wishes and instincts. She had not been satisfied with the hospital birth of Joya. Also, Charlie, a sometimes employed carpenter, had no medical insurance. The midwife and home birth were affordable.

So it happened in that beautiful old Carriage House, on the first day of spring, that Eli was born. It was a beautiful experience. To be there for the first breath of my first grandson was incredible. Giving him his first drink of water and watching him blossom like a precious flower, was beyond thrilling. Eli was a placid baby, a little Buddha, we called him. He seemed content to watch the world in wonder and contemplation.

Living in the Carriage House provided me with rich memories. We got through a horrific blizzard and were without electricity for ten days. The old fireplace and cistern provided us with heat and water which we could and did share with neighbors. We met and enjoyed several families because of that blizzard of 1978. Spring was the best in my memory. There was a field of daffodils, probably an acre between our house and the old covered bridge! It was breathtakingly beautiful.

Also, while living in that house I became close friends with Doodie and Dan Genthner who lived nearby. I had an awareness of them as they were also members of Trinity, but I had always felt that they were far more sophisticated than I. Dan was the only orthodontist in Easton for many years, and known and loved by almost everyone. Doodie had grown up on Long Island and was a gracious host and maintained a house that should have been featured in a design magazine. How wrong I was about them. They were the most genuine, caring and open people I had ever known, and were in my life ever thereafter.

However, after two years in that idyllic setting in Bucks County, Jim was bothered by the fact that we were paying rent and not building up equity on a property. He wanted to own his house and the Carriage House was not for sale. Marcie and Charlie were beginning to want a place of their own. Jim's sister, Mary, was in the real estate business and she found a house in Easton on College Hill which was perfect for us. Again, it was a house that easily accommodated both families and we moved there together.

CHAPTER 25

College Hill &
Hamilton Township

The six of us...Marcie and Charlie, Joya and Eli; Jim and I...moved to Layfayette Street on College Hill in Easton. During my early years in Pennsylvania, I never dared dream of living on College Hill. It was so far removed from my life...not even a possibility. Even at the time we moved there, a quarter of a century later, it seemed slightly unreal to me. This was where the doctors, lawyers, and college professors lived. Not someone of my background, or so I thought at the time.

We moved into a wonderful, modern, spacious house, more than adequate for our needs, which were extensive. As I recognized the impressiveness of the house, and the status that living on College Hill conferred upon its inhabitants, I felt like a bystander. It seemed that I was watching myself live this life...not really living it. Again, I wondered how I got there from where I started.

We had not been there long when Jim got a bad blister on his foot while playing basketball at a gathering of his Western Electric friends. I was alarmed when I saw it, as I know how important it is to keep the feet of a diabetic healthy. Jim was dismissive of the incident; he told me I worried too much. To him it seemed to be only a bad blister; to me it was ominous. Within a week after the incident his foot became swollen, red and painful. I took him to the emergency room of Moravian Hospital in Bethlehem. Because of his diabetes and the appearance of infection, he was admitted immediately.

This was the beginning of a long hospital stay. It was the first of many hospital stays. Looking back, it was the end of his life as a healthy active person. A pseudomonas infection had taken a firm hold on his foot. He was given intravenous injections of antibiotics. I visited him every day in the hospital for several weeks. Upon his discharge the doctor told Jim that he must stop smoking. He said that each cigarette Jim smoked was taking a saw to his toes and eventually to his feet and his limbs. Jim was told that he would lose the quality of life and shorten it considerably.

He disregarded the doctor's advice and continued smoking, drinking and indulging in ice cream just as he had before the hospitalization...perhaps a bit more, in defiance of the doctor's orders. I could not get the doctor's words out of my mind. Each day as I abraded Jim's wound I was further irritated by his self-destructive behavior. I wanted to feel kinder and more considerate than I was feeling but I was so angry with him. And I was full of loathing with myself for being angry with him. Of course, all the time I was trying to maintain a cheerful countenance. The incongruity of my inner and outer life took a huge toll on the quality of my entire life.

Mother came to visit for a few weeks early in the winter, and stayed through Christmas. For me it was great to have her there; I could talk to her about my feelings as I could with no one else. Jim did not like her being there. He seemed to be offended by her simplicity. She was not a sophisticated person by any measure. Her western heritage, and her direct ways were refreshing to me. She was without artifice. For Jim it was an embarrassment. His mother had been the President of the Women's Club of America. To him, she was what a mother should be. Jim did not want my mother around when his friends visited and he made that quite clear. In spite of that tension, I was happy she was with us even though created a further emotional distance between Jim and me.

Mother enjoyed being there with her family...her daughter, grandchildren, great grandchildren, Joya and Eli, and she enjoyed seeing me living in such a lovely house, but she was concerned about me and my life. She was far more concerned for Jim's health than she was about his feelings for her. She could see that he did not take his diabetes seriously. She, too, had diabetes and was very consistent with taking care of herself. There was an air of contention between them although neither of them could voice it to the other. They simply kept a cool and quiet distance from each other. She stayed with us through Christmas.

Throughout the holidays I wheeled Jim through the malls, to church and to various holiday parties. I tried to be gracious about it and put on a good show of caring. Sometimes I imagined, or perhaps it was true, that acquaintances we met along the way either felt sorry for me, or thought I was a martyring saint. I wanted neither their pity nor their adulation. The situation was tearing me apart. Inside I was very angry at him, in turmoil, feeling that he could have avoided this, and asking myself if this was how I wanted to live the rest of my life...and carrying an enormous burden of guilt for feeling this way.

Marcie and Charlie moved out of the College Hill house into their own little house early in the spring. They lived only about ten minutes away so we could still see them often.

Their second son, Ian, was born, a year later, and again I had the privilege of seeing another grandchild come into the world. Ian was a robust energetic little baby, so different from his brother. He was born at home with a midwife in attendance, and minutes after the birth was on his hands and knees rooting around for something to eat. The doctor who came to examine him the next day, said, "We don't get to see babies like this in the hospital!" Very early in his infancy Ian developed a raucous laugh that could keep all six of us entertained for an entire evening. Joya and Eli adored him and he enthusiastically responded to that, meeting all the expected milestones early, as if to catch up to them.

Continuing in my school social work I made another lifelong friend, Lexa Billera, also a school social worker in a neighboring school district. I introduced Lexa to Trinity Church where she became a very active and committed member, eventually going to General Seminary and becoming a priest. I was chosen to be Godmother to her little girl, Elonda. It is one of the failures of my life that I never lived up to that honor and responsibility. Lexa was very important in my life. I have called her "A Godsend." She was the one to whom I could confide the dissatisfaction and frustration of my life. Extremely intelligent, and objective she remained friends with my entire family, including Jim. She and her daughter Elonda, moved in to the upper floor of the house on College Hill when I left Jim in the summer, after that long, troubled period of my life.

Leaving Jim was difficult; each step of the process connected with so many conflicting emotions and I blessedly have forgotten most of them. However, one event remains in my memory and needs to be told.

Just one year before I left, he and I went on an excursion to Martha's Vineyard. That was a place I had wanted to see, and we had the time and money so we planned the trip with more enthusiasm than we had shown for anything else for quite a while. He was as healthy as I expected he was ever going to be, and he was able to travel.

However by the time we got to Martha's Vineyard and to our room looking out over the ocean, I was thoroughly annoyed. He had insisted on doing all the driving and throughout the long drive was chain smoking and tailgating every vehicle in front of us. I spent the trip in the back of the Volkswagen van trying to sort out my conflicting feelings. After we got settled in the room, I wheeled him out onto a board walk and to an alcove looking out onto the vast ocean. I was very troubled and sad and did not know what I was going to do. Perhaps I could get an answer from the wisdom of the sea. We sat in silence for a long time. After a while I could contain my feelings no longer. Words from my mouth spoke themselves: "Jim, if you are still smoking a year from now, I will be gone."

He answered dismissively, "Oh, you wouldn't do that!" I gave no answer then, but in a year, I was gone.

Of course, it wasn't that fast or easy; the drama was in-tense, even though we never had one fight. There is as much drama to a cold, deliberate ending as there is to a fiery and furious one. Leading up to the end was the cold and deliberate part.

The last day was attended with much drama. It was a hot day in June and I had packed up the few things I would take with me and was out of the house by mid-afternoon. Later that day there was a violent thunder storm, with raging lightening and piercing rain. Unfortunately, for her, Marcie was the one he called when he arrived home in the middle of the storm and found my note. He was stunned; could not believe it! I could not believe he had not known or seen the signs that were as clear as the TV blaring on about the oncoming the thunder storm...and had been there for him to see for a year.

I drove away from College Hill, away from Easton, away from my marriage, down the River Road that day, and as I reached the Delaware a glorious rainbow presented itself. I felt it was a good omen. It was the beginning of the odyssey that would last the rest of my life.

There were some weak attempts at reconciliation, but my heart was never in them. For me, it was over. I knew Jim was a gentle and kind man, that he had been wonderful to my children, and would be a beloved grandfather to my grandchildren. I hoped their relationship would continue and that he and I would not be bitter or mean to each other. By the Grace of God, all those hopes were realized.

Dolores

For Jim there was no lack of candidates for my replacement. He started dating within two weeks and by the year's end had found a new spouse, or she had found him. She was the administrator of the Volunteers at the Hospital. Jim sold the College Hill house and moved into his wife's home in the Old Orchard development...the one where Dan had begun his landscaping business.

Predictably, I found a small apartment on the Delaware River in Upper Black Eddy. I had attained my Master of Education Degree along with certification and license to practice Mental Health Counseling. I started a private practice in our home on College Hill and continued in my apartment on the River. I was having difficulty maintaining a practice so far from a town that I was dubious about staying there any longer, although I really enjoyed living on the river.

Another factor entered into my decision to move back into Easton. Social work meant writing long reports by hand and having a school secretary type them for the records. I began to have severe pain in my neck on the right side, and in my writing hand. I went to the Hunterdon Medical Center for a diagnostic workup. I was told that I had moderate to severe arthritis and the prognosis was grim. There was no cure, but I could alleviate the pain by medications. In ten years I would probably need assistance to walk.

I left the Medical Center in tears. I was an active person, loved hiking and mountain climbing, and frolicking with my grandchildren. After the initial shock and distress I had another thought. "I wonder," I said to myself, "If they ever had someone who would swim every day. I'll do that. What do I have to lose?" I moved into Easton right across from the YMCA where there was a pool...the one where Betty Berger had taught me to swim thirty years before. I swam regularly for two years.

My apartment was right in the center of Easton and I opened a Mental Health Counseling practice nearby. Both the apartment

311

and the practice were less than two blocks from Trinity Church. A few nights after my move into the apartment, a small parade, with cymbals, a drum, and penny whistles, marched down the street from the church right up to my door to welcome me back to Easton. The parade was led by Lexa, and Ed Krick. I was honored and greatly amused. We had a riotously good time that night and I felt beloved, blessed and very, very fortunate! How different this separation and divorce was from the first one. This time I felt liberated! And supported. I lived there for two years and I kept up the swimming.

For the following seven years I went through what I later came to call my "Menopausal Madness." Sometimes I called it "The Miry Bog" or "The Dark Night of My Soul." It was all of those things with its highs and lows in every aspect of my life. I had the richest time of my life, along with the most soul searching angst I could contain. Perhaps what I was going through could be labeled "Enchantment." Because much of that time it was as though I was under a spell. Along with the enchantment, I had great internal confusion and bifurcation; as much as one life could endure...the underside of enchantment. This one paragraph is all I am going to say about that period of my internal life because it would take an encyclopedia to cover the complexity of all that happened inside of me during those seven years. Except for one small thing...

One of my daughters, insisted that I tell about growing a single marijuana plant in my garden...my enchanted garden. A person from my children's generation gave me the seed. I had a wonderful vegetable garden so I planted it among the corn. That plant is a gardeners dream! Within a short time it was taller than the corn and continued to grow energetically. Then I became concerned...a policeman lived next door...so I harvested my plant and gave it as a gift to a friend. The end of my life on the wild side.

A few enduring external things must be mentioned that happened during that time because they are vital to the story of my life. First in importance are the births of four more grandchildren.

Lorie met and married a musician, Mark Murphy. It came about this way: I took her to a concert where I wanted her to see a fiddler I thought would be of interest to her. Instead of the fiddler, she was taken with the bass player, of whom she said with awe "Mom, he bows the bass!" Also he could not take his eyes off her. It was not a surprise to anyone that she would marry a musician. Molly was born to them in the spring of 1985 and Sally in summer of 1987. I was not so caught up in my enchantment that I missed their births and many of their milestones. I saw them often and delighted in their babyhood and early childhood. Molly showed signs of musical precocity at an early age, and by the time they were two and four they were singing harmonies. They were adorable, entertaining babies and toddlers.

Dan had become a successful and respected business man and had several girlfriends throughout his twenties. He was nearly thirty when he met Irene, a successful interior designer from NYC. Dan called me the day after he met her and said, "Mom, I have just met the most beautiful woman in the world, and I think she likes me!" He told me many more things about her. I had never before heard him so enthusiastic about a woman. She and I became friends on the first meeting.

Dan and Irene dated about a year and were married in a spectacular ceremony and setting in the fall of 1982. Dan obtained a permit from the City and turned the alley beside Trinity Church into beautiful garden where the reception was held. All his friends from childhood; the scouts, the church and his customers were there. Her friends and family from NYC were there. Dancing continued into the night. It seemed like a fairy tale. They went on a honeymoon to Nova Scotia, and returned to a somewhat complicated life. Irene maintained an apartment in the City and came home on weekends...or Dan would go to the city for the weekend.

They were totally in love. It was fun to be with them wherever they were.

The next summer they produced Jacob. He was a beautiful baby and became a handsome, intelligent, toddler and a delightful child. Dan seemed so happy in his life. He had waited a long time for the right woman and was ready to settle down to raising a family. His business was robust and satisfying for him.

Marcie and Charlie tried very hard to make their life together work for the sake of the three children. Charlie had all the post war afflictions that afflicted many of the veterans of the Viet Nam war. He drank too much, used pot to relieve the symptoms of malaria which he had contracted in the jungles. He had difficulty finding and keeping work.

One evening Marcie went to a meeting of families of Alanon, a group for the spouses of alcoholics. She observed the beaten down women that were trying to stay in intolerable situations and decided that she did not want to find herself in that circumstance ten or twenty years later. They divorced when the children were two, four and six.

Marcie was an attractive, intelligent woman, very committed to the Nuclear Disarmament Movement where she met interesting people and maintained a useful energetic life. She won a State award for the Unsung Hero of the Year.

It was not long before her activities brought her into the company of Gene Mater, an engaging, entertaining and enigmatic figure. Gene was a successful caricaturist who maintained a studio in Bethlehem. They were married in the fall of 1987. Gene took the parenting of Marcie's children seriously and was an excellent father to them. He and I became close friends. We seemed to understand each other, always laughed at each other's jokes and could confide deep feelings.

Life, with its peaks and valleys continued to present itself to me with wonder and amazement; matched with an equal amount of sorrow and pain. Two of the most important people in my life died during the time of my Enchantment, and I did get back to South Dakota to be with both of them.

First was Uncle Marvin. I flew back and visited with him and Aunt Mary in Whitewood SD, a few miles from Sturgis. Aunt Mary was teaching there and Uncle Marvin had been working at the fence post factory. I was summoned because he had been diagnosed with cancer. By the time I arrived Uncle Marvin was gravely ill. We had his last dinner together at their little table in Whitewood. He could scarcely eat but said he wanted to "Sit at the table with Sunshine."

The next day he was admitted to the hospital in Sturgis. The second day of his hospitalization Aunt Mary asked me if I would go over and see if he would let me say a prayer with him; or perhaps read something from the Bible. All the way to the hospital I was saying a prayer that the right and necessary words would come to me. When I arrived at his bedside, he was critically ill; his face a grave shade of yellow. He smiled weakly and reached out his hand to me saying, "I'm glad you came, Sunshine." I sat, holding his hand, waiting for words to come. When they came, I said, "Would you like me to read to you from the Bible, maybe a Psalm or something?" He answered, "I never had much truck with that kind of thing, Sunshine, but what I do know is that I loved a lot of people, and a lot of people loved me." Those were his last words.

After pondering over those words for several weeks I went to Jim Gill, in his priestly role, and asked him what he thought of that. He said, "I think Uncle Marvin got it just right. You needn't be concerned. He went to the right place!"

The second person to die during that period of my life was Grandma Michelson; Hattie, my mother's mother. She had suffered from asthma since childhood and from congestive heart disease during her last few years. In spite of her illnesses, or perhaps because of them, she lived an active life.

The last six years of her life she spent in Sturgis at Sunnyside, an assisted living apartment funded by the government, which took part, but not all, of her Social Security to pay for it. In her first days at the apartment complex she started making it into a community, by celebrating birthdays, visiting other residents, holding card parties, and other community building events. She told me that these were the happiest years in her life. It was the first time she did not have to work at a low paying job to pay rent on a substandard furnished room. Now she had a warm, safe and cozy place that she would never have to leave and she had enough to eat every day. Also she had spending money from her Social Security check. She was near two of her daughters and several of her grandchildren. She felt comfortable and secure which fulfilled exactly what Social Security Income was designed to do.

Mother had been calling me to tell me that Grandma was not doing well, but I did not arrive in Sturgis until the day after her death. I went to the funeral home, owned by the F.O. Jolley family and therefore had the unlikely name of the Jolley Funeral Home. We never realized the irony of that name until years later when we had been away, and heard it again, as if for the first time.

When I walked into the viewing room and saw Grandma's body in her coffin, I was unexpectedly overcome with sorrow. I wept, saying aloud, "Oh Grandma, Grandma, I wanted you to never, never die." I sat there a long time and my mind went through her place in my life...my birth, my naming; important milestones that came before my memory emerged. Then I remembered her being with me through the hard years of my mother's depression, I remembered her taking me to the circus and to parades, and of our time of working on the railroad together. For my twelfth birthday she brought me a ball point pen, the first one we had ever seen. I became sad when I thought of how we had drifted so far apart. I wished I had written more, called her, visited more often. Audibly I asked her to forgive me.

At her funeral some of the nurses who had cared for her at the end of her life told of how in her dying process she would tell the nurse who was with her, some little bit of wisdom, or perhaps a household hint, and then she would fall asleep. Upon waking she would say, "Oh, I am still here. There must be something more I am supposed to do," and she would dredge up one more helpful thing to tell the nurse. To the very end, she wanted to be useful and involved in life. She wanted to leave something useful to those who cared for her. Perhaps we had not drifted as far apart as I thought we had. A great part of her lives in me.

My mother came to visit me in December of 1988. She came to disengage me from the grip of the Enchantment. I was ready for her assistance, and together we extricated me from the spell. I rented a one bedroom apartment in Hamilton Township in New Jersey, near Trenton. It was not a very interesting place to live but I felt it would not be in use very long. I knew this was but a stepping stone on my journey.

At this time I was working for the state of New Jersey in the Division of Developmental Disabilities out of an office in Bordentown. I say, "out of an office" because social workers usually work "out in the field", rather than in an office. That was one of the reasons I liked social work better than teaching. I needed to be able to get out of a contained work space.

I met another of my lifelong friends Sally Liddie at this workplace. Sally and I had similar life problems and joys. We each had three grown children, two girls and one boy; we were each acquiring a grandchild nearly every year; both of us had been divorced, followed by a period of enchantment. We understood each other very well. She met and liked my mother. Sally and I took a couple of cross country car trips to see her. Once we went to see Mother in her little house in Sturgis and once to Seattle to bring her back to Princeton.

Memories of Sally are warm and rich. She was with me as I said goodbye to Aunt Mary in a hospital bed in Rapid City. Aunt Mary had been ill for three or four years, with complications from diabetes. I did not see her nearly as often as I wished I had. That last day in the hospital she was trying to read a book with a magnifying glass. To the end, Aunt Mary was a scholar. It was helpful to have Sally with me on that last visit. She filled the void that was part of this reconstructive period of my life.

The Christmas of 1988 was memorable. It was the first year I had been put in charge of the Division Christmas Party for the developmentally disabled adults we served. I wanted this to be the best party they ever had. I wanted each of the two hundred clients to know that they were valued, that their dignity was honored. I wanted them to really have fun at their party. I spent many hours choosing and wrapping gifts, each with their name on it. I obtained a hall and decorated it for the occasion. Setting up an attractive buffet...all the things one would do for their loved ones or for very important people. Mother got involved in the project and we had a joyous Christmas season that year preparing for that party.

After Christmas, on Dec. 30th, we were presented with a late Christmas present...a very important one. Lauralee was born to Marcie and Gene. Lauralee was my seventh grandchild and my mother's tenth great grandchild. Right from the beginning one could see that she possessed a unique character. In her early childhood she was sober and dignified; she did not easily smile or warm up to people immediately. One sensed there was an important presence behind that thoughtful countenance. Her adult life proved that to be true.

In February, Mother and I flew to California where Rosie and Allen had prepared a grand extravaganza of a birthday party...

celebrating 186 years, the total number of years of our three lives on this planet. Over a hundred and fifty people were there to help us celebrate. Dan, Irene and Jake came from Pennsylvania, Dorothy and Carl from South Dakota, Dorothy's daughter Anita and her husband, John Ramey and their six children, Bobbie and Jack from Rapid City, Ann Scott from Walnut Creek. So many people, such a great celebration.

When I went back to my life in Hamilton township, it was lonely in that apartment. I told my friends at work, that if you want to be really alone, don't go to some remote island or mountain retreat; go to an apartment complex in New Jersey. Every inhabitant there makes a studied effort to never, ever, make eye contact or speak to anyone else.

One day before Mother left to go back to South Dakota she was doing laundry in the central laundry room at the apartment complex. She tried to strike up a friendship with another older woman, and they had a conversation. Mother then invited her to our apartment for a piece of apple pie. Mother said the woman looked at her with fear, bordering on panic and quickly left the laundry room. That woman made sure she never again met with "that strange woman from South Dakota."

My loneliness lasted a short time. I've never been good at being unhappy. The loneliness prompted me to resurrect my hammer dulcimer, which had not been played for seven years. I bought an electronic tuner which was a milestone event for me. I did not spend money frivolously and that just seemed slightly so. Electronic tuners had come out during that seven years when my music participation was on hold. When I finished tuning my dulcimer, I was astounded by the beauty of the sound, and I played many songs I thought I had forgotten. It was sheer delight to play again. I went to the apartment on my lunch hour to play. I played it again every night. Marge Johnson, one of the women with whom I worked heard about it and came home with me at lunchtime to hear it. She invited me to go with her to the Princeton Folk Music monthly sing.

At the first Sing I attended I played and sang better than I ever had before. I was so thrilled to have music back in my life...to be surrounded by people making music together. After the sing, back in my apartment, I went to bed and had one of the most wonderful dreams in my life...I dreamed I was flying. Also I was instructing others on how to fly. "You just think of yourself up there, and then you lift your feet and you will be flying!" The dream was so real that when I woke up, I thought I could really fly. I could not, but when I went to the hammer dulcimer and played, it was as if I were flying. I know it has been said and quoted a thousand times, "Today is the beginning of the rest of your life." That is true of every day, but some days it should be surrounded by blinking neon lights that hover over you from morning to night. This was that kind of day for me.

CHAPTER 26

Princeton

Each month, looking forward to the Princeton Folk Music Sings. I practiced old songs and learned new ones, and attended each sing with high anticipation and was always satisfied at the end of them. I was meeting wonderful people there, who were in my life for years to come. Among many whose names I remember were Justin and Carol Kodner, Hannah and Rich Kaufman, Art and Arlene Miller.

I couldn't help but notice one particular man about my age, who came in from NYC, often late, and always with an original song to sing. His songs were about some significant current issue; one on the homeless on the streets of the city; another about Tiananmin Square. At my third sing, in March of '89, I found myself paired with him in a corner, where we were exchanging our important life data; such as he had been divorced twice, he had four children, all younger than mine, two of whom lived with him; he was a pacifist writer; and he was a fan of the folk singer Utah Phillips, also one of my favorites.

The next morning, I could not get him out of my mind. I wanted to see him again in a more personal setting than the Sing. I did an unprecedented thing, for me. I called the person who had hosted the sing and asked him the name of the man from NYC who sang political songs. I was told that his name was Sherwood Ross and was even given his phone number. Before I lost my nerve by thinking about it, I called him immediately. I asked him if he was interested in seeing Utah Phillips in a live concert. I told him about a small folk club, Godfrey Daniels, in Bethlehem Pennsylvania. I invited Sherwood Ross to go there with me two weeks later on a Friday night when Utah Phillips would be playing. He said he would be delighted to go with me. As I hung up, my knees were shaking. Never had I so boldly pursued a man. This was a new world for me, where a woman could be the initiator of a relationship.

The next two weeks were agonizingly long. When the night arrived, I made an apple pie that Sherwood and I could share, before the concert, or afterwards. I imagined the drive to the concert, I anticipated introducing him to Godfreys. I was a bit surprised that I had not heard a word from him in those two weeks while I was waiting, but...well...he was a busy man. The long awaited evening came, and I prepared myself for the event with special care. I straightened up the apartment and I waited and waited and waited.

Finally, in disappointment I went on to Bethlehem without him. I do not remember one thing about the concert. The next few days I resisted the temptation to call and see if he was all right. Had he become ill, or an emergency with one of his children; was there some explanation? Finally on Tuesday he called and was profusely apologetic, although he did not say why he had not kept our date. He invited me to a play, Murder in the Cathedral, which was to be presented in the Cathedral in Trenton the next Friday night. I accepted, and he did show up as expected.

We had a light dinner at my apartment before the play and became better acquainted. When I asked about his no-show for the concert, he said, "Someday, I will tell you the answer to that." I was puzzled, but also gratified; "someday" meant that there would be more time together.

During the play, we simultaneously, said, "Let's get out of here!" The play was dreadfully dull and poorly presented. On the way back to my apartment he asked if he could check out the baseball scores on the car radio. Of course, I said, "Yes," and was delighted. I remembered days more than a quarter of a century earlier when I would listen to the baseball games while I ironed white shirts and wished that there was someone, anyone, who would talk baseball with me. Sherwood and I went back to my apartment, watched the rest of the game on TV and talked long into the night.

As he was leaving he pulled me close for a goodnight kiss, and with my eyes open, saw that his were open too, and that he caught a view of my magazines resting in a basket in the corner. "You read *Mother Jones!*" he said with great enthusiasm. We both laughed. That was the beginning of a non-ending, usually delightful part of my life.

The events of the next few weeks were so enlightening, entertaining, and exciting for me that they blend into a medley of a new exuberant song. First in importance, I needed to meet his children. He invited me to dinner at his condo the next week. There was Elizabeth, age seventeen, then known as Libby. She was a tall girl, serious and intelligent. She accepted me, albeit, conditionally. She had seen many women come and go in her father's life and was not going to become attached to any of them...not again. I sensed that immediately. Then there was Drew, an incredibly bright boy of fifteen. His acceptance of me was withheld. I didn't take it personally.

Sherwood needed to meet my family. He first met Marcie, Gene and Lauralee when we drove to Bethlehem to see Ann Hills in concert at Godfrey Daniels. He liked them immediately, especially the baby. Lauralee was a sweet three-month old little girl. Sherwood has a soft spot for little children and tried to make her smile. She was uncooperative as was her nature for a few years. Lauralee never gave a gratuitous smile to anyone.

That evening was a spectacularly great time. We started on the drive, early in the evening, and enjoyed spring in Hunterdon and Bucks Counties. We had enough time to stop at Lehigh University. I wanted to show him the hundred-year-old library where I had done my graduate work. He was enthusiastic about the library,

"This is the best library I have ever seen!" he said. Then we went to one of my favorite eating places, "So Eat Already!" in South Bethlehem. Again, it was the best place in which he had ever eaten. The concert, also, was one of the best he had ever attended. I came to realize that when Sherwood was enjoying himself it was always new and the best he had ever experienced. I loved his enthusiasm and his ability to be totally present and view every experience with new eyes.

The next weekend we drove up to Belfast PA to the home of Dan and Irene and their two-year-old son, Jake. A wonderful day! Dan and Irene liked Sherwood and were happy for me. Sherwood and Jake played ball and chase, and hide and seek... they played and played. That bode well for our relationship.

Lorie came with her two little girls, Molly and Sally to my apartment one Sunday to meet Sherwood. The same day, Sherwood's oldest son, Sean, came to meet me. Lorie was her beautiful self and entertained us with her singing and guitar. Sherwood and the little girls entertained each other. I was becoming comfortable with Sherwood and assured that he would be accepted by my family.

One of those early days of our relationship I remember as clearly as if it were last night. It was the first time I went into NYC to meet Sherwood after his day's work in the city. I took the train from Princeton, got a cab at Penn Station to take me to The Brazilian Coffee Restaurant where Sherwood said he would meet me. I expected to find a simple little coffee shop and was surprised and impressed to walk in to a fine restaurant and have the manager say, "You must be Ms. Curry, Mr. Ross's guest."

I was escorted to a table in the back where Sherwood and Sean were waiting for me. After a very elegant Brazilian meal, which I enjoyed although I had never even thought of Brazilian food before, Sherwood retrieved his car from a parking garage and we drove to The Village; Greenwich Village, that is. We were going to a music venue, The Speak Easy, where he knew every musician and even I knew a few. I knew John Gorka from Godfrey's in Bethlehem, and another couple whose names have slipped into the abyss of forgotten things.

Sherwood was well known there and sang, upon request, *The Nightmare Room,* one of his originals, about a mentally ill person. I was offended by the song due to my seriousness about those with whom I worked. It was enthusiastically received by the audience. Sherwood had many songs that skittered along the edges of propriety, along with many lovely, sensitive ones.

At the end of the singing, about midnight, we decided it was time to go home and we drove out of the city. We started singing Irish songs and found we knew most of the same ones. Somewhere in the middle of the chorus of *A Jug of Punch,* he sputtered, "Damn! We are in the middle of downtown Newark!"

Sherwood tried to put a moratorium on all song and conversation until he found his way out of our dilemma. Newark is not a place for anyone to be in the middle of any night. It was an adventure we laughed about many times thereafter.

Sometime in those first years we took a train trip to Chicago to meet his stepmother Sylvia. She was to become one of my favorite people of all time. Sylvia lived alone in an apartment facing Lake Michigan. The apartment was decorated with several of her original paintings. She brushed off compliments of them with a wave of her hand, saying, "They are just little pieces I did in art classes downtown." Those were classes at the Chicago Art Institute. Her paintings were fine examples of a gifted artist.

She was also a careful and wonderful cook and made a Thanksgiving dinner that year for about a dozen of us, catering to everybody's likes and dislikes. She, herself maintained a vegan diet. Sylvia was a Bolshevik, a political persuasion with which I had no experience. She did not push her beliefs on anyone but could give an intelligent, rational explanation of her convictions. I respected her for that.

Sherwood's father, Boris, was in a nursing home, having been afflicted with Alzheimer's. He had been a powerful and opinionated man who left an impression on everyone he knew. Boris had emigrated from the Ukraine early in the 20th century; arrived in this country penniless, worked his way up from the stockyards to real estate in Chicago. His success was jump-started by his command of eleven languages, which made him valuable in Chicago in the early part of the century. He could enable people of diverse backgrounds to work with and understand each other. He was an avowed communist and Sherwood grew up under the surveillance of the FBI. Sherwood's mother was a teacher, who like my mother and I, had gone to college late in life and started teaching in her forties. She was a talented pianist. His parents were divorced just as Sherwood was entering early adulthood. Later, his father married Sylvia, and his mother remained single the rest of her life.

Sherwood, in his turbulent, young adulthood, while seeking independence from his father, had remained close to his mother. Her death, on his birthday, just a couple of years before we met, had nearly devastated him. He had broken off relationship with his father a short time before the divorce of his parents, and the breach with his father haunted Sherwood throughout his life.

We visited Boris in the nursing home...a tender and poignant reunion. Sherwood tried so hard to find a shred of the intelligence, the wit, the bombastic man Boris had been. When we got back to Princeton Sherwood wrote a heart-rending song, titled "My Father." The first line, "I know sometimes he knows me, I see it in his eyes," touches many people who have had such an experience with a loved person in their life.

I met his sister, Ludmilla, and her husband Harry Coven at a Thanksgiving dinner at Scanticon in Princeton Township. They were there with their entire family of four grown children. I felt welcomed and respected by all of them. I wanted to be part of that family. My oldest granddaughter, Joya and I were very close and wanted to be together on Thanksgiving Day. She had received her driver's license a short time before and was allowed to drive Gene's car to Princeton to spend the day with me. It was her first long distance driving adventure and I was honored that she chose to make it spending the holiday with me. She made a great impression on the Coven family.

Sometime in those early years when our lives were becoming interwoven I asked him again about that first date whereby he had stood me up...that Utah Phillips concert. I reminded him that he had said someday he would tell me the reason. I asked if he could tell me now. He looked earnestly into my eyes and said, "Because you were the most dangerous woman I had ever met. I knew that if I got involved at all...if I kissed you one time, I would never get out of it. You were never going to be a one night stand for me."

I was touched by that declaration. Even so, I had insecurities from two former failed marriages and other failed relationships with men, starting with my father. Those insecurities were clenched like a bull dog's grip around my heart. Try as I might, I could never believe there would be, could be a man in the world that wouldn't eventually see someone he felt might be more interesting than I, and for whom he would ultimately abandon me. And Sherwood...he had a complex that compelled him to hold on to relationships forever. Almost all the women he had ever loved, he kept in special tender regard, and he kept in touch with most of them. For a quarter of a century, our complex pasts hovered over our lives, even as we enjoyed the joyous and loving things we did together.

Along with all the good times in life were my bad times with the Division of Developmental Disabilities for the state of NJ. That work was not going well at all. I felt that I was never given work commensurate with my education, training or abilities.

My first attempt to deal with that was to take a leave of absence. I needed go away to view both my work life and my life with Sherwood, from a distance. I had been in close contact with Mother and she was lonely in the bleak winter in South Dakota. My son, Dan was eager to drive out there with me, so we set out in my car just after Christmas and drove across the country.

I remember that drive as a very rewarding time...four days in a car with my son...who could ask for more! We talked of many things and played music on the new CD player Sherwood had given me for Christmas. This was a new thing then and the only music we had was the double CD album of Bob Dylan. The rest of my life whenever I would hear Dylan, I would recall our trip across country.

The time in South Dakota, three months, was a time of exploration for me. I looked for opportunities to work in my area of expertise and found nothing available. I explored the terrain, often driving for entire afternoons on the prairie. I spent two days and nights in the Badlands, on a solitary camping trip. What a place to search your soul. There is nothing as solitary as a night there under the stars, and nothing as uplifting than the meadowlarks song in the morning.

At home, Mother and I got along very well. We were more like age matched friends than mother and daughter. She was still healthy and vigorous in her early seventies. We drove out to the prairie and to little towns in the Black Hills to explore and revisit places she had known in earlier years.

Sherwood and I were in close communication by telephone and mail. In February, for Valentine's Day he was going to be in Cleveland for a business trip and wanted me to meet him there. I made the trip by Greyhound bus, a long and uncomfortable trip, but my assessment was that it was well worth it.

By the end of March I realized that there was not a full life open to me in South Dakota, and went back to New Jersey. I had put my furniture and other belongings in storage and terminated the lease on my apartment in Hamilton Township before leaving for South Dakota, so I had no home to go to in New Jersey.

Sherwood met me when I returned to the East, and took me to his place. He said he could see no reason why I couldn't stay there permanently. I was dubious about it. The first night I happened to be the same night that his son Karl returned from Puerto Rico with his wife, Sophia. There was a joyous reunion between Karl and Sherwood, and the two younger children, Libby and Drew. I felt very much like an outsider, even an intruder.

I stayed a few days while looking for another place and soon arranged to rent a room from Sally Liddie, the social worker with whom I had forged a good friendship early in my years of working for the State of New Jersey.

Work with the State continued to deteriorate. When I returned to the office the supervisor called me in and told me he had a job I would love...sorting out files in a room in the basement of the old building in Bordentown, which the Division was soon to be vacating for a new office downtown.

I left the office feeling very deflated. This was surely not that for which I had worked so hard obtaining an advanced degree! I had scored highest in our division on the Civil Service tests we were required to take to assure the State that we were qualified for our positions. I knew I was qualified for more than sorting files. I went back to my office and sat at my desk in a numbed state for a long time.

The next day I went to the basement to assess the job set out for me. It was a mass of records which had been tossed into that room for more than a decade. There was no order or labeling of the records. Some were in boxes, many were moldy, some just scattered around, leaving very little room to walk.

I called the Division of Records to see if they could send out someone to advise me what had to be kept, what could be destroyed, what was the legal procedure for old state records. They sent someone out the next day who was appalled to find the condition of the files and records there.

That person contacted the supervisor who had given me this assignment. When the person from Division of Records left, my supervisor called me into the office and was very angry with me. Apparently he was scolded for letting records under his supervision become so disorganized. He swore at me and unceremoniously dismissed me from the office.

Again I went to my office, sat at my desk and put my head down on the desk contemplating my situation. After a while, thinking I was alone, I cried and cried in abject misery. I thought everyone was gone but a co-worker heard my crying. I told her the whole story; she listened attentively and told me that I had to contact the Union,

CWA 1039, was our local that handled unfair labor practices in our Division. I had been paying Union dues for years but had little contact with the Union itself. One of my best friends at the Division was Joan Brophy who taught me all I needed to know about the union.

A month or so before my own troubles, some nurses in a mental health facility in New Jersey were striking for long overdue wage increases and better working conditions, and we were told by our supervisor that we would have to go to that facility to work their positions while they were on strike. We were ordered to be strike breakers, scabs. We were told that our jobs were on the line and we could be fired if we refused.

I was confused for a while, thinking of patients who needed to be cared for versus the nurses who needed a living wage. Joan and I talked about it and I came to understand what labor relations was all about. Surprising myself, I found myself at the center of a group of the social workers in my office, surrounding me and asking, "What are you going to do?" I realized they were looking to me to lead them. Joan, who would have known what to say, was out of the office. It was one of the times I silently sent up a prayer, "Please give me the right words...I don't know what to say."

Then I heard my voice say, "We need to support the nurses not by doing their jobs, but by strengthening their quest for higher wages and better working conditions." In a body, we refused to go to the facility and work their jobs. Not one of us lost our job. That incident was my total involvement with the Union before that evening when my co-worker told me I must get in touch with the Union to help me with my problem.

I pondered my dilemma few days before calling the Union. They immediately sent out a representative, a bright young man who was just at the beginning of an important career. He told me to write out a report of exactly what had happened and he would do the necessary steps to get a hearing. I was buoyed up...felt I did have a case that was worthy of being addressed.

We worked on it for a few weeks and then it came to the hearing. Both the supervisor and I presented our cases and it was determined that I would be given an apology. An apology? That was it? No redress at all. I still worked in the same office, with the same supervisor. That particular job, cleaning the file room, was taken from me. Now I managed the fleet of vehicles for our division.

Work became even more difficult for me. Our division moved from Bordentown into a new facility in Trenton. I was put in charge of the unusual incidents along with the fleet management. My dissatisfaction was not because the work was too difficult or too much. Quite the opposite...it was not using my gifts, it was not within my motivated skills. I wanted to do more for the clients of the Division of the Developmentally Disabled.

I did my work, and facilitated the Christmas Party and the summer picnic for the clients of the Division. But it was not satisfying for me. It felt to me that it was window dressing, not the real work that needed to be done. A supervisory position in the Division became open for which I applied and was the mostly likely candidate, but I was passed by.

When I was offered a job by CWA 1039 as a Staff Rep for the Division I was happy and took the job. I would be investigating complaints from workers and determining what sort of case they had and what could be done about it. Often I would represent them at hearings on cases similar to my own. Taking that position meant taking a leave of absence from the State, and becoming employed by CWA. When and if the union employment was terminated for any reason I could return to the State.

Because of what was happening to me at the State, I jumped at the chance to be CWA employee. I worked hard at learning the statutes of labor law and the history of the union. How I wished that I had started earlier, because there was so much to learn, and so much that I felt strongly about. It turned out that I was good at the job of representing the white collar workers of the state. I won most of the cases that I took on. There were many projects where the union went in to secure favorable conditions for workers. I fell into it with a passion. Yes! It felt like a ministry and I had all the passion of a Bible thumping preacher. The Local President and Vice-President, were my capable mentors. This work continued for a couple of years, and I got better at it every week.

Many weekends were spent with my children and grandchildren. Sherwood was becoming a fixture in our family visits and holidays. It was a good time in my family life for those years.

It usually seems to us...I know that is how I viewed it...that personal tragedies happen in other families...not our own. Our family abruptly found that we were not immune to tragedy.

One day when Sherwood was taking me to work at the union office, he came in with me as he was doing some writing for the union. We were just in the door when the phone rang and the secretary said it was for me. I picked up the phone and Marcie was on the other end saying that Irene, Dan's beautiful, beloved, successful spouse, Irene, the interior designer, and mother of Jacob, had committed suicide that morning.

I screamed and collapsed on the floor. Sherwood helped me pull myself together enough to get in his car and he drove me to Wind Gap where Dan, Irene and Jacob lived. Where only Dan and Jacob lived after this sad day. Dan was not at home that morning; he had left the night before for a fishing trip. Irene shot herself with one of his guns, which he kept in a securely locked cabinet in a work shed. He didn't think that she even knew where they were.

Dan's father, Charles Lichtenwalner was the first one there after his foreman arrived and found her body. The foreman had called on a short wave radio for help which was connected to an emergency phone which somehow contacted Charles. He rushed out to Dan's place to get Jacob, before Jacob knew what happened. Marcie was the next one of the family on the scene. It was a horrific, nightmarish chore for her to handle alone. We were all stunned, and it seemed as if our world took on a pace apart from the rest of the world. Phone calls came in incessantly, people arrived with food, old friends from far away appeared. Her parents came from NYC. Sherwood and I went with her father to identify the body. Dan got home that evening and Father Gill was there to give him the news and to comfort him. Dan did not think he could live through this and maintain his sanity. He wanted me to commit him to the psychiatric ward at the hospital. I called Irene's psychiatrist but he could not admit Dan; there were no beds available. Dan pulled himself together enough to tell Jacob. The bereft little boy said, "If that is where my mother is, that is where I want to be."

The next day Dan and I visited her psychiatrist. We had pieced together the story, that Irene had abruptly discontinued an antidepressant which she had been taking for only a few weeks. She had been suffering from intermittent depression for several years and with supervision, tried various medications. Her psychiatrist told us that we could not even imagine the horror of the ideations from which she suffered.

The next few days and weeks were a blur for our family. The funeral was huge. Father Gill gave one of the most elegant sermons most of us will ever hear. All the people who had been at her wedding, all her professional friends from NYC, all the people in the Lehigh Valley who had come to love her gentle spirit, along with her grieving parents were in attendance.

It was a time of unprecedented grief in the history of our family. Irene had been beloved by everyone who knew her. I stayed with Dan and Jacob for a couple of weeks, getting Jacob ready for kindergarten and trying to comfort him. It was anguishing to watch this little boy mourn for his mother. When I could see that Dan and Jacob's life together was taking a shape and direction that would hold. I had a choice to make. Either make a commitment to stay indefinitely or leave and let them get on with their lives and me with mine. I decided on the latter. Dan and I talked about this for a long time one night after Jacob was in bed. Dan wanted his autonomy in raising his son and did not want to become dependent on me. We each had our lives to live. I could see that they had each other, and the strength to get through this.

When I got back to New Jersey, my personal life had fallen apart. Sherwood and I did not resume our former relationship immediately. Sherwood has an aversion to death so strong that his instinct veers him away from any contact with it. Death was a presence that stuck to me like nettles for many months. I knew Sherwood well enough to know he was trying to distance himself from death, not from me. It took a long time before I could shake off the aura of death. There was a huge chasm in my life for a long time.

I resumed work at the Union and that was the saving grace that got me through that black hole. The work was consuming and kept me busy twelve hours a day. Eventually Sherwood and I got back together, and resumed a relationship that was tempered by reality and less by romance, than had been the case before the intrusion of Death.

Work at the Union was going along at an interesting pace and absorbed me. I was offered an attractive early retirement package from the State and had signed on for it...to be enacted in ninety days. Then I would be totally a CWA employee and not have the State to return to. That was all right with me. I could see myself working at the union the rest of my life. The salary was good; benefits and pension were exceptionally attractive.

Local 1039 was always involved in crises work and even though we knew an election was coming up we did not do heavy campaigning. There was so much other work to do. Elections for the officers came up every three years. A new slate of candidates for the office of the local was presented which challenged the current officers. We were doing well with our cases and never felt that our officers we were in danger of being voted out of office. However, we were not aware of an underground Black Coalition that was campaigning strongly for their slate of candidates. It had not been seen or suspected because we had two Afro-Americans on our staff and were working well together. We represented many Afro- Americans at grievance hearings.

The evening of election day when we began to count the votes, we were in for a total shock. Within the first half hour of counting, it was clear that our side was voted out and that an Afro-American slate would take over the Local. We were devastated. Our officers vacated their positions the next day. My retirement from the state had become final a few days before. I could not go back to the State but I was sure that I could stay on with the Local.

The new president was a good union friend of mine. We had been on picket lines together, we sang all the union songs together, we had gone to conferences together. The two Afro-Americans on the staff of the local were kept on and I thought they would lobby for my continued employment.

The day after the election the new President, my friend, informed me that I was fired. She said they didn't want my kind around anymore. I asked, "My kind? Do you mean my color?" She nodded assent to that last part of my question. She could not say it aloud. I could not believe it! I continued to go to work every day for about a week. I was completely ignored; shut out of meetings, never spoken to. I refused to clean out my desk.

When it became public knowledge that I was fired, an unprecedented thing happened: The union members of the Local, picketed the CWA office. They carried signs begging to keep me on at the union. I was very moved by the demonstration. It was covered by the press and was on the front page of the Trenton papers the next morning.

However, the order that I was fired still stood. After a couple of weeks, I did clean out my desk, but left my elegant leather desk chair...my own personal chair. One of the Afro-American men, who was my friend and was the only one who would talk to me, offered to carry it to my car for me. I told him, "I intend to be back and sit in that chair." He looked at me with sorrowful eyes that were full of unspoken words.

While all that was going on at the union in Trenton, my family in Easton and New York were experiencing great life-changing events as well.

While Dan was in the process of trying to get his life back together, a friend had suggested that he go to a grief counseling group in Doylestown, quite a distance from Easton. This friend also had a friend, Joan Rush, who would take care of Jacob on the night that Dan would go the sessions. By the end of the sessions, Jacob had decided that he wanted Joan to be his mother and her boys, Jeff, Kevin and Danny to be his brothers. It was not long before Dan and Joan also thought that was a good idea. By January of the next year they were married in the chapel at Lafayette College, where Joan was employed. The wedding was attended by many of Joan and Dan's friends, and families, all of whom had supported each of them in the loss of their former spouses. Their four boys were an integral part of the celebration, as they all embarked on their life together. It seemed to be the beginning of new life for the couple and their children. They moved into a spacious house on College Hill, a house we all enjoyed visiting.

In New York, Lorie and Mark ended their marriage of seven years. She was working as nurse in Garrison New York, as well as for a photographer. She was also working for a financier there. She found many ways to make a living in this tumultuous time. She was singing in the choir of an Episcopal church and having a busy, active life. There, in the little nearby town of Cold Springs, she met Bill Ceccolini, a gentle, kind and handsome man. He was becoming a major part of her life in Garrison.

During that time, Lorie was on a photo shoot with her employer, doing a shot of her on a horse. The horse made an unexpected sudden turn and she was thrown off and was seriously injured. She was taken to the hospital and x-rayed which revealed severe injuries. The doctors said she would not be able to walk for many months. Mother and I went to see her immediately and did what we could to help with her children and her life. Bill Ceccolini was her main support at that time.

Back to my life in Trenton: I filed a grievance against the union and went to work preparing a case. A few months later the case was heard by an arbitrator, and my side lost on some very arcane ruling.

I spent the next few months trying every tactic I could think of to get my job back. I went to the Civil Rights office in Philadelphia, Rutgers School of Law, a dozen labor lawyers. No one wanted to take on the Black Coalition in New Jersey.

One lawyer, the last one with whom I consulted, and a very honest one, said he would take my case. He added that it would cost two thousand up front, and a thousand every month he was on the case and the chances that we would win were very slim. With that bit of information from a trustworthy source, I gave up.

Shortly after my debacle at the union, Mother visited us for a few months. She had a hard time comprehending what was going on. Things like this did not happen in South Dakota. Life was so simple there. Sherwood and I enjoyed her visit with us in Princeton. She was a comfort to me and a reminder that life can be simple and gratifying. She kept me sane. We had a great Thanksgiving at the lovely Scanticon resort with my mother and children in attendance.

Early the next year, in February, Sherwood had a surprise party for me in that resort. It was a Saturday and we often went to dinner there, so I was not surprised when he suggested that we go there for my birthday dinner. He was insistent that we swim there before dinner, which I agreed to, as I love to swim and there was a great pool at Scanticon.

I was speechless when we entered the swimming area and there in the pool were all my progeny, except for Lorie and her family. There they were; Marcie and Gene, Joya, Eli, Ian and Lauralee; Dan and Joan, Jacob, and Kevin. I quickly changed and got in the pool with them. Then I noticed that everyone had their eyes fixed on the steps into the pool area. There, walking down the steps with her girls, Molly and Sally, and Bill accompanying her, was Lorie. She, who was to be on crutches or in a wheel chair for a long time, was walking on her own! Soon they were in the pool with us and she told me the amazing story of her recovery.

Being a nurse she knew exactly what had to happen for those bones to knit and heal. She envisioned that happening as she lay in her bed after her accident. It was as if she knit her bones together by visualization. The doctors who had attended her, went back to check on the x-rays to assure themselves that their diagnosis had been correct. It was. She had healed herself in about one-tenth of the time they expected it would take for the bones to knit together. What a great birthday present that was for me.!

Mother stayed with us in Princeton a little longer. She greatly appreciated many things about Princeton, the old architecture, the new library and the senior center there. During her stay she became hospitalized with congestive heart failure. I took her to Emergency and they spent several hours getting her heart into an acceptable rhythm. Finally the crises stage was over and they put her in a hospital room. A social worker came to interview her, as was the standard procedure of the hospital. When he came to the question, "Do you take any recreational drugs?" she answered, "No, but I sure do like my Xanax." The social worker had to leave the room as he was overcome by laughter. Mother had an enduring sense of humor.

Her visit was a delight to us and to many Princetonians who came to know her. One of our friends, Laurie Lynn Strausser, a reporter for the *Princeton Packet*, interviewed Mother for a story on a blizzard that happened while she was with us in Princeton. Laurie wanted her perspective on blizzards, because of her many years in South Dakota, known for its epic blizzards. We were proud that she made the *Princeton Packet* during her short stay there.

I collected my unemployment checks from the State, and signed up for continuing education which the state of NJ would pay for as it would assist me to become more employable. Computer literacy was becoming an enhancement to employability so I found a program that would teach me computer skills. It was a three-month program lasting over the summer at the Cittone Institute in Princeton.

I liked going back to school. As well as computer skills, one was required to take a course in basic English. That class was a pure delight for me. The teacher and I became good friends and were more colleagues than teacher and pupil. I received an award at the end of the course for proficiency in English, but more surprising to me was that out of five hundred students; only two of us received perfect attendance awards. I would never have willingly missed one of those classes.

During my time at the Cittone Institute, Sherwood and I had optimistically bought a condominium in Princeton. We did it as a vote of confidence that I would soon be back at work and life would continue in a predictable and positive way. We moved in and fell into the pattern of domesticity which we enjoyed immensely...the decorating, keeping house, having a garden, and neighbors. I loved it!

However, it was a short love affair. I did not find a job immediately. I was sixty-two years old. No one ever said I was too old, but it was apparent to me that the newly hired people were under forty.

Sherwood had been employed by a large corporation to do a public relations video and he had invested a large sum of money in the project. Quite unexpectedly the corporation announced that due to their financial situation, they could not pay him for it. They had declared bankruptcy. This was the major source of Sherwood's income. Both of his younger children were in college. He had many expenses. He tried several ways to deal with the problem, but within a short time realized that he would have to declare bankruptcy.

We would have to disentangle ourselves from the mortgaged condo. Before complete despair consumed us, a plan began to develop. It was murky at the beginning but began to take on clarity.

Sherwood had always said he would love to live in the West. I believe that part of his initial attraction to me was because I was from South Dakota.

Mother returned to Sturgis after her visit with us and she had been calling me saying she was afraid she could not live in her house in Sturgis alone much longer and that she would rather die than go to a nursing home. Those events...my unemployment, the bankruptcy, Sherwood's desire to live in the West, and Mother's need for someone to help her...drew me to an overwhelmingly obvious conclusion. We would go to South Dakota and help her with her problem and it would certainly help us get through ours!

Any legal procedure is much easier in South Dakota than in New Jersey, so Sherwood's inevitable bankruptcy could be filed from there. We could find a place we could afford in or near Sturgis, and Mother would have the help she needed. Furthermore,

Sherwood's wish to live in the West would be fulfilled and I would be going home.

We sold the condominium in a few weeks but had little equity in it, so we lost money in the transaction. We were glad to be out of the financial debacle.

Rosie and Allen from California and Marcie from Bethlehem came to help us move. Those helpers were answering a call far above any call of duty. They were gifts of love. Rosie always knew when I needed her most and was always there. She brought lightness to it and we laughed through the packing and tying up loose ends. I treasured spending those last days in the East with her and Marcie. I was leaving my children in the East and that was like a stone in my heart but staying would have been an avalanche of disasters.

It was a tumultuous move, getting all our things in the U-Haul, leaving the condo in good condition, tying up loose ends, but we were finally on our way to South Dakota. Sherwood drove a U-Haul truck with our furniture in it, and I followed in my car across the country. We spent an overnight with his sister Ludmilla in Chicago, but mostly we drove on as if we were fleeing toward a new world of freedom. Leaving New Jersey felt like a deliverance for me. I had had enough.

CHAPTER 27

South Dakota

It doesn't take long, driving west from Chicago, before you begin to experience space. Space, that you forget the preciousness of, when you are having a busy life in an urban city in. Ah-h, that day in June, after getting through Milwaukee, you notice the terrain. Your eyes no longer bump into things as soon as they are open. Your sight can soar off into the distance. This day in June was as exciting to me as the first time Charles, the children and I drove back there forty years earlier. That first time, my gratification was that, only when I set foot on the soil of South Dakota did I believe I could get back there. This time, it was that I really planned to stay! Just as I had on that day forty-some years ago, I had a compulsion to get out of the car, pick up a handful of dirt, smell it, then deeply breathe in air that was as pure as heaven itself...look up and absorb a sky bluer than any sky I had seen in decades. It seemed to me that for the past forty-four years I had been experiencing second-hand pieces of the air, the earth and the sky. The source of it was here.

Mother was ecstatic when we arrived. She had a daughter back in her life and felt secure in her little house. The future looked good indeed. She and Sherwood got along well; as they had back in Princeton, way back in that other world.

We stayed with Mother a few days looking for a place to rent, but found nothing in Sturgis. We checked out the small towns nearby; Whitewood, Tilford, Belle Fourche, and St. Onge. Definitely nothing there. Sherwood had been scanning the newspapers and saw an ad for a house in Newell, a town thirty-one miles north...the town that was home to my first boyfriend. I was sure that Sherwood would not want to live there but indulged him in the exploration. I was indulging myself, too. I relished driving around the area and was absorbing everything I remembered about the prairie.

What we found in Newell on that hot day was a deserted town. We saw one person sitting out in front of the bar on Main Street. We were not sure if it was a live person or a stuffed dummy. We were stunned by the starkness of the town, and drove back to Sturgis in reflective silence.

The U-Haul, parked in front of Mother's house would be in violation of a city ordinance after one week. Towards the end of the week we found some teenagers who for a small fee helped us get our belongings into a storage facility and we returned the U-Haul. There is an abundance of storage facilities in Sturgis because of the Motorcycle Rally. Thousands of rally-goers leave their camping gear and sometimes their machines in storage awaiting the huge Rally in the first week of August. Our few belongings joined theirs at a storage place near Mother's house.

On Monday morning we decided to explore possibilities in Spearfish, a town twenty miles northwest of Sturgis. I loved Spearfish ever since Mother went to summer school there in 1945. Rosie and I stayed with her in a tiny cabin by Spearfish Creek and went to the Lab School on the campus of Black Hills Teachers College, now renamed Black Hills State College.

It was an elegant town by Western standards, influenced by the college and inspired city planners. It was named *The Queen City of the Black Hills* for good reason. The town is situated in a basin surrounded by the Black Hills on three sides and off to the northwest is the vast prairie. Spearfish Creek, a brisk and productive stream runs across the low end of town where the trout beg to be caught. Near the stream is a playground which was designed by the children in town, and executed by an architect who followed their ideas for the design. It is the only playground I have ever seen that has a gate for the children to swing on. Only a child would think of asking for that in a playground.

We found a realtor who showed us a few apartments and seeing no enthusiasm from us, made a call to a client who had been trying to sell her house but might be willing to rent it on a short-term basis. We fell in love with the house; there was no hesitation at all about renting it.

It was perfect, a two-bedroom with a small room for Sherwood's office, a large living room with a picture window looking out to the mountains, a kitchen that delighted me and a small manageable yard. We signed the papers that day and drove back to Sturgis elated. We retrieved our belongings from storage with the help of the same young men we had hired just four days before to put it in storage. They helped us move into the house in Spearfish.

Getting settled there was so easy! Setting up bank accounts, dealing with the Post Office and obtaining our driver's license, was all accomplished in one morning. The picture taken for my driver's license is one of the best pictures I have of myself. I was ecstatic! That afternoon we joined the fitness center at the college, which included a wonderful aquatic facility. I drove down to Sturgis later in the afternoon and told Mother all the details.

She had been apprehensive about this move because of the distance from Sturgis. She feared that I might not be able to get to her in the winter. We talked for quite a while and I mollified her by pointing out that we were a great deal closer that we had been in Princeton. Little by little, she became more comfortable with the situation.

Summer in South Dakota was glorious. Lorie, Bill and her girls, Molly and Sally, visited us there. It was Bill's first trip to the West and he was entranced by it. We went to Orman Dam for fireworks with my niece Jenice, and her daughter, Becky. The next day we drove to Belle Fourche for the Annual 4th of July parade and rodeo. Another day Bill and Sally went fishing in

Spearfish Creek and brought home several trout for dinner. I made a polenta souffle to accompany their fish, and Sally, who had been a picky eater, said, "This is the best food I ever ate!" Their visit was delightful, every minute of it. We drove out to Bear Butte; yes, the same Bear Butte that had been so important to me at age thirteen.

We went on east for seventy miles to the home of my mother's cousin, Mildred and her late husband Paul. I had spent many vacations and summers there when I was a child. Standing anywhere on their farm, you can see for miles. You see the glorious undulating river breaks rolling down to the Belle Fourche River, with nary an automobile or commercial sign in view. Above it all is the breathtaking dome of an azure sky, so deep and clear that it takes your breath away. Words cannot describe its magnificence.

This visit of Lorie and Bill's was a few years after Paul's death so Mildred was maintaining the ranch with the help of her grandson. She was in her late seventies at this time and could still climb the fences with agility and do the chores that had to be done. Lorie and Bill were impressed with the ranch but even more by Mildred. That was gratifying to me because Mildred was one of my major role models while growing up. I never felt I lived up to her stature, but Bill and Lorie's estimation of her, confirmed that I had chosen a good one to hold up as my model.

The last day of their visit, I got an urgent phone call from a daughter of one of my best friends in the East. Loy Zaremba had been married to Bob Tolson for a few years and they were enjoying a beautiful late-life marriage in Chevy Chase Maryland. She and I remained in close contact. Loy's daughter was calling to tell me that Bob had been electrocuted while installing an attic fan. Her mother, Loy, was in depths of grief and despair. Her daughter cautiously suggested that my presence might help Loy get through this tragedy. I said I would be there in two days.

The next day I drove Lorie and her family to Denver in a rented car so they could get on a plane to New York. I turned around and drove home, eight hundred miles round trip. When I arrived home about midnight I awoke Sherwood and he drove me to Sioux Falls to catch a plane to Maryland.

On the four hundred miles of the flat expanse of South Dakota, in the middle of the night, while I was fast asleep, our vehicle and a deer attempted to occupy the same space on the highway. I heard the deep thud and awoke. By the time I was awake enough to realize what had happened, we were well past the point of the collision. The rental car we were driving suffered moderate damage. The deer...well, it was dark and was over before you could realize what happened to it.

I was extremely upset, as Sherwood was not authorized to drive that car. There had not been enough time to go to the rental agency and get him signed on. There was damage, but not so much that we could not drive on to the airport. I reported the accident to my insurance agent by phone, although I did not tell them that I was not driving, and I actually told Lorie that I *was* driving.

I went on to Loy's and immersed myself in her life, trying to help her through the first days of grieving. One of the things we did was buy a puppy. It was a life affirming diversion and helped her through the difficult time after Bob's tragic death. With the opening of school she returned to her position as Speech Therapist, and did get on with her life, albeit much shaken.

When I returned to Spearfish after Loy's tragedy, I was obsessed with my lie to Lorie and to the insurance company. I simply could not get it out of my mind. Every morning, or almost every morning, since my confirmation some fifty years before, I started the day with a reading from the Forward Day by Day pamphlet which had been my textbook for confirmation. There is a credo titled "For Today", which I always read first. One sentence in that piece is this:

Dolores

Help me to keep my heart clean, and to live so honestly and fearlessly than no outward failure can dishearten me or take away the joy of conscious integrity.

I felt that by my lie, I had been *disheartened* and lost the *joy of conscious integrity*. I felt that I had seriously compromised my *integrity*, and suffered tremendously. I woke in the night thinking of it. I felt guilty and sullied. I spoke to no one I knew personally about this... only to a couple of attorneys from whom I can remember nothing, except that that they were not helpful.

Finally after about six weeks of agony I went to my State Farm insurance agent in Spearfish and told him the whole story. He was kind and understanding and not the least bit judgmental. He told me that under my insurance I was covered and anyone to whom I had given permission to drive was covered. Whew! It was as though a stone was lifted from my spirit. It was not the insurance or the expense of it that had been troubling me. It was that I had twisted the truth. That plagued me and sapped my energy. Telling the truth to the agent gave me back my energy and integrity. I called Lorie and told her the truth. She said, "I knew it was not true. You would never have hit a deer on the road."

Later in the summer Dan, Joan, Kevin and Jake, came to visit. Their visit coincided with a visit from Rosie and Allen and, Karen, and her four-year-old daughter, Stephanie. Much of that visit is but a blur in my memory but it is aided by some wonderful snapshots... one of Kevin and Jake in Mother's yard, playing with Stephanie. Another is of Mother showing Stephanie her garden, pointing to a corn stalk, as if she is saying, "Grow!" Mother cherished her garden and used it to teach children about growing things whenever an opportunity arose. Mary Lou came later in the summer and as we always do, we had a comfortable, companionable time together. A picture of her sitting among the poppies is one that has survived all the cuts and sits on a shelf in my room.

In the early fall Sherwood's bankruptcy hearing came up. We went to Rapid City for the hearing. Never had I seen Sherwood so agitated. At the lunch break we went for a walk around the area and it was there that he had his first intimation of heart irregularities. They were not enough to send him to the hospital, but nevertheless, were troubling. The bankruptcy was declared and we went on with our life in Spearfish.

Soon the Earth was tilting away from summer sun. In the fall Sherwood and I took rides up Spearfish Canyon, ate trout at the Latchstring Inn and were sure we had reached utopia. After that glorious fall winter came on gradually. Before Christmas it was a lovely early winter in Spearfish. Crisp, cold mornings warming by afternoon. Light snows that covered the town in sugar frosting, and some ice storms that coated every branch and flower stem with the clearest glass, sparkling in the low winter sunlight.

Christmas was glorious! I decorated a tree with white doves, blue lights and ribbons and angels; one of my favorite Christmas trees of all time. We bought a garden statue of St. Francis for Mother and she was as thrilled as a little girl who received for Christmas, her heart's desire.

After Christmas we entered a real South Dakota winter. There were a couple of days I could not get to Sturgis...roads closed. They were never closed for more than one day. I noted that they certainly know how to handle winter in those South Dakota towns...far better than Princeton where they can hardly believe it would dare to inconvenience them and in their unbelief are woefully unprepared.

Sherwood seldom got warm. The only time he was warm was when he was at the gym, working out at a furious pace. The college gym was always open and he was often there. One day after a blizzard, before the roads or driveways were clear he walked the two miles in the snow to the gym. I stayed home and shoveled out the driveway.

He was gone about four hours and when he came in I asked if he could shovel the front walk. Because he was so cold he helped himself to a hearty Scotch and water. Then he shoveled furiously for about fifteen minutes. After that he went to bed. In a few minutes I heard a heavy thump in the bedroom. He was on the floor and unconscious. I called the emergency squad. He quickly gained consciousness and asked me to drive him to the hospital...he did not want to go in an ambulance, so I drove him to the tiny Queen City Hospital.

They admitted him and worked for quite a while to get his heartbeat, blood pressure and respiration working properly. He remained in the hospital for a few days, and was seriously shaken by the experience.

Little by little winter subsided. By February it was warm and the roads were clear enough that we had a birthday party for the five of us who have celebrated so many birthdays together...Mother, Rosie, Jenice, Kayla and me. I had gone to great lengths to prepare food and get the house ready for that party. Picking up Rosie at the airport was a joy and we laughed all the way from Rapid City to Sturgis. There we picked up Mother and continued on to Spearfish. The event was a success by any standards, with many of my South Dakota and Wyoming family in attendance, laden with flowers and other gifts. It was such a treat to have another birthday together in South Dakota.

We did have a few more storms that winter but those late season storms had the hangdog appearance of late arrivers who missed the main event. With the arrival of spring I was working in the yard, doing all kinds of plantings and pruning in the mornings, swimming twenty laps in the gym and going to Sturgis in the afternoons to work in Mother's yard. Sherwood spent most of the summer at the gym. He was concerned about his health.

Sherwood always had time and reason to look for ways to earn money. As he had worked in Public Relations, Vern Bills, my

Dolores Curry

cousin Dorothy's son...yes, the one I had taken care of when he was two...now a successful business man in Belle Fourche, gave us a job trying to get an additional phone company accepted in the Northern Hills. We did the publicity and worked hard but were not successful. Through that endeavor, we came to know another aspect of the region and we had an enjoyable time working on it.

Then we were into our second summer...a typical South Dakota summer. Some days so hot you could not walk in the sunshine; some days achingly beautiful; so beautiful you could hardly take it in. And there were numerous dramatic thunder-storms and astounding rainbows afterwards.

A couple, Bobbie and Mort Meyerson, who had been friends of Sherwood's for forty years were coming from Long Island New York to visit us. We were thrilled with the prospect of showing this geographical and cultural wonder to people who had no previous experience with it. Bobbie was an accomplished artist and Mort, a writer.

The visit turned out much differently than planned. Mort was not able to come and Sherwood had a business trip to Oklahoma City that week. So Bobbie and I had a week without our men. She was awestruck from the moment we left the airport in Rapid City. Never had she seen so much open land or so much unobstructed sky. It appealed to her artist's eye. She and I forged an abiding friendship.

We took Mother's marigolds to the county fair, an affair so simple it astounded this native New Yorker. We went to the "Catch Your Own Trout" restaurant for dinner. One moonless night we drove out on the prairie to a place where there was no artificial illumination anywhere. We turned off the car lights and stood out there with our faces lifted to the sky until we were almost drunk with the grandeur of it. It was the last night of a great visit. When I took her to the airport to return to New York I asked her what had impressed her most. Without hesitation she said, "Oh, the stars, the stars!"

Another family of visitors was Dan and Jacob, now called Jake, Joan, and Kevin. They stayed about a week and enjoyed Spearfish and the wonders surrounding it. Jake stayed on after Dan and Joan's visit. He and I had a delightful couple of weeks together. Unobstructed time with a curious, active ten-year-old boy gifted with a keen sense of humor is one of the greatest gifts a grandmother could ask for. We explored all of Spearfish...the fish hatchery, the University. We went to the Buffalo Jump, a relic from the Indian days of hunting buffalo many decades before our time. It consists of a deep, wide hole in the land, where buffalo were herded into, and thereafter slaughtered. Buffalo were the source of food, shelter and more for the Plains Indians. It was unlike anything Jake had ever seen, and he was awed.

One of the first days Jake and I had alone, we went to a local ice cream parlor for a treat and after we left I realized I had given them a twenty and they had given me change for a five. I went back to talk to them about it and they said when they cleared the register that evening, they would call me. And they did. The honest and straightforward manager said there was no discrepancy on the register we had used, but on another one they were fifteen dollars over when they checked their balance at the end of the day. He told me to come in and he would give us some gift certificates. He gave me so many that Jake and I went in every day of his visit and had a treat. Jake thought that was so cool.

We also went to a little rodeo in the country near Spearfish, where he could get dangerously close to the corrals and bucking horses. He loved that! I knew we would experience events and places there that he would not see anywhere else and believed that he would treasure that visit for the rest of his life. Every time I think of it, I smile.

As it has for a zillion years, summer gave way to fall. The aspen trees trembled with gold lights. Other deciduous trees were exploding like flamenco dancers, whirling, twirling, pirouetting, until finally exhausted; they dropped their flamboyant gowns and then shivered in the breezes which grew colder every day. I had a front row seat to watch the performance through the kitchen window in our house in Spearfish.

One September day, through that kitchen window I saw Sherwood trudging up the hill that led to our house. His head was down and he was walking with fervid determination. What was going on in his head became clear to me in a single second. Winter was coming. He feared for his health, specifically for his heart. When he came in and sat at the table I sat down across from him. Almost as if another being were speaking through my mouth, I heard myself say, "Winter is coming. It will be hard. Why don't you go to Florida and stay with our friends, the Adkins? We have a standing invitation with them. I will go stay with Mother through the winter."

It was as if I had thrown a life preserver to a drowning man. By afternoon he had boxes lined up against the wall ready to be packed. I must admit that I was slightly deflated at his eagerness to leave. I had so loved this place and our life there.

That night I woke up about 1AM. He was not in the bed. I got up and listened for his presence and discovered he was in the basement packing up some of the things he had stored there. I went down to talk with him as he was working. As he unfolded the first box a dead snake fell out of it. We were both repelled by that sight, and with my aversion to snakes, I knew it was time to get out. Strange as it seems, the dead snake seemed to be a message for me and made the process of leaving that house much easier. Within a couple of days Sherwood was on his way to Miami, and I was cleaning up the house and arranging the move to Sturgis.

It was September 19 when I arrived, with all my furniture, at Mother's house and it was snowing, a wet slogging snow. Except for Mother's glow of happiness, it was a gloomy day. She now felt secure after a long spell of doubt and fear about the upcoming winter.

I had a whirlwind of thoughts and emotions going on in my heart, mind and soul. I had not lived under the same roof as my mother since I was a freshman in high school except for a few weeks one summer. My immediate action whenever I arrive in a place where I intend to stay longer than two weeks is to start nesting. Yet this was not my place to nest. It was Mother's house... once Mother and Tom's, and before that Mother, Tom and Rosie's house. I had never lived in this house with them.

They moved here after I married Charles and had my own house and babies. Mixed in among the feelings was some primordial comfort of being under the same roof as my mother...just she and I. Another part of my whirlwind emotions was that I did miss Sherwood. I worried about him, too. Like all whirlwinds, this one subsided of its own accord. You simply wait them out.

October became cold and cloudy; autumn ushering in winter. During that dreary fall I answered an ad in the paper and got a job doing the Gallup Poll in Sturgis. I wanted to do it because it reminded me of field work as a Social Worker. Also, I wanted an overview of the culture of Sturgis. Of course, in addition to that, it was an income, albeit, small.

I knocked on doors and presented my credentials and when I gained entrance, which was ninety-eight percent of the time, I asked many questions and filled out the forms. Having lived in the East for so long, it was amazing to me that people would so easily and willingly let me in. I was invited into many homes and made many observations. Furthermore, I was jolted by the recognition of how eager they were to talk to someone, anyone. One of the major cultural differences between the East and the West is the openness of people. Westerners, not all of them, but most, want to talk with other people. My Gallup polling was a short study of a small town...a small town where I intended to stay for an indeterminate period of time. I was committed to staying there as long as Mother lived. I was feeling increasingly comfortable with that commitment.

St. Thomas, the church where I had been confirmed, became my church again. Elizabeth Bryan, the priest, and I became very good friends. I was so gratified to find a soul mate, someone with whom I could talk about my spiritual life. I was quite involved with the church. Mary and Susan Wood were good friends of mine both in the church and out of it. I was building a support group of friends; Mary Wood, Susan Writer, also Maggie O'Neill, Karen Haynes, and Michelle Frye. Those friends made the prospect of staying there for a long time, possible for me.

Little by little I became comfortable in the house and started making some accommodations for myself to become more at home there. For example, I found a small portable dishwasher that would connect with the sink. Mother was somewhat resistant to having a dishwasher, but was so happy to have me living there that she acquiesced.

Having any carpentry work done while she was home was not possible. She needed her space to be unobstructed and the air free of pollution. So the first time she was hospitalized I had a carpenter cut a pass through between the kitchen and the living room, by the chair which she always occupied. I was apprehensive about making a structural change in her house but she welcomed it heartily. It gave more light and she felt more connected to what was going on in the kitchen. I felt easier about settling in the house. I could make it my home.

Mother and I enjoyed being with each other. Sometimes we watched an old movie on TV, but mostly we played cribbage. Often she woke in the night and we would play a couple of games until sleep came back to her. It was the conversational patter that went on during the game that we enjoyed the most. She always had a sense of humor and found many things to laugh about almost every day. She was generally cheerful. I went to the library once a week and checked out large print books for her. I apologized and said that perhaps I had brought ones she had already read. She laughed and said, "Don't you know; they are old friends. I can read them over and over again."

The next time she was in the hospital, not long before Christmas, I found a couple who would paint the living room. I chose a very light blue, as the furniture I had moved in from the house in Spearfish was blue and white striped, and her rug was blue. I framed the windows with white Bamberger lace curtains and had the rug cleaned and new linoleum put down in the kitchen. I had a beautiful collection of cobalt blue glass and found a corner shelf unit in which to display them. Little by little the house was becoming transformed. She was thrilled when she came home from the hospital that time.

That early snow in September was a harbinger of what was to come. It seemed the snow never stopped until May. Many times we had a hard time getting the driveway and walks shoveled. Mother was claustrophobic and any time she felt she could not get out created serious anxiety attacks, so I tried to keep ahead of that with shoveling. It was a difficult winter.

The only thing I remember about that Christmas is that, Sherwood, having arrived in Miami very broke but ever resourceful, had managed to find an inexpensive apartment in Miami Beach, abutting the causeway. He sent me a postcard of the building and talked about it in our daily phone calls. I was eager to see it. "What," a reader may be asking, "does that have to do with Christmas?"

What it has to do with Christmas is that the Christmas gift he sent me was a CD by Alex Fox, a Venezuelan guitar player, *par excellence.* Sherwood heard Alex playing on a stage on Ocean Drive in Miami Beach. In Sturgis on those cold snowy nights when I had trouble sleeping I would play Alex Fox. That hot Latin American music would conjure images of tropical scenes and would warm me and make me feel that Sherwood was not so far away. I gained cozy comfort from that music.

In February Dan came to visit me for my birthday. He arrived a day before the party and I met him at the Rapid City Airport. He was a son of whom I could not help but be proud! I never liked to say I was proud of my children. I usually said I was amazed by them or humbly grateful for them. This time, I was proud and could not deny it. He had grown into a man who exuded competence, kindness and good taste.

He wanted to take me out to the best restaurant in Rapid City, so, after a few that he rejected; we went to the Canyon Lake House. It met his standards and was better than he expected. He took me to a gift shop adjoining the Alex Johnson Hotel and wanted to buy me anything I wanted. I was so happy that he was with me that there was nothing left to want.

The next morning we went shopping in Rapid City for the dinner we would make for the guests who would arrive the next day. After our shopping we drove out to the prairie and he wanted to see all the places where I had memorable experiences in my childhood and youth. He wanted to hear all my stories. He loved the prairie. He expressed amazement that the government had set up electrification of the remote farms in the 1930's, via the REA program under the Roosevelt administration.

The following day, Rosie arrived from California, and every relative and friend we had in South Dakota arrived. It was a great event. We often wondered how we were able to pack so many people into Mother's little house, but through the fifty years she lived there we filled it many, many times. Often those times were in February for the family birthdays.

After the excitement of Christmas and February, I was restless. I really do not know how to be unemployed. As I was taking Mother to Dr. Jenter's office every week that seemed a good place to start. I was hired as a receptionist for his practice and found it interesting and absorbing.

Dr. Jenter was the doctor for many of the farmers and ranchers out on the prairie. I would listen to their conversations as they were in the waiting room. Once a rancher came in with a broken arm. A cow had butted him into a corner and knocked him down. He told another rancher that his cattle seemed to be angry with him. Many early calves had been lost to the extreme cold or mired in the deep snow. The rancher felt their mothers blamed him. The winter was treacherous for man and beast alike.

In many ways I liked working at Dr. Jenter's. I could go home to have lunch with Mother when I worked a full day. The young woman with whom I worked, Kari, and I became good friends. She belonged to a strict conservative Christian church. I was of a liberal one. We talked of our respective religion, church, beliefs and our spiritual lives. Neither of us tried to influence or criticize the other. Instead we both learned and respected how the other side feels and believes. We became close friends. After I had worked there about eight months I resigned in August as I needed to be at home with Mother. She was becoming more dependent at this time.

Almost immediately after my resignation, I went to Miami Beach for a short visit with Sherwood. Rosie came to take care of Mother while I was gone. Sherwood and I had a glorious time in Miami Beach. We went to see Alex Fox, of course. We also went to a concert of Rod McDonald, a friend of Sherwood's from Greenwich Village. Sherwood and I very much enjoyed being together again. I felt that Miami Beach was about as far as the moon from South Dakota. I stayed only a week as Rosie needed to get back to her life in California and Mother needed me.

In the spring, an ad for the Black Hills Blue Grass Festival caught my eye. Never letting an opportunity to hear Blue Grass music go by, I attended and had an incredibly good time. Part of that good time was meeting Dorothy Pulscher who was the president of the board of the Sturgis Arts Council. We became acquainted and talked several times during the festival. She told me that the Arts Council was looking for a Coordinator and asked if I would be interested in the job. They were looking for someone with computer experience and, *voila!* My Cittone experience, way back in Princeton, in that other world, was going to lead me into something at last.

I accepted the job with great enthusiasm. It worked perfectly into my life, as I wanted to be doing something wherein I could work from home, so that I would not have to leave Mother alone. Although the Arts Council took me away to many meetings and events, most of the time I was working on the computer in my bedroom. When I was away I had my as car phone; this was before cell phones. The first time Mother heard of that device she insisted that I get one immediately. Whenever I was at a meeting I expected a call from her. Most often my expectations were met. My friends at the meeting would call out, "It's her mother!"

The salary at the Arts Council was small, but the rewards were great. I met the most wonderful people in the Black Hills. There were artists, supporters of artists, theater people, musicians, writers and more. Western artists, and those who associate with them are a breed apart from ordinary people anywhere. It was surely one of the most interesting jobs I ever had.

Mother was becoming weaker and wanted me home more than ever before, and even when I was home she wished that I spent more time with her and less with the computer. After a short time I hired someone to be with her when I went to meetings and events. This was expensive and did not always fulfill her comfort needs or mine. It was time for me to leave the Arts Council.

Due to the Arts Council connections I was approached and hired by the Dahl Art Museum of Rapid City. I was to work on a commission, selling pieces of art at shows which I would organize and oversee. I did it only once. Loading the car, unloading and hanging the pieces, some of which were very large, and doing sales pitches were simply not in my catalog of motivated skills. I sold but one painting that night...and that was to Sherwood who happened to be visiting from Miami.

I did not have another job while Mother lived. I cut back on expenses and kept very busy taking care of her. Also I became more involved in the church. At St. Thomas, in their very small congregation was a trio of young men who were outpatients from Ft. Meade, the veterans' hospital just east of Sturgis.

Ft. Meade was an old venerable fort, established in the late 1800's and was the last post of the 7th Cavalry. It had been reestablished as a Veterans Hospital while I was in high school. A large part of it was devoted to veterans who were suffering from shell shock, war nerves and later on, post-traumatic stress disorder... the emotional detritus of the wars.

These three young men with whom I became involved had suffered from exposure to various chemicals in the Gulf war and were separated from the rest of the congregation at St Thomas, by their age, their experience and their conditions. They did not receive full acceptance from the body of the church. They were never mistreated in any way but suffered from the stigma and fear that mental disorders often engender. However, "The Guys" were my kind of people and I warmed to them immediately.

Gary, the most outspoken of the three, asked me if he could help me in any way. I asked if they would like to come and rake leaves, and they all showed up the next day and had the yard immaculate in a couple of hours. I offered to pay them and Gary said, "Oh, no! We couldn't take your money. We hardly ever get to hang out with decent people." He certainly found a place in the center of my heart with that pronouncement.

At Lent we began to have soup suppers at church. The Guys, Gary, Tim and George, were always there, and we always ate together. It naturally followed that I would have them over to our house for Easter Dinner. I made an elaborate dinner and told them to invite any additional guests they wanted. Two more veterans came for that celebration, one of the best Easters in my memory.

After Easter, The Guys and I were not willing to give up the weekly Lenten suppers so I started a Bible Study, and we had it in Mother's house because I could not leave her alone. She was very happy to have The Guys there. She was in bed most of the time but she could hear what was going on and they always came to her bedroom door and said goodnight to her.

We were using a simple Bible Study wherein a passage was read through three times and after each reading the leader asks a different question. One night we were reading the story of Abraham being called to leave his own country and embark into unknown territory. Tim, who was always shy, opened up that night and told of how he was in his home in Nebraska and answered a knock on his door. It was an officer in uniform who told Tim that he was going to leave with the officer and go to a new unknown territory. That's when Tim was brought to Ft. Meade for treatment of PTSD. As Tim was telling this story in a shaking voice, he said, "I know just how Abraham felt." It brought tears to my eyes and made that Bible story come to life as nothing had ever done before.

There were so many prescient insights The Guys brought to the Bible Study. They would put it into the context of their own lives. We became more than close friends, we were an extended family.

Late that spring Elizabeth Bryan was moving on and St. Thomas Church was getting a new priest. We eagerly awaited the arrival of this new person, and were surprised when, during one of our Bible Studies, he and his wife appeared at the door and asked if they could join us. That was our introduction to Tom and Elizabeth Campbell. They were immediately comfortable with us and we were comfortable with them. They came to Bible studies whenever they could for the rest of our time together.

Once The Guys and I went to visit a church on the Pine Ridge Reservation where Margaret Hawk, a friend of mine from days at the seminary in NYC, had lived for many years. The little church on the reservation was such a pitifully poor church, with earnest, honest, reverent parishioners. We expected it would be poverty stricken...all of Pine Ridge is...so we took several cans of food and bags of staples with us. The priest was heartbreakingly grateful and thanked us repeatedly. We asked what else he needed that we might be able to supply. He said that as he drove around, he noticed on the playgrounds that most of the children did not have warm coats. "Would it be possible," he asked, "that you could bring some coats for the children?"

We nodded and answered enthusiastically and in unison, "Yes, we certainly will do that."

It was early spring, still quite cold. The next Monday morning we went to the main dry goods store in Sturgis and found they had very few children's coats left. Their supply had been depleted by the winter's demands. We went to all four of the second hand stores, in town and they were eager to give us whatever they had left. We gathered up about fifty children's coats and were euphoric about our venture. People can be extravagantly generous when a need touches their heart. We took the coats out to the Pine Ridge the next Sunday along with cases of canned goods and other non-perishable food. We were jubilant!

In this early springtime, I wanted to visit Sherwood in Miami Beach. Rosie came from California to be with Mother while I was away. The blizzards do not give up easily in South Dakota and early spring is a time when some of the worst ones happen. And it did happen...with a vengeance, the very night Rosie arrived and we had finished dinner. It had been reported on the radio so we were not surprised by it. In South Dakota one is not surprised by a blizzard any time after August or before June.

We settled down cozily in the little house, nice and warm with the gas burner heating the house. Then Mother began to have breathing problems about nine o'clock. We called the hospital for an ambulance but they were all out tending a bad accident on the Interstate. I was confident that my Chevy Prizm would make it. That little car was good in the snow. "Should we try it?" Rosie and I asked each other. Mother was agreeable with that idea...she never liked ambulances, anyway.

We bundled her up, got her down the icy steps and into the car and drove the six blocks to the hospital. They were quite busy in the emergency room but took her in and worked on her for a long time until she was stabilized when they took her to a room. Again a social worker was interviewing her and she came to the question "What is your spouse's occupation." Mother answered, without emotion, "Shoveling coal, I suppose." Her sense of humor never subsided, even in the face of death. Perhaps near-death experiences made her realize the humor of life itself...or at least reminded her not to take herself too seriously.

The next morning Rosie and I visited her in the hospital and she told us of a vivid dream she had during the night. She woke up on a great expanse of soft grass and before her she could see a gate into the most beautiful flower garden she could imagine. She walked toward the garden but just as she got to the gate she woke up. She believed that she had glimpsed Heaven.

The strangest thing was that at Christmas time I had ordered a picture of the Peaceable Kingdom for my granddaughter, Sally, who loved animals. Along with my order, the catalog company had sent another picture. I had rolled it up and put it under my bed thinking that someday I would find a use for it. It was of a flower garden behind a fence with a white gate leading into it. I left the hospital abruptly saying, "I will be right back."

When I unrolled the picture to show Mother, she sputtered. "Why, that's my dream! How, where did you get that?" She had the nurse hang it in her room and after that, she had it in her room for as long as she lived.

After a long winter, spring again came to Sturgis, with its festival of lilacs exuding their aroma over the whole town, its perky daffodils, and the grass, greener than at any time of the year. Spring, so welcome! However there was a sadness then because Mother did not feel well much of the time. For one week we were both quite ill with the flu but recovered without complication or hospitalization.

Every Sunday evening Tommie and Al Leenknecht drove to Sturgis from Custer, about forty-five miles, to visit Mother for dinner. Before I came to stay they brought her dinner. When she felt well enough they took her out. After I arrived I enjoyed making a Sunday dinner for them. It gave me one more opportunity to cook for someone. Tommie had been Rosie's best friend in her childhood in Sturgis. She had been a part of our family for over fifty years. When Mother and I both had the flu they came and cooked dinner for her. I was too ill to eat that night, but was grateful for the few hours of sleep I had while they were there.

When Mother was well she often had visitors. She had many friends in Sturgis. There was Betty Ann who had been her cleaning woman for years and had become her close friend. There was Cindy Gray, whose children Mother had tended for many years, while Cindy was in nursing school and after she became a nurse at Ft. Meade. Sometimes I was slightly envious of the closeness of their relationship, but mostly I rejoiced in it, and admired my mother for her ability to make and keep good friends. Her cousin, Mildred, who had moved into town from out on the prairie, visited often. Her niece, Dorothy, although quite ill herself, came whenever possible, probably twice over the summer. Jenice brought her daughter, Becky Casey to spend a week with Mother. It was a delightful week. Mother was eighty-nine years old that summer but she and Becky related like good friends with no difference in their age. It was apparent to me that many of her visitors came believing it might be the last time they would see her.

Rosie and I decided that we should have a family reunion. The months of spring and early summer was given over to the planning of that event. We decided to have it at The Happy Holiday Campground near Rapid City because there were cabins, camping and a motel on grounds. We sent out word to all the family from Seattle, Portland, Wyoming, Kansas, California, Colorado, Pennsylvania, Virginia and New York, and they all came. About seventy-five people attended. Mother stayed in the motel in a room where everyone had to pass by on their way to the pool, to the kitchen where we prepared food, or to almost any activity in the campground. She had her oxygen tank in her room so she was comfortable with that. Also she could turn the air conditioning on whenever she needed it. The temperature went up over a hundred degrees that weekend! All of my progeny were there except one grandchild, Joya, the oldest, who could not take time off from her work in Boston.

Attendants at the reunion found many activities in the Black Hills to explore. They enjoyed the usual attractions, Mt. Rushmore, Crazy Horse Monument, Sylvan Lake, and other places, off the beaten track. Dan and Jake went fishing with Dan's cousin Steve Thomas and his son, Brock. One group went horseback riding. On Sunday T. J. Weichman, Aunt Mary's grandson, led a worship service at which Lorie led us in singing hymns. Gene Mater did caricatures of the members who wanted it done. Marcie organized a corn husking contest. It was a never-to-be-forgotten time.

On the way home Mother told me her face hurt from smiling; she had not stopped smiling from Friday night until Sunday afternoon. We had a professional photographer come to take pictures and in the pictures it was apparent that she never did stop smiling, the whole weekend.

One cloud, invisible to anyone else at the reunion, was hanging over my head. Many years before this, while in college, Rosie had given birth to a child and had given her up for adoption. I shall write nothing more about the college incident because it is Rosie's story and only she could tell it.

Mother and I were the only ones who knew of this child. Shortly after she was born and adopted, Mother had found the social worker at the State level who handled adoptions. Mother had followed her progress from birth until she was eighteen years old. Mother knew that she had been adopted. Shortly before the reunion Mother had received a phone call from a woman who said she was that child, and her name was Lisa.

Lisa had obtained her files from the adoption center. She found in the file a letter from Violet Olson which said, "You are now eighteen years old. If you ever want to find your maternal grandmother, here I am." Mother had left her address on the letter. Lisa easily found her phone number.

Mother got that phone call while I was away with Sherwood who moved back to South Dakota the week before. Mother excitedly told me about it when I got home and said she told Lisa that she must talk with Dolores before going any further.

The next day I called the social worker at the state level who had handled the case and she verified everything Lisa had said was true. This was the child, now grown-up. Mother and I decided we wanted to wait until the reunion was over to do anything more about it. It was too much to handle along with the reunion only a couple of weeks away. So throughout the reunion that weighed heavily on my mind.

The day after the reunion, I asked Rosie to go out to breakfast with me. Through breakfast I could not find the right words to say. Rosie, who knew me well, knew I was holding back something.

Finally on the way home, I pulled the car over by the fairgrounds and said, "If we knew something about the baby you gave up for adoption, would you want to know?"

She hesitated for an instant and said, "Yes, I would. First of all, I want to know, is it a boy or girl?"

From there I told her everything we knew. Rosie had so much to deal with over the next few months. True to form, she did it with grace, truth, intelligence and an unshakable trust in a loving God. Even with that, it was not easy. There was her daughter, Karen who had been raised as an only child. Allen, always doing the most kind and loving thing for Rosie, handled it well. He listened to her and always approved whatever she wanted to do next. There was a lot happening in Rosie's family as there was in Lisa's family.

Lisa was dealing with her family which consisted of her husband Casey Sherman and their eight year old daughter, Jessica. Rosie flew to Seattle to meet Lisa and her family. A meeting occurred in San Francisco where Lisa and her half-sister Karen met.

There were long and frequent phone calls between Rosie and Lisa wherein they explored the depths of each other's personality and discovered genetic similarities and differences, as well as preferences and dislikes.

In early fall Lisa and Jessica came to visit Mother and me in South Dakota. Mother was fulfilled by that visit. For thirty years preceding this, when people would ask her how many grand-children she had she would answer with the current number of acknowledged grandchildren, and under her breath she would say, "And one more." It was a great resolution for her to find this lost grandchild, Lisa and one more great grandchild, Jessica.

After Lisa's visit in mid-September we settled back into our routine of living together, playing cribbage, going for rides, visits to doctors, and getting ready for winter. We enjoyed sharing so much of our lives. It was a sweet time.

Every morning I would get up and get her breakfast ready and then wake her. Usually she woke quickly with a little joke or observation. If that didn't happen I knew she was probably ill and would be seeing the doctor that day.

One Thursday, at the end of the first week of October, she had a hard time waking up and I took her to the doctor. She was seeing a new doctor, only her second visit to this one. He looked at the lab work and said that she had an infection which he could treat with a broad-based antibiotic and she could go home, or he could admit her to the hospital where they could do more specific tests and treat whatever specific infection it was. He told her that the choice was hers to make. She said firmly and without the slightest hesitation, "Oh, home, home!" I took her home, and started giving her the prescribed medication.

Sherwood and I were going to North Dakota that weekend for a writing assignment he had agreed to do. I had never been to North Dakota and wanted to see what was there, if anything. Mother wanted me to go, on the condition that someone would be with her.

I hired Rose Derby, one of the women who had been Mother's favorite home health care aide, to care for her while I was gone. Rose was going to stay day and night until I returned on Monday afternoon.

Sherwood brought Mother a dozen roses when he stopped by to pick me up. She was thrilled by that. I made sure that the refrigerator and cupboards were stocked with all the things Mother liked best. I left detailed instructions for her care. Sherwood and I went off with satisfaction that she would be just fine while we were away. And she was just fine when we got back.

I got back early Monday morning and she seemed to be in good spirits. As I was doing the laundry which had accumulated while I was away a few tissues fell from something I was folding and I said, lightheartedly, "We have a problem in this house. Someone doesn't clean out their pockets when they put their clothes in the hamper, and someone else doesn't go through the pockets before doing the laundry...and these Kleenex just don't hold up worth a darn in the washing machine." She laughed heartily as if that were really a witty joke. She loved to laugh.

That night she woke up once to go to the bathroom, which was usual. I took her in and got her back into bed and she said, "Oh, Dolores, You've been so good to me. What are we going to do?"

"We are going to go back to bed and get the sleep we both need and feel good tomorrow." I answered.

Once, in the early morning, there was an audible sigh...the wall between our bedrooms was very thin. I waited and heard no more and went back to sleep until about seven in the morning.

I got up and made both of our breakfasts and went in to wake her. She didn't waken with a gentle shoulder shake. I went back to the kitchen. I looked at the calendar, and said to myself, "October 15th, is this a good day to die?"

I suppose I knew, but would not let myself accept the knowing. I ate my breakfast and then went in again. Then with a sob in my throat, I called the Home Health Aide office and said, "This is Violet's daughter, I can't wake my mother up."

The aide with said, "Is she cold?"

I answered in a strangulated voice, "Yes."

The aide said they would be right over and were there within five minutes. They made the necessary phone calls and Mother's body was taken away that morning. I called Rosie's house; Allen answered, saying she was substitute teaching that day and he would go right over and tell her. When she called back we talked on the phone, through our sobs, we assured each other that Mother died in her own house, in her own bed and in her own mind, just the way she wanted. We kept saying that through the days that followed to comfort ourselves.

Other phone calls were made to the rest of the family; a friend from church, Cherie Four Bear, came over to be with me; food started arriving at the door and the aftermath of her death took on a life of its own.

In the early evening, Sherwood, who has a powerful aversion to death and to anything having to do with death, came over to the house and wanted to go for a ride. I took him Bear Butte. There we parked the car and watched the sun go down in silence and drove in back to the house in the same comforting silence...a silence that exists between two people who know each other very well, and knows when words would be an intrusion
The next day Sherwood brought me this poem.

Bear Butte

You drove me to the crest of Bear Butte
Past colored colored ribbons fluttering from the breeze
High above a lake of silver paper
And we sat not touching
Looking out over the vast plain
Its mortal lights winking on at twilight
Like stars in another sky.

Between these two universes
The sun had fastened a colored ribbon
Of its own around the far pines
Until it melted into the horizon
Until in the gathering night
There was neither up nor down
Only a dream-field of Violets
Banishing alienation
With their completed beauty

Physicists state that matter
Is neither created nor destroyed.
So perhaps between the two sky worlds
Every thing is contained and no thing is lost;
Not a mountain or a stone
Or any speck of mortal dust
And surely no love that lives in memory.

Rosie arrived the next day, which was a great relief to me. It was pouring rain that day and the rain seemed appropriate. We visited the priest at St. Francis Catholic church where Mother had been a member for about thirty years. We talked with the young priest who had Mother's instructions, which told him Mother wanted to have a rented casket for a viewing and a funeral at the church. After that she wanted to be cremated and her ashes scattered at the Bear Butte Cemetery where her mother and Tom were buried. He demurred slightly and said, "That is not the Catholic way, but if it is what she wanted and what you want we can do it that way. However the cremation will have to be separate from the funeral and may be attended by family only."

Then the funeral home visit followed. Bobbie and Jack came from Rapid City to be there for the choosing of the casket and the viewing. That funeral home visit was not perfect, because Jack said he thought I should have taken her to the hospital, and Bobbie said she wanted to see the body. I was so emotionally fragile I felt they thought I had not done the right things. I let that feeling go shortly after it happened. Her own house, her own bed and her own mind, I kept reminding myself, "Who could ask for a better death?"

We wrote in her obituary for the newspaper that in lieu of flowers, donations could be made to the Sturgis Library for the purchase of large-print books. We were later told by the librarian that they received an abundance of donations and were able to buy many large print books in her name. There is a plate inside each book with her name on it.

The night before the funeral, the women of St. Thomas made an elegant dinner for my family. Marcie and Dan were there, my granddaughter, Joya, Mary Lou, Jimmy Dale, Rosie and several South Dakota and Wyoming relatives.

At the funeral I was surprised to see my cousin Marlene Buss from Colorado, the cousin with whom I had been so close in my year in El Paso. There were over a hundred others in attendance. All the Home Health Aides were there. Joya, read the obituary which I had written with the help of Rosie. She was chosen to read it because she was working in television, and was confidant in front of a crowd. About halfway through she was overcome by emotion, realizing that this was her great grandmother...it was not an ordinary reading. It was not television; it was real. She got through it and her emotional foundering added a layer of meaning to the reading recounting Mother's life. After the funeral the women of St. Francis served a gracious luncheon.

Then it was over. After all the friends and family had gone to their homes, I went back to the house on 4th street and felt very alone. I walked around listlessly, without purpose. I was physically and emotionally exhausted from the events of the last week.

As I was about to go to bed I realized I had lost my checkbook. I looked in every place I could think of and was becoming increasingly agitated. I was so tired. A wave of anger swept over me and I stamped my foot and cried out, "Oh Mother, why did you have to go. You could find anything! What will I do without you? Now I'll never find anything." That was my last thought before I climbed into bed.

In the night I dreamed that my checkbook was in a pile of newspapers in the laundry room. I woke up from the dream and went in and looked there. My checkbook was right where I dreamed it was. I knew that Mother's spirit was still there, watching over me.

Mother usually sat in her chair in the corner of the living room where I had the cutouts made in the wall so she could see into the kitchen. That's how she could keep track of what was going on in the house and how she knew where lost things would be found. By her chair was a low coffee table on which she kept everything she needed. It had a way of accumulating papers, books, cards, and other bits of the flotsam and jetsam of her life.

Also on the table was a figurine of a little Swiss boy with his a dog on a rotating platform. When wound up it played the song *"Doe a deer, a female deer; Ray, a drop of golden sun...."* It was what she used to make a connection with a child who came to visit. When little ones visited with their parents, often they feared her oxygen tank and tubes, or simply feared her old age. She would wind up the little figure and inevitably they would become interested. Then she would ask them if they could guess the song. A relationship would develop, which thrilled her and delighted the child.

When I decided to clean off her table, a couple of weeks after her funeral, I put the little figurine across the room for safety's sake. I cleaned Mother's table and as I finished and was turning away, from the tiny platform came a resounding "ding." I knew she was speaking to me through the little figurine. It made me smile. A bit of her was still here. Her life was over. The memories were alive and well. She was with me.

CHAPTER 28

South Dakota Altered

Slowly, I moved around the house. At first, it seemed as though my life's purpose was accomplished. It felt very much as it did when my last child, Lorie, left Stockertown. "What am I doing here? What is left for me to do, that matters," I asked myself.

Of course, the Bible Study with The Guys and the Campbells continued and that was my focus for the middle of each week. The food preparation became more elaborate. We came to know each other in a deeper way each week. We were able to weave our own experiences and stories into the Bible readings.

Mother had often told me of how she would like to have her room painted and refurbished, but she couldn't get out of it long enough to have that done. So, a few weeks after she was gone, I took out all the furniture and had the floor finished. I painted the walls a pale pink, her favorite color, and put up some attractive chambray curtains. When It was finished, and I had put the final touches on it, I turned to look and said, "Well, Mother, how do you like it?" From the shelf at the side of the dresser, the little Hummel figure, again, emitted a single, "Ding!"

Sherwood and I now spent more time together. He had rented a comfortable and attractive apartment across town, which in Sturgis, meant five blocks away. He bought a little red pickup truck from Carl Ogaard, my cousin Dorothy's husband. It was always seemed incongruous to see Sherwood in that little vehicle. Sherwood was a writer without an ounce of mechanical ability in his repertoire; a man who had lived most of his life in cities, whose passion in life was words. This man was fitting himself into the culture of a small western town and fitting his long lanky body into that little truck. He was held in high esteem by the library staff and visited there often. They knew no one else who had a weekly column in major newspapers. The staff at the gym admired him for his tenacity as he worked out almost every day. He and Carl, a native South Dakotan, a skilled mechanic and artisan, forged a strong friendship starting with their interest in history and expanding from that into genuine respect for each other.

Sherwood and I went weekly to a little coffee house in Sturgis, named Beatniks and soon became regulars there. Throughout the Black Hills there was a conglomerate of folk musicians. In that group were some very fine writers and performers. Sherwood became a favorite with the audiences and the musicians. I played my hammer dulcimer several times and spent much of my time at home improving my skill on the instrument.

By midwinter I was moved to start looking for a job. Settling upon me was a resurgence of my lifetime restlessness; looking for a structure to my day; having a place where I was supposed to be; that unrelenting drive that I should be doing something in the way of a job; earning some money, but above all else, using my gifts for ministry. I could live a simple, comfortable life in Sturgis on the income from my Social Security and pension from the state of New Jersey, but this wasn't about money. It was about my mission in life, about the years I had remaining, and the satisfying fulfillment of that time.

In *The Sturgis Tribune* I found the ad for a Park Ranger at Bear Butte, and the requirements were well within my repertoire, so I applied. Much to my surprise, I was granted an interview, and within a week was hired, and would start working in the spring. Bear Butte! The mountain that had been so important to me when I had, what I now know, was the spiritual awakening at age thirteen.

Dolores

It was in that winter, when I had a lot of time on my hands, that on a whim, I looked up my former husband, Jim online and found his number. With trepidation I dialed it and wondered what I would say to him. In answer that question I told myself that I would let the spirit move me and say whatever came out of my mouth. He answered the phone weakly, but with pleasant surprise in his voice. He said, "I suppose you heard how ill I am." I told him that I had not heard, and was sorry to hear it. He said he would probably not live until the 4th of July, his birthday. I told him how I remembered what a good father he had been to my children and an even better grandfather to their children. He replied that he loved them as much as if they had been his own flesh and blood. I asked if he could forgive me for leaving him and he said he had never blamed me. He knew I was not happy and deserved to find happiness. I thanked him for that and again told him that he had been a good stepfather and for that I would thank him all my days. He sounded very tired and we ended the conversation in a deeply connected way. He died within a week after our conversation.

I waited eagerly for the spring. Finally it came, with all the excitement of the first day of school, I set out for my new job. The very first moments of day one at Bear Butte I knew that this was one of the most important jobs I had ever had. Not in prestige, not in salary, not in status or recognition by anyone else, but for my own personal and spiritual growth.

I drove up to the parking platform and walked to the Visitors Center breathing in the air borne on a wind coming off the Black Hills to the west of the Butte. The air was an elixir. The day was perfect; that indescribably deep blue sky, the leaves just coming out on the aspen trees, the mountain awakening!

I walked in and met Chuck Rambow, chief park ranger. I was in awe of this man who understood every aspect of the Indian culture covering South Dakota, Wyoming, Nebraska, Montana, Colorado and beyond. Chuck was a great teacher and everyday

375

he taught me something about the ways and religion of the Indian tribes as well as the operation of the Visitors Center and what my duties were in that place. I listened to his amazing stories about miracles of the Butte, and by mid-summer I could tell many of those stories myself. I also witnessed extraordinary things on the mountain while I was there.

As mentioned before, Bear Butte is a sacred site for the Native Americans. It has been a place where they worship and feed their spiritual needs for as long as their tribes have wandered the plains, prairie and mountains of the West. The Butte can be seen from five states; South and North Dakota, Nebraska, Wyoming and Montana. It stands as a sentinel above the rolling prairie, so it was a logical place for tribes to gather for worship and guidance. It remains an active sacred place to the Indians of the Plains, especially the Sioux, the Lakota and the Cheyenne.

There is a mile long trail going up to the top, 1,260 feet from the base to the summit, along which there are pathways into the trees and brush, where today's Native Americans go to pray, to meditate and to leave their prayer cloths. One of my duties was to go up the trail every day to check for garbage or any other disturbance and to make sure the prayer sites were being used only for ceremonial purposes.

The temperature was hovering around 100 degrees on a morning as I was going up the path. I passed a Swedish couple and their two children. They spoke very little English and I spoke even less Swedish so our communication was sparse. When I stopped to rest they passed me and we communicated with each other in ways that were beyond words. Also going up the trail that day were two Native Americans in full ceremonial dress, carrying a red bundle. They walked deliberately with an attitude of reverence. We would pass each other resting or sometimes walking a few feet behind each other. We stopped often to rest and take a small amount of the water, very precious commodity on such a hot day.

When I reached the top there was one other family on the viewing platform, from which you can see the five aforementioned states. It is a truly awesome site from the top of the Butte and the family was drinking it in when I arrived. Shortly after I arrived the Swedish family came to the platform. All were looking at the landscape below and talking in hushed voices. It is a place where you want to whisper and gesture, never shout or make a disturbance. It has the feel of a natural cathedral commanding awe and respect.

Soon the two Native Americans were approaching the platform, but instead of coming onto it, they turned aside and went about forty feet away into the ever whispering pine trees that hold sway at the summit. Now there was no talking on the platform. Except for the trees, there was no sound at all.

In a few minutes the Indians opened the bundle and took out a pipe, lit it and sent the smoke upward towards the deep blue vault above. Because they were Native Americans, and because it felt so right, I did not admonish them about the fire and smoke. They began an ethereal chant, accompanied by a wooden flute. The music was directed for a few minutes in each of the four directions. This went on for a time that stood still. On the platform it was utterly silent. Even the children were awed and quiet.

After a while the Indians turned and began their descent and silently disappeared around the first bend on the trail. No one moved on the platform for a long time. At last the Swedish mother, her sun colored hair blowing in the wind, and her eyes matching the sky, put her hands to her heart and said, "I have it here. Always."

That event, that experience, is of such spiritual significance that I have it here in my heart, always, for the rest of my days. It also conveyed to me with absolute certainty, that everything of importance to me, I can carry in my heart. Always.

By the end of the summer I had a new friend, a young Cheyenne Indian, Phil Frame. At the beginning of the summer Phil did not think I belonged there. He felt that Bear Butte was a space that should be reserved for his people exclusively. However, after a few rainy days, when we were confined to the inside of the Visitors Center along with Chuck Rambow his annoyance with me turned into a solid friendship.

Phil had gone through many of the hardships and indignities that befall young Native Americans in South Dakota. He had none of the privileges of young white people. After the Visitors Center closed for the season Phil came to my house in Sturgis where I taught him to use the internet. This opened up a larger world for him. Eventually he got a job as a courier and crossed that vast state of South Dakota two or three times a week. I did not see him after that, but I treasured his friendship...and carry it in my heart. Always.

My children and I kept in contact through telephone and mail. I missed them acutely. Each of them called me to tell me that Charles, their father, was mortally ill. I called Easton hospital, where I expected he would be, and asked the operator to connect me to his room. The call quickly went through, and he answered, barely able to talk. He said, "How did you get through? I'm not supposed to get calls."

I inquired, "Do you want me to hang up?" With a surge of strength he said, "Oh my God, No! You are the one person I want to talk to."

I was in tears by this time, and said, without restraint, "Charles, you know I've always loved you."

He said, "I never had any doubt about that, and I loved you and still do." Then he said he couldn't talk anymore. He died a few hours after that call. I did not attend his funeral. He had a new family and was on to his third wife. I felt it would be awkward for my children if I were there.

In November of that year, my sister Bobbie died. She was only seventy-two and it seemed far too early for her to go. Bobbie and

Jack lived in Rapid City surrounded by five of their seven children and their families. They had a close-knit family and Bobbie was the strong force that held them together. She was quite ill for about two weeks, and I was kept informed of her condition and visited her in the hospital.

However, on the day Bobbie died, I had promised Elizabeth Campbell that I would help her with her booth at a cultural fair in Rapid City. I received a call from one of Bobbie's children that I should come to the hospital at once, so I called Elizabeth and waited until there was a replacement for me before I could go to the hospital.

All the way to the hospital I prayed that the words would be given to me, the words that needed to be said. I prayed aloud, "God, I do not know what to say to Jack. Help me. Put the words in my mouth and I will give voice to them."

Bobbie had been so strong, and Jack had leaned on her for support for over fifty years. When I arrived at the hospital, she had expired a few minutes before. Jack fell into my arms and cried repeatedly "What am I going to do without Mama?"

The words tumbled out of my mouth, "Jack, Bobbie left you all her strength." Those words were so effective! I could see him take strength from them. Never would I alone have thought to say that. Later that evening as we sat around the house of Bobbie and Jack's son, Steve, a disagreement broke out among the progeny. Jack, who had been sitting on the porch alone and quiet, stepped into the room like a nine foot giant and told them, with great authority, "You kids stop that right now! I don't want to hear another word of fighting. You hear me? Stop it!" Not another cross word was spoken that night. Yes, Bobbie had left her strength to him.

A week later, during Bobbie's service, I heard Jack say to someone who was offering condolences, "Mama left me all her strength." Those words that were given me to give to Jack were from another realm...a realm from which truth is spoken, where power is given to the powerless.

Through the winter, my South Dakota relatives came to Mother's house to visit me occasionally. Jimmy Dale, the son of Aunt Mary and Uncle Marvin dropped in on his way between Gillette, Wyoming, where he worked in the oil fields, on his way to Rapid City where he was actively engaged with AA. Jimmy Dale kept firm ties to the family. He stopped to visit Mother often in her life. He attended every family reunion and birthday party we had, often with his companion Betty Benedict, who had become part of our family.

He came to visit me on New Year's Day 2000. We decided to honor a tradition, not of our own family. We did not have a New Year's Day tradition. Jimmy Dale and I decided to borrow tradition from the southern part of the country and have Hoppin' John for the occasion. We went to the store and shopped for the black-eyed peas, ham hock and rice. We had fun cooking it and eating together.

Jimmy Dale is an interesting man. He told me things about the oil fields that I could not have heard from anyone else. He was a cowboy poet and brought the latest poem he had written.

He was born, raised and educated on the prairie of South Dakota and employed in the oil fields in Wyoming. From this and his stint in the Navy he is an open-minded, curious and exploratory person; interested in everything, and willing to step out of his culture to explore the rest of the world. Although on opposite sides of the political spectrum we have great respect for the thoughts and ideas of each other.

It was a sad time when we learned that my cousin Dorothy's cancer had returned and the prognosis was grim. Her daughter, Anita, now living in California came to be with her during the last few weeks of her life. I visited often, and always felt a mixture of sadness that Dorothy was failing, but a satisfaction of having had her in my life. It was a privilege to have grown up with her, as well as an honor to spend her last days with her.

The line, *Failure fails but once; Success fails many, many times* from a song written by Doc Gaskin, a South Dakota musician, exemplified Dorothy's life. Dorothy lived a difficult life and had turned that adversity into a testament of her strength of character. She died with great dignity, respect and success. Her funeral at the Mormon Church where she was a honored member, was a tribute worthy of her character. That funeral changed my assessment of the Mormon Church forever. The outpouring of help and active sympathy was overwhelming. The testaments to her life confirmed everything I knew about Dorothy.

Shortly before she became ill she and Carl bought a new house just outside of Belle Fourche. She took joy and satisfaction from living in this modern well-appointed house. Whenever I drove by the community of Prairie Homes, I felt a tug of emotion. I miss her being in this world.

That summer we had another family reunion. This time it was in the Northeast. The original plan was that it would be in Garrison New York where Lorie was living, but a few extraordinary, last minute things happened that changed the plans considerably. It turned out to be what we later came to call The Four State Reunion.

I had flown out to Garrison a week early, to help Lorie and Bill get ready for a move to Virginia where they had bought a farm and were going to be moving shortly after the reunion. We had done much of the packing and were on our way driving south to Bridgewater Virginia, when I got a phone call from Dan in Easton. His voice was anguished and he began with, "Mom, Jake is going to be all right, but I have to tell you something very bad...I ran over him with my tractor three days ago. He is in the hospital and they are quite sure he is going to be OK."

Dan went on to tell me how it happened. He had been demon-strating, to a new employee how to operate the tractor, and Jake, age fourteen, had been clowning around, running along aside, and tried to jump into the bucket, and missed, falling under the wheels of the tractor. I told Dan I would be there soon and was there within twenty-four hours.

I stayed with Jake in the hospital a couple of days and with him at home for a couple of days after. He made a quick and complete recovery, thanks to his excellent health, his youth and some very good doctors.

While Jake was recuperating, the Four State Reunion began. We met at a castle located near Garrison, overlooking the Hudson River that belonged to Fred and Anne Osborne, friends of Lorie. I picked up Jimmy Dale and Betty Benedict, at Newark airport and we drove from there together. They were both happy to have me drive in that urban area, which was vastly different from driving in Wyoming.

By five in the afternoon, in the courtyard of the castle, eight of us had gathered and piled into a seven passenger van Lorie had rented for the occasion. We were headed for Connecticut to hear Lorie's daughter, Molly sing. At that point the composition of the family reunion, in addition to Lorie, and Sally, was as follows: Rosie and Allen from California, my niece Lynn, her daughter Rebecca and boyfriend, Chris from Seattle; Jimmy Dale and Betty Benedict from Wyoming.

The concert in Connecticut was memorable! It was music of the Balkans which Molly could sing so well. She had been at sum-mer school with the Harmony School which was now touring New England. It was a good beginning to the reunion. The next day the tour stop was in Maine so Kay and Jim, longtime friends, who had been instrumental in Lorie's teen age years went to see the concert, and delighted to see Molly, the next generation, carrying on the music tradition of our family and friends.

When we got back to the castle, Marcie, Gene and their daughter, Lauralee had arrived from Bethlehem. We all slept in the castle, a unique experience for all. On Saturday morning we drove to the docks along the Hudson River and took a boat up the river. Lauralee asked the captain if she could steer the boat and of course, was not denied her request. It was a good experience for all of us. Later we drove to NYC where many of the people from the West had never been. We had lunch in a restaurant where a famous author, whose name I do not remember, frequented in the 1920's. Next we wanted to see The Cathedral of St. John The Divine. Joya drove one car, full of family and I followed closely behind with another, through the streets of Manhattan, which in itself was a New York City adventure. Then we found the Princeton Club where, Fred Osborne, the owner of the castle, had offered Chris, the young guest from Seattle, overnight privileges because it was his twenty-first birthday. The rest of our entourage drove back to the castle.

On Sunday we went to St. Philips of the Highlands, the church where Lorie sang in the choir. Before the reunion, back in Sturgis, I had discovered an old hymnal of Grandma Michelson's, in which she had marked her favorite hymn, *In Heaven There Will Be No Goodbyes*. We made copies of that hymn for the congregation and the entire congregation sang that hymn with the gusto of an Italian opera.

After church we went to brunch at The Hotel Thayer, connected to West Point, which was the most opulent brunch that any of us had ever attended. It was one of those moments when I look around and said to myself, "You just can't get here from there! And here we are!"

We drove back to Easton where Dan had prepared an elegant outdoor banquet for us. It was an interesting com-position of guests. In addition to the families who had come from across the continent, there were people from of many different sections of my life. There were friends from my book group: Faith Shireman, and Dan and Doodie Genthner. There were friends of Rosie's, people she had lived with before moving in with me in Stockertown, Shirley and Bimmy Van Norman and their progeny. And of course, many friends and relatives of Dan were there.

One memorable moment at that reunion was when someone asked Sally to sing for us. She sang two songs that day, *Crazy,* in an exact Patsy Cline rendition and a Disney song, *Somewhere Out There.* From the moment she opened her mouth there was complete silence among the guests. Everyone knew that she could command an audience, *a cappella*, with the power of her voice. We all knew that we would hear again from Sally.

After the reunion, I went back to Sturgis and resumed my life there...the Wednesday night Bible Study with The Guys, and maintaining the house on 4th Street. Sherwood and I often went to Beatniks in Sturgis and the Malibu Club in Deadwood where Sherwood performed his songs and I played my hammer dulcimer. Many Sundays he and I drove north beyond Belle Fourche to the grasslands that extend into the southeastern corner of Wyoming. We would drive for miles, drinking in the landscape, and always looking for antelope. Watching a herd of antelope startle and leap off in unison, is not surpassed in beauty by any ballet troupe.

In August, the Sturgis Motorcycle classic takes over Western South Dakota and Eastern Wyoming. Like a swarm of motorized locusts they descend on the country by the tens of thousands.

The crowd has been estimated by experts, to be surpassed only by the Mardi Gras. It is what has fueled the economy and kept Sturgis alive for over fifty years. Little did I know, when I played in the Sturgis High School band the year that the Rally moved up to the Fairgrounds, that it would become such an important event in the Black Hills. Mother loved the Rally and rented out her backyard to bikers. She made many friends in this way, and she felt safe and protected to have some of them on her property.

My friend, Mary Wood-Fossen, was employed as Executive Director of the Northern Hills Alcohol and Drug Services. Throughout the rally she was on duty at the women's section of the County Jail which was a block and a half from my house. Mary invited me to submit an application to work there through the rally, for a week in the summer of 2000. She said it was not hard work and was fun and made you feel a part of what was going on.

So, of course, I did. I realized that I would get no sleep at home during the early part of the night because of the roar of the bikes. Rather than be at home grumbling about it, I could have an interesting experience. I applied and was hired. I had my choice of shifts. I chose the 4 p.m. to 1 a.m. shift. I worked with four other women whose duty it was to book in and watch over the incarcerated women during the rally. When not doing that official work our job was to fold the laundry from the jail. Through the entire week, my coworkers and I booked in five women, and folded about five hundred pounds of laundry.

One very old biker who had been jailed had a heart attack his first night in jail and was taken to the local hospital. He recovered from the heart attack but was detained in the hospital for the week. For my last three days as Warden, I was sent over to the hospital to sit at his door to ward off anyone who tried to spring him. Nothing that dramatic happened. I read a book, took my charge out on the patio for a cigarette once during the night and talked with friends in the hallway. That was my exciting episode as Warden of the Sturgis Jail during the 2000 Rally.

However, what happened next was one of the most exciting things for many years past, and for many to come. One morning I got my mail out of the box, and there was a letter from my daughter, Lorie. I saw on the letterhead, *Innisfree* and recognized it from years ago. No letter at all from Lorie, just written across the page in her handwriting, "This is for you, Mom!"

The letter, addressed to former volunteers, was a request from Innisfree, asking if any of them knew of someone who might be interested in volunteering there, and if so, please inform them that there were openings and that Innisfree was eager to accept applications from friends or relatives of former volunteers.

As I read the letter a warm, wonderful feeling coursed through my body. It was like slipping into a warm bath on a cold winter night. So right! Such a good fit! No question at all...It Was For Me!

Much more than an invitation, it was a Calling...not a question. There was not a shred of doubt that I was going to answer the Call. It was as though all the magnetic filings in my body were turned toward Virginia.

My purpose was clear: get my things in order and follow my soul to where it was going.

CHAPTER 29

Innisfree

Of course, the move couldn't and didn't happen in a day. There were several difficult and complex tasks between leaving Sturgis and arriving at Innisfree. The first, and most onerous was telling Sherwood. He had rented an apartment, had become a true member of the Sturgis community and was liked and even held in awe by some of the people there. Above and beyond that, Sherwood and I had forged a lasting relationship. Not that we always agreed upon every issue and always wanted to do the same thing. We did not. Nevertheless, we enjoyed the same kinds of entertainment... folk music, books, poetry, physical exercise, eating out, live theater, good movies and endless discussions of worldwide political, current events, literature and ourselves and our children. We had conversations that mattered. Above all, we love each other. As I have told people, "Even when we were barely speaking, one of us made the phone call to be sure that the other one was all right." For twelve years we rarely missed a day talking, either in person or by phone...and much of that was before cell phones. We knew each other's family and were taken in by them as a family member. I was honored to be included in his Jewish family. He was comfortable with my down-to-earth South Dakota relatives and they were comfortable with him.

It was not an easy thing to tell him that I was going to disrupt this...that I was going away; that he was not invited to come along. This was a calling to me and to me alone. I spent many hours rehearsing my lines...and finally just blurted it out one day. He had come over to my house to hear a new arrangement of a gospel medley I had been working on with my hammer dulcimer. As he was telling me how I could perform this at a venue in Deadwood, I interrupted him and said that playing my hammer dulcimer was not my calling. It was a diversion. There was something calling me, something impelling me; a thing I *had* to do. And it would take me far away from Sturgis for an indefinite length of time. We talked for hours. He did not try to dissuade me. He knows me too well for that. In the end of that conversation he knew that I was going to go through with this. Although he was not happy about it he understood my need to go.

The next big thing was to get rid of things; my things, Mother's things, her mother's things; things that had become part of our lives and heritage. Rosie, Karen and Stephie came out and helped me. We had two big yard sales which were very successful. I contacted all the relatives who might be interested in preserving some things of our family history. It was a big undertaking, unraveling a hundred years of accumulation. Mother had been the keeper of Grandma Michelson's and of Aunt Mary's things.

Selling the house was easy in comparison to getting rid of things. I contracted with a local realtor, who found a buyer within a week from the list of motorcycle enthusiasts, who loved to own a little house in Sturgis which they would use for a couple of weeks and rent out the rest of the time. One of the things I admired about western South Dakota was the ease with which business could be done. This was in contrast to buying and selling a condo in New Jersey which I had done a few years before, and which took months and thousands of transaction dollars. This transaction in Sturgis took about an hour of face time and a couple of weeks waiting for the final papers to be signed and a check deposited into my Sturgis bank account.

By May of 2001, I was ready to go to Innisfree. The last days in Sturgis were poignant. Sherwood and I stayed the weekend in

Dolores

Spearfish Canyon, one of the most beautiful spots on earth. We ate brook trout in the Latchstring Inn; we woke to see deer outside the window on that last Sunday in South Dakota. We went to church in Lead because it would have been too painful to go to St. Thomas in Sturgis. The priest in Lead knew me and my plans and called me up front for a blessing of my trip and my future work at Innisfree.

After church Sherwood and I went for a long drive out on the prairie, saying few words, but communicating deeply through the sound of the prairie, a sound like no other. You get out of the car and stand still, breathing in air slightly perfumed with grass and hay. Then you are likely to hear a Western Meadowlark, with a song so beautiful it can make you cry. In the distance you may hear the whine of a truck out on the Interstate, and closer at hand the sound of cattle lowing peacefully. Occasionally there is a jet overhead but it seems inconsequential to the essential sounds of the prairie. It was a lovely day for being there, and like the Swedish woman at the top of Bear Butte, I remembered, that I have it here, always...in my heart and soul.

The next morning, a bright sunny morning on the 1st of May, I got into my little Chevy Prism and started across the continent to begin the next phase of my life. Sherwood was there to see me off, and it was painful; similar to a breakup of a young love-affair.

I couldn't hold on to the pain as it was overtaken by the gloriously beautiful crossing of my native state. Reaching the eastern edge of South Dakota I left the Interstate and headed to Pipestone Minnesota. This was a place that held great interest to me as it is important to the Plains Indians. Many of their religious items, especially the sacred pipes are made from the red jasper gathered from the quarries in Pipestone.

I found the beautiful little town, where most of the building fronts are embellished by jasper. I stayed in an old hotel in the middle of the town, and in the morning went to the quarry. Only Native Americans are allowed down into the quarry but there is an informative tour around the perimeter and an interesting museum. I spent the morning at the historic site of Pipestone feeling immense satisfaction.

Part of that satisfaction was the fact that although I had seen Pipestone on a map, and had read about it, always before, when driving across the country, I was in a car with at least one other person who was in a hurry to get to the destination. Now I was on my own, free to do whatever I wanted. The sense of liberation was intoxicating. There were gentle tentacles embracing me from my former life. I called Sherwood from the site, bought him a jasper letter opener and missed him, but not enough to counter my sense of freedom... not enough to turn back.

I had but one compelling issue concerning the time of my arrival. Lorie, now living on a farm in Virginia with her husband Bill, and teen-aged daughters, Molly and Sally, was pregnant and expecting a baby about the time I would be arriving. I wanted to be there for the birth although it was not imperative, more like a nudge forward. After the stop in Pipestem I continued eastward. Since there was no exact time that I had to be there...the baby would be born with or without my attendance...I decided that I would not take the Interstates except where necessary, for example, around an urban area such as Chicago.

I spent the second night in Highland Park, a suburb on the western side of Chicago, with Sherwood's sister, Ludmilla. Always before I had been an adjunct to Sherwood when we visited Ludmilla. We had met many times before but usually within a family gathering and had never spent even ten minutes alone, where we could get to know each other. It was very different being on my own. She is superb host and was interested in all that I was setting out to do. She, asked for a hammer dulcimer performance. I was reluctant to play for her, an accomplished pianist who could play a vast array of classical music with grace and competence. Nevertheless, I played my simple folk tunes, which I play by ear, and Ludmilla was a very appreciative audience. I spent a comfortable night at her elegant con-dominium in Highland Park after which she served me a sumptuous, healthy breakfast and sent me off with good wishes.

The next morning I was on the Interstate through the rest of Chicago and then back to the state highways on my way to Mansfield Ohio where I visited Bill and Marianne Bartlett, my close friends from The Golden Years.

When I arrived, Marianne was at work at the Children's Psychiatric Hospital so Bill and I went to the store and bought a large pork roast, with the prerequisite accompaniments. We took it home and made dinner for Marianne. We gathered as many of the Bartlett clan as we could find. There were fifteen of us around the dinner table and it was an outstanding celebration. Bill insisted that I get out my hammer dulcimer and play for the children. After that we sat around and sang every song we could until our voices gave out. It was a memorable visit.

The entire trip was enchanted. Everything I needed appeared just in time. For instance, when I was getting tired the next night and wondering how far to the next suitable motel; just around the next bend in the road, there it was! I took my luggage and hammer dulcimer in the lobby with me and the woman at the check-in asked me to play for her. She was having a slow night and was happy for the diversion. I believe that in my entire years of hammer dulcimer playing, this trip was the highlight.

The next morning, my windshield wiper was not working prop-erly so I stopped in a little town and asked at the breakfast counter of a small restaurant if they could tell me where to go to get it fixed. A man sitting nearby said he had a shop just down the street and would take my car down and fix it and have it back by the time I finished breakfast. It was the kind of place where you felt trust was an essential part of the culture. I finished breakfast, paid him the fifteen dollars he charged and went on. Little things like that along the way made the trip invigorating. Later when people would say to me, "You made that trip all by yourself! Weren't you afraid? You must have been so tired!" I would just laugh. "Tired?" I would say. "I was energized. I was liberated!"

On May 7 I arrived at Dudley Farm, the old abiding name of the place Lorie and Bill had bought in Virginia. Lorie was ponderously pregnant, and I helped with dinner and the clean-up. She had been to the hospital twice with false labor and was absolutely ready to have that baby. She was not worried or anxious. Her twenty-plus years of being a nurse gave her total confidence. It was more like Christmas Eve, with great anticipation of the magnificent gift that was to follow.

The next morning Bill went to work; Sally went to school; Molly was in boarding school in Staunton. Lorie and I decided to go into Staunton to have lunch. In the middle of lunch, Lorie said, "I think we should leave now and go to the hospital." James Madison Hospital in Harrisonburg was twenty-two miles away, by Interstate. I drove carefully and nervously north on I-81, looking at the side of the highway for safe pull-off places thinking, "What if I had to deliver this baby? Could I do it, like Grandma Michelson delivered me?"

Fortunately, we arrived in plenty of time. When we got to the reception desk, the admitting attendant said, "It's you, again!" Lorie responded enthusiastically, "This is the real deal!"

Within a couple of hours Bill was there with Molly. Sally had been invited but felt it would be too intense for her to endure. The four of us were there when Elizabeth May Cahalin, came into this world. Sally was right! The actual birth of a baby is one of the most intense experiences available in our lifetime. Lizzie, who attained that nickname within minutes of her arrival, was an active, enthusiastic baby right from the beginning. Anyone could see that Bill was going to be an involved and a good father. He was totally comfortable in holding and handling her. When I first heard of the pregnancy I thought of how he would be an excellent father because of his great care of and compassion for animals. When I bent over the bed to kiss Lorie goodnight, she said, "Oh, Mom I am so old to have such a little one!"

I answered her, "When you are my age, you will have a twenty-two year old daughter."

She seemed relieved and comforted and said, "Oh, That's not bad at all!"

At eleven p.m. as I was leaving, Lorie called me over to tell me that she had been taking care of a newborn kitten abandoned by the mother, and asked if I would give it a bottle when I got to the house. I picked up Sally from a friend's house and we went on to the farm. Somehow, it seemed fitting and appropriate that I should find myself feeding a tiny kitten from a doll size bottle at midnight while my newest granddaughter was adjusting to this strange new world a few miles away, and another granddaughter was sleeping upstairs. I savored the satisfaction of that moment.

In the morning I went to the hospital to visit Lorie and Lizzie. Bill had taken the day off work and was there to take them home. It was apparent that they had the situation well in hand, so I left for Innisfree, about twenty miles away.

I got off I-81 and onto country roads which became more narrow at each juncture. I became almost intoxicated with the beauty around me and the adventure ahead. I love the names of those last few roads leading to Innisfree...Via, Heartbreak, Mt. Juliet, Mt. Fair, Slam Gate, and finally, Walnut Level Road. As I drove up that last mile of a one-lane dirt road, bordered on both sides by thick trees laden with early spring blossoms and birds galore, I am sure my heart was beating at twice its normal rate.

The first person I met was Miriam, with her tiny baby daughter, Talia, in a sling on her breast. Miriam has been head of the weavery for over twenty years, although I was too excited to remember that at the moment. I told her I was the new volunteer and she greeted me warmly and told me they were expecting me at a house called

Amity. I drove past the Community Center, around the bend in the road and arrived at my new home.

With much enthusiasm I was introduced to Sharon, the only volunteer in the house at the time. She was very happy to have another to share the duties. I met Matthew, Robert, Jim and Paul who were to become among the most beloved friends of my life. When I was taken to my room, I began to weep. I could not contain the scene out my window, facing Pasture Fence Mountain. It was so beautiful only tears could express my feelings.

The next morning I awoke early, looked out the window and beheld a rainbow against the base of the mountain. I had never seen a morning rainbow in my life and could hardly believe my eyes, but there it was! If ever there were a sign given, this was it. My life at Innisfree was truly blessed. I took a picture just to prove to myself and others that I was not imagining it.

The first few weeks at Innisfree for any new volunteer, never mind that I had known and visited the place for twenty-five years, are a maze and haze of learning experiences. First there is the management of the house one lives in. There is medication training and First Aid, and different committees and protocols to learn about. Each volunteer has a different schedule, and each co-worker has different needs, medications and ways of relating.

Nancy Chappell, the Volunteer Coordinator, with whom I had spoken many times on the telephone was one who made my early days smooth. Nancy had lived at Innisfree for many years with her young boy, Alex. I respected her for her values, her integrity and the way she had lived her life. We became good friends that first year and will be for the rest of our lives. Another way they make life easier for a new volunteer is that they have a contact person, that is someone they can go to for answers to imponderable questions. Mine was Gillian Preston, a wonderful, gracious English woman... the best contact person one could have. Our lives intersected in many ways beyond our first contact relationship. We made trips with coworkers; we had many sincere and profound discussions. We were far more connected than volunteer and contact person. She brought peace to me in those early months of settling in and grace to Innisfree for many years. Sharon Snyder, the other volunteer in Amity and I got along well although our schedules did not allow very much one on one time together.

About the term co-workers: The nomenclature of people with handicapping conditions is sensitive and therefore ever changing. When Innisfree was new, the distinction between volunteers and those with handicapping conditions, was Co-worker and Villager. One of the Villagers did not like this as he felt it was a shortening of Village-Idiot. He petitioned the board to call everyone Co-workers, which was adopted as policy. Eventually, it was apparent that there is a distinction that necessarily must be made, so the designations became co-worker, volunteer, and staff, not by policy but by practice.

Getting to know my co-workers was both fun and challenging. Matthew was so in love with Sharon that he wanted nothing to do with me for the first month. Paul was the ever-helpful and polite host; Jim was interestedly aloof, and Robert, the perfect gentleman, friend, and helper. Little by little, I came to know what they liked to eat, how to engage them in a conversation, what activities they excelled in and what they liked to do.

Early on I started the Church Run. Innisfree is a secular enterprise, open to all expressions of belief or un-belief. When I pointed out that there were at least six co-workers who wanted to attend church I was allowed to take a van filled with our people every Sunday morning to church. It took several Sundays to find a good fit for us in a congregation. We tried several Episcopal churches, as that is what I know best. They were all kind but patronizing to us, and I was looking for something more inclusive. The last place I found, apparently the right one, was Sojourners, a UCC church in Charlottesville. My people slipped into that congregation as easily as if they had been there all their lives. They found their own places and people, and did not sit together as a group. They were easily and immediately integrated into the congregation. It helped a lot that Lee Walters, the director of Innisfree was a founding member and a vital presence in that church.

After my orientation period, I chose the bakery as my main work station. Pete, the manager, made it an entertaining place to work. He had managed it for years. One of the aspects I loved was the process: You enter at 9 am when the two rooms are spotlessly clean and orderly. By 9:15, to an unseasoned observer, it looks like chaos. Heyward is starting the granola, Chris and Bob are setting up and greasing the bread pans; Mitch is starting one kind of bread and Judith another. A flurry of action continues until the break at 10:30.

Then comes the tea and a sample of what has come out of the oven, perhaps a warm chocolate chip cookie or a hot roll with butter. Music, always there is music in the background and Judith loves to dance whenever the spirit seizes her. She pulls anyone in her orbit to dance with her. After break, the granola, cookies and rolls are taken out of the ovens. The bread, which has been rising atop the ovens, goes in and the clean-up begins.

Julie oversees the dishwashing and others take care of the kneading machine and the flour mess on the floor around it. Everybody has something to do, or if they are worn out or finished with their task, they sit in the chairs and companionably converse or observe. Minutes before lunch time the bread comes out of the oven and is put on racks to cool while we all go to the community center. Heyward goes a bit ahead and rings the bell summoning the whole community to lunch.

We all walk to the community center, except for some of the gardeners whose work is further away and are exhausted from the intense work of providing a large supply of our food. They drive in a pickup often laden with vegetables for the houses to take home. You see volunteers, staff and coworkers converge looking satisfied with their morning's work and anticipating the wonderful lunch Sharon and several co-workers have prepared for the community. Lunch is a gathering time where birthdays are celebrated, announcements made and community happens.

We come back to the bakery after lunch and put the bread, cookies and granola in bags. Jim and Philip deliver them to the houses and the rest of the crew cleans up the area, making it ready for the next baking day.

I had not been there long when Pete wanted a change of work stations and I gladly accepted the job as manager of the bakery. I loved the work and felt I made positive contributions to operation, but after about three months I had gained fifteen pounds. Try as I might I could not refrain from sampling just one roll, one cookie and one bit of granola every day. I announced sadly that I must change my work station. I told the steering meeting that I had an all-consuming passion for my work and must find less enticing activities. I went to the gardens where there were healthier choices.

Several people came to visit me that first summer at Innisfree. The first one was Sherwood. Having grown up in Chicago and spending his teen-age and college years in Miami, and adulthood in NYC and Princeton, this was totally foreign to him. He was interested but not really engaged. He found some secluded places to get his writing done. We had a good time together but it was apparent that it would never be his choice to live at Innisfree.

One weekend, quite early in my stay, Musicalia was being celebrated nearby. This was a music party that had started twenty-seven years before, as a birthday party for Lorie. The next year it was the site of the wedding of Pete and Ellen Vigor. The Vigors had worked along with several other music veterans to make this an annual celebration, a reunion of musical families whose strongest tie was music. It has grown into a yearly music festival with a couple of hundred old time and bluegrass musicians attending.

Lorie and her family, Lizzie, Sally, Bill and I met in the afternoon at the field and set up a temporary camp. Always before Lorie brought tent and stayed from Friday night until Sunday afternoon, but this year Lizzie was such a tiny baby that Lorie and Bill left early on Saturday night. Sally, age thirteen, wanted to stay longer. So she and I stayed an hour or two longer then went to Innisfree for the night. She opted to sleep on the floor beside my bed rather than the bedroom across the hall from me. We stayed up talking until dawn. It was a great night for us and forged an everlasting friendship that will remain as long as we both live.

Marcie, Gene and Lauralee came to Innisfree for a weekend and Lauralee stayed on with me for a week. Sally stayed most of that week as well. They helped me in the bakery and loved it. Lauralee told me that she had always longed to immerse her hands and arms in a barrel of flour. Her wish was satisfied. Her inquisitive energy endeared her to many of the staff, coworkers and volunteers at Innisfree. Sally worked in the bakery for a couple of mornings and sang for them. Co-workers mentioned that for years thereafter.

Eli, my oldest grandson came, and as I took him around, visiting worksites, he was politely interested. Eli's forte has always been with literature, computer skills, and computer games. So the workings of the farm were not of great interest to him. However at age twenty-two, he was impressed with a young Irish volunteer, Cath Standley, who had arrived a few days before. She was, he said, the most beautiful woman he had ever seen or ever hoped to see.

Jake came for a week and helped a work crew from Korea build a ramp to the house named Halcyon. He was wonderful to have around, helpful and inquisitive.

Months before I was accepted at Innisfree Marcie, Joya and I planned a trip to Ireland. When Innisfree accepted my application I told them that this trip was planned for late May and they had no objection to my leaving for ten days, even though I had barely started as a volunteer.

What a trip that was! I had never travelled to Europe or any place outside of the US, except Canada and Mexico. This trip to Ireland was exciting for me. Not only seeing Ireland, but seeing it with my daughter and granddaughter made it sevenfold more worthwhile.

I was to meet Marcie and Joya at the Shannon Airport but missed my connection at Heathrow. That was the only time in my life that I lost my composure at an airport. I sat down and sobbed. I had no way of contacting them. I tried so hard to make it but the busses at Heathrow go at their own speed...slowly. A helpful Irish flight attendant took an interest in my case and with great resourcefulness was able to procure a seat for me on the next plane to Shannon. What a relief to find Marcie and Joya waiting for me when I arrived. They had total faith that I would be on the next plane.

They were already having fun. They had rented a car and Marcie had knocked over a mailbox never having driven on the wrong side of the road before. They were laughing about it. They had found our first bed and breakfast and soon we were on our merry way. We started driving and drove from one little Irish town to another, as the spirit moved us. By a blessed miracle we were always in full agreement. We drove north to Dingle where we heard real Irish music in a soggy pub with the attending grog. It had been raining all day in Dingle, and there had been a horserace at the track just outside of Dingle in the rain. Everyone was wet and soggy but the musicians were not fazed by that. The fiddlers and other Irish musicians played on and on.

We stopped at beautiful little villages, graveyards, churches, country stores, and anywhere there was a vista...a place where we could get a good look at the ocean or a vast hillside of partitioned fields looking like a cozy quilt in shades of green. And, yes, we did kiss the Blarney Stone. It was a great trip and I anticipated getting back to Innisfree which gave me almost as much pleasure as the trip itself.

I resumed my work and life at Innisfree with many satisfactions, few disappointments, and always, challenges. After I had been there almost a year, an opening for a volunteer was available in Plum Tree, one of Innisfree's town houses.

This is a program in Charlottesville, which is home to co-workers who are able to work in town, or who have a background that makes town living more attractive to them than the rural village. I had spent enough time in Charlottesville to appreciate its unique charm. In my estimation it is a perfect small city. The house I moved into was within walking distance of the down-town mall in the center of the city. The coworkers in the house were Andy, Annette, Marny, and Mark. Later I moved to Walden, the second town house, and lived with Ellie, Willie, and Chris. Those six co-workers became another family with whom I felt fully integrated.

Four days a week I drove out to the village with a van full of the town people, who worked in the workstations. Most of the town people did not go to the village everyday as they had jobs or volunteer work in town. Chris had a full time job at UVA, where he loved his work and was highly valued by the staff. Andy had a job at a bakery. Annette moved into independent living shortly after I moved to Plumtree but we remained in close touch with her. Willie stayed in town one day a week building models for an architect in Charlottesville. Marny volunteered at the day care center of the synagogue in town. Ellie volunteered at the hospital.

While living in the Innisfree houses in town I became involved with the Live Arts Theater in Charlottesville. Sherwood moved to Charlottesville about that time and we did theater work together. There was a late Friday night theater group, the No Shame Theater where one could sign up to do a ten minute skit, a reading, or performance of some kind. It was an exciting time for us and any spare time we had, we were writing, practicing or performing. Sherwood's play, *Baron Jiro*, was produced in Charlottesville.

It was produced on the day of my seventieth birthday. Many guests were invited to the birthday party to be held in a restaurant in the Downtown Mall of Charlottesville. Before the party we all attended the play. Rosie was there from California, my cousin Bill and Pat Waterson from North Carolina, Joya from California, Ian from DC, Marcie, Gene, Lauralee, Dan, Joan, Jake and Kevin from Pennsylvania. Naturally, Lorie, Bill, Sally, and Lizzie, and many Innisfree and Sojourner friends were there. What a great celebration that was!

I left Innisfree for a short while when Sherwood and I rented a little cottage together. Once again he was struck with Florida fever as winter approached. I was not ready to leave Charlottesville and while I was turning that dilemma over in my mind, I got a call from Lee Walters. She asked if I could come out to the village and care for an elderly resident, John D who was deemed to be near death. I was asked to try to make his last few weeks a little better. I fell in love with John immediately. He responded to my care and concern and began to improve rapidly. Every morning, as he got out of bed, he looked out to the mountains, gave a broad wave and exclaimed, "Oh, my God! Oh, my God!" John saw the mountains anew every day. He made me see them that way too.

He never walked by a flowering bush or plant without stopping to caress a blossom and talk to it. He was the sweetest person I've ever known. I bought him new clothes; very gentlemanly clothes, and dignified hats. I demanded that he be treated with extreme dignity. John had ceased talking for several months before I took care of him. He began again with these words to the director, Lee Walters, "She likes me!" John said, nodding to me. I was very moved by this.

John responded to any attention with a broad smile and it had become easy for the younger volunteers to tease him. This, I demanded, had to stop. He was moved to a house named Amity where he sat in a place of honor and wrote his memoirs, which consisted of his name, written repeatedly again until each page was a work of art. There is a framed copy of a page of this above the chair where he sat in Amity. He paged through his *National Geographic* avidly and was held in love and respect until his death about four years later.

In October of 2004 my first grandchild, Joya, who now lived and worked in TV in Los Angeles, was getting married to Josh Weinroth. Her wedding was a grand occasion and the entire clan gathered for the great event. Marcie's entire family, Dan and Joan, Rosie's family and a large contingent of Josh's family were in attendance. Both Joya and Josh had many young friends so it was a huge celebration.

The wedding was elegant and the first Jewish wedding in my family. The service was beautiful with all the solemnity and joy one could hope for in a service. Food was beyond expectation. Just as the last dinner was served, the sky opened as if it had been held back by a sheet, and let loose with a torrential California rainstorm. It was a warm rain with no wind, and became more of a joke that an interruption. The people who did not want to get their clothing or hairdo damaged went home immediately. Those who wanted to stay and celebrate danced in the rain and carried on until they could go no longer. The rain made the event exceptionally memorable. It was the last time my family celebrated all together. There were events and factors in the works then that we could have never imagined.

After the wedding I went back to Innisfree. One day as I was straightening up the house where John D lived, I picked up a book, *The Magic of Findhorn*. It really grabbed me and I read the entire book by mid-afternoon. I was compelled to go and experience this place; an eco-village, a spiritual site, a learning center and a community. Gail Ford, a fellow volunteer at Innisfree, became as excited as I about the prospect and soon we had tickets and a plan to go to a little spit of land twenty six miles northeast of Inverness

Scotland on the coast of the North Sea for a ten day workshop in community building. This was the most exotic trip I had ever planned.

We flew into Glasgow, rented a car and drove toward the North Sea. The first night we stayed in a bed and breakfast above a country bar. My but the wind blows cold up there in northern Scotland! The next day we arrived at Findhorn and it was all I dreamed of, after having read the book and anything else I could find about it. It was not quite as cold here as it had been inland, as the Japanese current runs through the North Sea at Moray Firth where the village is located. We were housed in a thoroughly sustainable little cottage with five other workshop attendees. The people in our workshop came from Brazil, Ireland, Wales, Scotland, Northumberland, England, France, Korea, South Africa, Australia and from the states, Ohio, Maine, Illinois, and Virginia. We learned about diversity and how to live with it productively. We learned about living in community and working in fields and kitchens. It was a place to which, if not for my family in the states, I would have committed the rest of my life. The ethos of that Findhorn is close to what I expect "Thy Kingdom Come" would be. It will always be with me.

I returned to Virginia in time to have Thanksgiving dinner with Lorie, her family and neighbors in the countryside around Bridgewater. It was an idyllic Thanksgiving on the farm she and Bill were restoring. They invited all their farmer neighbors, who were entranced by my stories about Findhorn, which was still fresh in my mind. I left the farm that day feeling contented, wondering if anyone could ever have predicted that I would have such a complete and satisfying life. Certainly not me. My life was a wonderment to me. I thanked the Power that made it all possible.

Little was I prepared for the phone call that arrived from my son, Dan, the very next day. I was ill prepared; is anyone ever prepared to hear such words, "Mom, I am not going to try to soften this or lie to you...I know you are not ready for it, and I am sorry. I have leukemia." There was more to the conversation but nothing I remember. My entire body and soul were wrenched from their moorings. I knew it was a major shift in my life. It was like B.C. and A.D... an intersection of time.

I told Dan I would be there the next day. There is much I do not remember. Ah! Blessed forgetting! I spent Saturday with him at Easton Hospital, listening to nurses educate us in what was going to happen next and what the likely outcomes would be. His chances of survival were fifty percent, providing we found a perfect bone marrow donor.

That night I was walking near Marcie's house and stumbled on an uneven sidewalk; fell on my face, broke my glasses and the bone around my left eye, and incurred many cuts and scratches. Marcie and I spent the night in a hospital in Bethlehem, where I had stitches and treatment for my damaged face. Sunday, it happened that Lorie was driving through Easton with some music friends and would be dropped off at Easton Hospital and would visit Dan and then drive me back to Virginia where I had to wrap up my life. I was resigning from Innisfree and planned to devote all my time to Dan. I did not see Dan that day as I did not want him to see me so damaged and pathetic looking.

On Monday morning I arrived at Innisfree and told the outgoing director, Lee Walters, and the in-coming director, Carolyn Ohle, the circumstances. By the end of that meeting we were all in tears. After that I went to the herb garden managed by Catherine Boston, where she gave me some fresh calendula cream to apply to my stitches and wounds. I used that cream Monday night. Tuesday I packed my things from Walden, with the help of Pete and Willie. We took the boxes to Lorie's barn where they would be stored indefinitely. I started driving Thursday from Virginia to Easton hospital. By the time I saw Dan on Friday the damage to my face was scarcely noticeable. I have wondered since if the calendula cream had some magical properties, or was it the care and compassion

I was receiving from many directions and many people. One of life's mysteries, never to be forgotten. Nor will I forget to be grateful for whatever it was.

The next weeks, months and year were such a mix of emotions and events that an entire book the size of *War and Peace* could not contain them. It was as though we...that "we" being Dan, Joan, Jake, Lorie and Marcie, and about a hundred good friends, co-workers, doctors, nurses, chaplains, priests, ministers, social workers...had all entered into something like *Dante's Inferno*. Yet it was blessed with so much love and care that we weren't consumed by the flames. Each of those people mentioned above has their own story of that year. I can only tell mine.

I have heard it said that a person's character is not measured by the successes in life but by how they get through the difficulties life presents to them. Dan had many successes. His business was going well; his was one of the most respected land-scape businesses in the area. He served on the Township Council; his home was a place where many people were served by his impeccable hospitality and his exquisite cuisine. In his year of dying, his character became stronger. He was well loved by the hospital staff. The friendships he had developed before his illness became even deeper.

On Christmas Eve 2004 he was transferred to the University of Penn Hospital. He was given the executive suite, but it was small comfort to those of us who were there. His half-brother, Robbie, and his wife Sarah sat with us through that long night.

Dan's spirituality, which had never weakened, came closer to the surface. Every time I departed his room I would say, "The Lord bless and keep you." Dan would say, "The Lord let his face shine upon you," then together we would say, "and be gracious to you. The Lord look up on you kindly and give you peace."

One day when he was in remission and allowed to go home, I called Lexa Shallcross, a fellow social worker who had become a priest, to come to the house and give him communion. Dan was as thrilled as I have ever heard him when he realized that he was going to have his own private communion. It was important to him. There were so many rising hopes followed by devastating despairs that went on that year. His faith prevailed through all the trials.

One day in November of 2005, he awoke to tell me that he knew he would die that evening, at seven o'clock. We had profound conversations that day; he did not seem depressed in any way. About a quarter to seven an old friend, Susan Barnett, came to visit. He spoke a few words to her and then his eyes drifted off to a place in the farthest recesses of the hospital room. He exclaimed, "What about all these people in here?"

I asked, "What people, Dan?"

He replied, "There's a great crowd of people over there."

I asked, "Dan, do you know any of them?"

With a little laugh, he said, "Well, heck, yes!" and then drifted off into unconsciousness.

Those are the facts of that event. As for myself, I believe that Dan saw something from another realm. Dan slept well that night, and I slept just as soundly beside his bed in a chair. In the morning I awoke a few minutes before he did. When he opened his eyes he looked to me and smiled and said, "I guess that wasn't a good day to die," a line from the movie, *Little Big Man*, one of our favorite movies in his early years. His sense of humor was alive and well.

From that day on, there was no fear of death in Dan. Yes, there was discomfort, impatience, concern Jake, Joan and about his business, but no fear about Death itself...not in Dan. I carried a mountain of grief, a boulder in my heart and a sickness in my inmost self, but also a knowledge that it was going to be all right. Not that I ever harbored the fantasy that he was going to recover, just that it was going to be all right, sometime in the future. Somehow we lived through Thanksgiving and his fifty-second birthday, with acknowledgement, but no celebration.

Around the middle of December the transport crew arrived in his room to tell Dan that he was to go down to the lab for one more test on his liver. I asked, "Just what is the procedure for this test?"

The technician explained it, and Dan said, "No, I am finished with labs and tests."

The memory of this is surreal to me, but it seems that very soon his room was filled with people; Joan, Jake, his step sons, Danny, Kevin and Jeff, and his doctor. The doctor asked, making sure we all heard the interchange between him and Dan, "Are you certain you want to discontinue any further treatment for your condition?"

Dan said, "I am certain. I am ready to die."

Dan called each of the people in the room over to his side and spoke to them individually. I do not know what he said to each of them but it was profound. The doctor was the last one and when Dan had spoken to him, the doctor came to me, with tears running down his face, and said, "You certainly did something right. You raised a spectacular human being."

I answered, "Dan was perfect when I got him, I simply nurtured him and watched him grow into the person God intended him to be."

I stayed at the hospital that night, went to the family waiting room after Dan was asleep. Around midnight the nurse came in and said, "Your son wants to talk with you." I went to his room and sat holding his hand and we talked about Jake and what Dan wanted for him in the future.

We talked about the many losses he had, starting with Irene, Jake's mother, and his friend Terry, who had died of cancer just two years before. Dan said he expected to see them soon. Then a long period of silence and he reached for my hand and said, so earnestly, "Mom, how do you die? Tell me how?"

I wish that I could tell you that I said something profound but all that came to me was, "Dan, I do not really know. You are the pioneer here. I will be with you, but I can't lead you into it. It is something you have to do yourself."

At that point a nurse came in and said, "Can I get you something, Mr. Lichtenwalner?" Dan answered her, "Yes, bring death in, please bring death." She administered a drug of some kind, with a needle, and he fell asleep. His beautiful heart beat for several more days but he was never conscious again.

This was the week before Christmas but so many people dropped anything else and made this sacrifice...to be with me in my grief, to do honor to his life...to pay tribute to this great man who was my son. My friend, Loy Tolson-Jones was with me the evening when he breathed his last breath.

Most of what happened for the next week or so is blurred in my memory. Rosie arrived from California, niece Jenice from South Dakota, niece Cleanne from Illinois, the Bartletts from Ohio, the Gills from Maine, Sherwood from Florida and many others. I remember that Joan and I went to the funeral home to arrange his service.

With us was the priest who served Trinity Episcopal Church, the place where Dan was baptized and confirmed, sang in the choir, was acolyte, was married there and landscaped the grounds and built a memorial garden. The funeral would be at Trinity. This minister did not know Dan well and was not prepared for the size of the crowd. Joan and I had some inkling of what it might be, but even we were surprised, even overwhelmed. It was huge. I was told that people were standing in the street unable to get into the church. This I did not know because I was in a receiving line that seemed to go on forever.

I learned many things about Dan that day. There was a large contingent of Puerto Rican people at his funeral, because his employees were largely from that population. One woman came to me weeping profusely and said, "Mr. Dan! Oh, Mr. Dan, he made our Christmas every year." A person from the Tree Commission of Easton told me that Dan had contributed many trees for the beautification of Easton.

I could not possibly remember all the things that were said, or the flood of tears that were shed. Marcie read a scripture passage. His boyhood friend, John Letson, known to Dan and friends as Hip, spoke of their boyhood times together, fishing, hunting and pondering life. The Chaplain of the hospital in Philadelphia came to speak of him and his genuine spirituality. One of his later life friends, Dave Reifsnyder spoke of his friendship with Dan. Dave later dedicated a book he had written on fishing, to Dan. His nieces, Molly and Sally sang Amazing Grace in their incomparable harmony. Jim Gill gave a short and loving message. He said we had all suffered enough grief and now it was time to go to the reception and tell stories of Dan.

The reception was a blur for me. Lots of people, lots of tears and laughter, pictures and relics. I wanted it to be over. After the crowd dispersed, people were taken to airports and went back home to attend to their own families and Christmas. Rosie stayed until Dec 24 and we made a very sad visit to Joan and the boys at the eerily empty house on Tatamy Lane, the last place inhabited by Dan.

Then it was over...almost. Jake went to church with me on Christmas Eve, but sadly did not feel the spiritual pull to the church that his father had. Jake and I flew to Seattle because Dan wanted me to take him to meet and talk with John Graham, who often was a speaker at graduation ceremonies and a co-director of the Giraffe Society on Whidby Island. Dan felt John Graham could help Jake get through the immediate aftermath of his death. While Jake was talking with John for a half day, I wandered the main street of Whidby Island and left a trail of tears in the little shops along the way.

Back in Easton there was the burying of the ashes in mid-January which had a bitter sweetness to it. His ashes were buried in the remembrance garden he had designed and built at the side of the church of which he had such a great part. Irene's ashes were in the same garden.

Sherwood stayed with me for a few days or maybe it was weeks. It was quite a while before I could keep track of days, or weeks or months.

What pulled me out of that ennui was a call from Carolyn Ohle, Director of Innisfree in February. She told me that the house of Amity needed someone to help with morning routines. It was certainly the best therapy I could have had. There were two young people, Stefani from Switzerland and Florian from Germany managing the house. They were energetic and competent. However both of them were extremely grateful to have a morning person there. I love to get up early in the morning, always have been that way, so it was no chore for me. Everyone who came by the house on those crispy, snowy days was in some way an antidote for my grief. Lorie came to visit me there. I remember one day when she came at the end of her work day, exhausted and we both lay down on my huge bed, facing the window, looking out to the mountains. We listened to music and held hands and watched a sun dog in the sky. It was a precious time together.

Little by little the healing happened. I came to see that having Dan in my life was an extraordinary privilege and that to mourn and be sad would be doing him a disservice. His life was a gift to me and his dying was a gift in an unexpected way. How many mothers are given the gift of a year to spend with an adult child where they talk of things that matter day after day?

I stayed at Innisfree for about a month and then went back to my little apartment on the Delaware River that I had rented early in Dan's illness. That charming apartment fulfilled one of my major desires...to live intimately with that river. I stayed there until the flood in July 2006. I got out just before the water was up to the road leading out of the village along a bend of the river, outside of

Harmony New Jersey. I was the last car to go over the bridge into Pennsylvania for several days to come.

I fled to Innisfree where I had sent an inquiry asking if I could come and be the community counselor in late summer. They had responded positively and even though it was a few weeks early, they allowed me to start at once.

I set up an active counseling schedule immediately and saw co-workers on a regular basis, volunteers and staff as needed. It seemed to me a service that the community needed and I felt equipped to fill it. Eventually I moved into Trillium, the house halfway up Pasture Fence Mountain. For a while I had the honor of sharing the house management with Gillian Preston, the one with whom I had forged a firm friendship in my first days at Innisfree. I felt I had reached the pinnacle of success at Innisfree. After Gillian and her husband Scott left Innisfree, a few months later, I really put my heart and soul into managing that house and maintaining an active counseling practice.

Rosie and Marcie came to visit. Lorie and Lizzie came from over the mountain for a sleepover. We had an Empty Bowls dinner in the Community Center where the pottery of Innisfree was sold, then filled with a wonderful soup made by Kristin Meyers who had set up the event. A program followed the convivial meal after which Rosie, Marcie, Lizzie, Lorie and I sat out on the porch of Trillium and watched the stars. A supremely satisfying evening.

In the summer of 2007 I tore the tendons in my right foot, and it was in a cast for two months. I used a motorized scooter to get around the house and a golf cart to get around the village.

In late October I had a TIA and subsequently carotid artery surgery. What an outpouring of help I had for that! Gail Ford, my good friend with whom I had gone to Findhorn, and who was a nurse, came to stay with me at Trillium for ten days. It all seemed to be pointing me toward retirement. I did not want to become a burden to Innisfree. I could imagine a volunteer meeting where the subject would be, "What do we do about Old Dolores?" I was convinced that I should leave now of my own volition and with my dignity intact. "But what will I do then?" I asked myself.

As I might have expected, Rosie came to the rescue. She had visited me shortly after the carotid artery surgery, and wisely, waited for the right moment to say that she would fly to Virginia and we could drive my Chevy Prizm across the country together. I could stay with her and Allen as long as I wanted...for the rest of my life! She was so enthusiastic and eager, I knew it was a genuine offer... one might say, too good to pass up.

The night before I left, after the car was packed and there was nothing left for me to do at Innisfree, I drove the golf cart down into the village and visited every house. Most of them were dark and quiet but I found a few inhabitants to bid farewell. I woke before dawn and quietly left the village; was in Charlottesville as the sky turned gold and by the middle of the day was at the Richmond Airport where I met Rosie. We drove my car across the country with nary a storm cloud, either in the car or in the weather.

When people comment on how hard it must have been to drive across the country in January we laugh, because for us it was a gratifying, satisfying and purely delightful trip. For me it was release and a new life beckoning on the other side of the Continental Divide and just before my seventy-fifth birthday. We laughed most of the way from Virginia to California.

CHAPTER 30

California-Revisited

Traveling has always meant adventure and most often been with the idea of not staying, but moving on. I might stay as long as a school year, but not much longer. The first time I had the feeling that a move was permanent was fifty-some years ago when I moved into the Stockertown house. It was thirty-five years later that I made the next move I believed might be permanent...moving back to Sturgis to take care of Mother. After that were the Innisfree years which I knew were limited and now this. I was approaching California with an intention of living there for a long time. I can hardly use the word *permanently*. But it was vastly different from going for a week or weekend as I had so many times since Rosie moved there in 1965.

We left Arizona and crossed the state line into California and my inner space began to shift, to accommodate myself to this experience. This was really going to happen! I was going to live, really live in California. Not just a pass through for an exciting weekend but to become a resident!

As we drove through the Bakersfield area, Rosie changed routes, leaving the I-5 and getting onto 99N. Rosie made the route change, so I would get a look at the towns and cities nearby, a feel for the geography and culture of the area. Elk Grove, a small city abutting Sacramento was going to be my home. This is where I would possibly spend the rest of my life. I was about to celebrate my seventy-fifth birthday. I felt there were probably not very many moves left for me.

This was a positive move. I was not running away from anything but embarking on a new life. Rosie and Allen's house was comfortable with a bedroom, bath and a guest room in the front corner of the house. That part of the house was primarily for me. From my bed I looked out a large picture window into the small orchard, viewing the dwarf fruit trees. There were oranges ripe and ready for eating. The window was close to the fence, which was laced, with naked vines. As spring progressed I watched them become covered by a curtain of new pale green leaves, soon to be ornamented with an abundance of luscious little green grapes. The wonder and amazement of the bounteous gifts of nature never failed to delight me, anew every season, and caused me to give thanks. I was reminded of a favorite line of mine in a psalm, "The boundary lines have fallen for me in pleasant places."

Along with having a garden in the back yard I was delighted to find that only a few blocks away was countryside, still a productive farming region. Elk Grove was formerly an agricultural center and home to an indigenous group of Native Americans. I could live here. Yes, I really thought I could become a Californian.

The first morning I set out to find a gym where I could resume my swimming and exercise program I had maintained for many years. There was a gym with a pool about a half-mile away, and I went there to swim. After the swim I decided to join that gym. It was close to home, was clean and I could afford it. As I was filling out the papers I heard a voice say, in wonderment, "Don't I know you?"

I was about to say, "I don't know anyone; I just got here."

She said, "Dolores! Sturgis! Mary Wood!" It took but a moment to recognize Michelle, a woman I had met through my friend, Mary Wood, and with whom I had some very good conversations in Sturgis seven years before! What a surprise! What a coincidence! We agreed to have lunch in a quiet Thai restaurant in the same complex as the gym. By the time we were five minutes into the lunch, we knew we had found a kindred spirit in each other. After lunch she followed me back to my new home and met Rosie and Allen. The next day I drove out to Galt where she and her husband Mike had a little farm.

The cold windy day surprised me. I had visited Rosie and Allen many times in the Santa Clara Valley where winter was wet but mild. Elk Grove is in north central California and has four distinct seasons. That was good for me. I like seasons...celebrating equinoxes and solstices and noticing the difference in the length of days that goes along with them.

When I got to Michelle and Mike's little farm house, I came in from the wind and found a warm fire and cup of soup ready for lunch. It was exhilarating to have such an experience on my first day out on my own in California. It certainly felt to Michelle and me that something more than coincidence brought us together. Having my own friends gave me a sliver of independence that made it easier to settle into this new life.

Some of the big boxes I had sent ahead had arrived at Rosie and Allen's by the time I got there so we spent the rest of the first week unpacking and getting my paintings hung in my room and throughout the house. My hammer dulcimer found a good space in my bedroom where I would be reminded to play it every day.

Rosie and I laughed and talked as we unpacked the things that I felt would be essential in my new life. The things I brought along with me informed me of what I valued; or what I thought I valued. Many of them had no place in my new life and discarding them was easy. It was liberating. The less I had of stuff, the more I had of me.

Getting connected with Rosie's busy and involved family was a natural thing that happened easily. She and Allen took care of their grandson, three-year old Brian, and had daily contact Karen and fifteen year-old Stephanie. They were at Rosie's house a part of every day and I was becoming integrated into this close-knit family. Also a big part of Rosie and Allen's family was their friend, Jeanne Hamel and her three children, Mark, age eight, and the twins, Annie and Jay, six. Many family dinners and celebrations gathered around the dining room table. We celebrated every possible event.

Rosie, Allen, and Karen took me to Monterey for my seventy-fifth birthday. We stayed at a time-share with a view of Monterey Bay. In the morning we were graced with a double rainbow...the second morning rainbow I have ever seen. Good omens were abounding.

Finding a church home was more difficult. I went to the closest Episcopal Church and earnestly tried to feel a part of it, but could not. I found a second one which was twenty miles away and after a year I realized that it was too far for me to be part of the church family. I left that church when I went back East for the summer of 2010, and did not return to it when I came back.

When I came back to California, I found Trinity Episcopal Cathedral in Sacramento. It felt just right, very much in the spirit of Trinity Easton where I brought up my children, which was an essential part of my own development. I attended their newcomer's group which made me feel a part of the church immediately. One of the great breakthrough's in my life came when I attended their Creative Writing Group led by Canon Lynelle Walker, a priest at the Cathedral. I had not been able to write one single paragraph on my book since Dan died. I started writing the book three years before his death. After that I would open my MacBook and find my mind as blank as the page in front of me.

I went to the writing group on that breakthrough day with trepidation. I wondered if a laptop was permissible. I wondered what other restrictions applied. I found there were few hard and fast rules with this group. It was about *writing* exclusively. It seemed friendly with a common interest holding the group together. When they met, each writer wrote for about twenty minutes on a prompt written on the board. On this day the prompt was "The Perfectly Orchestrated Lie."

I started writing cautiously, measuring and weighing each word. Within a few seconds, a dam broke; words were flying off the ends of my fingers without engaging of my critical mind. The unrepressed part of my brain took over. I wrote and wrote until the time was up. I was so excited! My heart was beating as if as fast as if I had run nine minute mile. I volunteered to read mine first, and I knew they liked it. Lynelle said that I had made everyone confront their own lie. I was soaring! I was a born again writer! Immediately upon arriving home I read it to Rosie and then called Ann Scott, my friend of the Golden Years, an excellent writer and a sharp editor. She loved it. Everybody did. I could write again, and got back to my book.

Soon thereafter I drove to Martinez to visit with Ann. We connected again as easily as if we had seen each other the week before. We shared our precious memories of the Druthers, and the Bartletts, the Gills, Trinity Church, and other people from the 70's and 80's. Ann's beloved Scotty, the newspaper man, had died a few years before, and we reminisced of our times together when we were both part of a couple and part of the Easton community.

Ann was actively involved in the lives of her daughters, Sarah and Amy and Amy's children. Ann was involved with a church, played on a Bocce team and loved living in Martinez. She had a circle of older wise women and I was invited to join them for their monthly Trivial Pursuit game. These were all retired professional women and I feared being embarrassed by my lack of knowledge. Very soon I realized I could hold my own. Furthermore, this was not a contest. They were there for the pure enjoyment of each other. It was a playful game and no one could tell who won. I know no one lost.

During the years that Ann lived in California she and Rosie had become close friends so she was an important part of the many celebrations at the house in Elk Grove. I cannot imagine a February birthday party without her.

For the first year I was quite content in getting to know California and finding my place in it. I loved the Jazz Festival in Sacramento and through that festival formed a friendship with Rosie's friend, Pat da Silva. Pat lives in a beautiful house with an ocean view at Pajaro Dunes near Watsonville. Mother used to visit there with Rosie and Allen years before. She called it *The Glass House*. After our connection at the Jazz Festival I usually visited her on my way up or down the coast and enjoyed Pat's gracious hospitality. She comes to Sacramento every year for the Jazz Festival and sometimes for family parties.

I drove to Los Angeles and spent time with Joya, Josh and Hattie and admired their community of Studio City. Los Angeles can seem daunting to an outsider, but their area feels like a small town, where neighbors walk their babies and dogs and share their lives. It was good to be just a day's drive from one grandchild and a great-granddaughter as well. They came to Elk Grove for a glorious Easter celebration. We had an Easter Egg Hunt for Hattie, Brian and the Hamel children at our house in Elk Grove. One of the best videos I ever made was of that event. The last scene in the video was made near the end of the day when both of the little ones were tired. Hattie has inveigled Brian to playing house with her. The picture shows them, each in a rocking chair holding a doll. Brian has a weary expression on his face and Hattie an anxious look on hers. I titled the picture, "We didn't know it would be was so hard."

Marcie and Gene were my first visitors from the East. They were enthusiastic about everything...my bedroom, Trinity Cathedral, and the old Victorian houses in Sacramento. We celebrated Mark Hamel's birthday while they were here. Gene, a professional caricaturist, did a wonderful pencil drawing of Mark. The whole family, including Michelle and Mike, went to Guisti's, my favorite place on the Delta, for dinner. I cherish the pictures from that dinner and the memory of our time together.

What an honor it was to have my granddaughter, Sally from Virginia choose to celebrate her twenty-first birthday with me. We did so many things that week that it seems it would have taken a month. Rosie and Allen took us to San Francisco where we had dinner at the Cliff House. We walked through the red-woods at Henry Cowell State Park. We had a delightful time at the Golden Gate Bridge; we played and had a birthday dinner at Santa Cruz. Another day Sally and I drove north to Cotati in the wine country, for an accordion festival. It was the only music festival I could find while she was here, and we both enjoyed the music, our afternoon together and the beautiful drive through the wine country. The last night we had another birthday dinner at a restaurant in Freeport with Karen, Stephie, Rosie, Allen, Mike and Michelle, my miracle friend in California.

I go back in memory and try to capture the next few years of my life. It is like a tapestry filled with so many people and events...as though I am trying to fit into my life everything and anything I may have missed. It is a beautiful tapestry, colorful, loving, varied, and ambitious. However, I am immersed in that tapestry, an integral part of each scene and it is difficult to step out of it and get a perspective of how it fits into my whole life. I go through my four thousand photographs in my iPhotos, and they fill me with joy and questions. They show the surface of my life but not the depth.

One of the deeper, darker things lurking in the background was the illness of Marianne Bartlett my longtime, abiding friend of many years. She had contracted a virulent infection and was hospitalized from April until October. I scarcely know how to write about it. She was always on my mind and I was trying to find the right time to see her. The summer became very busy and I put off the visit to Ohio.

That same summer, Sherwood came to visit me in Elk Grove. We spent much of our week exploring the possibility of living together, or near each other, in or around Elk Grove. We looked at apartments near Rosie's and others in downtown Sacramento. By the end of his visit I believe we both knew that he would never be satisfied in any place but Florida, and that I would never feel at home there. I concluded that I could be satisfied with daily phone calls, and a few visits a year. At the same time I knew it was unfair to him, as he really wanted a full time relationship. It remained an unsolved problem. He returned to Florida and I resumed the task of making Elk Grove my home.

In early fall Sherwood and I met at Dudley Farm, Lorie and Bill's place in Virginia. Sherwood and my granddaughter Lizzie had forged a strong bond when she was a toddler, and they still loved to be silly and laugh together, so that was a good place for us to meet in 2008 to start our epic tour of the Northeast. We spent a couple of days at Dudley Farm after which he went on to DC for some business writing and research and I went to the Rockbridge Festival, where I met with the Green Grass Cloggers, who had been to our music parties in Stockertown. It was one of the best festivals I had been to for a long time.

Sherwood and I went a week later to Bethlehem where Marcie and Gene lived, and we spent a few days with them. I was just in time to attend a meeting of my old book group for a session that was as comfortable as if I had never been gone. Inevitably, realistically and sadly, I had to recognize that we were all growing older.

From there Sherwood and I continued our odyssey. We drove to Ursinus College near Philadelphia to visit granddaughter, Lauralee, a Resident Assistant at one of the dorms. What a gratifying visit that was! We could get a glimpse of the competent woman she was becoming and that was very satisfying. While I was with her was assigned the task of checking each of the dormitories for the working of the fire alarm. I got a good sense of the friends and respect she had on the campus.

We stopped at the apartment on the Delaware River where I had lived during Dan's illness and death. It brought back poignant memories but was not depressing. I was bold enough to walk up the steps and knock on the door. The current tenant invited me in and I went for one glimpse of the river through that window where I had sat and practiced acceptance during the time of Dan's dying. That was an important part of my life and I will not forget it, nor will I try.

In Maplewood New Jersey we spent time with Sherwood's son Sean, his wife Linda and daughter Anabel. We took Anabel a gift of fairy wings, tiara and ballet skirt. Her mother, Linda, has been employed at Carnegie Hall for many years so Anabel knows all about show business. She has seen the best. She performed magnificently that evening and we delighted in it. I captured that in a video and it is still fun to watch it with Sherwood.

On northward, we stopped in Boston and visited my grandsons, Eli and Ian. Sherwood, Eli and I went to dinner to a restaurant managed by Ian. With his careful attention to our meal and service and Eli's witty and intelligent conversation, it was a great evening.

After Boston, it was a short drive to Amherst where we attended a conference. I left the conference on the last afternoon and drove up to East Winthrop, Maine to visit Kay and Jim Gill. I was a sad visit because I could see that Kay was not as well as I wished her to be. In spite of her condition, we had a deep and spiritually nourishing time together. We talked about death and what it meant to us. We were both very concerned for Marianne, one of the integral people in our lives.

She had been a major player in the close circle of best friends of my adult life. We had helped each other with our children and other difficulties of being a woman in our time. Now she was in a hospital bed in Columbus Ohio, still fighting the infection she had contracted in the spring. Kay and I said sincere prayers for her and talked about what her life meant to us.

Kay herself was facing surgery later in the month. I felt guilty for being healthy. Nevertheless, it was a sweet visit with Kay; we were gentle with each other. Both of us suspected that it could be the last time we would see each other. I intended to see Marianne when this trip was concluded and promised Kay that I would keep her apprised of the situation.

After the visit to the Gills, Sherwood and I drove south-ward and that evening made it to Annapolis Maryland. Once, many months before, I had read, in the Sacramento Bee, a short article by a traveling writer who told of the ten best places he had eaten while traveling around the country. I had that list with us and we, with much difficulty, found Jimmy Cantler's Riverside Inn, which was on the list. It was unique and charming, and served large portions of especially good seafood. It was the second place on the list we had found and enjoyed. I enjoy a quest and appreciate Sherwood joining me in fulfilling it.

Sherwood and I have driven I-95 many times from Bethlehem to Miami and this time, as always, we are gratified to finally reach Jacksonville. There begins the intimation of tropical air as we enter the land of perpetual summer. From there I am eager to get to St. Augustine.

However, before St. Augustine there is a big treat awaiting us. We are afraid we might miss the sign. It is a small sign about eye level and if you didn't know what you're looking for you might miss it entirely. As we have done for twenty years we found our way to Cap's on the Water. The first time was quite by accident. "Let's drive down this dirt road and see if it takes us to a waterfront."

At the end of that road was a quaint little wind and water-worn shack with a makeshift Tiki bar and a few picnic tables in the sandy beach which sloped down to the Inter-coastal Waterway.

On a table in the sand we had the most memorably good food that we had ever eaten. Was hunger the reason for our high opinion of it? We were convinced it was more than that. This was especially good food! By 2008, Cap's on the Water had been discovered by everybody! There is a huge deck surrounding it, the tables in the sand have given way to a parking lot. They now serve hundreds of people every night. The one thing that has not changed is the food. It is still incredibly wonderful and served by exuberant young servers.

I could explore St. Augustine a hundred times and never get tired of it. The superb layout of the old town, the tree-lined streets where the tops of the trees form a canopy dripping with Spanish moss over the street below, combined with the smell of the ocean fresh air, are balm for the soul. We walked around the city and then went to the "Fountain of Youth" where Ponce de Leon landed in 1513, on his quest to find the island of Bimini. I have a snapshot of Sherwood standing by a statue of Ponce, with a sign overhead: The Fountain of Youth. Sherwood is smiling broadly; this is his desire...to be young forever...one of his endearing qualities.

We finally reached our destination, Sherwood's apartment in Coral Gables. Three days later I received word that Kay had died of a blood clot after her surgery. It was a very hard time for me. A great light had gone out of my life. Before I could process that, and imagine life without Kay somewhere in it, I got word that Marianne Bartlett had taken a turn for the worse and was gravely ill. I felt that I was being buffeted by a great cold, hard wind. I flew back to Elk Grove and planned on going to Ohio very soon, to be with Marianne.

I had been back in Elk Grove only a few days when I received a call from Josh in Studio City. He and Joya needed someone to be with Hattie in the evening so Josh could go to work. I was honored to be asked, and eager to forge a bond with Hattie, my first great grandchild. Joya, a writer for a TV station, worked from midnight to eight in the morning and needed to sleep in the early evening. It was a difficult choice to make, but I thought I had time to see Marianne and would go to her when this short-term predicament was over with Joya and Josh. I bought some material and was in the process of making a hat for her, as she had lost most of her hair.

Death, an imperious force, comes not when bidden, but on its own schedule. Marianne died at the end of October, while I was with Hattie, Joya and Josh in Studio City. I flew to Columbus Ohio where I rented a car and drove to Mansfield. I met Marcie at a motel the night before Marianne's funeral. It was a time of reflection for Marcie and me, and it meant so much to attend Marianne's funeral together. The service was, more than anything else, a celebration of her unforgettable time on earth. Our friendship was one of the great gifts of my life. She left a legacy of strong, healthy children and grandchildren who would give substance and grace to the world. I was honored to be a part of the celebration with Bill, their progeny, and a host of friends. After the ceremony, I was given a hat that I had made for Marianne thirty years before, and which she wore often.

After the funeral I went back to Studio City and stayed until a few days before Christmas. Rosie flew down to the Burbank Airport where I met her and we drove north on the 101, because the Grape Vine was iced over. Again, traveling with Rosie is a treat...for both of us. We find things to laugh about, always. We celebrated a glorious Christmas at Rosie and Allen's home in Elk Grove with their Karen, Brian and Stephie, Jeanne Hamel and her three children.

After Christmas, perhaps because of Christmas; perhaps because of the loss of Kay and Marianne, I began to feel an acute longing for my children. Loving your sister and her family, and your bedroom, and the climate didn't quite fill the void I was experiencing with my children available, but out of reach. I wanted to spend as many holidays with my children as I could in the time I have left in this life. I was also missing the community of Innisfree. Many people there had become a surrogate family for me. Those two holes in my soul led me to decide that I would spend half of each year in California with my sister and the other half in the East with my children and Innisfree.

I wrote to Innisfree and asked if they had a place for me in the coming summer; their reply was positive. I would be in the house named Meadow, helping the volunteers, Melanie and Zackey. I could resume my counseling sessions, which were never called counseling, but *Time with Dolores*. It seemed to be a perfect solution for my aching void.

Before I left California I had two important west coast visits to make; first to see my sister, Mary Lou in Portland and second to Seattle to visit my sister, Kitty and her family.

It felt so right being with Mary Lou and reconnecting on a more profound level than we had at family gatherings through-out our lives. She liked to get out of her apartment, so every day we drove somewhere...to the ocean at Seaside, or to some site in Portland of which she had fond memories, such as The Grotto, a religious shrine and botanical garden covering sixty-two acres on a wooded rocky cliffside. I had visited there with Aunt Chrystal when I was fifteen and loved going back as an adult. For me, it calls forth awe and wonderment at the natural beauty and of human-kind's endorsement of it.

We also ate out in many restaurants where Mary Lou had worked as a waitress. In the evenings we would play Scrabble or gin rummy and then the conversations would flow. Remembrances of those who populated our lives, old questions answered, feelings revealed. I visited her several times in the past few years. We watched each other grow older and ruminated about our health and our families. We became closer friends and sisters. What a gift for us in our later years!

The visit to Mary Lou also includes a stay with her grandson Michael and his wife Toni and their son, Jake. There I have a delightful little bedroom in the eaves of their beautifully decorated home in Portland. Toni is a wonderful homemaker. Her meals, her gardens, and everything about being there is one hundred per cent enjoyable. My great nephew Michael and I always find things to talk about and to enjoy. He took me out to the garage to show me a car he had restored to perfection. It is a beautiful shade of deep red, almost maroon. I commented on the color and he, almost blushing, told me he chose it because it matched the fingernail polish Toni was wearing one night when she came out to view his work. He is a fine craftsman, and metal-worker. Jake, my great grand-nephew is a personable self-assured athlete. He is a teenager who takes time to sit down and talk with me and to show me features of my cell phone and how to use them and to always make certain that he carries my luggage in and up the stairs and down again when I leave.

After Portland I went to Seattle. There I stayed with Mary Lou's daughter, Mary Lynn. She and I have a personal and genuine relationship. Our outings often consist of shopping in consignments or secondhand shops, and going to interesting sites, such as the Seattle Space Needle for lunch. But mostly with Mary Lynn the pleasure is talking and listening. Lynn and I have shared many of the same difficulties in our lives and have a common bond because of them. Her daughters Rebecca and Suzie usually came to see me, taking time out of their busy young lives, which I appreciate and always enjoy.

Next I visited Connie and Lee Linne, Kitty's daughter and son-in-law. Connie took me to Kitty's senior apartment, and was sensitive to our need to talk to each other alone. When she picks me up we go to her home in Federal Way, a suburb of Seattle. Staying with Connie and Lee in their house, so tastefully adorned with interesting antiques and a magnificent view of Puget Sound, is an extraordinary treat. We have candid conversations which stay with me long after I have departed. Connie and Lee have taken me to amazing places for vacations, for instance, to their retreat at Los Cabos, Mexico. We always visit their daughter Deb Linne-Figgins and the children, Kitty's great granddaughters, Ellie and Charlotte. Deb is a vibrant and intelligent woman with whom it is a wonderful treat to spend time. She has invited me to several special occasions in her life; I always accept those invitations and they provide me with colorful and joyful memories.

Kitty and I always find things to laugh about and things of great sorrow to talk about. She will be forever missing her home in Bothell where she lived with Jimmy, the love of her life and where she raised their children. They had bounteous gardens outside, and inside she had collections that had special meaning to her. She misses the organ which Jimmy bought for her because he enjoyed listening to her play and sing. She inherited her musical ability from our father, Bob Curry.

Her son, Cliff visits me when I am in the area. He is very close to Dan's age, and we relate very well. He, too, is a fisherman and sometimes brings fresh fish which Connie prepares magnificently. Cliff owns and operates a vacuum cleaner business which thrived for many years in the Seattle are. He is now retired.

When I had completed this time on the West coast, I flew back East, into Dulles Airport where Lorie picked me up. I was ready to be back to Innisfree and to resume my place in Meadow and my listening sessions with the beloved coworkers. Homecoming there is warm and inviting. It is a community to which I will always belong.

In May 2009 one of the first things I did was to attend Musicalia. This year I saw it in a different way than any year before. Perhaps because I had gone to California and didn't expect to be back, it now took on a dreamlike quality.

For nearly forty years I have had the joy of watching the Musicalia families grow up. People I knew as babies and toddlers are now accomplished fiddlers, banjo players, guitar and ukulele players in addition to being business men and women, lawyers, entrepreneurs...grown-ups everyone! The young adults I knew in their courting days are now grandparents.

The setting remains the same. As you approach the site you see an open field filled with colorful tents and if your windows are open you will hear the sounds of strings and occasional drums and wind instruments. In the early years parking was haphazard...park where you want, a no-boundaries event. Through the years it has become more organized. Now you must have an invitation and show it at the gate. Now there are porta potties on the site. One thing that distinguishes these, is that someone graces them with fresh wildflowers every morning. People who have been coming for years now have loosely defined neighborhoods wherein they set up camp, bringing out food, tables, lounge chairs and most important of all, instruments! Now there is a crop of children and teenagers belonging to the adults I knew as children. A new element has been added to the music. That is a direct experience of evolution.

A never-changing element is the sound of children playing, running around, tossing balls, hula-hoops, bicycles, with the ever present background music of the guitars, fiddles and banjoes.

The terrain of Musicalia never changes. A large field slopes gently down to a river which has a huge outcropping of rock, a boulder, on which the parents and grandparents watch the young ones tubing, canoeing, fishing in the river, always with the music in the background.

From Friday to Sunday there are ever-present melodies filling the air. On Sunday morning there is a Gospel sing down by the river after which the festival begins to fade away. Families make plans with each other, for the next festival where they will camp and play again. They help each other take down tents, pack up cars and pickups. The dismantling is as much a part of the event as anything else that happens throughout the weekend.

After Musicalia I go on to Innisfree. I immerse myself in the community. Sometimes I am in one of the town houses, and other times I am in the village. Sometimes I have mixed them up and stayed for about six weeks in each setting. Whatever place in Innisfree I am staying feels like home to me. Every week brings something authentic and satisfying; be it a garden event, a birthday party, volunteer meeting or something unexpected, something that has never been done before. Innisfree is staffed by volunteers from all over the world and is able to weave cultural characteristics into the fabric of the community of Innisfree.

In the summer of 2009, I went to the Lehigh Valley in Pennsylvania several times to be with Marcie and whichever of her children were in the area at the time. Marcie and I enjoy our time together. She always says that we are the same age. We have many ideas, thoughts and values that coincide. I highly respect all that she does. She has been employed in Human Services all her working life. In the '80's she started being the community resource person at Trinity Church in Bethlehem where she has been a major force in tending to the needs of the homeless and destitute people of that city. Marcie could run for mayor and not even need to campaign to be elected. That is how well known she is for the good she does in Bethlehem.

I visited her several times that summer and each visit was unique, and memorable. One in particular was significant to my own personal quest in finding out exactly who I am. Lorie, Lizzie and I drove up to Bethlehem because we were all invited to the Bartlett Family Annual Pig Roast, being held in Easton at Suzanne Bartlett's home.

Deja vu! All those little Bartlett teenagers and children, bearing the genetic resemblance and exuberance of the generation I had known so well. The sense that Marianne was with us was more pervasive than the knowing she was not. I saw Marianne in the smiles, the eyes, and the mannerisms of her progeny. I saw her in the hospitality of her daughters and in the respectful demeanor of her sons. As I entered the garage where the pig was being carved and served, Bill appeared and made way for me as if I were royalty. He treated me kindly. I do not remember what we talked about but will never forget how I felt. He ordered his sons to wait on me, serving me the first morsels of the delicious pig which had been tantalizing us with its aroma, promising a feast to be remembered. That was a day not only memorable for itself but for what came afterward.

The weekend ended and Lorie, Lizzie and I went back to Virginia; Lorie and Lizzie to Dudley Farm and I to Innisfree.

Who started the communication? I don't remember and it doesn't really matter, but Bill and I started communicating by e-mails. We were reconnecting with the past and sharing our present lives with ever-increasing frequency. He invited me to come to Mansfield for a weekend and I accepted his offer.

At this point, I made a firm decision that I would let happen whatever seemed right and natural, but above all, I would be totally honest with Bill, with Sherwood and with myself. As usual Sherwood and I were in close contact, talking almost every day. I told him what was happening and that we might not talk quite as often, but I had to work through this in an open and honest way. Sherwood accepted this.

Bill and I packed so much into that weekend. We walked to Marianne's grave, about a quarter of a mile from his house. We both felt that she would approve of what we were doing. After that we went on to the house and planned dinner. He had a giant edible mushroom growing in his yard that he had been saving for my visit. He knew how to prepare that but needed some accompaniments. We shopped in a farmers market for other delectable vegetables and fruits for dinner, and cooked the dinner together, with precious camaraderie. We listened to music from The Golden

Years, and watched a documentary of the gathering of the cast of *O, Brother, Where Art Thou.*

On Saturday we took a day trip into the Amish country and visited Ruthie, who had been a teenage friend of the Bartlett clan when they first moved to Ohio. Ruthie, now called Ruth, was the matriarch of a large Amish family. She was shelling peas on the porch in the shade when we arrived; she offered us a glass of water and invited us to sit a while with her. I have always felt privileged to be accepted into the Amish community through the Bartletts. The genuine character and integrity of the Amish individuals I have known touches me in a profound way. How they live simply in concert with the seasons and the land, the graceful sparseness of their homes, exemplifies values I have cherished. I felt gifted to be invited to sit and share a slice of life with Ruth that day.

On Sunday morning Bill and I went to church. Although Bill was still involved with the Catholic Church, singing the responses at Mass every Sunday, on this Sunday he asked if I wanted to go to the Episcopal Church in Mansfield. I took him up on the offer and so we did. Even there, he had a presence. He had taught computer classes at the Catholic High School so there were young people who knew him and looked surprised to see him there. They greeted him with a respectful, "Good morning, Mr. Bartlett," with a decided questioning look. I felt their question, "Who is this woman?"

We spent the afternoon with his friends Roger and Sherry. Sunday evening I flew back to Virginia. I finished my work at Innisfree in September and at the end of summer went back to Elk Grove, the place I now call home.

The e-mails between Bill and I continued and somehow it evolved into the plan that Bill would visit me in Elk Grove. We spent some time in Elk Grove with Rosie and Allen. We drove down to Long Beach to visit his daughter, Robin and her family. He planned to stay there for the winter. I would visit for a week, have Thanksgiving Dinner with his son Bill's family in San Diego and then return to Elk Grove.

There was no particular time or incident that made it happen... just a growing realization that my freedom was in jeopardy. I had to make a decision very soon or the hurt and damage would be tremendous. If I allowed it to go on any longer there would be dependency issues. It was difficult to say, but I said it as clearly and simply as was possible for me to do. I told him that my freedom was the most precious thing I had, and I could not let it go. Bill is a wise man; he said that he understood that I had to do what I felt was the right thing. For me it was a matter of integrity and honesty. That was who I am at the core, a free woman.

I drove back to Elk Grove with satisfaction that having been tested I came out of it with my self intact. I had been totally honest in this intricate relationship with myself and with Sherwood. I called him on my drive home. He was extremely happy to hear from me and to hear my decision.

Much later I realized that both Bill and I had wanted to recapture the past. Wanted to relive just a sliver of The Golden Years. Each of us thought we could find a bit of Marianne in the other. One more of life's important lessons: I can live genuinely and with integrity, only as my authentic self and only in the present.

CHAPTER 31

Complete and Unfinished

This is a difficult chapter to write. Perhaps because it is the last chapter and I am not finished with my life and I suspect that if I wait until the end, it may be too late. Also making it difficult is that I am too close to what is happening. I cannot back away from my life far enough to have a perspective on it. As I remember the distant past, I can see which events were changing my direction or my perception of life. In the immediate present, I cannot see that. The story that follows is the story of my life up to the end of 2012.

After the Bill exploration, I returned to Elk Grove, to Rosie and Allen's home...my home, now. There was relief and resolution for me here...a place to call home. Still I did not allude to it in my mind or in conversation, as my permanent home. "You never know," is how I answer questions about what I intend to do next. "You never know."

When I was younger, I never expected that so many things would happen after my seventy-fifth year. I thought that was when one starts to wind down. Many things happened since my seventieth-fifth birthday that were lifesatisfying, albeit not life-changing.

One of those events was attending the family reunion in South Dakota in June of 2010. Rosie set the ball rolling for that. Bobbie and Jack's family, who lived in South Dakota, Colorado and Florida, fleshed out the details with great energy and enthusiasm. All of Bobbie and Jack's children and grandchildren were there. Three of Dorothy's children were there with their families; Vern, Tucky and Peggy. Also attending were Jimmy and Betty from Wyoming,

Rosie, Allen, Karen, Stephanie, Brian and Terry from California; Lynn and John from Seattle and Sherwood from Florida.

I flew to Atlanta and met Sherwood. On our way to the family reunion we drove to Paducah Kentucky to visit the Quilt Museum. It is one museum that if we are within a hundred miles, will go out of the way to visit. After our appetites for that were satiated, we drove on to South Dakota. We stayed in a time share with the California contingent.

The main day of the reunion, in early June, was uncharacteristically cold. None of us from out of the state expected anything but blistering heat, so were not prepared. The Thomas family rose to the occasion and brought to the picnic at Canyon Lake Park, sweat shirts, jackets, gloves and warm socks for every visitor from warmer climes. We had a terrific family picnic at that park where our family has picnicked for seventy years or more. We got to know Marshall Adkins, the youngest of Bobbie and Jack's grandchildren, his mother being their youngest child, Shannon. The next day the entire family took a historic train ride to Hill City, the nearest town to Curry Canyon where I was born. It was hosted by Steve Dutton the husband of Kayla, the fifth of the Thomas children. Family reunions become more touching as I grow older. I ask, "How many more will I be given the chance to attend?"

A day after the reunion we got a phone call from our cousin Dorothy's son, Vern. After Dorothy's death he had been given a box containing squares of fabric, each embroidered with flowers and a person's name. The names were all relatives or friends of Aunt Mary, his grandmother. We discovered that these were squares of a quilt that had never been finished. Aunt Mary's name was not on any of the squares, but in the box, in her handwriting, was a list of the names of those who had contributed squares. We reasoned that the squares had been for a quilt that was to be given to Aunt Mary...a tribute of some kind. Vern took the squares to the High Plains Museum near Spearfish. He was not present when the curator opened it for us. As they came out Rosie and I saw, in handwriting we knew so well, the names of our grandmother, our mother, our aunts and cousins, and people we knew from days long ago on the prairie. We both wept. We could flesh out some of the history of the quilt for the museum. A few months later volunteers at the center pieced them together into the quilt that had been conceived long ago, and it is now on display at the High Plains Museum. Probably not life changing for me, but certainly life affirming. It was a testament to the spirit of community that prevailed on the hard country plains in the '20's and 30's.

One more life changing event occurred later that year on Christmas Eve. I was back in Elk Grove, had been there since October. In the afternoon of that day I began missing Christmases past with my children and missing the season with my children and grandchildren at the present time. On the internet I received a version of "Silent Night" sent to me by granddaughter Molly. It put a very different spin on the images usually summoned by the song. Some of the moving lyrics of this song by Andrew Peterson are:

It was not a silent night.
There was blood on the ground.
And you could hear a woman's cry in the alley way
that night,
In the streets of David's Town...
Little Mary full of Grace,
With tears upon her face and no Mother's hand
to hold.

It was with those words in my head that I attended the Christmas Eve service at Trinity Episcopal Cathedral in Sacramento. At the service, the priest, Brian Baker gave a sermon which followed the spirit of that song so exactly that I was sure he had heard it too. I wept through the entire service.

435

All the Christmases my children and I had spent at Trinity Easton flooded back to me. I remembered one Christmas Eve in particular, when Marcie was seventeen years old. We had a silly argument or misunderstanding in the afternoon and had not reconciled before the Christmas Eve service. At the end of the service that night, everyone was given a candle and the lights were turned off. The choir sang "Silent Night." Marcie soloed on the last verse from the loft at the back of the church. It knew it was a beautiful gift for me, even before she told me it was my Christmas gift. I shed many tears that night, too.

Tears are never wasted on me. They wash away all pretense and bring reality and clear decisions to the front of my mind and prompt me to action. At that point I decided that I would divide my year into a triangle of time...four months in California, four months in Virginia and four months in Miami. I want to spend my last years visiting the people I love the most. My children and grandchildren, Sherwood and Rosie make up that triangle.

After Christmas, I left for Miami, to spend New Year's Eve with Sherwood. It was our twenty-first New Year's Eve together. Such an alliance cannot be easily set aside. Our times in Florida together are gentle and enjoyable. He writes while I go out exploring. That January I walked around the Miami University area and found a waterway in which manatees were lounging in their sleepy, easy way. I interrupted Sherwood in his writing, to come and see them. He, too, was surprised and thrilled.

Then we went to one of our favorite places for lunch. We usually enjoy food from the various ethnicities of the area...this time, an authentic Spanish restaurant in a strip mall, where the bread dough is flown in from Barcelona and baked at the restaurant every day. Usually we are the only English-speaking people in the place. On New Year's Day we went to see Alex Fox. After all these years he now recognizes and acknowledges us in the audience. We also drove up to Daytona Beach to see Rod McDonald perform. He always sits down to talk with us at the break and we reminisce about the days in the Village and update each other on our present lives.

When I returned to California I started settling into this part of my triangular year. I spent the rest of the winter in California, with visits to my sisters and their families in the Northwest.

When Lorie heard of my plan she asked if I could help with Lizzie for the summer. Lizzie had many day camps throughout the summer but would need transportation and someone to be available when camps were not in session. I thought that would be a great opportunity to get to know Lizzie better and to spend time with Lorie. That is exactly what happened and there were many benefits I had not anticipated. I spent precious time with Molly and Sally, attending music venues where their band, "The Judy Chops" was featured. When it was time to pack up my boxes which had been in the barn at Dudley Farm, I could not have had a better helper than Lizzie. She was strong and tireless, carrying hundreds of pounds of boxes from the house to the car and then to the post office for mailing. That summer was not exactly life-changing but certainly, life enriching.

Life for me was becoming much easier. I was free to come and go without tethers binding me to one place. Once, while in Elk Grove I decided I wanted to take a car trip down the coast and visit several people who had invited me.

First I visited Robin Bartlett Pherson in Garden Grove near Los Angeles. Robin, the oldest Bartlett child, is a gracious, intelligent and successful woman. I am unreserved and comfortable with her and her husband Eric. Robin has chosen a career in social work, and so we had a commonality of careers, as well as a lifetime of experiences to share.

From Robin's I traveled south to San Clemente to visit Deb Weinstein. I met Deb and her husband, Bob at a Thanksgiving dinner at her mother, Sylvia's, in 1989. Technically, she is Sherwood's step-sister, but her mother and his father were married long after

Sherwood had left home. We had met again at several gatherings of their family. Whenever we were at the same gathering Deb and I would find ourselves, apart from the others, having rich private conversations. The last time I saw her in Chicago at Sylvia's memorial service, she told me she was moving to California and if I was ever able to visit her, she would be delighted to see me.

When I called her after leaving Garden Grove, she was delighted, and said to call her when I was close to Laguna California, and she would give me directions. I called and she gave me directions to her studio in Laguna Canyon. I had no idea that Deb was an artist, and wondered what I would find there. When I walked into the studio I was stunned! The beauty of her paintings is astounding! Like her mother, she minimizes her talent, but I predict that she will be well known among American artists. I spent the night and next morning with Deb and her husband Bob looking at her paintings, talking of our lives and what we valued and what we did not. We had years and years of our lives to fill in with each other. For example, they had spent their early marriage and child bearing years on a Kibbutz in Israel, which was fascinating to me. My childhood in the American West was equally foreign to them. The glow from the visit with the Weinstein's went with me as I moved on toward Santa Maria.

There I reconnected with Teresa Grubl Graves. Teresa, with whom I had spent my teenage years, lives with her beloved little dogs in the house where she and her husband Fermin raised four children. He died two years before my visit. She was still missing him very much. We looked at old pictures and told stories of long ago and of our present lives. I felt closely connected to her. The next morning I went with her to her ukulele band practice and it was gratifying to see her well integrated into a community. She has a close and involved life with her children and grandchildren nearby. It was a rich twenty-four hours. Re-establishing that old friendship seemed to give my life cohesion.

Another part of that trip was an overnight stay with Pat da Silva in her home at Pajaro Dunes on Monterey Bay...in the Glass House. I watched from her balcony as the moon was going down and was aglow over the ocean. What a gift! It was a treat to be there and enjoy her spectacularly beautiful home and her gracious hospitality. We talked long into the night about our childhoods, marriages, careers and how we got from there to here. She grew up in Iowa far from the sound of the ocean. In a day I had moved from one of my friends of long ago to a friend of just one season's acquaintance. Loose ends were coming together.

At the end of that trip I felt blessed and rich to have visited many homes where I was not only welcomed, but became a part of their lives for the few hours we spent together. I do not feel the lack of a home. Instead, I feel gifted with an abundance of homes. People I can visit and feel warmly received...even cherished.

The next summer, I decided that I had traveled by plane enough. I was constrained by not having my own car when I arrived at my destinations. My dear Chevy Prizm had over 250,000 miles on it and I thought it might be asking too much to take it across country. So I left it in Elk Grove to be sold and I flew to Virginia and bought a blue Hyundai as soon as I arrived. I've made my trips by car since then. Having my own car gave me more freedom to explore and allowed me to be independent wherever I visited.

That summer I lived in Waynesboro, taking care of a house and garden for Scott and Gillian Preston, my old friends from Innisfree. While I was living in Waynesboro there was a Hammer Dulcimer Festival in town. It was delightful and I met many kindred spirits there. It was one more community I came to know well. It was not far from Innisfree and I drove there a few times a week for my *Listening Sessions* with co-workers. When Gillian and Scott got back home I moved out to the village for the month of August and part of September.

Then it was time I was for Miami. Sherwood and I resumed our life as seamlessly as if we had not been apart at all. We filled our time with food, music, poetry readings, conversation and all the things that make our lives richer for being together.

I made a great Florida discovery. Until then, I had not found a church that felt right in that area. As I was surfing the internet looking for an Episcopal church where I had not yet attended I found St. Stevens in Coconut Grove. This, I knew right away was my Florida church home.

I loved everything about the church. It is one of the most beautiful churches I've seen, one of the oldest churches in Coconut Grove. The people of the congregation and the staff are real, genuine, and caring. Location is so important. This church is located beside a park where many homeless people hang out. There is an outpouring of ministry from the church to the poor and homeless. In a short time, I made many friends there. Having found that church, and having my own car, made living in Florida seem like a possibility to me. Not that I can say I definitely would stay there for the rest of my life. I cannot say that about any place, not Florida, not California nor Virginia.

The morning I was leaving Florida for California, about ten miles away from Sherwood's apartment, on I-95 I swerved to avoid a barrier in the road and felt the tendons tear in my right shoulder. I pulled off the road to assess the damage. Although it was painful, if I didn't move it the pain was bearable. I reasoned that the best thing for it was rest and I could rest my right arm in my lap and do most of the driving with my left, so I went on westward.

When I got back to Elk Grove I had it x-rayed and found four major tears in the rotator cuff. Surgery was scheduled for May 25th. However, between January and May it had healed enough that I consulted with my three trusted medical advisors...first, Lorie, my daughter, the nurse; then with my primary care doctor back in Elk Grove and with a wise gerontologist I had met at Mt. Sinai Hospital on Miami Beach. They all agreed with me that canceling surgery was in my best interest.

With surgery off the table I was free again. My wistful dreams of the summer ahead began to take shape. They start with an expansive canvass in my head showing a map of the United States, with shimmering images of family constellations and geographical names that stir up my energy. I fantasize that I can do everything this summer. How it works out is never the same as it starts in my fantasies; often better than I could have imagined.

The last week in May Sherwood arrived in Sacramento by train; we went out to breakfast and filled the days in Sacramento exploring and enjoying being together. In early June we drove my Hyundai south to Los Angeles to say goodbye to Joya, Josh, Hattie and Chandler my newest great granddaughter. I would be going East and would not see them again soon. Sherwood and I were there to see Hattie perform in a production of "Annie." It was a thrill to see my great granddaughter on stage. She reminded me of myself except I didn't get started until I was almost in my teens. Hattie, at age six shows great promise. Her little sister, Chandler, who was very much her own person, is a challenge for me. While she is funny and animated and charming, it takes her a while for her to warm up to anyone but her immediate family. The time will come when we have fun together, but not yet.

The day after Hattie's play, Sherwood and I drove on to Albuquerque to see his sister Chaia and her husband, John. It is interesting to see Sherwood in the context of his family. I get to know another aspect of his personality and the forces that shaped him. Chaia and John are good company and gourmet cooks. Our time there was short and delightful. From Albuquerque Sherwood returned to Florida and I drove back to Elk Grove to finish my packing for the summer.

The next week I drove up the coast of California, to Silverton Oregon where I spent a night with Lisa and Michiel, a young couple I had known at Innisfree. They now live in her home-town with their two children, Alexander and Anabel. Alexander was the first baby to be born at Innisfree during my time there. This started a trend, as four more were born in the next few years. It was satisfying to connect with an extended part of my Innisfree family. Another important connection I had with Lisa was the very first time I read a chapter of this book to anyone; it was to an Innisfree writing group at Trillium. Lisa gave me many helpful suggestions to improve it. She is now writing children's books.

As I drove from Silverton to Portland I saw a part of Oregon that I had never seen or had forgotten...the lush orchards and farm land. There were vegetable stands that could have detained me for hours, but I pushed on to arrive at Mary Lou's before it became too dark. That night we talked and talked, of our childhoods, our mar-riages, our children and of nothing at all...just filling the air around us with comforting words. I stayed, as I usually do in Portland, with Michael Peterson and his wife, Toni. After a short, easy conversation there, I went to my little room under the eaves, like a pilgrim at a familiar comfortable way station.

I drove to Des Moines, a suburb of Seattle...always a bit un-settling because with a name like that I feel it should be in Iowa. Probably it was settled and/or named by someone who moved there and wanted to preserve a bit of their homeland. I arrived at Lynn and John's house in the evening, tired and ready for bed. But the next day I was ready and eager for the party that we had on their new deck with a glimpse of Puget Sound through the trees. Both her daughters and their husbands were there. After the sumptuous dinner on the deck, Suzie and Mike had to leave but Rebecca and Chris stayed. They wanted me to read what I had written of my book. I was honored and they were surprised. There were many stories in my book that are a part of their history, which they had never heard before.

Dolores

After Des Moines I drove to Federal Way. Now that name always strikes me as a place with an odd name. I imagine that so many people settled there because of the logging industry or because of the beauty of the Sound, bordering it to the West, that they compromised on a rather unimaginative name to appease all and offend no one. An inquiry revealed that it was named after Federal Highway 99, the major road in the early days of settling the area. Connie and Lee...it is as warm and comfortable as visiting my own children. There, too I have a bedroom that feels like my very own. Connie made a wonderful meal and her brother, Cliff and Mona came over for food, fun and conversation. The next day Connie took me to Kitty's apartment where we were left alone to visit for a few hours. Later Connie came back and took us to the home of Connie and Lee's only daughter, Deb. She is married to Ryon and they have two adorable little girls, Ellie and Charlie. Those little girls are lively and entertaining and have the run of a large house. It was almost like watching a ballet.

The last significant visit in that area, was lunch with Lisa and Eli, Rosie's daughter and grandson. We met at a place Eli liked to eat and had a light lunch and a deep talk. Lisa, an extraordinarily intelligent woman can fit so much information, humor and deep sharing in an hour's visit that I felt they were with me during my long drive that afternoon.

After that last visit, I began my eastward journey, arriving in Bend Oregon quite late in the evening. It was too late for a visit and I was tired by then, so I stayed in a motel. In the morning I was met by Mary Lou's daughter, Michele and her husband Dave. This is the same Michele who was my mother's first granddaughter, and who I took care of in Portland when she was a toddler. Here she was, a mature and beautiful woman with her husband Dave. We had a short, satisfying time together. We went out to breakfast and then to a lovely park where a beautiful trout stream runs. Conversation flowed as easily as the stream. When I encounter a trout stream and am with a fisherman, conversation turns to stories about Dan. Most people seem to want to hear them, and I am always willing to oblige. This was no exception. Dave and Michele would have spent the entire day with me if I could have, but I was on my way and had to leave.

When I drove out of Bend, I was not prepared for the long stretch across eastern Oregon. I had not filled my gas tank when I left, never dreaming that it would be almost three hundred miles to Boise and the next acceptable gas station. Oh, there were a couple of small ones with only one attendant and one pump where I did not feel safe. I experienced some tension, but made it with the warning signal on and a smidgen of gas.

After one night in a motel in Utah, I moved on toward Boulder Colorado. I stayed in the Foot O' the Mountain Inn, a little place with unique charm, very unlike the chain motels. The city of Boulder radiates young energy. Jake was working at the ski lodge the night I arrived so I had dinner with his girlfriend, Ashley. There were so many places to choose from we took a long time deciding just where to eat. The street where everything is happening, Pearl Street, has quaint little restaurants interspersed with tattoo parlors and marijuana dispensaries. That was just too cool for me, so we decided on an Indian restaurant decorated ornately with tiny tiles from India arranged into exotic murals. Ashley, a good conversationalist made it a memorable night. I was too tired to do anything after dinner but retire to my little rustic inn. In the morning, Jake met me there and we went to breakfast at a pancake restaurant where one of his good friends is a chef. He came out to meet me and when he dis-covered that I ate gluten-free, went back to the kitchen to make an elegant gluten-free pecan pancake for me. Jake and I shared a short visit, satisfying, nonetheless.

By noon I was on my way to Topeka Kansas. The drive is not particularly picturesque but as I came upon the town itself, the sun was going down and I got a photo of a spectacular sunset. I stayed overnight with Tracy and AJ Schmutzler and their daughters, Shelby and Rachel. Her brother, TJ and his wife came over and we had fun piecing together parts of the puzzle of our families and geographies. Tracy and AJ are Aunt Mary's grandchildren. The next morning I felt privileged to be asked by the little girls to walk them to the school bus stop and wave goodbye from there.

Driving eastward, Paducah was right on my way, of course, I made that my stop for the night. It was not as much fun to visit there without Sherwood, but nevertheless I could not drive by without a glimpse of those magnificent works of art. Even without him to share the wonder, they are something to behold.

From Paducah it was a long day's drive to Charlottesville, and I arrived at the townhouse of Walden which would be my home for the summer. The townspeople, Ellie, Chris, Willie, Marny, Mark and Andy were enthusiastic about my return and it felt like coming home.

Thus began the summer of 2012 in Virginia. Now I look at my calendar and read the scribble on every date. It is hard to believe so much could be condensed into July, August and September. The most important thing I do is the *Listening Time* with people in the village and in town. As I listen to their stories, confessions, fears and triumphs, their worries, the slights they have received, and the hopes they have for the future, I look them in the eye and know that this hour makes a difference to them. It explains them to their selves. "Yes, my life is valuable; I am a unique human being" is what I strive for...what I hope each one feels when the session is over. One other thing I do is to make a special dinner twice a week. Sometimes other volunteers admonish me and say, "You don't have to do so much. They are happy with a hot dog or a frozen pizza." But for me it is an offering. It is one more way to show that I love them and they are worth this effort. The coworkers and volunteers are always appreciative.

One evening I had not paced myself well and my foot...the one which had the torn the tendon a few years before, was giving out. A fellow volunteer, Eric, noticed that I was limping and asked if there was anything he could do to help. "There is my therapeutic boot in my closet across the street...if you could...would..." Before I had finished he was out of the house and back in a flash with my boot. He put the meal on the table and I was relieved of any more work that night. I adore community! What I do is but a drop in the bucket compared with what most young and long-term volunteers do for the community. Eric, for instance, has been there for about four years and had brought the community into the computer age, and keeps it going. It has not been an easy thing to do, but he persists.

Most Friday evenings in the summer are spent at *Friday After Five* in downtown Charlottesville. This event takes on a festival atmosphere every Friday night in the summer. There is music, dancing and street entertainment such as jugglers, and acrobats. The downtown mall in Charlottesville is a phenomenal place. There are a plethora of restaurants from that covers the gamut of styles, flavor, atmosphere and ethnic food choices. Two ice-cream parlors are the busiest on a hot summer night, and the most convivial for conversations on a cool day. Each has a set of tables out on the mall under the trees which are adorned with tiny Tivoli lights. There are several book stores, where you can browse, and sit and read unimpeded. Usually one or two buskers are playing violins, guitars, or unusual instruments, with the cases open inviting contributions. Oh, yes, I almost forgot the ever present vendors who sell exotic and colorful goods from Tibet, Andalusia and other exotic places.

When I set up the summer with Innisfree I told them that I would be going to Maine for ten days in August as I had been invited to a retreat by Jim Gill, the husband of Kay, my closest friend. The retreat was being given in her honor as she had done some memorable creative work there. I assumed it would be using her material. She developed a unique workshop/retreat titled "The Seven Stations of the Earth," and I expected that would be the material used for the workshop.

I was in for several surprises! The first person to meet me was Claudette, who had been Kay's closest friend for several years at the retreat center, Spiritual Waters in Waterville Maine where our retreat was being held. Claudette and I had made instant connection. As soon as our eyes locked, and we began to talk, we were friends; much the same as when I first met Kay fifty years before. The next thing I learned was that almost all the participants were nuns....very modern and unhabited and uninhibited nuns. We sat around a circle in casual clothes and introduced ourselves. I found them to be the most interesting group of women I had ever been with. Their life experiences were phenomenal and their faith lively and untethered! Among them were missionaries in the Sierra Leone, social workers in the slums of India, teachers, administrators, lawyers....all with professional, impressive backgrounds. And they were the most approachable, down-to-earth women I could imagine. The retreat was led by Mary Southard, an artist who taught at Loyola University in Chicago, and has produced paintings and sculptures on display around the world. What a soul-satisfying enriching week it was.

I had barely returned to Innisfree when I got e-mail after e-mail from my grandchildren entreating me to be at the Jersey Shore for a long weekend to celebrate Marcie's birthday. At first I told them I could not be there as I had a commitment to Innisfree, but in the end they convinced me that I must go. What a celebration that was! All of Marcie's children, their spouses or significant other and her grandchildren were there. But the biggest surprise of all was that Lauralee had been given a leave of absence from the Peace Corps and was there from Paraguay along with the love of her life, John Beacher. I was so surprised they thought I might be having a heart attack and wondered if surprising an almost eighty year old grandmother had been such a good idea. But my surprise was of pure, unadulterated. No ill health dared show itself to anyone that magic weekend. It was a spectacular family gathering and we are all grateful to have had it, especially because that part of the Jersey Shore was devastated by Hurricane Sandy not long after our celebration. I am so happy to have many photos of our time there.

When I got back to Innisfree they needed someone out at the village in the house of Amity...where I had started eleven years before. There was plenty of coverage in town so I willingly took the opportunity to be out in the country and spent a totally perfect September there.

At the end of my summer I drove south and met Sherwood in Savannah. We had driven through Savannah and spent one New Year's Eve there years ago but had never explored the city thoroughly. This time was perfect. With no other people but ourselves to accommodate, and nothing on the agenda we gave ourselves over to each other and to this beautiful city for several days. There were trolley tours, the Civil Rights Museum, the art museums, the waterfront and more to explore. But mostly we enjoyed that special time together. Whatever we did was precious.

After Savannah I retraced my route back to Sacramento, once again staying in Topeka KS with Aunt Mary's progeny, which was even better than my visit in the spring, because Tracy called her brother TJay and he and his wife came over. I had not seen him for fifteen years. There are few things in life as soul-satisfying as talking with grown people who are reincarnations of loved ones of long ago, and are, at the same time their very own present selves.

I drove on to Boulder CO and stayed at my favorite sleepover, *The Foot O' The Mountain Lodge*. My grandson Jacob met me early the next morning when the air was mountain-fresh and crispy with intimations of a serious winter in the near future. He took me out to breakfast. Once again I was brought up short with the realization that I could never get enough of him. He is as good a conversationalist as his father, Dan, and so like him in many ways. However, he is his own person and has his own ideas and values. When I left Boulder, I realized I had started this summer visiting my two sisters in the Northwest, then Eastward to spend time with Jacob. Now I had made the full circle. I had spent time with all my sisters, all my living children, grandchildren, and great-grandchildren. Surely, my cup runneth over.

To complete my story I must get back to Elk Grove. There were still some surprised and adventures. I left Colorado, planning to go north to Laramie WY to visit my great-niece Becky Carey, her husband, Tony, and son, Nolan.

However, I heard someone on the streets of Boulder talking about a blizzard coming in from the north. I checked the weather and decided I must move on West as fast as I could. Even in my haste I could not ignore the sheer and unabashed beauty of the red rocks and canyons of Utah and into Nevada. Sometimes I laughed out loud at the grandeur surrounding me. Sometimes it brought tears.

I arrived in Wendover NV about five in the evening and stopped at an elegant motel attached to a casino. A kind and generous young man at the registry discovered that I was headed to California, and said, in all earnestness, "Ma'am, if you want some advice from a native, I think you should get back in your car and drive across the mountain to Elko. By morning it will be impossible to get there. The snow is about an hour away." I gratefully accepted his advice, got back in the car and drove on to Elko.

In the morning, it was quite cold and I shivered as I filled the tank with gas. I noticed one of the tires looked a little low, and when I got back in and drove away, the icon on the dash indicated a tire problem. Back at the gas station I asked where I could get a tire fixed and was directed to a full service station one block away. When I got there the interior was closed. A young man, really only a teenager, had just finished filling his pick-up and noticed my distress. He asked if he could help. I told him my dilemma and he said he would check my tires if I would drive over to the air pump. He checked all my tires and put air in the ones that needed it. We had a good conversation while he worked and were friends by the time he finished. I told him that he was my Angel for the day. He was pleased and surprised by that.

By mid afternoon I was back to share life in Elk Grove with Allen, Rosie and their extended family. However, that was not yet to start because they had booked a time-share in Capistrano many miles south of Elk Grove. They invited me to come with them. I thought about the delight Mother would take in this. One of her favorite songs, under the Black Hills pines, eighty years ago, was one my father sang: *When the Swallows Come Back to Capistrano*. Oh, life! How incredible that you provide me with turns and events that take me away and bring me back again like the currents of the ocean, like the paths of the ever-swirling winds. It is almost more than I can hold, much less comprehend.

It was a delightful week in Capistrano. Even though I never saw the swallows come, it was compensated by a whale watching trip where Rosie and I enjoyed, not whales, but thousands of dolphins cavorting around our boat that would be the envy of the Bolshoi Ballet. A big bonus to the week was a visit to Deb Weinstein's studio in Laguna Canyon, enjoying her paintings and a delightful lunch with her and her daughter. It was a week and a place that I never dreamed my life would take me…and oh, so far from Curry Canyon.

The next week I was excited to resume my connections with Trinity Episcopal Cathedral, my true church home in Sacramento. Basking under the glow of Dean Brian Baker as he delivers the most erudite and inspiring sermons one could ever hope to hear and attending classes every Thursday and Sunday. I also re-entered the creative writing group. This church is everything I could ask for on the pathway to enlightenment. It was good to be back.

It was better than good…it was complete. It was whole. It was where I wanted to be.

The first three weeks in November I settled into my place, began to get in the swing of living here and soaking in the sun of my rainbow-studded bedroom, enjoying my paintings on the wall. The warmth of the family, which was not only Rosie and Allen but their daughter Karen and her children, Stephie and Brian, and his father Terry, fulfilled my life here with the exuberance of two younger generations.

Probably, in order to balance all those good things, on the day after Thanksgiving, I walked out in the meadow behind our house and tripped on an unseen root, falling and fracturing my hip. The next two and a half months were devoted to getting beyond that serious misstep. Rosie cared for me all along the way, from the first doctor's visit through the emergency rooms, hospitalizations, and rehab. Along with everything else that happened in my life, it has been a learning experience, albeit a humbling one.

I am well on my way to health and am thinking about my plans for the next adventure. I never look up in the sky without thanking the Universe and the benevolent presence that carries me along.

My life continues to be a miracle to me. I still cannot fully grasp that I have come from where I started and have been given and have taken all the opportunities that came my way to propel me to where I am. I am not a theologian and could never explain the mystery of God or of the divine guidance that got me from there to here. Trusting the Process is the best I can come up with. Everything evens out. In Eastern thought they call it yin and yang…believing that there is a balance to the Universe and that I am privileged to be part of that miracle.

I seldom see them now, but throughout my life I felt them…the Pleiades, Orion, the North Star, the Big Dipper, and Cassiopeia are there to guide me and the meet me in the fullness of time.

My wanderings are as free and fixed as the stars!

Made in the USA
Middletown, DE
21 April 2017